Learning Resources Center
Collin County Community College District
SPRING CREEK CAMPUS
WITHDRAWN
Plano, Texas 75074

075800

COLLIN COUNTY COMMUNITY
W9-BKH-077 1420

DATE DUE

E
184
K6
E27
1996

East to America.

$25.00

BAKER & TAYLOR

East to America

EAST ASIA:

KOREA AND HER NEIGHBORS

East to America

America

Korean American
Life Stories

Elaine H. Kim
and
Eui-Young Yu

THE NEW PRESS

The New Press
New York

© 1996 by Elaine H. Kim and Eui-Young Yu

All rights reserved.
No part of this book may be reproduced in any form
without written permission from the publisher.

Map courtesy of Hollym International Corporation

Library of Congress Cataloging-in-Publication Data
East to America: Korean American life stories /
[edited by] Elaine H. Kim, Eui-Young Yu.
              p.   cm.
Contains edited transcriptions of interviews
conducted by Kim and Yu presented as oral histories.

ISBN 1-56584-297-9

1. Korean Americans—Interviews.
2. Korean Americans—Social life and customs.
3. Oral history. I. Kim, Elaine H. II. Yu, Eui-Young.
E184.K6E27   1996 973'.04957—dc2095-32555CIP

Published in the United States by The New Press, New York
Distributed by W. W. Norton & Company, Inc., New York

Established in 1990 as a major alternative to the large, commercial publishing houses,
The New Press is a full-scale nonprofit American book publisher outside
of the university presses. The Press is operated editorially in the public interest,
rather than for private gain; it is committed to publishing in innovative ways works
of educational, cultural, and community value that, despite their intellectual merits,
might not normally be commercially viable. The New Press's editorial offices are
located at the City University of New York.

Book design by Paul Carlos
Production management by Kim Waymer
Printed in the United States of America

96 97 98 99 9 8 7 6 5 4 3 2 1

To Oliver, Lisa, and Jennifer

This rain gouging already gouged valleys
And they fill, fill, flow over

What gives way losing gulch, mesa, peak, state, nation

Land, ocean dissolving
The continent and the peninsula, the peninsula and the continent
Of one piece sweeping

From "Into Such Assembly," in Myung Mi Kim's *Under Flag*
(Berkeley, Calif.: Kelsey Street Press, 1991)

Contents

Foreword

Once, just as I was about to embark on an ambitious and demanding performance experience, my acting coach suddenly had to leave the country before the opening. When she left she gave me a beautiful stretch of printed fabric. It was meant to be a talisman against stage fright, but, because it was malleable, I ended up using it to carry my makeup. It allows all my bottles and tubes to fit and it conforms to a variety of suitcases and boxes. When I arrive at any venue, I can plunk my bundle down on whatever half-painted or laminated plastic board that is serving as my dressing table, open it up, and have a beautiful and familiar surface. I can also use it to protect my neck and voice from the cold, both physically and spiritually.

In Korea, the *pojagi*, or wrapping cloth, which is described in the intro duction, serves a similar purpose. The *pojagi* is used in Korea to carry functional items, as well as to wrap gifts. I am told that this book is meant to be a *pojagi*, because, like that traditional cloth, it is comprised of fabric fragments of many shapes and sizes. Each piece is stitched to another of a different hue and texture. As the reader unwraps this *pojagi*, surprises await at every turn.

My first steps into *East to America* reminded me of walking across the threshold of the Oriental Mission Church (O.M.C.) in Los Angeles, which I visited on Mother's Day 1993, roughly one year after the Los Angeles riots. (The pastor, the Reverend Tong Sun Lim, is among the voices included here.) Although I had passed the church many times when I drove down Western Avenue, once inside, I found myself in a world that previously I had no idea existed. I was stunned to find a full orchestra accompanying a church packed full of parishioners singing hymns. I was fascinated by the power of the speaker, though I couldn't understand him—despite the efforts of my hosts who were whispering English translations in my ears. The Reverend Lim was as dynamic as the Reverend Cecil Murray, the charismatic pastor of First African Methodist Church (F.A.M.), which had hosted many meetings during the days of the riot and its aftermath. I wondered if the black choir at F.A.M., an oasis for politicos, movie stars, and locals, had any idea of what was going on just a few blocks away. At F.A.M., they were praising the Lord with organs, riffs, and hollers, while at O.M.C. they were doing it just as passionately with violins. The best gifts are full of surprises.

I am also intrigued by the idea of "perpetual marginality," which Sookhee Choe Kim introduces in this book. As an actress, perpetual marginality delights me, largely because it goes completely against Western naturalistic acting technique. The traditional acting method, a product of the nineteenth century but still popular today, is to enter the center of a character and fully inhabit him or her, contributing one's personal identity and experiences to the character. I have long questioned the feasibility of this technique in a world where the idea of a "center" is increasingly challenged. Given the difficulties of being both Korean and American, which are explored by many of the storytellers, Sookhee Choe Kim welcomes the alternative of marginality. This seems to be a sane position. After all, fitting in is impossible if there is no space reserved for one. Like Sookhee Choe Kim, I see the benefits of perpetual, deliberate marginality. It alleviates the need to prioritize aspects of one's identity. Remember the days of "I'm black first, American second" or "I'm a writer first and a man second?" In perpetual marginality, there is constant life; marginality is volatile and fluid. It is always in a state of becoming. There seems to be less need to eliminate one part of the self in order to let another part live. It's exciting, but it isn't easy.

When I was preparing for the play *Twilight*, I took Korean lessons from Kyung-Ja Lee, a filmmaker whose story is included in this collection. And, although my spoken Korean was criticized by some (primarily academics and artists), I welcome the idea James Ryu puts forth in his story: "In order to really speak Korean, you have to think of yourself as Korean." I am grateful that his conclusion was not "In order to really speak Korean, you have to be Korean," which, of course, some purists might contend. I have taken Ryu's conclusion a step farther: In order to represent a Korean on the stage, you have to think of yourself as a Korean. I like the possibility of the *as* when it comes to representation. It allows me the freedom to explore multiple points of view, just as this collection of stories pursues many voices.

When Kyung-Ja Lee was struggling with me to get the proper sounds to come off my very stubborn African American (or was the American part alone the problem?) tongue, she told me the history of the heartbreaking

Korean opera Sim Ch'ong Jon. I remember her saying, "supposedly you can only sing that kind of opera if you cough up blood." It is a beauty born of pain. Similarly, in the stories that follow, there is pain and there is rage, but they lift. What remains is the passion. There are accounts of people finally reuniting with parents and family members they hadn't seen for years. There is humor and there is change. The pressure lifts. As we meet some of the younger historians, and some of the unexpected ones—a gang member, a drag queen, and a police lieutenant, for example—we are relieved of a certain burden. I can only imagine how that must feel for the Korean American reader. As an outsider, I experienced my own ignorance lifting when I shed the burden of some of the stereotypes I had been carrying.

The Los Angeles riots introduced Korean Americans to much of the nation for the first time. Part of what the media brought us in covering the riots were images of Korean Americans and African Americans at war. I was both surprised by and oddly appreciative of the frank remarks. As Elaine Kim points out, the idea of an easy coalition among people of color has been called into serious question, and we are likely to find a growing race dynamic which looks yellow and white rather than black and brown. If that's the case, and if we care at all about ending racism rather than merely watching it transmogrify, there's much to be gained from the candor found in the pages that follow.

The authors describe this project as an attempt to take apart a congealed image. To hold those parts one needs a *pojagi*. The *pojagi* is a wraparound that can contain disparate items. It can also be laid out to display its rich variety, its diverse textures, colors, and patterns. *East to America* is a *pojagi* that combines thirty-eight voices, spanning generations, social classes, and a wide variety of experiences, into one sweeping chorus. Their voices project upward and out. It is the healthiest stance from which to project the voice. What I hear is a symphony of voices, strong, distinct, and beautiful.

ANNA DEAVERE SMITH

Preface

Ordinary people's lives are so often effaced, transmuted, or covered up in history and sociology books. Because of the hierarchical relationship between the researcher and the object of study, even ethnographies designed to describe how people live and think can erase their individual histories and contexts, placing them as "native informants" at the service of the anthropologist's worldview. As a collage of fragmentary testimonials that express, by class, gender, generation, religion, sexuality, places of origin and settlement, multiply determined and irregularly formed subjectivities, this collection of oral histories cannot be an "official history." It can only be an intervention of sorts into History, capturing some Korean Americans at a particular moment and offering a neither explicit nor linear glimpse of some Korean American perspectives on history, identity, and community. We've chosen oral history because it disturbs the hierarchical relationship between writer and subject, allowing us to speak not *about* the subject but *with* and *beside* him or her.

Though we could never hope to approach the diversity of experience reflected in the pages that follow, we, as coeditors of the book, do have vastly different perspectives in terms of gender, nativity and generation, religion, social class, and academic training. As a result, we complement each other well. Yu was particularly interested in how people shape and view the community around them and how their lives are affected by larger institutional forces, while Kim focused a great deal of attention on how gender figures into people's thinking and experiences, as well as how they adhere to and rebel against conventional definitions of family and community. Each of us conducted about half the total one hundred or so interviews, of which thirty-eight appear in the book. We interviewed some people together, and others separately; whenever we interviewed people alone, we tried to be mindful of each other's particular interests.

Because we could not offer the Korean-language interviews verbatim and because we recalled vividly how Korean immigrants were cast in the media as inarticulate aliens during the Los Angeles riots, we decided against using verbatim transcript data. We edited and rearranged them, taking pains to follow people's words as closely as possible. Since the Korean-language material underwent several processes before being made into stories, it was difficult to capture in English the idiosyncratic way speakers of Korean expressed themselves. Except in cases when certain Korean words, especially place names and people's names, had already been romanized, such as "Yonsei University," "Syngman Rhee," or "Kim Il Sung," we followed the McCune-Reischauer romanization system.

East to America reflects the changes we went through during the two and a half years we spent on this project. Taking our cues from our interviewees, we gradually shifted the focus of our interviews. Along the way, we had to struggle with the temptation to try to create a Korean American typology so that our collection would "accurately represent" Korean American experiences. Did we have too many immigrants and not enough 1.5[1] and second-generation Korean Americans? Too many social activists or merchants and not enough wage workers? Were there too few right-wing conservatives, too few Christian fundamentalists? Were there too many men born in the 1930s and too many women born in the 1950s? Did it seem that every marriage was poisoned by patriarchal practices? We worried that the women's stories would be more compelling than the men's, especially since so many middle-aged and older immigrant men seemed preoccupied with what they considered their proper image and uncomfortable with anything besides listing the events in their lives in chronological order. We wondered if there was too sharp a division between what readers might think of as exotic immigrant life stories and quotidian U.S.-born Korean American ones. We knew that many of the immigrants we interviewed wanted other generations of Korean Americans to understand their histories and their nostalgia about a period they hoped the younger generation, having no stories of comparable pain, would long to know. Then we remembered one young woman, when asked for advice about what to include in our book, saying that she was fed up with her parents' tales of relentless suffering and sacrifice. She wanted to read something hip and humorous. By the end, we determined that we should simply offer a sense of the range of interesting Korean American experiences, with some attention paid to diversity in age, gender, generation, occupation, political perspectives, sexual orientation, and length of stay in the U.S. We could see that the stories themselves revealed how Korean American subjectivities are multiply formed and how the Korean American community, like all communities, is multiply organized. Instead of taxonomizing by theme or by people's ages, we arranged the stories rather randomly, so that readers would be taken by surprise by the overlapping lines of affinity and difference among them.

In the course of our work, we learned how to be better interviewers. We also learned how to be better listeners. From listening intently to tapes and poring over transcripts, we realized how much we usually miss because we don't listen closely enough to what people say. We carelessly interrupt the natural flow of their narratives, and we are often so busy mentally preparing to express our own views, or so preoccupied with how what someone is saying bears or doesn't bear upon our own lives and self-images, that we miss, reject, or look askance on a great portion of what is being said. We were reminded that true listening occurs only when one is keenly attentive without passing judgments on what a person is saying. While conducting three to eighteen hours of interviews with a person, and then working closely with his or her tapes, transcripts, and story drafts, we enjoyed such a feeling of intimacy with our interviewees that we found ourselves falling in love with each one of them.

Acknowledgments

We wish to thank Dawn Davis of The New Press for soliciting the project, for encouraging our work, for providing detailed editorial suggestions, and for being such a good friend; Chungmoo Choi, Laura Hyun Yi Kang, and Susan K. Lee for their ideas, advice, assistance, friendship, and support; Julie Ha and Eithne Luibheid for their excellent transcriptions, comments, and criticisms; Jerome Chou for his intelligent readings of the manuscript; John Cha for commenting on the story drafts; Yunshik Chang, Patricia Chu, Eungie Joo, Lisa Lowe, Nayan Shah, Ronald Tsukashima, Hertha Wong, and the faculty and students of the University of Chicago American Studies Workshop, especially Elizabeth Alexander, Bill Brown, Helen Koh, Theresa Mah, Vicki Olwell, and Ken Warren for their helpful suggestions on how to tackle methodology problems; Mina Chu, Youn Jae Kim, Sandra Kim, Michael Kim, Sun Kim, Dave Koo, Christy Lee, and Sandra Liu for their translations and transcriptions; Hyungwon Kang for his support; Janet Chang, Suk Sam Chung, Y. David Chung, Bong Hwan Kim, Eunhee Kim, Henry Kim, Janet Kim, Ji Sung Kim, Myung Mi Kim, Yusang Kim, Angela Oh, Helen Oh, Rok Park, James Ryu, Julie Yu, and Young Im Yu for helping us locate and meet interview subjects; Yong-ho Ch'oe for information about Korea immediately after World War II; and Tiffany Bachtel, In Sook Cho, Leonard Cho, Peter Chung, Michung Gilbert, Young Lee Hertig, Unhei Kang, Byungsuh Kim, Chayoung Kim, David T. Kim, Eunhee Kim, Gene Hyung Kim, Jane Kim, Keith Soon Kim, Ilhwan Kim, Jisu Kim, Young Bin Kim, Ko Won, Kilsang Kwon, Chung Lee, Hwa Soo Lee, Kapsoon Yim Lee, Pyong Yong Min, Angela Oh, Hyun Mi Oh, Indong Oh, Ken Kil Nam Roh, Jai Lee Wong, Jerry Yu, Kent Yu, and Susan Yu for their time and assistance. We thank Chris Ahn and Larry Mock for the work spaces they created. We are grateful to the Committee on Research of the University of California, Berkeley, for Humanities Research Grant support, and to Eric Fong of the Asian American Studies program at Berkeley and Ruth Martinez of the Sociology Department at California State University Los Angeles for their skilled and efficient help with the production of our manuscript. Most of all, we are grateful to the thirty-eight people who shared their lives with us and whose stories are contained in this book.

Introduction

Both of us have been quite involved in Korean American community affairs, and we thought we understood fairly well how Koreans figured in American life. We were used to viewing the world through more than one pair of lenses. But neither of us was prepared for the brief but intense and telling public discussions of Korean Americans that took place during and immediately after the 1992 Los Angeles riots. While Americans of mostly African or European descent discussed the significance of what was happening, Korean Americans remained for the most part silent and invisible except as grotesque stereotypes.

The two recurrent images most frequently beamed by the commercial news media into American living rooms were of Korean men on rooftops guarding their stores with guns or seeming to fire randomly into crowds and of Korean merchants, mostly female, screaming hysterically or begging and crying in front of their ruined stores. Korean American opinions were scarcely solicited, except as they could be used in the already-constructed mainstream discourse on race relations, which for the most part blamed African Americans and Latinos for their poverty and scapegoated Korean Americans as robotic aliens who have no "real" right to be here in the first place, and therefore deserve whatever happens to them. We knew that relationships between Koreans and African Americans have to be viewed within the context of U.S.-Korea relations and the history of racism and race relations in this country. We knew that not every looter was African American, as represented in the news. We also knew that not every Korean American is a merchant, that no two Korean American merchants are alike, and that no Korean American merchant is *only* a merchant. At the same time, we knew that if Korean American merchants were begging and crying or standing on rooftops with guns, it was not because they cared only about their money and property as opposed to other people's lives, but because they had probably spent the last decade or more working twelve to fourteen hours a day, six or seven days a week in those stores, which had come to signify for them the sum total of their American lives.

During the week following the riots, both of us wrote personal opinion pieces, Yu for the *Los Angeles Times* and Kim for *Newsweek*. We coincidentally asserted that the roots of racial violence in the United States lie not in the Korean immigrant-owned corner store situated in a community ravaged by poverty and violence, but reach far back into the corridors of corporate and government offices in Los Angeles, Sacramento, and Washington, D.C. We chided the news media for diverting attention from the larger issue of the centuries-old problem of racial hierarchy in the United States by focusing on tensions between Korean Americans and African Americans, positing instead that Korean Americans and African Americans were ignorant of each other because educational and media institutions erase or distort our experiences and viewpoints.

We both consider ourselves Americans: Yu has been in this country for three decades, having studied, worked, and raised his family here, and Kim has lived here all her life.[2] We did not expect that our opinions would position us as part of a congealed group of Korean "outsiders" whose "anti-American" views made us worthy of deportation to Korea. Some of Yu's longtime European American colleagues were offended by his use of the term "Eurocentric" to describe public school curricula in the United States, especially since they had always thought of him as one of them rather than as a "Korean." Kim was deluged with letters reminding her that she should be grateful for having been saved from starvation in Asia, warning her not to "bite the hand that feeds" her by siding with African Americans—and presumably against whites—and letting her know that if she could not say "good" things about America, she should go "back" to Korea. Someone even tore the essay from the magazine and mailed it to her, covered with angry red-inked obscenities scratched across the picture and the words: HOW MANY AMERICANS MIGRATE TO KOREA?? IF YOU ARE SO DISENCHANTED, KOREA IS STILL THERE. WHY DID YOU EVER LEAVE IT? SAYONARA! BYE-BYE!

We decided to gather materials for a book that might intervene in the discussion from the flanks instead of head on, by bringing forth a variety of viewpoints to demonstrate how Korean American lives are linked but at the same time are multiple, layered, and non-equivalent. We thought that a collection of stories would show that there can be no real spokesperson, that no one can tell the "whole story," and that there can be no typology of Korean American identity, family, or community, since a collection of perspectives would insistently point to the absence of thousands of other stories that remain as yet untold. We wanted to bring forth something that would recall the traditional Korean *pojagi*, or wrapping cloth, which was constructed of fabric scraps made into artistic designs by anonymous women for everyday use. Beautiful and functional, the *pojagi* was used to contain and carry ordinary household items as well as to wrap gifts. We wanted this collection to be a gift to our readers and an intervention into the misunderstanding of Korean Americans. The task was a crucial one for us because of what we knew to be our stake in the outcome: for us, representations of Korean Americans are never merely academic questions because, in a sense, arguing for the humanity of Korean Americans means arguing for our own humanity as well.

We hope that readers, whether Korean American or not, will find something in this collection that takes them by surprise as well as something by which to recognize themselves and their lives. The average American might be surprised by the revelation that Korean American history does not begin on American soil, or by how much adult immigrant Koreans' lives have been shaped by the Japanese colonization and later, the partition of Korea, the Korean War, and Cold War politics.[3] Those who think that Korean immigrant families are fraught with "East-West conflicts" of the kind described in the ABC-TV sitcom about a Korean American family, *All American Girl*, might be surprised to find in the stories that follow how energetically Korean American children strive to understand and how deeply they love and appreciate their immigrant parents. And stereotypes might be challenged by these stories' diverse array of complicated gender relationships formed within the context of Korean—and American—patriarchy. Even some Korean Americans might be surprised to discover that Kyu Min Lee's Spanish is better than his Korean, that Dredge Kang is *both* a gay rights activist *and* the son of immigrant merchants, that Janine Bishop, who was adopted as an infant by an Anglo-American family, grew up unfamiliar with Koreans and Korean Americans, that new immigrant high school student Youn Jae Kim's tormentors were other Korean immigrant students who had arrived a few years earlier, or that Brenda Paik Sunoo's fourth-generation Korean American teenage sons, who blend in rather easily with children of recent immigrants from Korea, are embarrassed that their parents "talk white."

The average American might also be surprised to learn of the professional or vocational trajectory that many Koreans experience once they come to the United States. In large part because it is difficult for them to find employment commensurate with their education and experience, Korean immigrants are three times more likely than other Americans to be engaged in small business enterprises such as dry cleaning, small grocery and liquor stores, fast food shops, clothing stores, and photo processing businesses. Because of the high rate of business failure, they often move between wage labor and entrepreneurial activities. Intense price cutting wars among Koreans competing in the same line of business have frequently brought small business owners to the brink of financial ruin, as suggested in the stories of garment factory owner Y. Chang and cab driver Kun Soo Kang. Success in Korean American small business has always depended on long hours and unpaid family labor, as many whose stories unfold in the pages that follow testify.

It is apparent from what they told us that many of the immigrants' children are acutely conscious of their parents' sacrifices and want to demonstrate their gratitude if they can. Most parents think that fluency in English will guarantee their children's success and acceptance as Americans, never dreaming of the hidden barriers the English-speaking generation so poignantly describe. As Bong Hwan Kim says about the debilitating effects of racism, "You can't really participate in society if your humanity and your sexual identity are always in question. You are just too distracted to find a goal, much less focus on it."

For Korean immigrant parents, displacement helps shape experiences of and attitudes toward America. As for their children, constructions of race in U.S. society are a powerful cultural script to which they adhere and against which they struggle in turns.

The Korean American community is delineated along generation and language lines. It consists primarily of the *il-se,* or immigrant first generation; their U.S.-born children, the *i-se,* or second generation Korean Americans; and those who came before completing high school, often referred to as the *il-chŏm-o-se,* or the 1.5 generation. The majority of Korean Americans are foreign-born immigrants. They are also young: according to the 1990 census, the median age of immigrant Koreans was thirty-five, while that of U.S.-born Koreans was only nine. Korean is the language of the *il-se,* who usually read Korean-language newspapers, attend Korean-language church services, and tune in to Korean television and radio stations when they can. Many *il-se* direct their attention to political issues in Korea, and South Korean politicians tend to view the Korean American community as part of their territory, jokingly referring to Los Angeles as "Seoul *si* [city],

Na-Sung [Los Angeles] *ku* [district]." The *il-chŏm-o-se* speak Korean and English with varying degrees of fluency, and the predominant language of the *i-se* is English. In recent years, as the *il-chŏm-o-se* and *i-se* have been graduating from U.S. high schools and colleges, they have been leaving their mark not only in various occupations but also on a widening range of American cultural institutions, including journalism, visual art, literature, music, and theater. The younger generation's interest in cultural critique is apparent in the stories of students Sandy Lee and Hyun Yi Kang as well as in those of newspaper editor James Ryu, film maker Kyung-Ja Lee, and artist Kyu Min Lee. Bilingual Korean Americans have moved into previously unlikely occupations, as has Los Angeles Police Department Lieutenant Paul Kim. But limited opportunities and the pressures of family circumstances often limit the social mobility of even those with the best educational credentials, and a significant number of *il-chŏm-o-se* find themselves working in the ethnic community after completing college, like Alexander Hull. At the same time, some young Korean Americans, such as Bong Hwan Kim, Kathy Kim, and Youn Jae Kim, choose to do advocacy work there.

The early Korean immigrants who came at the turn of the century to work on the sugar plantations in Hawaii were 90 percent male; today, more women than men are immigrating. Among them are wives of U.S. servicemen, like Kyong-Ae Price, Kyung-Ja Lee's sister, Hyun Yi Kang's aunt, Kook Dean Kim's mother, and Kun Soo Kang's aunt; wives of other U.S. citizens, including naturalized Korean immigrants and U.S.-born Koreans; and single women who wish to move away from the marriage and motherhood mandate in South Korean society. Whether they are *il-se*, like Yanny Rhee and Nataly Kim, *il-chŏm-o-se*, like "Maeun Koch'u," or *i-se*, like Sandy Lee, many of the women we talked with were acutely aware and sharply critical of patriarchal practices in the Korean community. Some, such as Dredge Kang, Imjung Kwuon, and Sandy Lee, devote their energies to educating the Korean community about heterosexism, homophobia, and domestic violence.

The Korean American community is diverse and heterogeneous. Despite their national and cultural affinities, which are sometimes intensified by feelings of displacement, there are important generational, gender, and class distinctions, each formed within the other. To some of the people we interviewed, America is a sanctuary, a promised land. To some, it is purgatory. To others, it has been a prison. And to still others, it is the only home they have ever known.

Whether their American life is experienced as sanctuary or purgatory, many Korean Americans consider their ethnic community organizations essential to their immediate psychic and material survival. Christian churches, most of them Protestant, have become the most important community organization for Koreans in the United States. There are approximately three thousand Korean Christian churches, as compared with fifty Korean Buddhist temples, in the country today. The compatibility of charismatic Christianity with shamanism and animism may help explain Christianity's appeal to many Korean Americans, including Kyong-Ae Price, Nataly Kim, and "Maeun Kochu's" father.

In the Korean American community, no other organizations can match the Christian church in terms of size, influence, and financial resources. For many Korean Americans, church is the principal place for making friends, forming support networks, and exchanging information about jobs, business opportunities, social service programs, and schooling for children. Churches can provide spiritual and psychological comfort as well. Even for English-speaking Korean Americans, the Korean church, like the family, functions as a haven from what Bong Hwan Kim describes as the "strong backdrop of white male standards" in the society at large.

Other support organizations include business associations, such as the Korean American Grocers Association (KAGRO) and the Korean Dry Cleaning and Laundry Association. Unlike in Chinese or Japanese American communities, clan- or region-based associations are rare. Instead, high school and college alumni associations and *kye* [rotating credit associations], a crucial source of capital for business and for children's college education often organized through high school and college alumni networks or church congregations, are key organizations in immigrants' social and business lives.

Though Koreans are more widely scattered across the United States than other Asians, such as Chinese or Japanese, for this book we decided to interview mostly people who live or have lived in Los Angeles. We did so because the city has one of the largest concentrations of Koreans outside Asia; because Los Angeles Koreatown is a kind of symbolic community center for Korean Americans all over the country; and because the Los Angeles riots threw the Korean American community there into the spotlight. During the past two decades, Korean Americans have helped reshape Los Angeles, whether other Angelenos are aware of it or not, although their participation has been more in the informal economy than in political or cultural arenas.

At the same time, this is not exactly a book about the Los Angeles Korean American community, for Korean Americans are not quite "from" Los Angeles. Some came to Los Angeles via Buenos Aires, Argentina, or perhaps Louisville, Kentucky. Some think of their *kohyang* [native place] as P'yŏngyang in North Korea or Taegu in South Korea. And although they might live in Los Angeles now, some will eventually move to Atlanta, Georgia; Fort Lee, New Jersey, or even back to South Korea to live and work. Like many other contemporary Americans, they straddle many borders and are tangled in involvements that are seldom limited to Los Angeles.

It is popularly thought that Asians come "West" from the "East." Most Korean immigrants, including the ancestors of U.S.-born Korean Americans, moved *east* to America, although their paths have been circuitous rather than linear or unidirectional. Thus, while our title has its shortcomings, it does call into question the centrality of the "West."

Korean American communities are not a homogenization of "there" and "here," and Korean American experiences cannot be read as stories about fitting into one place or the other. But because they are often able to view cultures alternately as if through different pairs of eyes, Korean Americans can suggest new ways of thinking about America and different ways of being American.

Our purpose, in any case, is not to render Korean Americans transparent and knowable, but to open up spaces for engaging heterogeneities of many kinds, without losing sight of shared pain and common struggles. For us, bringing together many different narratives is not simply a call for Korean American visibility, but also a bid for Korean American participation in establishing the terms of that visibility.

K.W. LEE

Urban
Impressionist

K.W. (Kyung Won) Lee is a pioneer Korean American journalist in English. He came to the United States by boat in early 1950, when he was twenty-one years old, half a year before the outbreak of the Korean War. After studying journalism in West Virginia and Illinois, he began a long and successful career as an investigative reporter for dailies. He has received dozens of journalism awards, including those from the AP News Executive Council, the National Headliners Club, the Columbia University Graduate School of Journalism as well as the John Anson Ford Award from the Los Angeles County Human Relations Commission, and the Freedom Forum Free Spirit Award. Affectionately referred to by colleagues as dean of the Colombo school of journalism, Lee has a slightly disheveled look and an intense, almost gruff, manner of speaking.

I was in Korea in 1988, doing research on Ahn Chang Ho.[4] I went to the March First Movement[5] Patriots Archives to get a picture of him in prison garb at West Gate Prison, where he died in 1938. There were the names of all the inmates — Ahn, Kim, Lee, and so on. I was curious about Lee because I had been told that my father was involved in the March First movement. Then I came across my father's name! What an eerie experience.

There were court documents on my father, translations made of the verdicts in 1973 by the National March First Patriot Commission: how old he was, his occupation, what laws he had violated, and the summary of the trial itself. He was sentenced in April 1919, nine years before I was born. He admitted leading 2,000 people to march through the city of Kaesŏng, and he had ripped Japanese flags from the front of the Japanese colonial government buildings. Isn't that incredible? This guy was provoking the Japanese. Twelve people from Kaesŏng were imprisoned, most of them in their twenties. My father was the oldest. He was a merchant, running a confectionery factory. A thirty-six-year-old man leading high school boys and girls!

My father was not a well-schooled man. He went to a *sŏdang*,[6] but two of his brothers went to Paejae Haktang.[7] He got involved in the movement because of his brothers' involvement. All three went to prison. They never made a big thing out of it; they considered these acts of heroism a part of their duty. He never mentioned it. I wish to God he had. I feel like I've been cheated by life, because it had been a family secret, and I came to know it too late.

According to my sister-in-law, by the time my father came out of prison, he was completely crippled. He was just skin and bones. He should have been a hero, but the average Korean then would have stayed away from you if you had a prison record. You are just a condemned man. He was considered an outcast. The family collapsed: all the children had to drop out of school, and my older brothers went south for *mŏsŭmsari* [to be live-in servants]. That personal misfortune completely wiped out our family's social status. My mother sold the shop to bribe him out of prison, and he couldn't make a living because he was branded as an ex-convict and people were afraid to be associated with him, so he became a peddler of farmers' summer raw cotton fiber summer work clothes. He would travel on foot or oxcart to remote country villages after the harvest, when the farmers would have some money. He'd be gone for three or four days at a time, carrying a huge bundle.

I recall the word *sabok* [literally, private uniform; the Japanese thought-control police]. My mother and sisters-in-law whispered that word often. I knew something was strange, but I didn't try to find out more. The *sabok* were always trying to ferret out anti-Japanese elements in every city in Korea. They harassed my father constantly, checking on him every week, like probation officers. That kept him from ever being productive.

I heard that my father grew up in a *kiwajip* [tiled-roof house, or a nice house] in the mercantile section of Kaesŏng. I was born in Namsan-dong [literally, south mountain street], which was for the have-nots. Although my main family was *petit bourgeois,* I had that vague sense of envy and fantasies the have-nots feel about the haves.

I didn't know that it was the worst part of town at the time, because I was living an insulated life. But I had to go out, and every time I opened the door, there was a bloody fight going on outside. I saw low-life that I never forgot. When somebody was down, they threw rocks at him. The neighbors were mostly A-frame laborers.[8] Drunken, and oh, they were bloody! They stayed drunk almost all the time. I never saw a sober Korean laborer. They would put their A-frames down and stretch out in a drunken stupor.

When I was six, we literally slipped out of Kaesŏng. My mother woke me up suddenly one night. They had a little bundle. It was just the three of us: my father, my mother, and me; I was the last child in the family, born when my mother was forty-nine years old. We were going to take the midnight train to Kwangju. Kwangju was like Australia, a colony for the undesirable.[9] I was crying, "Why?" But then when I thought about it, it was exciting: it was my first train ride. There was a big steam engine with a whistle. They bought me *hottŏk* [Chinese steamed buns], and that was the first time I ate *ppang* [bread] and my first time eating on a train.

My parents decided to move because there was no way to make a living. Peddling is a young man's job, and my father was not getting any younger. It was physically taxing for him and also demeaning, because we were always singled out by our relatives. My mother felt sad every time we went to *k'ŭnjip* [literally, the big house; the oldest uncle's house] because I would insist on staying there. It was a *kiwajip*, and they had good food, including meat. My mother decided that we'd better get the hell out of there, so we came down to Kwangju.

In 1942, Koreans were first admitted to the high school established in Kwangju for Japanese students. Three hundred Koreans applied for only three slots, and I was one of those admitted. Children of the Japanese colonial rulers were a mean bunch, different from the Japanese in Japan. I was a constant target because I disturbed their sensibility. I was Korean, and I beat them in academic subjects every time. But I was always number two because they gave me low scores in Shushin, Japanese ethics. The upperclassmen hazed the freshmen, but usually the hazing stopped when you became a sophomore. They continued to beat me. I had practically no lunch hour. It was very ritualized: they would summon me during lunch hour, and upperclassmen would ask me questions and order me to sing Japanese songs. They would make fun of my Korean accent and order me to repeat the pledge of loyalty to the Japanese emperor. If I made a mistake, they beat me. When they stole my lunch box and found *kimch'i* [pickled vegetables, a dish traditionally eaten at every Korean meal] in it, they started *really* beating me up like hell, four or five guys, every one of them with pimples. Many times, I could not eat because my mouth was all bloodied and my gums were messed up. My buddies at Sŏ Jung, the rival Korean high school, would beat up the Japanese kids who tormented me after school, and the next day the hazing would get more intense. My constant obsession was how to avoid these bullies and how to help my buddies from Sŏ Jung ambush them after school.

There were two other Korean kids in the school. They were from the countryside, so they had to stay in the dormitory. I asked them, "How come you lucky dogs are never beaten?" Then they told me that they were sexually abused by upperclassmen. Sex was forbidden between men and women, so these guys were victimizing newcomers, and Koreans were easy targets.

The airplane was the obsession of my generation. We were frustrated and earthbound; the airplane represented our flight of fancy. Everyone wanted to become an air force pilot. Lower classmen from my school applied to Japanese Air Force cadet school. Only five from my class passed, and I was one of them. The Navy was closed to Koreans. I joined the Japanese Army

Air Force to stop the Japanese bullies from beating me up every day. That was my daily concern. Then, for two glorious months after I was selected, the hazing stopped. When I look back, it was stupid to join the air force. But I now understand the juvenile gang syndrome. Joining the air force cadet school was like gang behavior, a power trip.

When I told my father that I was going to join the special Japanese volunteer cadet corps, he looked at me with unspeakable sorrow, but he couldn't tell me that the Japanese had ruined his life and his family. For their own survival, my family had kept my father's imprisonment a secret from me, as did the families of many other patriots. My mother thought I would never return. I remember her wailing, "Die for the *waenom* [derogatory phrase meaning Japanese, literally, dwarfs]."

The Japanese military was very savage. They spent all their time beating up their subordinates. That's why Japan lost. Between December 1944 and the end of August 1945, I was on Kyushyu Island with a bomber squadron as a radio operator, and later waiting to be trained as a radar operator in a search plane for the Sixth Air Division, which had the cream of the crop of navy and army bomber pilots. They were exclusively for the Okinawa Operation. I was continuously beaten, even when I was on combat duty. The noncommissioned officers who had become sergeants after many years resented us because we had a lowest sergeant's rank even though we were in our teens.

By mid-1945, it was near the end of the war. Almost everyone was on special mission. It was not the *kamikaze* mission, but it was a one-way trip. By the time we located the enemy without any radar, we would be shot down. I was to be trained as a radar man. I had a tremendous memory; I could remember a hundred three-digit code words. Luckily for me, though, I flunked the pilot test because of my [poor] peripheral vision. We had only six months' training. All I knew was the manual. *Kamikazes* learned dive-bombing and landing, but many planes conked out not long after take-off because of mechanical failure. The planes were being built by female peasants, since the men were all fighting. At that point, near the end of the war, even the radio receivers and transmitters usually didn't work.

I saw the Japanese in the worst hours of their lives. At that time, the Japanese would defend their motherland to death. I can understand why they love their land. They love their landscape, the fields and the mountains of the land where they were born. Japan is a verdant land. When you fly over it, oh, it is intoxicating. The sea and land are deep green, hardly

5

distinguishable except for the white caps of the waves. I would see the hundreds of little islands with fishing boats floating on the ocean like flower petals. Their love of the land was reinforced by the folklore that their land and islands were inviolable.

All the air bases were outside the cities, and many of them had *buraku-min*[10] living nearby. At the time, I didn't know who they were, but I knew they were different. They were rural people, with complexions darker than other Japanese. They all seemed to be involved with cows and horses. I used their rest rooms many times when I was far from the runways. They used straw as toilet paper. Somehow they seemed ethnically different; I think they created a new species when they were inbred.

Our bomber base was huge, so we were the main target of U.S. B29s and Lockheed P38s. At that time, there were hundreds of conscripted Korean laborers working at my air base. They were the expendables. The bombing and strafing were like hell: every day, three times a day, the base was car-peted with huge bombs, which created enormous craters on the runways to keep us from flying. It was terrifying. The conscripts were brought in to fill up the numerous craters while the Lockheed P38s were strafing overhead. Many of them died there.

Chosenjin [Japanese word for "Korean"] villages started popping up near the air base. My name was Umeda,[11] meaning field of plum blossoms, my favorite Korean flower, but my face was distinctively Korean. I would run into these Korean laborers who figured out I was a Korean. They wanted to comfort me because I was a young boy away from home. Isn't that incredi-ble psychology? They invited me to their village miles away. It was like a ghetto, an all-Korean village. I had never seen such a feast in my life: every kind of contraband, every illegal food and drink was there.

We were one of the main *kamikaze* bases; most *kamikaze* sorties had to pass through to be refueled and outfitted with bombs. Usually the pilots stayed there overnight; I met hundreds of them.

I met four or five Korean *kamikaze* boys while I was on Kyushu. They were two or three years older than I was, tough-looking, muscular guys from Ham Kyŏng Province in northern Korea. You could tell they were Korean because they had chosen Japanese names that had distinctively Korean meanings, like Kanagawa [gold in the river] or Kanayama [gold mountain].[12] I asked one guy from Hamhung how many Korean *kamikaze* pilots there were, and he told me there were many. They had passed the very rigorous pilot test after three to six months of training in landing, and dive-bombing.

After three months, they were sent on a special attack mission. They just stayed overnight at our base and left the next day for their advance base. They never returned. Either they reached their target or were shot down or they had engine trouble.

I saw "comfort women,"[13] but I didn't recognize that they were Korean. Most comfort women there were Japanese daughters of peasants. There was a red-light district in Kumamoto with a comfort women section. I could see soldiers standing in line. Everybody had ten or twenty minutes in the little cubicles. Can you imagine that these comfort women had sex every ten or twenty minutes? Women were considered just extra. The reason why I never had contact with them was that I was still a cadet, and our motto was virginity. Each class had a motto, and that was ours. Can you imagine?

I found my identity when I saw Koreans at their most wretched and miserable. After they had been conscripted, used, and discarded on the way back home to Korea from Japan at the war's end. I was bunched together with a sea of refugees, conscripted laborers and their families, coal miners, and women whose husbands were wounded and dying. They were crying *aigu, aigu,* and begging, with children clinging to their emaciated breasts. People were in rags, almost naked, thousands of them, lying in the open field, dying like flies. It was like hell on earth. We had been herded onto a beach near Hakata like herds of seals and quarantined there to wait for boats to take us to Korea. Everyone was weak and hungry; we were afraid people would start killing each other for food. Once you went in, you couldn't get back out; the Japanese MPs were guarding the place, bayonets in hand, because Koreans were considered dangerous bandits.

About twenty of us young cadets, aged fifteen to eighteen, grouped together like a pack of stray dogs. We thought we'd be the first to be killed by the Americans. I burned my air force uniform and wore a borrowed high school uniform. We bargained with a Japanese fisherman, who agreed to take us across the strait to Korea. It took us five days and four nights. It seemed eternity. It was a miracle that we were not killed; if the weather had been windy, we would never have made it. The U.S. bombers had dropped thousands of mines into the ocean. The ocean was still like a mirror, and we could see them floating on the water as our boat glided by. To avoid stirring up the waters, the fisherman just let the boat drift for two days, starting the engine only after we had passed through the mines. Along the way, we passed hundreds of capsized Japanese transport and war boats belly-up in the water. We regretted every mile. We kept lamenting to each other, Why did we come? We found out later that hundreds of Koreans died on the way home from Japan in boats overloaded with coal miners from Hokkaido or the Sakhalin Islands.

On the fifth day, we finally landed on a small inlet outside Pusan. We were among the first to arrive back in Korea after the defeat of Japan. It seemed that there were a million Koreans on the beach when we arrived. We were almost stomped to death by the crowds of peasants in sweat-stained clothing, thrusting photographs of their family members in front of us, wailing and asking us if we knew what had happened to their sons or daughters in Japan.[14] Scenes like that are burned forever into my memory.

I spent my youth as a brainwashed tool of the Japanese military, and overnight I was on the other side. I was a brainwashed young punk who knew nothing, but I literally found my identity there. After that, it was smooth sailing; my DNA just burst out. When I look at second-generation Korean Americans, it's hard to persuade them about their identity. They have to meet it, eyeball to eyeball, by themselves. It has to be very personal.

The first thing I did when I got back to Korea was to spend two weeks making the rounds and beating up the bullies from the high school. They were still in Korea, waiting to be evacuated back to Japan. It turned out that most of them were cowards. They had avoided military service. They were working in factories. Together with three other naval academy and cadet returnees, we beat up those bullies in front of their crying parents. We told them their sons had made our lives miserable and we were going to teach them a lesson. It was heady: two years had changed my physique, and I was lean, mean, and tough, a macho stud. I had returned alive, and now I could have revenge.

I enrolled in a Korean Methodist missionary high school back in Kaesŏng and spent the year picking up Korean. I had such a passion to learn that I was one of the best students. I memorized the poetry of Kim Sowŏl and Han Yong-un,[15] as well as other anti-Japanese resistance fighters. People were never accusatory about my early adolescent Japanization; they embraced me more because I had been through hell.

When the Japanese occupation was over in 1945, patriots returned from overseas, luminaries from China and Manchuria, nationalists and socialists who fired our romanticism and patriotism. In the post-liberation period, ninety percent of Korean young people were influenced by sweeping ideologies—not just university students, but also high school students, and intellectuals. The sheer absence of patriotism among the Korean domestic elite during Japanese rule drove them to draw inspiration from these patriotic fighters from overseas.

In Kwangju and all over the Chŏlla provinces there were incredible injustices. It was a feudal state. Every spring, the peasants would dig roots because there was not enough to eat. After I returned from Japan, I saw people eating roots and weeds. In the season called "hunger pass," before the barley ripens, the peasants would dig down five feet deep for bark and roots to chew. The mountains around us were bare; they had been picked clean. I grew accustomed to the strange, semisweet, ripe smell of poverty. Ninety percent of the people were oppressed by injustice. I was not especially sensitive. I was just normal; you can see why so many Korean young people became revolutionaries.

I was involved in the student movement. Those were chaotic times. Students spent their time in tea rooms and *makkŏlli* [rice wine] houses and all sorts of demonstrations in the streets. During three years at the university, I spent only a few months a year in class. What were we demonstrating about? Everything. We were demonstrating against corruption. We were demonstrating against dictatorship. We were drunk with the chaos of the times and the sudden freedom we were enjoying after the end of the Japanese occupation. I entered Korea (Koryŏ) University in 1946. Korea University was popular because resistance was nurtured there.[16] In demonstrations, Korea University students always marched in front. We pasted up thousands of antidictatorship or anti-corruption handbills all over the city. If you were caught by the brutal police for doing that, you'd be half-dead.

At one bone-chilling winter afternoon demonstration, as police oppression mounted, the armed guards in black uniforms started shooting into the student demonstration. We had been instructed to always link arms and move forward in a line, never looking back. People around me fell, and I kept running forward. Although I had been told not to look back, I did, and that was when I saw that there was no one behind us. I ran as fast as I could. I was so scared that I urinated in my pants, and the air was so cold that my pants froze. My pants were like sheets of glass. Finally, some people living in the neighborhood let me into their house and hid me.

The bloody Sunch'ŏn revolt in late 1948[17] was a harbinger of what was to follow in the divided, troubled peninsula. The rebellion, in which I later learned Park Chung Hee was an alleged ringleader[18] and during which a relative of mine was executed by communist rebels, was a wake-up call for me.

The relative was a Japan-educated professional and a popular figure in town. When the rebel forces occupied the city, it was like the French Revolution. Hundreds of educated and titled people in that town were rounded up and executed. Then the South Korean Army came through and killed many suspects. It was Korea's Rwanda.

My mother told me to go find the relative. When I entered the city, I saw so many corpses lying in the streets everywhere. That was my defining moment. I never knew how a revolution would end up until I faced that bloodbath, eyeball to eyeball.

In the 1940s, Koreans had what I call the "Yankee disease." Everything American, even American feces, oh, smelled good. The whole country was like a chicken running around with its head cut off. Corruption was rampant. Here I was, a so-called flaming campus activist, but I used to look at *Life Magazine* as if it were the Bible. On my wall, I hung a big poster of Deanna Durbin, the movie star dream girl of the 1940s. She was the neighbor-next-door type. Since it took years for American trends to hit Korea, I was worshipping a girl who was no longer on the screen in the United States.

I had a cousin who was never involved in the student movement. He was the quintessential son of a Korean doctor who wanted to be a doctor himself, so he went to the Seoul National University Medical School while I was involved in the dissident movement. Somehow he befriended an American major in the occupation forces who had a cousin or nephew at a prep school in Tennessee. This cousin of mine was so infatuated and afflicted by the American "disease" that he just went there, only to find out later that it was a prep school for rejects from the public schools. And I followed in his footsteps. Can you imagine? My cousin was a Kyŏnggi graduate,[19] the elite of the elite. He was a senior in the nation's top medical college. And he found himself in an American private reform school with a 10:00 P.M. curfew. He told me to apply, so I followed him six months later, since my father and brothers also pushed me to leave the country.

I was one of the original FOBs [fresh-off-the-boats]. I took the slow boat to San Francisco. I was on a student visa that took two years to get. I arrived with fifty or sixty dollars, enough for the train fare to the school in Tennessee. You could count on ten fingers who the Korean American families were when I arrived in 1950. Our group was mostly Christian; we were targets of the Christian embrace. Any Korean who had some connection with a church could get a scholarship, but I never had any connection with the church, so I came on my own. The others had scholarships.[20] Most of them became doctors and are millionaires now.

That summer, I decided to go to Detroit to join my cousin, who was then a student at the University of Michigan. He rented a room in Detroit from an American military man he knew and worked on the auto assembly line. Since I was broke, I had to hitchhike from Tennessee to Michigan. I got fifteen or twenty different rides, sometimes for half a mile and sometimes for a hundred miles. It took me four or five days. It was then that I learned how to give the finger and say "fuck you." While I was passing through southern Kentucky, for instance, some young guys in a pickup truck slowed down, but when I ran up and put my hand on the truck, they started kicking my hand, jabbering in fake Chinese, and speeding up the truck. They gave me the finger and cursed me out. I'm sure that was the first time they had ever seen a real "Chinaman" before. When I look back, I was like a little Marco Polo in America. Every encounter was the first time, not only for me, but also for whomever I met.

My cousin and I lived in the black section of Detroit. We were the first Koreans to live in that community. It was relaxed and easygoing; everybody had a party on weekends. The early 1950s was a period of prosperity in the U.S., and it seemed that every black man had a job on the auto assembly lines. My cousin had a job on the assembly line also. When I joined him in Detroit, we had a living room with one bed. I slept while he was working at night, and when I got up, he slept. The landlord was a black soldier who had served in Korea.

Five days in a row, I stood in line for an assembly job, but I never got any work because I always got up too late and was always at the end of the line. Finally, I said, "Fuck you." I got a job as a busboy at a hotel. The first Friday night, I saw a gum-chewing blond woman coming in with suitcases. I was supposed to wait in the basement in case the guests signaled that they wanted something.

There was a buzz for bourbon and Coca Cola, so I went up and knocked on the door. Come in, a woman was saying. I went in, and there was a big guy and this woman having intercourse. I said, So sorry, so sorry. It was an absolute shock to me; I felt I was really invading their privacy. I thought I must have really screwed up, but she said, "Come in, come in; it's all right." While she was having intercourse, she had me put the drinks on the table. I went in with my back toward them, asking myself the whole time what I was doing there. I was in shock. To them, I was not a human being, just a typical Chinese houseboy. The women were not even embarrassed. I was penniless, but one week was enough of that job.

Walking in the black town after a summer rain was like a poem. Everything was limpid, but there were reflections of light. We could hear the robust voices of black women bantering with black men. Black guys would say, "Hi, there" to us in a neighborly way. Whenever we went into a bar, they were kind to us. They gave us free drinks and asked us questions. People were in a good mood. The Korean War had brought an economic boom to the community, and everyone had a job. Maybe I am romanticizing it, but I felt that life was really good there. You can see how important jobs are to a community.

No one was hostile to us, though Korea was so alien to them, and we were like celestials from a celestial body in outer space. It was funny. Each of my Korean buddies was like a Marco Polo at that time. He had to live by his wits and his guts. One time, in the summer of 1953, while I was a graduate student in Illinois, five of us Koreans in Chicago got together, drank, ate *kimch'i* and everything. We were out in the country, urinating against a fence, when a farmer approached us to find out what the hell was going on. He thought we were trying to get into his farm. We ran to our car. Then one guy suddenly stopped and shouted, "We are from China." I'll never forget that. We had a sense of honor; if we ever got into trouble, we were from China.

One of my friends had a menial job and wanted to make some extra money, so he made *kimch'i* to sell. He had twelve jars of *kimch'i* with lots of garlic and anchovies in them. It was a hot summer day in Chicago, and the jars all exploded. The *kimch'i* juice started dripping down the stairs. The other tenants in the apartment building didn't know what that smell was, so they called the fire department. They thought maybe there was a dead body in my friend's room. The fire department flushed out the room with a water hose, and my friend was kicked out the next day.

In those days, Koreans were only allowed into the U.S. as foreign students. To maintain our visas, we had to keep going to school no matter what. The immigration authorities watched us like a hawk. If you missed one semester, they could catch you for deportation. I was almost deported myself. I was freelancing for a couple of papers in Monterey, California, because I couldn't find a job after getting my M.A. in journalism at the University of Illinois. In April 1955, Syngman Rhee was declared "president-for-life" in South Korea. I had been a supporter of Rhee, but I was disenchanted when his government turned into a dictatorship, so I wrote a column for the *Monterey Herald* satirizing the "happy celebration" in South Korea. I hadn't realized that there were many *Tongjhuoe*[21] people in northern California. Someone apparently mailed a copy of the clipping to Rhee's Austrian wife, Francesca, who was in charge of all foreign affairs, including every South Korean passport. Suddenly, I received a notice commanding me to appear before the consul general to answer some questions. When I realized what was happening, I played stupid and offered profuse apologies, saying I was just a brash youth. I knew that without a passport, I was dead.

My visa expired, and I faced deportation hearings. I received a one-year extension. Then I was offered a job at the *Kingsport Times and News* in Tennessee. At that time, the congressman from my district was a good friend of John Foster Dulles, who was then U.S. secretary of state. I obtained an exception to the quota for Korean immigrants, which was one hundred at that time. My publisher supported me, and I became a non-quota immigrant. I became a U.S. citizen in 1958, a year before I met my wife.

I met Peggy in Charleston. I was covering weekends at the *Charleston Gazette,* and she was the nurse in charge of the emergency room at the local hospital. Her shift ended at eleven P.M. and my deadline was midnight. I needed facts, and I had to get them from her. There were five Korean medical residents there, and I persuaded them to tell her I was a good guy so that she would help me. I was very persistent. She was a quintessential nurse, and her face and manners were a dead ringer for Ingrid Bergman. Whenever I called, I was struck by her soft voice. She was dating a German doctor at the time, but I was very persistent. I was one-track-minded, and she finally got tired of resisting. Two months after we started dating, we got married. I must have been thirty-one years old.

I have three children: a daughter in her early twenties, a daughter in her early thirties, and a son who is thirty-three. All of them had to put themselves through school because I could not afford to. My son is an accomplished welder, undeniably normal, steady, and gifted with his hands. I like him very much. There is something about American blue-collar people that has always attracted me very much.

I have always identified with the people who reminded me of Korean peasants, hardworking, honest, decent, poor, with something spiritual about them, whether they were Appalachian mountaineers, Del Paso Heights blacks, or Filipino migrant farm workers. I covered black lung disease among coal miners, and civil rights struggles in the South, and massive vote-buying practices in West Virginia. I was born under a grass roof. I have always hated bullies. In America, I was in a position to get even for the bleeding hurts of my whole adolescent life.

The publisher of the *Charleston Gazette* was an unconventional and independent-minded guy. He was one of those natural aristocrats; his father was a U.S. senator, and his classmate at Yale was Bill Buckley. The state government was rotten to the core. He wanted to clean up corruption in the Democratic state. But it had never dawned on him how the blacks were suffering in the Jim Crow years. Then one day, an Indian diplomat who was not served at any restaurant when he was passing through West Virginia on his way to Florida because he "looked black" wrote a nasty letter to the State Department, which sent a copy to my publisher. Suddenly the truth hit: "Hey, we have Jim Crow right here." I had been starting to raise hell myself at that time, and he ordered, "Hey, K.W., come on! Get the hell out there and open up all the Jim Crow places." I said, "Yes, sir, yes, sir!" That's how I became a "black" reporter. I had to wear many hats. When I look back, those were glorious days.

As an investigative reporter, I felt insecure because I was afraid they would pick on my Asian background. I could not afford to make a mistake, so every time I did an investigation, I had to have overwhelming supporting documentation. I never slipped, because if I had, I would have been gone. It took me thirty years of super-human effort to win some respect among my peers in the trade.

The late 1950s were exciting but dangerous times in the South. Responses to sit-ins and demonstrations were unpredictable. Everything was unpredictable; there were no guidelines. After three years, when things were popping all over, I said, "I'm getting tired of being a black reporter. Why don't you hire a black person?" My boss hadn't even thought about hiring a black reporter. He was responsive, so my buddy and I called this professor at Northwestern named Curtis McDougall, who recommended Ed Peeks, one of the best students, who became the managing editor of *The Afro-American* in Baltimore or Washington. I told my boss, "Don't just hire a token. Why don't you hire an editor?" Ed Peeks had tried to get into the *Philadelphia Inquirer*, the *Washington Post* and the *Washington Star*, and the *New York Times* for years, but they paid no attention to him. He fought in Europe in an all-black combat unit. In 1961 or 1962, he came and worked as labor-business editor.

I came to California from the mountains and hollows of West Virginia. After almost ten years at the *Sacramento Union*, I started a Los Angeles-based weekly paper, *Koreatown*, in 1979 and operated it for two years. Chol Soo Lee (Ch'ol-Su Li)[22] had a lot to do with my starting the paper. Two other partners and I took turns traveling eight hundred miles between Sacramento and Los Angeles every week for two years. It was like a mission I had been given; if I had said no, nobody would have given a shit, but I had to answer to myself. I had to keep going. Koreans need an English voice. The Chol Soo Lee experience taught us a lesson. It took a big chunk out of my life.

In 1990, I started the weekly English-language edition of the Los Angeles *Korea Times* at a time when tensions between Korean American merchants and African Americans were escalating. I spent all my adult life as a practitioner of daily journalism. I was infatuated with the First Amendment and all the best traditions of American journalism, until I ran into *sa-i-gu* [the Los Angeles riots]. That was when I saw the beast, the demon in the mainstream media; I realized that the metropolitan newsroom was the last bastion of ignorance and arrogance in America. I'm talking about the editors and assistant editors who control the flow of information. These people still manifest their insensitivity and indifference to Asian people as if it were some kind of badge of honor. They almost flaunt it. They don't apply their standards of professionalism to Asians; they think we are some kind of aliens from another planet. Because they don't know us, it takes a great deal of effort to write about us. But they don't try. Why should they? We weren't invited. They are there because they are good with words; but they are devoid of conscience when it comes to Asian immigrants. They seem to have completely forgotten about their own immigrant ancestors. You have to either own newspapers or force them to change their coverage. Moral persuasion doesn't work with them.

Nowadays Americans are genuinely bewildered and confused. They are unprepared for the new social demographics of this country. For the past fifty years, American intellectuals wore their ignorance as a badge of honor reading "No tickee, no washee." At least U.S. institutions are grappling with guilt about black Americans, who were familiar [to them]. There is ambivalence about Latinos. With Asians, it's just a vacuum.

Sa-i-gu is our [Japanese American] internment experience, our Warsaw, our baptism by fire. Our twilight struggle is far more vexing and troublesome than black and white racial issues because it involves language, culture, generation, and race. But in a way, *sa-i-gu* was a blessing in disguise. Yesterday, I spent all day as a judge for the Asian American Journalists Association's national scholarship. We had to select six winners from among 150 applicants. Of the six, four were Korean Americans, and every one of them wrote about *sa-i-gu* in their personal story. They talked about their obligation to speak up for their parents, who had been misunderstood and punished by the media for sins they did not commit. The children understand and feel that their parents' immigrant life is nothing but drudgery, exhaustion, and fear, completely devoid of joy. It's a life of unending melancholia and frustration. And things are getting worse. What sustained Korean Americans is the illusion that there would be life around the next corner, that there is always life after loss. But now that illusion is gone. *Kukmuldo ŏpta* [literally, there isn't even any broth/juice; nothing is left]. Since urban problems in America have yet to bottom out, Koreans will continue to be a vulnerable target for more crimes, more violence, and more scapegoating. And it won't be just in L.A.; it will also be in Detroit, Chicago, Washington, Baltimore. Koreans are sitting ducks everywhere.

They built their dream on the unprecedented rise in real estate values in southern California, which coincided with their immigration. Their purpose was to create a down payment on a house, which would open the door to their American dream. But real estate values crashed, the golden egg disappeared, and *sa-i-gu* put an end to their seemingly optimistic beginning in America.

With their eyes wide open, Koreans walked into violent inner-city areas. They just dived with reckless abandon into the places where the most deprived people live, without thinking about the dynamics of the neighborhood. They built their little world where the desperate converge. Take Koreatown in L.A. It's going down the drain; it's easy prey, isolated, a target for robbery and murder. When I work in Koreatown, I have to watch my every move. For three years, I deliberately took off my necktie every time I went out. It is a killing field; many people are desperate. They mug you. Koreatown is among the most violent places in the U.S.[23]

I'm an urban impressionist; I watched them put up their big shop signs in Korean letters, a riot of chicken scratching. They thought they could jump into the ghetto, stay a few years, and get the hell out. But it doesn't work that way. The Jews were burned out in 1965 and were soon replaced by the black businesspeople, who gave up and left a long time ago. Now, the Koreans can't leave. They have no options.

Most people in the poor communities are law-abiding citizens, but they have to play the game of the street to survive. Koreans, lacking in language and street manners, behave just as if they were in Myŏngdong [a very crowded shopping district in downtown Seoul where people push and shove each other on the sidewalks]. They have struck the most sensitive chord in central city black culture, which has to do with respect. Koreans don't understand what respect in street culture means. Every time a young black person, not to mention a middle-aged black person, goes into the store, the Korean merchant's behavior seems disrespectful. The people in the neighborhood define respect in their own terms—meaning body language, language, eyes. Koreans don't know any of these terms at the outset, but they aren't dumb. They can learn quickly.

In a couple of decades, we have replaced the Jews in the black American psyche. The intensity of resentment and contempt for Koreans among many black people is amazing; it should not be underestimated. We occupy a very dark spot in black consciousness. Black people regard us as strangers with unfamiliar customs and language. They feel no bonds with us. To them, we are just strangers barging into their neighborhoods.

I think that the onrush of immigration during the last two decades has made many black people feel threatened, that the gains they have made are being diluted and that they are being squeezed out by the newcomers. They may feel under siege and seek refuge in group loyalty and identity. That's why I can't judge anyone; I think I understand the dilemma.

Vocal black nationalists are prone to wrap the class issue with a racial thing. This is self-deception. Their outrage tends to be selective. They are not aroused by blacks who rob welfare mothers and elderly people in the ghetto. Their outrage is reserved for outsiders who come into their territory. What happened after Malcolm X is a big divide between the black middle class and the underclass. Middle-class activists from the suburbs, in alliance with white liberals in the media, created the theater, which is the press conference, on the outskirts of South Central, where none of them live. Afterwards, they return to their upscale neighborhoods. Three-piece-suited civil rights leaders like Danny Bakewell[24] provide good ammunition for the guilt-ridden in the media who are afraid to go into South Central. They are useful to each other's own agendas, but I still say we Koreans should blame ourselves. We could change things, but we are not doing it because our community is also divided between the voiceless, fragmented merchants and the new mandarins[25] with their degrees. Each ethnic group has to take

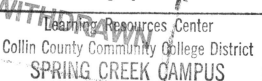
WITHDRAWN
Learning Resources Center
Collin County Community College District
SPRING CREEK CAMPUS

care of their own; that's the beginning. Only when they have done that can they build coalitions with other groups.

On our part, Koreans are unprepared for even a basic dialogue with blacks. In the American republic, each ethnic group has to fend for itself. Freedom is not a given; you have to crawl your way to freedom. That's what black Americans had to do, and Koreans partook of the benefits. Since Koreans came after the civil rights struggle, they have no memory of how hard it was for blacks to bring about such modest gains, not overnight, but over long, dark years. Koreans did not participate in the learning process, so they don't have a sense of affinity with blacks. Neither Koreans nor blacks are in an advantageous position for understanding the other. They can't see that all Korean Americans and African Americans share common sorrows and struggles, that inside they are spiritual brothers and sisters.

We Korean Americans have yet to define our place in U.S. society. The immigrants thought all they had to do whenever they faced a setback was to work harder. But now, the American dream has collapsed; the old ways don't work. In Los Angeles, the safety net of the aerospace industry, the defense industry, and rising property values are all gone. Los Angeles is the place where crisis and opportunity converge! This is the home stretch: in Los Angeles, we will see either Bosnia or the Eden of the West.

Jews wandered the world as pariahs, but Jews in America have achieved the normal lives they yearned for for two thousand years. It's like a beautiful ending to a long story, an epic with a great ending. Ironically, *sa-i-gu* is the beginning of a group of new Jews wandering the earth—the Koreans. It's almost biblical, like Armageddon coming. When you think about *sa-i-gu*, Korean Americans seem almost like God's choice for suffering. It's almost messianic. Maybe a messiah will emerge. Maybe God is making us angrier to save us. Maybe God is fair. He knew about our weakness, so he endowed us with one glorious gift: stamina. The question is, how long will it last? Koreans are a fascinating people, warts and all. I am one of them, but I have the misfortune of being able to see the larger picture.

We are deeply afflicted people. It goes beyond the Korean War and the Japanese occupation. It goes to the very heart of the dark legacy of the Yi Dynasty.[26] Koreans are very private people. We lock each embarrassing episode in our hearts. We are not even honest with each other. We can't say yes, we can't say no, even for the sake of our own survival. We say *kŭlsse* [well...]. That's moral evasion. We lack a value system of our own. That's why we don't have any heroes. We won't let people live long enough to become heroes. Korea is a nation of scoundrels and martyrs.

Korean history really is made of nothing but bitter years of defeat and death. There is not one victory; it's all an endless series of betrayals, frustrations, self-immolations, and self-destructions. Mostly it's self-infliction; we have to redeem ourselves. Cultural victimization is seeping into our consciousness, just like it has done with blacks for the past fifty years. Blacks and Koreans both tend to be self-deceptive people; in our hearts, we can't deny it.

Ever since Korea was opened to the West, I don't think it has had the time, energy, or space to sort things out and create core values. Our millennium of experience has been put on the back burner in favor of two alien ideologies, communism and capitalism.

In the absence of our own value system, we have no dialogue, no sharing. Koreans use their incredible feeling and passion, or *chŏng*. *Chŏng* is giving without expecting anything, but by giving you are totally recognizing your own being and existence. *Chŏng* means unconditional bonding; once the bond is broken, you have mortal enemies forever. Koreans are enamored of and supported by this *chŏng*, which seems to work under oppression. If you don't have *chŏng*, you can't survive domestic or foreign oppression. *Chŏng* and *han*—a grudge that lasts forever, an eternal unrequitedness—are a dangerous, vicious cycle that imprisons us. It's a symptom of affliction; that's how I see it. America is a new laboratory where we can see how we do without it. Or at least we can try to refine it. *Han* will recede with the passing of the immigrant generation.

The indigenous moral value of the Korean family is the only shield Koreans had against cruel outside and inside elements, and it is the main source of energy and passion, of energy and discipline, for Koreans in America. The sheltering family unit as a last refuge has been reinforced by outside forces. I call it the "piggy-back syndrome": the children on the parents' backs are continually aware that they must lighten their parents' burden by succeeding in school. The immigrant parents will have fulfilled their historical mission when their children's generation comes of age. The immigrants provide a cocoon for their children. To ask more than that is to ask too much. Their energy and pride are reflected in the visibility of young Korean Americans in the best American colleges.

The upheavals in Asia are taking centuries to heal. They go from brutal colonization to their own holocaust killing fields and cultural revolutions.

The struggles between capitalism and communism have been played out in the blood of millions of Asians, who have had no chance to nurture their own values and legacies, no time to choose their own destiny. The price, in terms of broken dreams and broken lives, has been beyond calculation.

The Korean War might flare up again at any time. I worry about these Koreans beating their breasts over nationalism. How can we Koreans tout our national homogeneity and the purity of Korean culture when we are the only people left on earth with the devastating firepower for nuclear genocide? Many Korean intellectuals in the U.S. are involved in national reunification drives here, which is self-deceptive escapism at its worst. I've never seen so many unification conferences in Los Angeles as right now, when their own people are burned out, looted, mobbed, and murdered. I don't understand it.

When we talk about the Korean community, we are talking about two separate societies: the U.S.-educated professionals, or new mandarins, in America and the struggling and stumbling inner-city merchants and inhabitants who are called the mainstream of the immigrant community.

Do you know how many American-educated Korean professionals we have in this country? I suspect we have at least 60,000, which means more than ten percent of the Korean work force in the U.S. They stay put in their upscale suburbia, sheltered by their institutions, away from the madding crowd. Korean American doctors say they go through a great deal of suffering to make it, so they believe they have literally no obligations to anyone else. We Korean intellectuals tend to be selfish people. We can expect little from the children locked into the academic track by their professional families, who mostly live outside the Korean American community. Even when our Warsaw *[sa-i-gu]* came, how many of the American-educated new mandarins volunteered to help? I can count them with my fingers. This is an undeniable indictment. It shows that the Korean professionals brought the dark habits of Confucianism with them here. After crossing the ocean, they have merely adapted their Confucian elitism to the new environment. They are the last legacy of Yi Dynasty *yangban*ism.[27]

Korean elites have never washed their hands in the mud of real life. We Koreans pride ourselves that young students rise up in protest against injustice, but we let the young people die and pay the price for us. I have grown weary of so many polished men with all the right words and gestures and their degrees from Ivy League colleges. Many are latter-day palace eunuchs. Their veins are filled with antifreeze. They obey dictators from inside and out, and they manage to stay in power—never attacked, never sanctioned. Hungarian people didn't let collaborators thrive. The French are a cowardly bunch, but they didn't let Vichy take over after the liberation. But we have no sense of shame. We always complain that we are under somebody's domination. We are like this because we were under the Japanese. Everything is explainable; nobody is accountable.

We are not endowed with the genuine Judeo-Christian foundation, even though most Koreans go to churches. We share the work ethic, the pursuit of education, and the belief in the family; but we don't share the sense of community conscience—public charity or civic culture. Lately, I have been reading about the Jewish experience in America. When they arrived here, they brought with them their centuries-old messianic vision of morality, which reinforced their desire for better social conditions in America. What motivates them is not goods but ideals. Wherever Jews go, they want to better the society, so that they can have a better life. What separates us from them is our lack of moral fervor and moral passion. When Koreans arrive here, we don't have such enduring moral values. That's why we are so lost. Koreans observe personal decorum, but beyond their own families and their jobs or crafts, community issues have little or no meaning. That is the Confucian world.

Maybe I'm a romantic, but in my book our heroes are the immigrants. To me, these ghetto Koreans are more miserable than *lumpen* proletariats, who at least have government checks coming in. These ghetto merchants are condemned like Sisyphus to push the rock back up the hill only to have it roll down again, forever. But these grunts in the urban trenches are a pragmatic people. Through blood and tears they will acquire the survival skills needed for an urban society in the global economy, not through formal education, but through everyday experience. They will learn how to behave and conduct themselves in a more democratic way. And hopefully their children will participate in the Korean community and fill up the great void in the Korean character, the absence of social or community conscience.

It's time for us to look at ourselves. We've been lost ever since we came here. We Koreans lack the social, political, and economic infrastructures [that the Chinese and Japanese enjoy] in this country. Successive generations are very important in terms of a community's continuity, stability, and direction. The Korean American community is marked by a very distinctive dichotomy. The first wave of immigrants—seventy-five years of Korean existence in America—is gone with the wind. When the second wave, of which I am the vanguard, came, we did not receive the benefit of any infrastructures left for us by the previous generation. As far as I'm concerned, they have left hardly any impact on us.

Take the San Francisco Korean Methodist Church. That church was more than just a church; it was a depot; it was a homeless shelter; it was the first day-care center for Korean American families. I was a nomad before I entered that place. Nomads are always tense; they are very lonely people, fraught with danger because they don't know what's around the next corner. When I attended that church in 1950, I felt continuity and sanity; it was a place to hang your aching heart on. There were ten or fifteen Korean American families with little kids. Look at that church now! They are selling it to a Chinese mortuary, and the landmark will disappear.[28]

Numbers count. Early Korean immigrants had no numbers.[29] We have a vacuum of leadership after *sa-i-gu*. The current second generation are considered just kids by the immigrant community. We are also saddled with the indifference of educated Korean Americans to community affairs and the riotous growth of churches that siphon off our ethnic capital, each church preoccupied with raising funds for itself.

Right now Asian Americans—and Korean Americans—are in an enviable position because of our magnificent marginality. Away from Asian upheavals that devoured the hearts and souls of our compatriots—the end of Asian feudalism, the Sino-Japanese war, the Japanese occupation of Korea, the Indochinese wars, the civil wars in Korea, China, Vietnam, the Philippines, Burma—we have an opportunity to look deeply at the beginning of diaspora. The future defies all the wisdom of the past. We must be "bi-oceanic," not just bicoastal. We can't create values just from listening to our mothers in the kitchen, like [Chinese American author] Maxine Hong Kingston. Values are like stalagmites—they drip down for thousands of years. It will take generations to sort out the years of pain and passion wasted in the short years from the 1949 Chinese Revolution to today.

Korea and China are inseparable—culturally, ethnically, and geopolitically. Asian Americans were not created in San Francisco with the California Gold Rush. Even Europeans in America trace themselves back to Chaucer and Shakespeare. We can't just flip off the legacy of a millennium when we arrive here. We have to go back to the origins of our language and our imaginations. Today's China looks dismal, but still it beckons. Asian American studies must go back at least to the opening of feudal Asian societies. They've got to write about Korea, Japan, and China. So many people just disappeared from the face of the earth; we have to restore our collective memories. The task falls on the shoulders of the best and brightest Asian Americans, and I don't mean those professors or leaders who only participate in community activism when the evening news broadcast needs a spokesperson.

There is no such thing as race. Race is nothing but the continual evolution of genes. There was no Korean in the beginning. In the modern world, race no longer applies. When we talk about Asian Americans, for instance, I am conscious about the growing number of interracial people. I see a lot of mingling among Asians and Hispanics. The emergence of Africa is changing perceptions of blacks. Many of our children are culturally black. The trend is toward cross-pollination. Our grandchildren will be ethnic Americans, and that will be the end of this curse, this scourge of race.

If I believe in the cosmic fraternity, and if America is the last and only place where race could become the obsolete trash of history, why am I still concerned, then, with Korean American well-being? Because the legacy of the millennium of our forefathers' experiences deserves attention. The only thing we can extract from this legacy is aesthetic—poetry, spirit, folklore. Poetry as expressed in songs, stories, and plays. These have to be preserved. People with only oral history cannot transmit their noble visions in written words to succeeding generations. History without memory is hollow.

I think about these things because I've had a few close calls in my life. Many Koreans are afflicted with hepatitis B virus, but most of them develop immunity to it. Unfortunately, a significant minority do not, and so they die of liver disease. Hepatitis is the Asian sickle-cell anemia.

I was attacked with acute hepatitis in 1984, and I knew it was a progressive disease. I knew I was ordained to knock on the door. I didn't know a transplant was available. All my siblings had died of liver disease and my turn had come up. I took comfort in the fact that I had outlived them by twenty years. When I was going to get the transplant, the doctor warned me that the virus tends to come back to Asians within a year.

I was not in the state of mind to listen to him. I had the transplant, and I beat the one-year rap. I felt invincible. Then my doctor said I was on my way out again, because the deadly virus had come back. He told me to tidy up my affairs. My immunity was at zero, and they couldn't even draw water from my belly for fear of infection. I would just die with a big popped frog belly. Even if they could give me another transplant, I wouldn't go through that again. I was ready to die when they asked me if I'd like to experiment with a daily intravenous treatment now being given to AIDS patients to slow infection. Now my liver indicator has stopped going up, which means that the drug is suppressing the virus and the liver is slowly rejuvenating itself. But we don't know, so I am constantly under surveillance.

Every day is a bonus. I don't know what future lies ahead for me. I don't know for how long; the fact is that we all die. I think I have had more than my share of life. During all of those peaks and valleys after the transplant, I was constantly thinking back to good memories and laughing my head off. I was activating all the marionettes of my life. Right before the transplant I was silently crying to reach out to some divinity. But just admitting your sins is not enough. You must be accountable, and you must pay. I feel unworthy of knocking on the door.

Oral history is so fragmented that it's like parachute history. The remarks people make have to be put into a total context. You need a rifle, not a shotgun. Otherwise you can't make a point. You have to be focused. I think *sa-i-gu* has to be the focal point. It's an all-defining event. It almost wraps up Korean history and opens a new chapter. It is a Wagnerian opera: everything goes up in flames. Reach out to the victims first. You have an obligation to put them on record. You are chronicling the Korean community in transition.

Subjects provide you with sound, smell, and their own points of view. You have an obligation to mingle with their testimony. Every subject doesn't deserve equal space. For some, maybe one paragraph is enough. For others, even a hundred pages won't do.

I'm sick and tired of books on Asian Americans that use only secondhand sources. There are so few first-person accounts. You are writing a here-and-now story. This is not a dried-up textbook.

Korean immigrants are blind, deaf, mute, and without spokespeople. It takes a generation to grow spokespeople who will be the ears, eyes, and mouth of the voiceless immigrant community. Immigrant life means thirty years of silence, and then it will take another thirty years for the second generation to find a place in the sun. Two generations of silent struggle! Our ordeal has just begun—a twilight journey.

Korean life in America is mostly a caricature, because the host culture doesn't care to know about us. It's myth and misconception—Koreans as greedy, gun-happy, and exploitative of blacks. You must tell another story by insisting on the human dimension. The larger picture will emerge a generation from now. It will become an epic.

JANUARY 1993; APRIL, MAY, AND JUNE 1994

STELLA SOON-HI KOH

Dirty Laundry

An accomplished seamstress, Stella Soon-hi Koh [pseudonym] makes the elegantly simple clothing that adorns her delicate frame. Born to upper-class parents who attended American colleges in the late 1930s, Koh came to America in 1948, when immigrants from Japan and Korea were still excluded from this country by law. Like some of the 1.5-generation Korean Americans who were born decades later, she came as a teenager and is thus neither quite like a native-born American nor a Korean national. Although delicate in appearance, Koh's voice is husky, and she still speaks English with the slightest trace of a frisky Taegu accent.

My brother and I were both born in Kyoto. We stayed there until I was a first-grader. My parents were attending Doshisha University in Kyoto at the time. In 1939, when I was five, my parents left me, my brother James, and my younger sister Sara to go to the U.S. They had both gotten scholarships to study theology at Oberlin College in Ohio.[30]

My parents were both from Taegu. They had known each other in Japan, but my father went back to Korea to look for a wife. He didn't find anyone better than my mother, so he came back and married her. She married him because she was very ambitious; she wanted to go on studying, unlike what a Korean woman was supposed to do. She wanted to go to the university and to go abroad, and she married my father because he was the only one who consented to her going on for more education with him.

It was terrible for me in Korea because I had to stay at my uncle's big house, where my grandmother was living. My uncle was rich. He had a famous apple orchard. He even supplied apples to the emperor. His first wife had two sons. He lived in the orchard in the small town of Kŭmdang, in a magnificent white mansion with his second wife and two more children.[31] I lived in Taegu City with his first wife, who was like Cinderella's stepmother. It was like a nightmare every day. I was wearing a beautiful dress when I arrived at that house. The next thing I remember was not having any clothes. All I had to wear was a Korean *chi'ma chŏgori* [Korean women's traditional clothing], a black skirt, and white blouse. And no shoes. If I had shoes, they were wooden *geta* [Japanese platform sandals for working in rice paddies]. I had to do lots of housework. My uncle's wife would make me clean the *maru* [wood floor of a traditional Korean house's entryway] in the morning. I had to wash the breakfast dishes. She would make me do it even though they had a maid.

During the war, my aunt gave me only leftovers. They were all gone after one or two bites. My grandmother knew I was hungry, so she always wrapped her covered bowl of rice in a blanket and put it on the hot spot on the *ondol* [oiled paper flooring heated from underneath with charcoal briquettes or firewood] floor.[32] She was so sweet all the time.

I lived like this until the war ended. Then my father came to Korea. We were taken from [my] uncle's place to our own house. It was huge and beautiful. All of a sudden, I had everything I had not had: beautiful clothes, maids doing the work. Before they arrived, I knew I had parents, but I couldn't say anything about them. I had to pretend to be an orphan because Japanese killed Koreans with parents in the U.S.[33]

I always prayed to have a mother. But after my mother arrived, I started praying to God, "Why did I ask for a mother? If a mother is like that, please take her back." I didn't have any rapport with my mother then. Now, at least we talk civilly.

She was not kind. She was not compassionate or loving, not a warm person like I thought mothers were supposed to be. She was very devilish, always angry and screaming. When I think about it now, I realize that she was very unhappy. But I was only ten years old. How was I to understand?

I think it was because my parents had an unhappy marriage. Nowadays, Father says she was not having any "fun" with him. It was a boring life. I think any marriage has a boring side.

She worked full time for the U.S. military, assisting General Hodge.[34] She was very fluent in English. My father had a lot of jobs; one of them was overseeing the Korean education system. Both my parents were big shots. We had everything: chauffeur, gardener, seamstress, cook, bellboy or butler. They were always out all day, and they would come home to eat in the evening. I was at school pretty late, and I would eat whatever the cook had made. I never had dinner with them.

After about three years, we left for Hawaii. I have to admire my father, because at that time Syngman Rhee, then the president of [South] Korea, wanted to give him any kind of job he wanted—foreign minister or whatever —but my father refused, saying he was not a politician. He had studied to become a minister and could not accept any political job. For three years, he refused. Finally, Syngman Rhee said his church in Hawaii was having a big problem, and that he should go and fix it. My father had refused other government jobs, but he could not refuse this one. The church had two factions; one liked the minister and the other didn't. They finally had two services, one in the morning and one in the afternoon. After my father arrived, there was one service only, filled to capacity. We went to Hawaii for a three-year term, but the congregation voted to have him stay another year; then the Korean War broke out, so we couldn't go back to Korea. We went to Washington, D.C., in 1951 to join my mother, who had taken a job there the year before.

In a way, my father was more there like a mother than my mother was. He was the one at the hospital when I was sick. He paid for the luxury liner when I came to Hawaii with my youngest sister, Grace. Grace was in the hospital with pneumonia when Mother left Hawaii for [Washington] D.C. She never quite got over being sad and angry that Mother left while she was sick.

We had the feeling Mother was always leaving. If she was there, she was always negative. She was critical of everything. For example, I kept house for her ever since I was thirteen in Hawaii. Every meal, I remember, I cried because she was critical about something I had made. She never said, "This is good." She would complain that the rice was too hard or too watery, or that the vegetables were too salty, too spicy, or too bland. Eventually I figured I was not good for anything. My brother liked to tinker with mechanical stuff. He'd take apart broken watches and radios. Instead of encouraging him, she would say, "What do you know about fixing anything?" She would never give him the confidence that he might need. It was always [her] negativity that drove us nuts. Today, it would be called child abuse. We were thoroughly abused, both emotionally and physically.

My father once got furious with my mother, but he couldn't take it out on her, so he whipped me with a leather belt. I had stayed up all night fixing *panchan* [side dishes] for a church picnic. When we got to the picnic grounds the next morning and unloaded everything, we discovered that the *kimch'i* jar was missing. My mother was screaming, "Stupid! How could you forget?" Father said, "Let's go pick it up." He could have gone alone, but he wanted me to come so he could beat me up. At first, I didn't know why he started taking off his belt. That day I couldn't swim because of the red welts. I just sat on the beach with all my clothes on, watching the others. I just felt numb. My father apologized before we came back to the picnic, but it really didn't make any difference to me anymore.

When I was sixteen years old, we moved to Washington, D.C. Staying with my parents' friends, the Kim family, I was still pretty shy. I didn't speak English well then. Auntie Anne was so kind and nice. I felt she was the ideal mother I had missed.

Whenever I received a letter from my mother, I would shake as if her letter was screaming. Later, when I was a college freshman, I couldn't study because I kept imagining my mother screaming at me. I was a poor student.

I thought I didn't belong to this world. I figured I'd better die, I'd better kill myself. Through my teenage years and early twenties, for years and years, I wanted to die. I wanted to die as soon as I found out who my mother was.

She never had any idea that I felt this way.

From the Kims' we moved to a red brick apartment building in Maryland. Father was getting ready to organize a church. My mother was working for the map service. When I was in high school, I was a good singer. That was what saved me. My music teachers immediately discovered my voice, and I was always given solos in Christmas programs. I was having fun at school. At that time, I was so shy that when I walked down the hallway I kept my head down for fear that someone would speak to me. I was even more shy because we moved around so much; I had to change schools thirteen times.

For a while, we lived at a rooming house for old Chinese men in Washington D.C.'s Chinatown. Father did most of the work cleaning the rooms. The men were incontinent and soiled their bedding every night. I remember changing the sheets.

I graduated from high school in D.C. in 1953. McKinley High School was all black the following year because of the *Brown v. Board of Education* decision. I had very good friends there. I was so quiet that other students tried to help me because they thought I needed help. After high school, I went to a small Methodist college in Maryland. I didn't do very well, so I left after one year and started working. Father said I should finish college, so I enrolled myself at D.C. Teachers College in elementary education. I found out I wasn't cut out to teach little kids, so I quit.

I always had lots of boyfriends; I don't know why. My mother gave me the impression I was ugly, yet every time I went to school or somewhere, I attracted boys. I said to myself, "I'm not pretty; why are they attracted to me?" Eventually, I thought I must not be too bad-looking. Having lots of boys attracted to me changed me; somehow, it helped me live. When I was a freshman in college, the very first day, boys picked up my luggage and took it to my room. Within an hour I got a telephone call. All the girls were shocked, wondering who was calling Stella already. That was my first American date.

He was such a nice young man. His father was the consul general in Japan. He was pre-med and handsome. The girls were dying to know how I had attracted a person like that. I later asked him what attracted him. He said the way I dressed and what I brought—other girls had mountains of luggage, but I didn't.

We saw each other daily and on weekends. At Easter vacation, he brought me home. I was ready to go back to school. Father asked, "How often do you see this guy?" I said, "Every day." He said, "I don't want you to marry some white boy, so I want you to stop seeing him." Stupidly, I obeyed. I told him, tears rolling down my face, that my parents would not allow me to see him anymore.

Earlier, when I was fourteen, I had fallen in love with my father's friend's son, who stayed with us in Hawaii. I never said a word. He came to my college to see me. I had gotten a job as a YWCA camp counselor in Pennsylvania during the summer. He proposed over the phone. I was deliriously happy. When my mother found that out, she sat him down and said, "Call Stella tomorrow and take back your word." So he called, his voice shaking, to say, "I can't marry you." My brother James knew what had happened. At that time, James was already very unhappy and wanted to leave home. He was leaving, so I left with him.

I had lots of Korean boyfriends by then. Some men fell in love with me, but I was thinking I should die cleanly without a mistake. I was planning to set the date and do research on less messy methods. When one of the guys showed up at the door with flowers every day, I would slam the door in his face. One day I was sick, lying on my couch with an earache. I screamed, "Go away! I'm sick." I was lying there with my back to the door. He asked, "Where are you sick?" He gently touched my ear with shaking hands. Then he called his brother, who was a doctor in New York, and told him to send medicine. When the medicine arrived the next day, he came and gently administered it. This man was 100 percent Korean, but he made something and brought it out for me to eat. I was so amazed that I ate it.

I was still thinking about dying, so I told him, "I'm not worth it. I already have a date set to die." He cried and cried. "If you have to die, I will die with you," he said. We set the date. The day before, he cried his heart out. He said, "Please marry me, don't die." I decided that marrying him was better than dying.

He was so happy. My parents were in Korea. When they heard about this, they told his boss to bring him back to Korea, and he got recalled. He wrote twice daily. By that time, I loved him and wanted to marry him, so I decided to go to Korea. I was twenty-three. I borrowed money from a friend and flew to Korea. The boy came to the airport, and so did my father, who shoved and punched him in the men's room. My parents kept me imprisoned at home. I was not allowed to talk to him or see him. All I could do was go back to the U.S. My parents were powerful people at that time.

I decided to marry whoever came along next. My husband-to-be showed up in D.C. He had been in Tennessee as a foreign student. He was so clever that he went to my mother first. He told her all about his ambitions and plans. My mother was attracted. They planned for him to call a certain day, and my mother would make sure I was there to answer the phone.

Our first date was July 24, and by August 15, 1959, we were married. My mother was scared I wouldn't say yes, but after we were married, she terrorized us. When we were leaving for Colorado, where my husband had a teaching job, she beat me because I wanted to give the old furniture to my husband's younger brother. I was bruised all over. I knew that what my mother did was wrong, so when I had my own children I never got nasty with them. I always felt I would never repeat what my mother did to her children. It came naturally to me to be good to my children.

My husband's first teaching job was in Alamosa, Colorado. After a while, he got a job at a university in Arizona. I was happy when I moved away from my family. Our marriage was "parallel living." He did his research and his traveling, and I took care of everything else. We had a nice house and a comfortable life. Unlike my mother, he always thought I was very smart; he didn't degrade me like my mother did. Since I didn't have enough confidence, I tried to prove myself, and I took care of the bills, the car, the children. In fact, I was too capable; he wanted to use me too much. Like a good secretary or wife, I had to remind him of everything. He never participated in anything for the children. He didn't know what was going on. He didn't even know where the car radiator was. I managed the household. If he had to go, he went. He was never around when I had a baby. I thought that by helping him to do his work by giving him all the time he wanted, I was doing my wifely duty, but actually I was making him into a dumb idiot.

I didn't care what other Korean women wanted for their kids. I just wanted my children to do what they loved and be happy and healthy. I didn't care about them being doctors and lawyers, and I wanted them to marry anyone they loved. Their father wanted them to be "somebody" so that he would not be embarrassed about them. He always had conflicts with them. He was always angry at them for playing. Once he told me to go to the teacher to get more homework for Hugh. The teacher said, "Your son is a good boy and a good student. He needs to enjoy his life." My husband would not believe me when I told him that she had said that.

In 1979, after twenty years of devotion, I got sick with rheumatoid arthritis. I couldn't even get out of bed easily. I was going back and forth to California for treatment. School was out, and my husband's brother was running for Korean Federation president. He would go out all day. Other husbands were so devoted they would not accept evening invitations. My husband took our one car from 7:00 A.M. to midnight. He never called to find out how I was. I asked him what he would do if I were paralyzed. He said, "I was born to leave my name in the history books, not to take care of a sick wife." I hadn't eaten and I couldn't stand up, but I was suddenly energized. I got up and said, "If you can't take care of me when I'm sick, I don't need you when I'm well. Get out." He said he would leave when he was ready. In ten days he packed up and moved to his mother's.

My three children were so angry at him. From then on, they were after me to get rid of him as soon as possible. For a time, he walked in whenever he wanted, taking this and that. I discussed the problems with everyone. It was November 1979. They all said I should get rid of him. I was divorced in January 1980. I got child support until the children were eighteen. I also got the house.

Five months later, he married another woman. All the time he had had a woman. I didn't know it, of course. He had never been a good husband or lover. She would only get his title. He teaches in Korea now. Whenever I see my ex-husband I say, "Did you leave your name in any history books yet?"

My children went to college after my husband left. He couldn't imagine that they would still be doing well without him, although he didn't care about them when he left. They don't go out of their way to call him. My kids worry about me. He once called to say he appreciated that I had raised our children well. His current wife is ambitious and didn't want to raise the kids, and now he realizes what I did. I said, "Don't ever call me again." The problem is that if he keeps on doing that, I will forget about the bad he did. I used to cry when I talked about him. I admired his hard work, and I gave him all my life, and yet he disregarded everything. He didn't even care. It was just shocking.

The kids were in junior high school and high school when we got divorced. I stayed in Arizona until my youngest finished high school. I studied for a real estate license and took in sewing. I tried to get a job at the university library. My friend knew I was a professor's wife without any money, and she got me a job at her husband's company in Los Angeles. I came to California in November 1983. At first, I handled parts bidding over the telephone. Later I became an administrator overseeing the contracts. It was a pretty good job. I got a little apartment. I liked living alone. I had a lot of friends in Los Angeles.

I had been divorced four years, I hadn't dated anyone, and I never thought of remarrying. Marriage was the furthermost thing from my mind. I thought, "I'll never wash any other man's dirty clothes again." Then I met J.K. It was one week after I got to L.A. I had gone shopping one Saturday and felt like going home to eat something Korean. I stopped to pick up some noodles. I was coming out of the store when the bag boy put a Korean newspaper in my bag. I said, "It's difficult for me to read this, so you might as well give it to someone who can read it." He said, "You read English better than Korean? How long have you been here?" The people in the store couldn't believe I was a middle-aged person who had been here all my life.[35] The man standing next to me listening to this conversation was J.K.

As I was leaving, he picked up my bag to take to the car for me. He asked me where I was from, and I said, Arizona. When he saw my car tags, he figured I was telling the truth. He asked about my husband. He said he was single too; and then he asked, "Can we have a date?"

We met for lunch the next day. The first thing he said was, "I'm going to make you my wife." I didn't have a chance to disagree. He said he never found such a naively honest Korean woman. He had heard so many lies he couldn't believe that someone was telling the truth. He had been alone for ten years. He had been in the U.S. for two years. In Korea, he had been in the military. I was attracted because he was forceful, direct, definite about what he wanted. I told him I didn't want to be left alone by some man, and I didn't want to do any man's dirty laundry. He promised he would not leave me alone or make me do the laundry.

We got married, and at first he packed a lunch box for me every day. We started doing a produce market in 1985. I put in all of the money I got from the sale of the house in Arizona. Since I always help out a husband, when J.K. decided to have a market, I helped out as a cashier. We toiled for seven years. We were there from 7:00 A.M. to 7:00 P.M., seven days a week. I had never done this kind of work before. I had been in a protected environment. As a minister's daughter and then a professor's wife, I didn't really know the downtrodden. When I started being this "produce Mom," there were all kinds of customers. I didn't know Mexicans that well. I admire them because they love their kids. The parents could be dressed shabbily, but the children would be dressed so prettily. Everyone loves children, especially the men—they adore their children. I could not speak Spanish, but I could feel their happiness. I had never been in that kind of situation myself.

There was a colored man who collected all kinds of stuff for recycling. He worked so hard. He was around seventy. He walked so many miles a day. He'd come in smiling and say, "Today I made fifty dollars!" He was always so energetic about working. I thought, "God! A person can be so happy." I had so much to learn. As a young woman, I thought I should die. I was always so negative about myself.

There were so many people like that.

I saw many sad cases, too. We got a lot of bad raps from people complaining about our produce. Some would just scream and leave. We were also mugged and robbed. J.K. was mugged at gunpoint several times by young Latinos and African Americans. You are never prepared, but I was never really that afraid. People come in and talk to you. Then they turn out to be robbers. One time, a bunch of black boys came in. They were talking to us and being friendly. All of a sudden, they grabbed my cash drawer and ran. You can't control things like that. You have to learn not to let down your guard. You feel you have to be suspicious of everyone who comes in. I disliked that very much.

The destruction in April[36] was such a waste. I couldn't believe that such a thing could be happening. We had finally gotten rid of our store, but I could imagine what those store owners were going through. It's a shameful thing. And yet, it seems to be a no-no to complain that this was done. I never heard anyone say, "I'm sorry." They act like they did the right thing, like they had the right to do it. They had no right to destroy people's livelihood. Where did they get that right? Because they are poor?

Judge Karlin was stupid. Du Soon Ja should have gotten a prison sentence.[37] Her reason was that it didn't do society or her children any good. If she were thinking about her children, she would not have pulled the trigger in the first place. Karlin should also have been aware of the feelings people had at the time. It is very difficult to understand how [Du] could pull a trigger on someone who was walking away. What is a bottle of orange juice, anyway? I hate these people who say they looted or stole and had a right to do it. But to kill someone who is turning around and leaving is something I can never comprehend. That judge had no more sense than a three-year-old child. Why did Du Soon Ja pull out the gun and shoot her? It shows that she hated not only that teenager but all black people.

With all the things I went through, I am still optimistic. We should recover. I think the relationships between the races will be better. Now race relations are advertised more and we are more aware, but race problems are not worse. They are better. My closest friends when I was young were black. I had no concept of color discrimination. I used to think "colored" meant white because they have so many different colors and are colorful— red, brown, yellow hair, blue, brown, green eyes. I could not figure out why black people were called colored.

When people ask me where I am from, I don't know what to say. After living here and becoming an American citizen, I say, "I don't know where I'm from. I'm from all over."

JANUARY 1993

DONG HWAN KU

War Zone

Dong Hwan Ku [pseudonym] was born in Korea in 1958 and came to the United States when he was twenty-six years old. He and his wife operate a small sundries store close to a college campus. His father was a military man, and Ku himself seems influenced by his own experiences serving in the South Korean Army. For example, he would not hesitate to use Mace on customers he fears are unruly because he views Mace as a way to defuse violence. Ku is slightly built. His dark face is imprinted with an expression of perpetual anguish. He speaks rapidly, tears occasionally filling his eyes when he recalls the past.

When I was growing up in Korea in the 1960s, life was very difficult. We were very regimented, forced to have our hair cut short and forced to wear uniforms to school.[38] I faced a lot of economic hardships. We did not always have enough to eat. Sometimes all of my family members had to share one egg.

I came into contact with American soldiers when I was young. It seemed to me that they were all able to eat well every day. They ate lots of meat. I remember thinking that if I went to America, I could eat like that too, even if I was a beggar in America. Like all other Koreans, I had to serve in the Korean military. I remember being always hungry and always cold. The U.S. soldiers would come out of their tents in weather that was twenty degrees below zero Centigrade wearing only their underwear. In those days, blue jeans from America were so popular. If I could ever afford a pair of blue jeans, I would not wear them, I would just look at them. To me, America seemed like heaven.

After I finished my military service and attended college, someone offered to introduce me to a Korean immigrant woman who was living in the U.S. I agreed to the marriage, and that's how I happened to move to America. I landed in Dallas, Texas, in July 1984.

Since I could not speak English, I was very handicapped. But I worked so hard. I tried everything; I was a janitor for the first three and a half years, then I worked as a white shirt presser at a dry cleaners, and then I was a dishwasher and a hamburger cook. I got a job working for a white shopkeeper in a neighborhood where ninety percent of the customers were black. I got into trouble because I started giving away the ends of salami and other meat chubbs to the customers, since the boss was not able to sell them anyway. When he ordered me to stop doing that, I was threatened and cursed by the customers. I was harassed a lot; even though I could not fully understand what people were saying to me, I could tell it was unkind. They slashed my car tires and wrote "Fuck you, chink" on my car with razor blades. It was a poor community, and there was always some stealing at the store. The white owner had promoted me to a supervisor position, but I took my old janitorial job back to avoid all the hassles.

I learned from my experience in Texas not to give away anything. People get used to it and start expecting it. If you can't give them something, they get angry. I used to live near a black area. I see that black people don't have a chance to get an education. They come from broken families. Sometimes there is no food in the house. The parents drink, so the kids steal when they are hungry. They can't get a job and they take drugs. Most of the drug dealers I have seen are black. I think it's white people that made them like that. If you go to Harlem, you will see that it's not fit for human habitation. People are born there and they die there. When buildings are torn down or condemned, they are not rebuilt. The city does not invest in that community. The message people get is, "You guys just live and die there." There are many old folks who have never been on an airplane. They just stay in the neighborhood. It's like the countryside in Korea, where people just live and die in the area.

Survival was very difficult, and then the economy fell due to the oil crisis in Texas. I moved to Flushing, New York. It was a very mixed area—about twenty percent black, twenty percent Asian, thirty percent Latino, and thirty percent white. The neighborhood was rough. Kids were learning how to give people the finger. After working for about a year, I got a little produce stand. Then I heard about the store here in California. My wife's brother knew about it. So we moved here and put down all of our savings and a loan from our parents for the down payment. My wife and I both worked and saved up all our money.

I wanted to have my own store because when I used to work in the hamburger shop or the sandwich shop, I would hear the customers complaining about the mustard or whether or not the food was cooked the way they liked it. I thought that if I had my own store, I would not have to listen to these kinds of complaints. I would buy my merchandise from some supplier, so no one could complain about anything being my fault.

I feel very disabled because I am not good in English. I have never had time to get any education in America. Even if school were free I would not have time to go. I work in this shop fourteen hours a day, seven days a week. My wife works here nine hours a day. The only other thing we do is go to church. But even then, we can't even go together; one person has to mind the store. I have two children, five and six years old—Mary and Steven. But I only see them in the morning when I drop them off at preschool before opening our store. By the time I get home at 2:00 A.M., they are already asleep. I only really see them once every four days or so. I have to keep this place open late so that we can pay the rent and service our debts.

My wife and I together work twenty-three hours a day, seven days a week. There are no days off. I figure that our hourly wage is less than minimum wage. Even if I died right at this moment, I have nothing to leave behind.

Hundreds of people come into my store. I can't satisfy all of them perfectly. Sometimes dozens and dozens of people want change for a $20 bill in one day. They get the bills from the ATM machine next door. When I refuse, they curse me. I can change money twenty or thirty times, but not hundreds of times. People don't understand.

I always work so hard. I eat at the store. There is a little hot plate upstairs. I just wear jeans and a T-shirt to work. I don't spend money on eating out or on clothes. I know that many Korean store owners have been killed.[39] I feel like this is a war zone and that my life has become like a battle. If I close my eyes or relax my vigilance for a second, I might lose my life. I always have to be on my toes.

After the Rodney King verdict, the other stores around here were broken into. The windows were smashed. One market down the street was completely looted of everything of value. People broke down my door and started looting until I showed them I had a gun. At first, they said, "Go ahead and shoot," and kept putting things into their pockets. So I shot one round into the air. They threw down what they had and left. The police didn't even get here until much later. They advised me to carry Mace instead of a gun.

I am scared every day. I have been beaten, cursed, and spat upon. Sometimes young kids demand cigarettes, and if I don't sell to them, they get angry. Once someone threw a bottle at me. If I hadn't blocked it with my arm, I would have been hit in the face. The bottle broke on contact, and I had to go get stitches on my arm. The police only come after everything is over. They ask for descriptions, write a police report, and leave.

Last year about three hundred students tried to break down the door with a battering ram. The window didn't have steel rails, so they broke through the glass. Again the police came when it was too late. Sometimes street people who are drugged out come in here and start harassing me or throwing things around. Once a drunk came in here and threw merchandise on the floor, broke the window, and ran away. I had to chase him several blocks down the street. I handed him over to the police. Later, when he got out on probation, I signed the release on the condition that he not come back to my store. Last summer, I was badly beaten when I tried to block the doorway as a man who had stolen something before was trying to enter the store. I was alone, and several men beat me up so badly that I had to go to the hospital. After that I got health insurance. Life was hard in Korea, but over there I would not have to endure this kind of abuse.

This is war. There's no end to war. It's just continual escalation. I've tried everything: video cameras, Mace. It's a sign of social disease; there's no end, no solution.

When I first came to this country, I saw banks in certain neighborhoods in Dallas and New York with bulletproof teller windows. As a customer, I felt insulted. It was like assuming that I was going to commit a crime. Now I understand.

Now when I compare the dream I had of America with the reality, I know this is not an easy country to live in. When I finish paying off my debts, I hope I can go back to Korea. People are always saying that anyway: "Fucking Chinese, go home!" I hear that every day.

It is very hard to live as an immigrant here. Race discrimination is far too strong. It's impossible to overcome the limitations on first-generation immigrants. There is a real limit to how far a person can go.

In the old days, it was hard to live in Korea, no matter how hard you worked. But during the last ten years, it seems to have become possible to survive there if you try. My parents are in Korea. They have seen how I live here in America, working like a dog in this crowded little space. They say, "Hurry up and come back home."

I am sick and tired. I feel defeated. The prospects for my further growth are very limited. What kind of future is there? American-born Koreans, when they grow up, will face race discrimination, even if they are born here. It's not fair. Will the second, third, or fourth generation born in the U.S. ever be equal? I know one man who doesn't let his two U.S.-born sons work in his store. They speak fluent English and can understand everything people say and do, so they feel worse. They get into fights with the customers.

In my own case, I am a cripple without any American education. There's no way out. I just have to continue to work hard. I have a college degree in architecture from Hong Ik University in Seoul, but look at me now. Look at what happened to me. When people criticize me, why don't they think about my circumstances? I have worked so hard only to have so many shameful things happen to me. I cannot understand; if other people are partially at fault and don't acknowledge it, they aren't human beings.

I have never broken the law. I have never even been cited for a moving violation. I have never written a bad check. I have always paid my parking tickets. I have tried my best to be an honest person. If I hire a black employee, they don't work very hard. I have hardly seen any African American grocery owners. This business is one of the toughest, and you have to be willing to work hard. Ask any American citizen about these small businesses. Which one of them would do a small business? Only an immigrant is willing to do what no one else will do.

No one knows what I have been through. When I was working as a janitor in Dallas, I had to clean the bathrooms. People's diarrhea would be in the toilet, women's used sanitary napkins, everything. To save money, the owners of the office building would turn off the air conditioner while we were working, and the smell was overwhelming. The smell would linger, making me lose my appetite for a long time. Sometimes I would just clean with my bare hands because it was faster. I have had my hands in American people's shit.

If people read my story, they may come to know how hard I have tried to live in America. People who like to drink, none of them are bad. They relieve their stress that way. I have no friends here; I am lonely. I don't have time to do sports or go anywhere. I look forward to having a drink after work, just to make me feel better for a short while. I don't drink a lot, but I really feel better after I numb the pain with a drink. I have nothing else.

Right now, the American dream is unattainable. I want to sell this store and move back to Korea. But who would buy this place? Once you get into this kind of work, it never ends.

MARCH 1993

41

IMJUNG KWUON

Launched

Imjung Kwuon was born in Korea in 1958 and has lived in the United States since she was four years old, when her parents decided to immigrate. A marriage, family, and child counselor, she writes an advice column for the English language section of a Korean language daily newspaper in Los Angeles, where she professionally counsels men who abuse or kill their wives and children. "I do this work because I believe that it's always possible for a person to change," she says.

There were not many Koreans in Los Angeles when we moved here from Korea in 1962. I remember that I didn't know what was happening. I just remember me and my younger sister causing a lot of trouble on the plane, making noise, crying—I was so unhappy, and the food tasted awful. My parents were carrying a grill pan. I know there's a name for it in Korean—it's the one with the holes for the barbecue juices to drip down over the charcoals. Anyway, I remember them carrying that on the plane and how difficult the plane ride was for us.

When we first got to L.A., our parents had to leave us somewhere so that they could work. I think we went to some nursery school. I remember not liking the food and not being able to understand what the lady was saying, so we caused a lot of trouble crying and not being like the other kids, who already understood the routine. Finally, I think our parents had another Korean mother watch us while they went off to work.

My father tried his hand at all sorts of small businesses—import-export, wigs, laundry—the kind you don't see anymore, where the sheets go around and around in automated giant rollers. I remember the wig stores. We would get boxes and boxes of wigs from Japan. My father spoke Japanese and was able to make some connections there. He would sort out the wigs according to color. There was a little office where he would take orders, and then we went around delivering wigs to mostly African American shops.

We lived on Catalina and Pico in a quadplex. There weren't many Koreans at my school, but there were lots of Hispanic and African American children. The classes were mixed, and there was a lot of sharing of food and fantasies. We made up imaginary families. I remember it clearly because I needed that when business wasn't so good, and I noticed my father's rages more. They had happened in Korea too; he had a horrible temper. We used to run and hide. He would be yelling and screaming and hitting. But I remember more clearly that after we had been in L.A. for a couple of years, the weekends always included drinking. Even though there weren't many Koreans then, every weekend Korean families would visit us, play *changki* [Korean/Chinese chess], and have dinner at our house. The men would drink vodka or whatever, and my father drank every day. For him, it was like eating rice. It was part of his routine.

There were lots of episodes where he would be very unhappy about something. I'm sure it had to do with business not being good. He would feel frustrated and come home. We'd all be sitting around at the table, and he would pick a fight about something. Maybe the rice wasn't prepared right, or there was a little piece of stone or a hair somewhere in his food. He would sweep everything off the table. All the dishes would break. For a long time, we didn't have a complete set of dishes. We were always replacing them. He used to throw ashtrays and glasses.

One time I tried to interfere. I think I was about six or seven. I could hear my parents arguing in the kitchen, and of course my sister and I were out in the front yard. Then, I don't know why, but I must have run in and said "stop" or something. He hit me. It wasn't like punishment, like spankings— we understood those, when we had done something bad. When he hit me, I flew across the kitchen. I don't remember the pain, only being stunned and blacking out for a second. Then my mother came over and said, "Don't come in; don't interfere. I don't want you to get hurt. Please go over to the other room. It only makes it worse if you come in, blah, blah, blah." So I learned very early that to interfere caused more trouble, because then he could say, "Look at the way you are bringing up your daughters! They are getting worse, they won't obey, blah, blah." We were afraid for our mother. And I would hate my father. There would be periods of quiet, and then there would be a blowup. Then there was the drinking.

I think the immigration experience was very stressful for him, so he had a hard time. This was his way of releasing some of his anger and frustration. I know that the bad temper stuff runs in the family.

My father really wanted a son. In 1964, I recall my mother being pregnant again. She had to eat all kinds of special stuff and ask fortune-tellers for predictions. That was a huge part of my parents' pregnancy! I say "their pregnancy" because both of them were involved. My mother had to eat special food, do all the right things, all that superstitious stuff. I can remember someone holding a needle above her wrist—if it went one direction, it was a girl, and if it went in the other direction, it was a boy. If the stomach hangs low or wide, and all this stuff. Everyone said this time she would have a boy. That was before amniocentesis or ultrasound. My father picked out a boy's name, Hugh—because it was like "Phew! I finally got a son." It was his private joke.

When my fourth sister was born, he didn't even want to look at the new baby. He would have nothing to do with her. I think his disappointment was so strong that he might have given her away if he could have. I don't know how my mother felt. I'm going to have to ask her. Dad just left her at the hospital. She had to come up with a name in order to get the baby released. She wanted the name Joanne, but she could not spell it, so she spelled out J-O-A-N.

Dad acted like Joan was some dustball. He no doubt felt humiliated because he had told everyone he was going to have a son. Babies can sense what's going on from day one. After about six months, when my father realized that she was kind of cute and tried to interact with her, she tried to avoid him. Every time he went over to her, she would burst out crying. She would not go to him and didn't want him to carry her. He had to really work at winning her affection.

My father was the first son of a first son of a first son. He was the leader of his family. His father had died when he was in his twenties, so he became the top person in the clan. He still does *chesa* [ancestor commemoration] and abides by all the rules. It bothered him that his brother had three sons, while he had none. For a long time, he blamed my mother for not giving birth to sons. Even as a teenager, you learn in health education about X and Y chromosomes. I would argue with him, but he would say, "That's nothing! What do you know? There is such a thing as ancient human knowledge that has come down over ages and ages."

My father had affairs, using the rationale that he wanted a son. He planned to impregnate some woman and have his son come live with us. My mother must have felt betrayed by his adultery, but she felt that all the other stuff, the beatings and abuse, were just her destiny, the fate of women, whatever. She used to always tell me, "You're lucky if a man doesn't beat, cheat, or drink." It was some formula that I wrote down in my diaries.

The one time my mother tried to leave was when my father was really openly flaunting this one woman he wanted to have a son with. He had sponsored her immigration as a nurse. She stayed at our house for a day before going to her job at the hospital, which he had helped her get. When things finally dawned on all of us, especially my mother, she poured out her anguish at the dinner table in front of some guests who were there. I was fifteen at the time. She said she was leaving. He said, "To hell with you, go ahead if you want." There had been a series of events like this, but this was like the last straw. Up to this point, she had said she would not leave because she worried about who would marry her motherless daughters. She stayed for our sake, for our future. But this time, she was going to leave. I had a hard time forgiving the dinner guests, who stopped her by literally dragging her back into the house and sitting her down in a chair. Someday, I will have to tell them what I think, because they are still around in our community.

My father wanted us girls to be pure and innocent. He thought that by putting up barriers, he was doing a good job as a father. He would not allow us to have bicycles or roller skates because we might get hurt. My mother told me how she fought with him to let me get some skates. Even then, he would only let me practice in the backyard. He was afraid I would not stay a virgin, that someone might rape me, that I would learn immoral values in American society and become loose and wild. He knew about good girls and bad girls, since he knew about adult male society in Korea and America, and he definitely wanted his daughters to be good girls and marry good men. Good men would not be attracted to women who were open about their sexuality.

I would ask if I could go to the graduation night or the prom, and that always caused a lot of trouble, since I was the first kid. We were pretty isolated, because of our culture and because of our family pattern. My friends knew nothing about my family life away from school. We never talked about our families. I didn't invite anyone home because Dad didn't like us to be friends with people of different races. They could not come through our front door, and we could not go to their houses either. At Hollywood High School, I used to ride the bus home on Sunset Boulevard with my friend Denise. Once my mother picked me up and I asked her if she could drop Denise off. My father found out about it and screamed and yelled for a couple of days about how I should not associate with black people or let them get into the car. He would lecture about inferior races, bad influences, rootless people, bad blood, all that stuff. I think he would have been surprised about the friends I had, if he had ever followed me around in high school as a sort of invisible person. I never shared anything with him. It was better that he didn't know, because he would have been very upset. I think he really didn't want to know. My mother sort of went along with the program. It was one thing they were very united about.

I was depressed for many years. I figured somehow that my parents' marital problems were my fault. When I was seventeen, I tried to kill myself. I got a bottle of sleeping pills. I took two, because I had never taken any before. I had written a good-bye letter. My sister and I were living in an apartment above a garage, while my parents were living in a little house in front. There were only two bedrooms in the house. Anyway, my mother came up for some reason. It was in the afternoon, and I was by myself. She saw the letter and the bottle and realized what I did. She said, "You stupid, stupid girl!" and tore up the letter and threw away the pills and woke me up. We never spoke about it afterwards. She never asked me why I did that. She couldn't understand why her intelligent, lovely, educated daughter would feel like this. She had no idea that what was going on in her marriage was affecting me.

I dropped out of high school in my senior year. I had enough units to graduate, so they let me graduate. I had had a 3.66 grade point average. They wondered how an A student could suddenly start getting Ds and Fs. Maybe they asked me what was wrong, but I couldn't answer.

I started working at the Carpeteria. Once, while I was working there, my father beat me up so badly that I could not go to work. I had done something pretty stupid. Not stupid, maybe, but immature and foolish. It was not a big deal. I talked to some of the salesmen at work. I didn't really know anything about male-female relations. Anyway, one of the men asked me, "Is your mother as beautiful as you are?" I said, "Of course, she is better looking," or whatever. I must have repeated the comment to my mother when she picked me up from work. Or maybe I said in front of my father that Mr. So-and-So said that Mother was beautiful. Then my father beat me up because I allowed a strange man to—I don't know what, exactly—invade his family? bring dirty stuff into the family? He was inordinately jealous.

When I got beaten up, he said, "You're not going back to work." I said, "I am going back to work." That was the only thing I had outside the family. I thought that if I didn't have my job I would be stuck in hell. But I had a huge black eye and bruises all over, so I called work the next day and said I would not be coming back. She said it would look really bad on my employment record and tried to convince me to come into work, but I told her I couldn't, and that my father wouldn't allow it. I am sure that if I had tried to go back to work, I would have been beaten to death. He wanted to stop me while I was only having little trouble, before big trouble could start.

He used to beat me whenever I got back from a week at Korean American camp with a bunch of crazy Americanized Korean kids. He would detect that I had acquired a kind of attitude, so he would beat me up. I was beaten through high school. My last beating was when I was in college. I used to write it all down; I have a box full of diaries filled with all my childish unhappiness. I documented it all in diaries, because I had no one else to tell. A couple of years ago, I tried to read them over, but I just couldn't. It brought back all the tears and pain.

I argued a lot with my father about going to the college of my choice. I wanted to go somewhere away from home so that I could move out, make choices, make mistakes on my own. But he definitely wanted to have control. I lived at home and went to UCLA, but I was really unhappy and depressed seeing my life unfold just the way they wanted it to. I would get a college degree, marry some Korean man, and lead my life the way they led theirs. I knew I didn't want anything like my parents' marriage.

I absorbed all that unhappiness. I felt so helpless in the family unit, absorbing the pain without knowing what to do with it. I don't think my father's trouble with my mother was really about not having a son. It was about his personality. He was not aware of the effects he had on other people. He always thought he was right. He was not open. Now that I look back, I see that he was an intelligent, skilled man, dynamic and fun. But he was very insecure, abusive, psychotic. He hurt a lot of people.

My sister ran away when she was nineteen or twenty. I think she saw me arguing with our father and figured that it was no use to fight. I was always identified as the troublemaker for always asking "why." The others would say, "Why don't you just shut up and eat?" My mother thought I was constantly making trouble, and my father thought I was disrespectful. My sister decided she did not want to argue. She planned it all out ahead. We were both attending UCLA on and off, living at home and going to school for one quarter, dropping out for two quarters. One day, I woke up to make breakfast for myself and feed the dog. I went to her room and knocked, but no one answered, so I opened the door. Everything was gone—even the sheets on her bed. It never occurred to me that she would run away. Then I found the good-bye letter. I can't remember the details; I wish I had saved it, because it was a record of what she saw was wrong with her life and our family. I woke up my mother, but I didn't dare wake up my father, for fear he would explode.

We were so upset. I can only remember that when we sat down for dinner, he cried. We were waiting for him to take the first bite, as always. I thought to myself, "Wow, she really got to him." He never cried for any of us, for any reason. He was always angry with us, mostly at me. She was the daughter he didn't love as much when we were all little. She resembles the brother he didn't like, and she used to get more punishment. Even now they don't have a good relationship. They pretend, but she's not ready to try a new relationship with him.

A year after my sister ran away, I told my father I was not going to run away like her, but I was going to move out. He said, "If you move out, I am going to shoot your dog. You can't take him, and you can't have someone else take care of him. I am going to blow his brains out. That is the price you will have to pay." The dog was the only being to ever give me unconditional affection. So before I moved out, I took him to the pound and had him put to sleep. Only recently have I forgiven myself for putting a healthy, loving dog to death. I covered it all up and never told anyone, and no one in our family mentioned it. One day the dog was there; the next day, he was gone. No one asked me about it.

I moved out. I lied to my parents, telling them I was in school when actually I was working. They were unwilling to help me financially if I moved out, so I said, fine, and I got a job as a bank teller. But I made so little money that it was impossible to live. I didn't have enough for food and barely enough to cover the rent. They wanted me to go to school, and I thought of school as something for them, not for me. I just kept signing up for classes and then dropping or failing them for forgetting to drop them. All those years went by, with me sending checks to the University of California but never finishing the classes. I was lying to them, saying I was in school. My parents were uncomfortable and ashamed of me, and I was uncomfortable and ashamed also.

When I was about twenty-five, I tried to commit suicide again. I was dating, and by that time had become sexually active. One thing I did agree with my parents about was marrying a Korean man, so I met everyone my parents wanted to introduce me to. I didn't want to marry an American and live the American life-style, because there are so many things I don't like—divorce, immorality, all the things I heard about when I was growing up. But I didn't like Korea or Korean values or life-style either, because it made me depressed. It really tries to squash me.

I was dating a Korean man and we had broken up. He was someone I really thought I was going to marry. He was going to dental school at the time. He said he wanted a very traditional wife. He wanted his dinner at exactly 5:30. He would come over to my apartment to eat. I would help him with his homework. If he had an exam, I tested him with flash cards. I would stay up all night or go to the dental school to keep him company when he was working on a project. I remember sleeping in the dental chairs. We had been together for a year and a half. Then, when my finals came, he disappeared. He had gone to Las Vegas with his parents. I yelled at him, and he laughed. I couldn't believe it. So I pushed him, and he slipped off his chair. Then he was really angry. How dare I express my anger? He punched a hole in the wall and said, "The next time, it's going to be you." After he left, I thought, "I am going to relive my mother's life." I looked at the broken plaster and thought, "This is my skin."

I broke up with him. I felt like such a failure: I could not fit into American society. I was not succeeding in American schools, with American men, in American careers. I could not fit into Korean society. It was hopeless. So I drank a fifth of Scotch and smoked pot every night, thinking I would over-dose or die of alcohol poisoning. But I always woke up the next day. Finally, I tried to find an Asian American woman therapist. Instead, when I was twenty-five years old, I found a third-generation Irish American man who had studied t'aekwondo [Korean martial arts].

I went to see him every week for five or six years. I still go every other week. Now it's more like consultation. He is sort of my adviser; that is how I see him. I don't always take his advice, but I like to hear his opinions, know-ing that he knows about my personality and history. Therapy does not work for everyone, but I was open to it. It fits me because I am a talker, and talk therapy is important to me.

I had been in therapy a year when I met my husband in 1984. I think if I hadn't been in therapy, I could not have experienced a relationship with a man that was intimate and supportive. I used to think of men like my hus-band as wimpy, boring, and weak, because the only thing I knew about male strength was yelling and beating. I didn't know about quiet strength. My therapist encouraged me to see the value in Brian.

My father and I had some sort of sexual connection: he always used to say that if I were the same age as my mother, he would not have married her, he would have married me. It was so inappropriate. It made him crazy to imag-ine that any of his daughters might be having sex, or being women in any way. When I was twenty-one, I told my father I was having sex with a forty-two-year-old man, and he beat me up. I think I wanted to get at him. My mother and sisters thought I sort of deserved it. They only stopped him when he said he was going to tear off my pants to check to see if I was still a virgin.

That was the last time he beat me up. I used to visit my parents' house from time to time, but the next time we had an argument, I just freaked out and ran out of the house. I didn't have any shoes on; I didn't have my purse or my car keys. I just ran into the dark and hid. Then I thought to myself, "This is really stupid. I don't have any money, I have no ID, no shoes on. What would I tell the firemen or police? Who is going to help me?" So I waited around the corner until he finally left in his car. Then I went into the house, put on my shoes and got my purse, and left.

Just leaving while my father was yelling was a very significant gesture. When I was growing up, no one was allowed to leave the room until my father was finished with his rages. If he started screaming at the dinner table, we just had to sit there. It was unthinkable to just get up and walk out. He used to wake us kids up in the middle of the night, make us get up and kneel on our heels while he yelled at us for one or two hours. Then he would tell us to go back to bed. Our legs would be in such excruciating pain that we'd have to crawl back to the bedroom. Sometimes he did that twice in one night. Usually he was up late at night, thinking over something that made him angry during the day, and he would wake us up to vent his anger on us.

Later, my therapist encouraged me to be prepared, whenever I visited home, to leave at the first sign that violence might erupt. He told me to keep my shoes and purse close by. He said I should say, "Dad, I don't think we are really communicating. How about I come back some other time?" The first time I tried it, I was so scared, but I tried it. I had my shoes on, my purse was right next to me, and he was so angry he didn't notice. I said, "*Appa* [Daddy], I don't think we are really talking." I was shaking and my voice was trembling. "I think I will go. I will come back, but I will go now." He didn't believe me, but I got up, got into the car, and drove away. When I got home, I found he had left messages on my answering machine: "Imjung, did you really leave the house? Are you really gone? Are you really at your place?" I couldn't draw a breath. I didn't pick up the phone. But little by little, I had to establish my own safety.

For a long time, he did not let me come home. Finally, when I started visiting again, I was prepared to leave each time. I had to show how I could be strong, how I needed to be safe. It was such a long process. I used to think that old dogs can't learn new tricks, but they can. He began to accept me as a person, even if I was promiscuous, even if I wasn't succeeding at school.

The first three years after I got married, my husband and I visited each week. We had rules. He would still drink, but I would say, "Dad, you can drink. It's your house and your choice. But I need to go home if you drink.

I can't stay here. I can't love you when you drink." Often he would ask, "Imjung, can I have a drink?" and I would say, "Sure. You can have a drink. But I think I'm going now." So Brian and I would put our shoes on and walk out, even in the middle of Thanksgiving dinner, even if there were guests. But for three years, every time I visited, he would ask me if he could have a drink, and I would say, "Go ahead, but I'm leaving." He would not drink, but he would test me each time. If he was in a rotten mood or could not stop himself, he would say, "Fine, you can go. Who cares about you? I am going to have my drink!" And I would get up to go. My mother and sisters would say, "What's your problem? He always drinks. Why should he change for you?" My relatives would say, "Your mother has made a big meal for you. Why don't you just stay?" They would make me feel guilty, but I would go.

Later, he tried drinking before we arrived, so I would say, "Maybe we should meet for lunch instead of dinner," because Dad doesn't drink at lunchtime. I told him he is boring and repeats himself when he's drunk. He's sloppy, mean, nasty, and not fun. He drinks double or triple scotches, depending on his mood. For me, drinking means trouble. My body has learned to be scared. My husband comes from an alcoholic family. That's why we agreed about the way we were going to deal with it. We are united about this.

I also have this rule in my head: that if he starts hitting someone when I am in his house, I am going to call the police. That is the only way I can love him. It hasn't happened so far, but I am prepared. I think it still happens when I am not there. Sometimes when I call, my mother or a sister will pick up the telephone, sounding like they have been through hell, crying and whatever. I tell my mother if she ever wants to leave him, I will help her.

I think that their relationship is better now. Still, I keep imagining her slowly and secretly feeding him poison. She always says that now that he has less power, she is more powerful. She says that he is stupid, that the art work he does as a hobby is stupid, that he is wasting money and time. I think she learned how to be passively aggressive. But they are a lot better now, as far as I can see. He is retired, and they play golf together and watch a lot of Korean soap operas on television.

What really launched me as an adult was one time I told him after dinner that I didn't appreciate all the stuff I saw him doing when I was growing up. I had been preparing for the moment for a long time. I did it only once, in front of everybody. I said it slowly, clearly, and quietly. I am sure I sounded nervous, because I was really scared, but my husband was there to protect me. My father said nothing. He got up and went outside to smoke a cigarette, and then he came back. We pretended nothing had happened. But for me, it was a real turning point. It was like I stopped being a child. I had been launched. Marriage, career, children—none of that was important. I had an opinion, I said it in front of him, and he didn't attack me. My friends asked me why I didn't get him to apologize. I don't need an apology; I just wanted the witnessing and the acknowledgment. He didn't deny it. He didn't say I was a stupid person, as usual. That's when I forgave him for what he did to my mother. I didn't like it, but it happened; it was their life.

Now I have been able to learn about him as a person. There are many fathers and mothers out there who refuse to let their children be launched. When my husband says to his mother that it was bad when he was growing up, she says, "No, it wasn't. What are you talking about?" My father had the courage to deal with the person his daughter became. In my eyes, he's a true hero. It's not the past that defines him or anyone; it's what you do with the past, now and in the future. I speak out against oppression, and he no longer oppresses me.

Now I have an advice column [in the English section of a Korean American newspaper]. The teenagers who write in are like my substitute brothers and sisters. I want to help them get launched. I know there is such a thing as mutual respect without obligation; I learned that from my father. I am also talking to my parents through my column, and I know they read every word.

SEPTEMBER 1993

Revitalizing America

Reverend Lim is the pastor of the Oriental Mission Church, a conservative evangelical nondenominational church with close ties to the Holiness sect. A tall and strikingly handsome man with a deep, sonorous voice, Lim gestures expansively and his speech never falters. Born to a large family in 1923 in Puchŏn, Kyŏnggi Province, he grew up in Inch'ŏn and Seoul. Like many other Korean families, his family moved to Japan-controlled Manchuria and returned to Seoul at the end of World War II.

I am optimistic about the future of the Korean American community. Things are opening up; we are beginning to see Korean city council people, state legislators, and congressman. I always say to people, Look far ahead. Our children are our great hope. They are much better educated than their parents, better at handling interethnic relations, better at conversing. They have a much wider view of things and are less prejudiced against other people. They know about democracy, and they respect other people's integrity. The immigrant generation wants to maintain Korean culture, tradition, and language, but Koreans must become American in America while maintaining their Korean heritage. It's hard for the immigrant generation to achieve this, but the second generation can. They may be a little short on Korean identity, but if they go to church, they can learn the meaning of "minority" from the Bible, through the stories of Joseph, Moses, Esther, and Daniel.

We Koreans are spiritually blessed people. That's why we have hope. There are two thousand Korean churches in the United States,[40] and our young people will carry them on. We extend our mission to nonbelievers in America. We want to help revitalize American churches.

I prayed to God for the first time fifty years ago in North Korea, the night before I was to be executed as a South Korean spy. Ironically, I had been jailed in South Korea earlier, for working for the leftists. I had joined the South Korean Coast Guard with some friends from Manchuria and was an instructor at the Navy Military Police School. Soon after I was released from the jail in southern Korea, I went up to the North with several friends.[41] People were saying that communism was good for our country, and yet people were leaving the North to come down to southern Korea. We wanted to find out what communism really was. In North Korea, I entered the Military and Politics School, which was headed by Kim Chaek.[42]

I got arrested because people in North Korea were saying bad things about Kim Ku and Rhee Syngman.[43] I had to speak: "Do you really know about Kim Ku and Rhee Syngman? They are both patriots who devoted their whole lives to the independence of the fatherland." I was arrested as a South Korean spy and sentenced to death.

The night before I was scheduled to die, I prayed to God, "If you are there, please save my life, and I promise I will study for the ministry with my brother (he was in a seminary in Seoul). Like the Wesleyan brothers in England, we will serve you and the country." Then I heard the voice of God, saying, "Don't worry; you will not die. You will become my servant." After that, I fell into a deep sleep.

In the morning, two soldiers with rifles and bayonets took me to the communist headquarters in front of the P'yŏngyang railway station. I thought they were taking me to the execution site, but they led me into Kim Il Sung's office. There I saw someone who knew me, a man who had been a student of Yŏ Un-hyŏng[44] in Manchuria and who, as a captain in the Manchurian Air Force, had flown a plane carrying the Manchu emperor. He was now an adviser to Kim Il Sung. He knew me, and he said, "This man is not a South Korean agent. He was suspected to be a communist and put in jail by South Korean authorities. He may not know how to be patriotic, but he is not a spy." Then Kim Il Sung said, "Comrade, you have suffered enough. Go and work with the People's Committee."[45] I realized then that I would have to find the right way to be patriotic; having a good heart alone was not enough. I had been jailed in both South and North Korea. So I said, "I am still young. I want to study economics under a communist professor at Seoul University and then come back."

Kim Il Sung ordered his secretary to issue a permit for me to cross the 38th parallel. I was escorted south by the North Korean soldiers. As soon as I had crossed over, I tore up the permit. I was bursting with joy: I was free and alive. I went directly to find my brother at Seoul Seminary.

After a year's preparation, I took the entrance examination and entered the seminary. Before school started, students went through a one-week religious revival session. Hearing the sermon, I realized all my sins, and the Holy Spirit touched my heart. I wept all night long. I confessed my sins, and the preacher put his hand on my head and prayed that I would be like the apostle Paul. That was the second time I felt great joy in my life. Before that moment, I had thought of Christianity as a Western religion. I realized for the first time that it is a religion of life and resurrection.

When I repented my sins, my value system and frame of mind completely changed. Even the colors of *sanch'ŏnch'omok* [mountains, streams, grasses, trees] looked different. I studied the Bible and carried on with a life of prayer, and my faith grew stronger and stronger.

During winter and summer vacations, I traveled with a classmate all around the countryside, spreading the good word. One summer, I went with a friend to a Buddhist temple in Odaesan, Kangwŏn Province. We asked the abbot for an *amja* [prayer chamber], and we fasted and prayed there for six days. One day, when I was alone in the room, I suddenly experienced the fire of the Holy Spirit for the first time. It seemed that the whole room was engulfed in flames, but my clothes and body were not burning. I was overwhelmed by a sudden sense of strength. I still believe that the strength and good health that have enabled me to spread the good word are from the power of the Holy Spirit that I was given at that moment.

During my first two years at the seminary, I was making a living as a *chigyekkun* [porter with an A-frame on his back] in front of Seoul railway station. I was twenty-three years old and didn't want to rely on my parents for my living. Also, I wanted to experience hard labor and see the underside of society firsthand. I carried rice, persimmons, and other cargo between the railway station and the South Gate market. I learned a lot about life at that time. Several classmates from the seminary joined me, and eventually other university students joined as well. We formed a *chigyedang* [A-frame association] and discussed current affairs and theological questions. Many of the members are leading figures in the Korean church community today.

In my sophomore year, an important man in the Holiness Church[46] saw me leading a student revival and asked me to join him as an apprentice in charge of high school students' education. After I graduated, he asked me to go to Yŏju in Kyŏnggi Province to try to build up a church. It was a very small place; only about five families were attending the church, which was just a portion of the inside quarters of a house that was also being used as a wood shop. After one year, however, the church grew to about 300 members. We were able to put in a bell tower and buy an organ. Then the Korean War broke out.

We took refuge in Pusan, where I was ordained as a minister. I was called by a small church at a nearby village. Again, the attendance grew to about three hundred after two years. When we moved to Yŏju, I was recommended as a Korean Air Force chaplain, so I joined the Air Force Chaplain's Corps in 1953 and served for eleven years.

While in the service, I graduated from the U.S. Chaplain's School in 1960. At that time, I decided to go to the U.S. for further studies, so after I retired from the air force, I went to Los Angeles. I arrived alone in May

1965. To earn my livelihood, I worked in a print shop for six and a half years. It was the third largest printer in the Western region. When I applied for the job there, the supervisor said I was too old. I was forty-four. I asked him to let me work without any wages for just one week. I said, "If you like my work, you can hire me." They agreed. The factory was sixty years old, and the machines were coated in grease and dust. Using my skills and experience from the Korean Navy and Air Force, I cleaned them until they were spotless. When they saw the machines, they were gasping. So I was hired. While I was working there, I never forgot I was a Korean and a minister. Sometimes I would come in and work when everybody else was gone. When I told the print shop that I was starting a church and wanted to quit, they said that if I ever had to leave the church, I could come back anytime.

For two years, I went to language school to learn English; then I got my M.A. at the American Baptist Seminary and my Ph.D. at the Fuller Theological Seminary. Altogether, I studied for nine years. I wanted to return to Korea, but a Korean professor at Seoul Theological Seminary suggested that I start a church in Los Angeles, since the population of Korean Americans was growing rapidly; so I started a church. At first we met at my house. We sent $400, the total offerings from the first service, to two village churches in Korea. Ever since then, we have been sending money to churches in Korea every month. When I retired in 1988, we were sending money to 178 churches every month, and now we are sending missionaries all over the world.

When I arrived in Los Angeles in 1965, there were about 5,000 Koreans here and six Korean churches. The churches were meeting places for the immigrants, places where students and immigrants could get some help. Their main function in the past was collecting money for the Korean independence movement.[47] The evangelical aspect of the churches was weak. Some people asked me to start a church right away, but I thought that six churches were enough for Los Angeles. The number kept growing; a few years later, there were thirty churches. We started our church in 1970.

My wife joined me from Korea just before I started the church. She worked twelve and a half years at a sewing factory in L.A. She continued working long after I had started the church because I refused any raise in salary. The church members were mostly workers and students, and I just didn't feel right about accepting a raise. Then other pastors started complaining, saying that their churches were setting their salaries according to our church's standard. So I finally accepted a raise.

The church grew very fast. Within two years, we were able to buy a building on Crenshaw Boulevard. After three more years, we needed a bigger space, so we bought this church on Western Avenue. This building used to be a Ralph's supermarket. That was eighteen years ago, and the price was $625,000. We used the proceeds from the Crenshaw building sale as a down payment and borrowed $500,000 from the bank. The monthly loan payment was $5,400. We had a difficult time for the first few months; I had to borrow money every month, but we stuck it out, and three years ago were able to pay off the loan entirely. Also, we built a $3 million education building next door, as well as a second $2 million education building, which is now used as our seminary. We are planning a 3,000-seat capacity church building. We also plan to acquire an adjacent lot for a 500-car parking lot, and we want to buy the four buildings surrounding the church. We are targeting $10 million for these projects.

When we bought this building, many people predicted we would fail. Rumors traveled as far as Korea. People were saying we were too greedy. Now people are saying we had vision. This is the center of Koreatown. We don't want to move away from this Koreatown location. We want to put our roots down here. That's why we want to buy all the properties surrounding the church. We are looking ahead a hundred years.

As long as there is a good pastoral message, location is not important. People will come. When I was in the air force, I saw many pilots from Suwŏn at a Seoul *naengmyŏn* [cold noodles] restaurant one day, so I asked them why they didn't go to a *naengmyŏn* place in Suwŏn. They said, *naengmyŏn* is for taste, not for just filling the stomach. It's the same with a church. People will come to the church if the Lord's grace is there. We are going to suffer and rejoice with Koreatown. We are not going to leave even though the riots have left Koreatown devastated.

In the U.S., there are three kinds of Korean churches: the denominational, the regional, and the nondenominational. We are a nondenominational church, which results in our having more new converts and younger people. We have five Sunday services for adults as well as Sunday school and Bible study classes. Most people come from nearby areas, but some come all the way from Ontario, Irvine, and Thousand Oaks. Registered members of our church number about 6,000, including children. We have twenty-one branches in South Bay, Gardena, Fullerton, Irvine, and elsewhere. They are all doing well. Elders, deacons, and members of nearby churches are encouraged to join the branches. There are more women than men in the church; this has always been the case. There are women prime ministers, senators, legislators. I am in favor of ordaining women as pastors. Fifteen churches have been established by missionaries we've sent overseas. We have a church in Moscow and another in Vladivostok and a beautiful mission center in Paraguay with a middle school, a high school, a seminary, a vocational school, and a hospital. We are thankful to God.

We established our own seminary five years ago because before, our young people would grow up in our church and then attend seminaries elsewhere to become ministers of other denominational churches. We also established the World Mission Evangelical Association, which has about forty member churches. We have a certified four-year college and a permit to offer graduate studies. We want to establish education and social work departments.

I think the church should serve the community. Our doors are always open. Seminars, concerts, and many other community events take place here. Russians, Armenians, Guatemalans, and El Salvadorans come to our church to study English at the adult school operated by the city. We have afternoon programs for the children of working parents. Several hundred students are enrolled at our Korean language school. During and after the riots, our parking lot was the center of relief activities, which were offered here for over a year.

I save money from stipends I receive from the church and honoraria from revival meetings and donate them to community causes. One time, the Korean School of Southern California invited me to their initiation meeting about purchasing a site for the school. I told them that when we raise money for the church, the elders donate first then the deacons, and then the lay people, so the board members should start first. We all wrote down pledges; I had them open mine first. At first they thought it was $500, but then they saw another zero. They were embarrassed, because they had written down $1,000 or $2,000. They rewrote their pledges, and everyone wrote down $10,000. They said that since Reverend Lim had given $5,000, business people should give at least double that amount. Since then, you have to donate $10,000 to the building fund in order to be a member of the board.

Once an elder from a South American country who was visiting mentioned in passing that he needed a car but it was too expensive, so I gave him $5,000 right there. This is how I live my daily life. My daughter once said to me, "Thank you for showing us life by your own deeds." I cried when I heard her say this.

In my sermons in relation to the immigrant experience, I emphasize the pioneer spirit of John the Baptist, who paved the way for Jesus. A pioneer is fired up with the desire and strong will to accomplish. He has to pave a wide, straight, solid road. He has to design and invest well, and he has to be willing to sacrifice. All the pioneers who came to this country have sacrificed a lot. They overcame hunger, disease, wild animals. To understand America, you have to know about the blood of those buried in the valleys, mountains, and plains of America. In Jeremiah, chapter twenty-nine, God gives lessons to the immigrants: first, I am with you, you are not alone; second, you must put your heart into this land, for you will not return home for seventy years; third, you must marry with the people here and multiply.

This means that intermarriage is not a bad thing. I'm not saying that everyone should intermarry, but in the Bible, Moses, Joseph, Esther, Ruth, and Timothy all intermarried. Rhee Syngman intermarried. The violinist Chung Kyung Hwa also intermarried. Reverend Han Kyŏng-jik's son is intermarried. Reverend Ryu Hyŏngki's grandchildren are all intermarried. Reverend Choe Hi-dong, a leading figure in the Holiness Church, is also intermarried. Intermarriage is not a bad thing. If you cannot find a Korean spouse, it is perfectly all right to marry a non-Korean.

God says that we should have a long-range outlook for the future. The Jews have a three-hundred-year history in this country; the Chinese have one hundred fifty years, and the Japanese have more than a hundred years. There were Koreans here at the turn of the century, but they were only a few laborers; the real history of Koreans in this country is only thirty years long, so we have to look far ahead. It takes three generations to reap the fruits of our efforts.

Some people say that when Korean Americans become more affluent, they will move away from the church and the Korean communities and lose their ability to speak Korean. They will not be giving money as their parents did, and their Korean identity will be weakened. I don't think this will happen. Look at the Jewish temples: they continue to grow. I'm optimistic about the future of our churches, if our ministers provide our children good bicultural education along with evangelism.

That's why we emphasize education. Otherwise, we will lose the children, and eventually the church will have to close. Thank the Lord, our young people fast, do overnight and mountain prayers, and are capable and dedicated leaders. Many are attending seminaries. There are about a thousand 1.5 and second-generation seminary students in the U.S., and several hundreds are at Fuller Seminary. There are hundreds of Korean students at Princeton, Westminster, Southern Baptist, Trinity, and Calvin theological seminaries. I used to think all our young people would go to business, law, and medical school. But I was mistaken.

I am optimistic about the future of race relations. Korean merchants generally have negative attitudes toward black people. They have preconceived notions about them and cannot talk with them because of language and cultural barriers. The younger generation are much less prejudiced and have a much better understanding of black people.

Black people's situation has improved a lot. They were brought as slaves and liberated after two hundred years by Abraham Lincoln. Then, due to people like Martin Luther King, their lives have gradually improved. Now there are black mayors, governors, legislators, and congressmen. Many jurists are black, and I don't have to tell you about athletes. Martin Luther King's dream is slowly coming true for them. It will also come true for us eventually.

Koreans made money, but instead of using it for the neighborhood, they drive luxury cars and look down on black people. One of our deacons has a grocery store in a black community. He employs many black people, who take charge of the store when he goes out. He attends the black church and sometimes teaches Sunday school. He donates to neighborhood youth and senior citizens programs. When the riots occurred, his neighbors guarded the store. Now he sells four times more than he did before the riots.

When you look back at history, there are peaks and declines in every major civilization, whether it is Babylon, Mesopotamia, Greece, or Rome. It looks like America has just passed its peak. The decline is apparent when we look at the people's morality and spirituality. I don't think that the U.S. will fall suddenly; the Puritan roots are still strong. The churches that are evangelical are still flourishing. These believers lead a humble life; Koreans cannot match them. I know one family that adopted five physically and mentally handicapped Korean children. I really bowed my head to that family. There are still many families like that here in America. How many orphans have been brought here from Korea?

I think that there will be a slow decline, though. The Lord's good words have moved from America to Korea.

OCTOBER 1993

Hot Pepper

"Maeun Koch'u" [hot pepper; a pseudonym] was born in Korea in 1968 and came to Los Angeles when she was three years old. She has lived in Virginia as well as Louisiana, where she attended college before returning to Los Angeles. She attended graduate school in Latin American Studies at UCLA. After working several months for a Korean American community organization, she took a job as an accounts executive and special events coordinator at an Asian American advertising agency in Los Angeles.

When I was fourteen, my parents thought it would be easier to raise their kids where the crime rate was not so high, so my father sent us to Virginia while he stayed in L.A. He was going through a lot of financial problems at the time. He was even contemplating suicide so that we could have his insurance money. He told me later how he'd planned everything out.

He hardly ever went to church; he used to hate it when we'd go. Whenever he did go, he'd fall asleep. He traveled a lot on business, and he'd say, "I'm only here once a month, and this is my only Sunday; I want to spend time with the kids. I want to go to the beach." But my mom would want to go to church, and there'd be family arguments about that. I'm not sure how devoted to the church Mom really was. To be honest, the church was like a social scene—status and all that—for her.

Then my father got the calling. It was just like one of those things where you get blinded by a light. He changed from being an international commodities broker to being a minister. Many people who knew my father before are really shocked when they find out he's a minister now.

He had been coming to visit us in Virginia about once a month. Then one time he sat us all down and started praying. We didn't know what was going on. We'd never done that and weren't sure what we were supposed to do. After about a year and a half, my father just packed us all up and said, "We're going to New Orleans." He gave us two days' warning. He found a Southern Baptist seminary in New Orleans that he liked. Now he's working on a Ph.D. in theology.

He has a small church in New Orleans. He specializes in crazy women, like women crazy from their marriages to American soldiers. They live in these small southern towns, where there aren't many other Koreans to talk to. A lot of them have psychological problems, especially the first wave of GI brides. Many have actually been put into insane asylums in New Orleans. Some are just walking around crazy. They'll just go off. My father helps them out by praying for them. If he hears about a crazy Asian woman, he goes to look for her. Usually they are Korean GI brides whose husbands dumped them after several years. My mother and father go to these halfway houses and boarding homes to meet with them. My father will talk to them, pray for them, and bring them food. Even *kimch'i* is a thrill for them, because they haven't eaten it for so long.

Other Koreans don't want to bother with them, but my father takes them to church. He keeps a constant vigil on them. Usually after about four years, even the most psychotic women that he sees on the streets, women who don't talk to anybody, become sane. His only failure was one woman he worked with for three years. Her husband was Korean—a pharmacist, I think. She came from a very educated family. She played the piano and graduated from college in Korea, but something went wrong. My father tried to work with her for three or four years without success. He's been successful with everyone else. Even now, he drives to a little country area an hour and a half away every week to a mental ward. He sits there and talks to the patients from seven in the morning until seven at night.

He believes that insanity is caused by sin. That used to scare me. Once, we were dropping off one of these women, and he was in the car saying, "In the name of Jesus Christ, demon, leave her body." I was scared: if it left her body, where would it go? We were in the car with the windows closed. My dad said if my faith was weak, the demon would jump into me.

It was kind of frustrating, because he gave away everything we had. When I came back from college, the clothes I hadn't taken with me had been given away. Or some of my furniture would be gone. Everything was donated. We always had guests, like Korean seamen who jumped ship. Dad was known because he would drive to the dock and pray for the seamen. He had a seamen ministry on the side. There would always be this knock on the door, or a phone call saying, "Reverend Kim, I'm downtown. I've just jumped ship. Come pick me up." So we would have another houseguest. We would help the seamen find jobs and clothing. Sometimes there were five or six seamen at our house for two or three weeks. I was cooking and cleaning up after them because my mother was working. Our life was not our own. I couldn't just walk around in shorts. Finally we sat down with Dad and said, "Listen, we can't live this way. You can, but we can't. If you want, go become a missionary. But you have a family; you have obligations to us." We complained so much that my father decided to have people stay at the church.

His church is a small converted house. The congregation is only twenty or thirty people. He puts all his money into it, and mother supports him with her T-shirt shop in the New Orleans tourist area by the river. If the church needs a new roof, my mother pays for it. The other ministers' wives don't work, so my mother gets a lot of flak about not having the house clean all the time and so on. She's a target because she's not a "minister," so she gets all the blame for everything that goes wrong at the church. Sometimes I get aggravated about it. They are both very strong in their faith, but they're not very realistic.

Our parents forced us to read the Korean bible every night. If we couldn't finish reading it, we sometimes had to stay up until two in the morning on school nights because we kept missing the same word three or four times. My younger sister, who's at Barnard College in New York, doesn't go to church now; she despises the dogma and sees the ideology as male chauvinist. Lately, I'm a little in line with her. I went to a Korean church here in L.A. for a while, but some of the things they said really bothered me. In the pulpit, the minister would say something about Hillary Clinton or make snide remarks about "feminazis." After Clinton was elected, the young girls were crying and praying, saying they were going to leave the country because now we were going to have abortion everywhere. The young deacons were saying, "We're going to have feminists and fags killing babies." And then his new deacon announced that he had a petition to Clinton not to allow homosexuals in the army. I'm still kind of shocked, and I can't step back into the church. I respect my parents, but sometimes I wish they'd just go off and do their own missionary work and leave us alone. All of us, like my brother and I, had to take summer jobs to help support the family. In college, we had to take jobs and get scholarships. Before, everything was taken care of, and then at such a late age, we had to take care of things for ourselves. What was hard for us was that, even though they really love us, if God told them, "Leave your kids and come to me," they would—the next day, without turning back.

In L.A., I had lived a very sequestered life. All my friends were white; I don't think I ever had a Latino friend or an African American friend. I was very racist, like, "Oh, those spics, what are they doing here?" The Korean community in Virginia was very intellectual. All the Koreans were professors and doctors, and the kids were valedictorians in every school. As soon as people at the school found out I was Korean, they put me in all the honors classes. I was under a lot of pressure to excel. The kids at the Korean church were straight-A students. All they wanted to talk about was going to

Harvard. I felt I really had to succeed. And being the only Asian girl at the school in Virginia Beach was really fun. I was like a novelty. Everyone was a surfer; the beach was right there. All my friends were tall and blond. I really lived the life; I dated the quarterback and went to beach parties that you don't even dream about here in L.A.

I was so upset when we moved to New Orleans. That was in the middle of my senior year in high school. I pictured the people there as being hill-billies with no shoes, living in swamps among the alligators—a nightmare. When I went there, I found that there were actually cars and cities. But people were so racist. There's a large Vietnamese community in New Orleans. In Virginia, the view was that Asians are high-class, smart, intellec-tual people. In New Orleans, they were just refugees. So instead of excelling, I became an introvert; I was like a total nerd. I didn't talk with anybody. It was hard to make friends with white kids in New Orleans, so I hung around with the Vietnamese kids. I had never seen a Vietnamese person in my life. I was still very racist, and it was really hard for me to adapt, but the more I got to know them, the better it was.

I think I stopped being a racist when I was in college. I was a microbiol-ogy major at Louisiana Tech University. The first African American com-munity I encountered was in New Orleans. It was very rough because they were so discriminated against. When the Vietnamese came, they saw another ethnicity they could discriminate against, so they were very rough on the Vietnamese. I received some of that, and I couldn't believe it. They were so cruel. Yet, I had some African American friends who protected me and helped me out. But I would never give them a hug or anything. I thought that African Americans were loud, but white southern girls were genteel, kind of like how Korean girls are supposed to be. At college, I acted white, so it was easy for the fraternity and sorority people to accept me. That was fun for a while, but after I met one or two African American friends, one girl really opened my eyes. She said, "You are a racist." She pointed out that when I was with her privately, I'd be comfortable and relaxed, but when my white friends were around, and I was with her, I tensed up.

The Latino kids at Louisiana Tech were exchange students from wealthy families, and I got along with them well. But the Mexicans! In L.A., I had these images of them screaming on the streets or something. Then I saw this movie called *El Norte*, and I was in tears by the time the first part ended because I realized that they were immigrants like my family. It wasn't just the stereotype of living off welfare in America, but struggling to survive as immigrants. That really opened my eyes. I hate to admit that I was so racist.

I still have Latino friends from school, but I rarely see them anymore. I moved back to L.A. after college, and lately I realized that all of my friends here are Korean. There are very few Koreans who are able to hang around with *both* Korean and non-Korean friends. You usually only hang around with Korean people, or you are so Americanized that you buy into the main-stream life-style and try to escape from the fact that you are Korean. Some Koreans date only white men and women, even if they find Korean men and women attractive. We call them "funky white Asians." Their parents speak English at home. They want to have this country club image, like they're not Korean at all, and their kids become like that—kind of Americanized and kind of Korean at the same time. A lot of Koreans want to affiliate with the white community, not the black community; to them, that would be like taking a step down.

Look at L.A. If a Korean kid drives a junky car, he'll park it a block away. That just reinforces the Koreans' value system. When I brought in my Hyundai to a Korean restaurant parking lot, they parked it far away and didn't even lock the door. I mean, the guy with the Mercedes has an alarm system and I don't.

I've decided that a lot of Korean parents feel guilty. When they first come to America, they are working all the time; their kids are latchkey kids. They push their kids to succeed and send them to private schools. If they do suc-ceed, the parents are so relieved that they overcompensate for the fact that they weren't there for their children when they were growing up by giving them the money they make now. The mothers have these Korean American business associations where they meet to match up their kids. The eligible bachelors and bachelorettes sit at one table, and the mothers sit at another. They usually don't match. People say it's because everybody's too stuck-up and selfish, but I think it's because they are all the same.

It's really funny, because now that the parents finally have the time, now that they've made the money, they could sit down with their kids instead of just giving them money. They should at least tell them about their struggles, so that if the kids get to spend $500 they at least realize that their parents had to struggle many hours to get that $500. Money that is easy to spend might have been hard to get.

I have so much respect for my parents. When they were already adults, they came to another country with a totally different culture, where they look completely different from everyone else, and they survived. I'm so amazed. That's courage. They gave up everything for us. They could have stayed in Korea, but they didn't. I'm not sure I could have done as much as they did. I have so much to learn from them about our culture that I still don't understand.

My father came to America because he had daughters and knew that we would never have a chance in Korea. He wanted us to do something with our lives. He sat us down when we were old enough to understand Korean history and told us about the two or three Korean queens. "Be proud that you come from a lineage that respected women," he said. He told us that once when the Chinese [sic] were invading Korea many centuries ago, all the men had died, and there were only women left. The women put rocks in their aprons and fought and died too.[48] My father would say to us, "This is what you are, Korean women. You can bleach your hair and get your eyes done, but you are always going to be Korean. So you have to outshine everybody. You have to show them what a real Korean can do, because Americans have the oxcart image of Korea. You have to fight that image."

Mom is very pragmatic about men. She says if your husband's a bastard, leave him; don't screw your life twice. She says, "Don't ever trust any man. You should always have your own bank account, and don't let him know about it. Don't be 100 percent dependent on your husband, and never let him take you for granted. Let him know that he should thank God and kiss the ground you walk on. Make him dependent on you." She says to be like *chagŭn koch'u* [small hot pepper]; you're small, but when someone bites into you, you've got a big kick.

My father has a lot of respect for my mother. He knows that if he didn't have her, he wouldn't be able to do anything. In my opinion, she's really got him well trained. I think I could learn some lessons from her.

Korean men don't know how to handle me, because if I don't like something, I'll say something about it. Like a couple nights ago, this Korean guy who goes to law school and drives a Porsche was making fun of Chinese and Latinos. He said that UCLA was stupid compared to his school, USC, so I said, "At least we have a Latino program," and he said, "We do too; Jorge and Manuel—they wash our toilets." My eyes popped out, I was so offended, but no one ever says anything to him, so I told him, "I don't appreciate that. That is not funny. I am going into another room where the atmosphere is better." I also have arguments with my Korean women friends; they don't speak up because they don't want to be labeled as feminists, but in my opinion, a feminist is somebody who wants equality and doesn't discriminate by gender. A lot of women constantly worry about finding a decent man. It's so scary; they don't judge him by how much they love him, but by whether he's firstborn or secondborn, or if his mom is a widow, things like that. They're so calculating. There are a lot of gold diggers who are my age.

I see women, girls my age, students at UCLA or USC, having sugar daddies who pay for their nice apartments on Bunker Hill, or their Mercedes, or their Lexus, or they give them spending money for shopping. The sugar daddies are usually "Korean-Korean" married men in their late thirties. And these women aren't street prostitutes or anything.

My dad always told me that there are "bad" and "good" women. When I was in college, I had this image of college women as saintly and pristine. Then I came to L.A., where I saw them at church, but I also saw them at nightclubs with those married men. They are 1.5-generation women usually. They're pretty, they wear nice clothes, and they drive nice cars. What's amazing to me is that some of them go on to law school or medical school, and then they get married.

Some of these girls are so cold about it that it's scary to me. They have both boyfriends and sugar daddies, and they have no guilt about it. And they still go to church! One of them just got married and had her photos taken at a big photo studio. She acts so virginal now that you'd never know. Her husband doesn't know, and no one's willing to tell him. No one's going to say, "Hey, do you know what your wife did before? She might have a degree and everything, but how did she get it?"

I asked one woman once if her sugar daddy had any kids, and she said he had one little boy. I asked her, "Don't you feel guilty? What if that was your dad?" And she said, "Why argue about this? I'm not asking him to leave his wife. I only see him every week or so. There are no emotional ties. I'm not going to grab him; I'm not going to call him in the middle of the night." I know one girl whose Korean American boyfriend lives with her. Maybe he never brings his clothes there, or maybe he lives out of a trunk; I don't know, but when the sugar daddy is there, he leaves. When the sugar daddy is gone, he comes back. The boyfriend is also a student at UCLA; he gets free rent out of the deal.

It's not just that these women are selling sex, but that what they are doing makes a statement about the community. Look at so many Koreans: as soon as they make more money, they don't just get a car—they have to get a

Mercedes, a 300 Mercedes. Then, when they get a little more money, they have to buy a bigger Mercedes. They'll have a tank in the end! They could drive a used car. But no, they want to drink that Crown bottle that costs a hundred bucks! You see these small Korean women driving huge cars, and 15-year-old kids driving Porsches with ski racks on them. They don't even ski! We value material stuff so much that we're willing to sell our soul for it.

The other thing is that a girl's value is determined by her beauty and how "ladylike" you are, and how you dress, walk, and talk. When people compliment a girl they say *"mŏtjaengi"* [smartly dressed, trendy person] or *"yeppŭda"* [pretty]. They never say, "You're so smart, you're so successful." They say those things to guys. Even though our parents say they came to America to give their daughters a better future, they still think it's important for them to be beautiful. My aunt is a makeup artist. She's been suggesting that I get eyelid surgery. After hearing about it so much, I started thinking maybe I should do it. I called my sister, who's the only sane person around, and she says, "I'm going to hang up. I can't believe you're talking this craziness. Good-bye."

Korean women are so pretty, but some of the funkiest looking men I've ever seen are Korean. Maybe the men are the ones who should get the surgery. For instance, one of my major complaints about Korean men is that they have no butt. Once I saw this guy in a cafe and I said, "God, did you see that?" That's what men are always doing when they see women, so I decided to do that to him. I said, "Wow! Look at that butt! My God, it's chiseled." He stopped smoking for a minute and said, "I can't believe you said that." So I said, "Well, you just commented on that women's breasts." That's when he said, "You're too sexually progressive for me."

There's no way I am going to marry a Korean man. Maybe I'll become a civil rights attorney and work for women's and minority rights. If I don't find the man that I want, I'll adopt a kid from Korea and have a happy life anyway.

The thing is, I have the habit of venting all my anger; I can't keep it in. I have to buy a punching bag or something, because I'm always running around screaming and stomping. It's better for me, because I can relieve my stress. If I held it in, I'd have an ulcer. When I get stressed, I drink and cry and cry until I'm so exhausted that I fall asleep. The next day I feel refreshed because I got it all out.

I have to learn the art of being subtle, the art of humility. But it's really hard acting subservient and docile, not letting them know you're smart. It's frustrating to me. A friend advised me to learn the technique of letting a man think he's getting what he really wants while in fact I am actually using my wiles to get him to do what I want. Part of me doesn't want to do it because it's demeaning. But working with first-generation Korean men has made me realize I have to acquire this technique. I have to smile even though I'm insulted. If I were older and had prestige, men would think I had proven myself and that I know what I'm doing.

Even in Korean American organizations of 1.5-generation people, all the top positions go to men. The women get slave wages. I think this will continue until the women on the bottom get experience. I'm constantly being reminded that I'm inexperienced, young, and female. I have to overcompensate by being aggressive and showing that I can do more than a guy.

After the riots, I saw that Koreans have very little power. I want to facilitate more integration, and I don't mean blending into the melting pot. I don't want my community to be this little ethnic place tucked into some big town. Maybe I have my head in the clouds, but I want fairness.

Although my parents do missionary work, they hated it when I was doing community work. They say that the community's going to crap on me and not appreciate me anyway, no matter what I do. They see the Korean community as ungrateful and easy to forget about; they don't think it's worth it for me to fight chauvinism and age [hierarchy]. They tell me I'll never make money and will just get my name tarnished, and that I should go to law school. They say that after I have my own law practice, money, and power, I'll be respected instead of just used.

JULY 1993 AND FEBRUARY 1995

KYONG-AE PRICE
Spiritual Tension

Petite, well-dressed, and supremely confident, Kyong-Ae Price has
a take-charge attitude. But she was not always so self-assured.
Price was born in Osaka, Japan, during World War II. Like many
other Koreans in Japan, her family moved back to Korea when the
war ended. They settled in her father's hometown in Hadong-kun,
South Kyŏngsang Province. As if in an attempt to explain why she
became "a problem child" and later, "a troubled woman," Price says
that the neighborhood children made fun of her because she spoke
only Japanese at first. She recalls that during the Korean War, when
villages all over the country were sites of partisan conflict, her family was harassed by other villagers as the North Korean soldiers
entered the village because her uncle was in the South Korean Navy.
Finally, she explains that when her father found a job as an animal
caretaker at a Pusan zoo and moved the family there after the war,
she found herself a country girl attracted by the lure of big city life.

I started smoking when I was nine. My grandmother used to give me her pipe whenever I had a stomachache, because the smoke would calm down the parasites; but then it became a habit. I liked dancing, but my parents said I couldn't learn dancing because I would turn out to be a bad person. My attitude was that if they wouldn't let me dance, I didn't want any education. At the time, I thought education was for my parents' sake, not for my own life. I stopped going to school after the fourth grade. After that, I transferred to many different schools and was in and out of school. I ran away from home many times, and finally moved out of the house when I was fifteen. After staying with an aunt for a while, I moved around here and there.

In 1959, I went to Seoul alone. I did a lot of different things in Seoul, until I met my husband at the U.S. Eighth Army compound. I had given up hope for my life; I tried to commit suicide three times. Then one day, I went with my friend to see a show at a club. There were no empty seats, so we were standing in the back. An American soldier approached us and asked if we wanted a drink. That's how I met my husband. He had just arrived from Vietnam the week before. He was nearing the end of his tour of duty when he was injured in a battle, and since the wound was not serious enough for a discharge, they had shipped him to Seoul.

My husband wrote to his mother saying that he wanted to marry me, a Korean girl. She replied that he should not marry a foreigner, especially a Korean girl. Korea was so tiny and different, she said; a Korean girl could not survive in a big country like the United States. She didn't want to see the girl suffer from the marriage. We waited one year for her consent, but she would not approve. I suggested we break off the relationship, but my husband said that we should not give up.

We got married in July 1970 and came to the United States in March 1971. A week before we left Korea, I told my father that I had married an American and we were going to America. He was shocked, but he could not do anything. Anyway, he wasn't responsible for my life. He told me that he would consider me dead and not think of me as his daughter. Now we are close again and love each other, but deep in my heart, there is still the unresolved issue of my parents not approving of my marriage. For my friends who married non-Koreans, not getting their parents' approval was no big deal, but somehow for me it is.

Even though she regretted that we had gotten married, my mother-in-law was kind to me. Now our relationship is very good. My husband is her only son, and she and I are the closest of friends.

My husband is from Waco, Texas, about seventy-five miles from Dallas. There weren't any Koreans in Waco when we moved there, but there were about two hundred fifty in Dallas, where we moved after a year.

In those days, there weren't any Korean churches in Dallas. I was a more or less shamanistic type of Buddhist, like most other Koreans. My husband and his whole family were devout Christians. He went to church without me. He never tried to make me go with him. I found out later that he prayed for me for seven years, until I became a Christian.

Because we were worshipping two gods within one family, there was spiritual tension. I think that Satan was taking me in, telling me that my husband was no good. My husband is the quiet type, very different from me. I was young, and I wanted to go to parties and have fun. All he ever did was work all week and go to church on the weekends. I was working two shifts as a waitress, morning and night, instead of having fun. I told him to go to school, and he got a master's degree in engineering; but things didn't get better, they got worse, because he spent more and more time at work. He was a workaholic.

We were both unhappy. I hated him and gave him a hard time; I didn't like anything he did. I wouldn't even let him take off his glasses. I even hated it that he was generous to other people. I told him that he should focus first on his wife. Four years after we got married, I almost divorced him. I went to New York secretly to find a lawyer, who promised to get me a lot of alimony. But two days before the final signing of the divorce papers, I accepted Jesus Christ. That changed my life 180 degrees.

What happened was that a Korean neighbor in Dallas asked me to drive her to the Korean church for a revival. When I returned to pick her up, the service wasn't over, so I stayed. The preacher, who was from the Central Baptist Church in Seoul, was talking about the prophet Hosea, God's chosen person. He said that Hosea had a wicked wife who blamed everything on him, betrayed him, and fooled around with other men. Then he said that love is to cut open the wound, cure it, sew it up, and wrap a bandage around it. I realized that my situation was my fault, and that I was a sinner.

At the reception after the service, the pastor asked the sinners to raise their hands, and without even realizing what I was doing, I raised my hand. He made me realize who I really was, and I was born again. My life completely turned around.

When I got home, I told my husband that I had accepted Jesus. I told him all about the secret plans I had been making for the divorce and said that if he didn't mind, I would cancel the paperwork. He cried and said, "Jesus won," but I didn't know what he meant. That was when he told me that he had prayed for me for seven years.

My husband immediately joined the Korean church, and he's been a loyal member ever since. He knew that my English was poor and my education level was low, so I would be more comfortable in the Korean church. He is the English program coordinator; he teaches Sunday school and helps people who need translation or interpreting, like when they have to go to a government office or something. My husband is a liaison between our church members and the larger society. He's the only non-Korean ordained deacon. There are about a half a dozen people at the church who ignore or don't care for him, but many people respect and envy him. He isn't much concerned about what people think of him; he just does his job.

I get along fine with my husband's American friends now. Becoming a Christian really changed my life. I married my husband because I loved him, but when I came to America, I thought I had made a big mistake, not because of the way he treated me, but because of my own self-consciousness. When we went to parties, everybody had white skin, blond hair, and blue eyes. I was the only one with a short body and slanted eyes. That's why I wanted a divorce. I told my husband that it bothered me, but he said it didn't bother him and that it was my own self-consciousness that was causing the problem. Now my short body and slanted eyes don't bother me, because I have accepted Jesus and have no inferiority complex or guilty conscience. Nothing in this world bothers me. Living a Christian life gives me confidence and self-respect. It's true that if you can't respect yourself, you can't respect others.

Our church has about five hundred members, including about one hundred fifty young people. We have a full service for the second generation. We have a 100,000 square-foot gym with two basketball courts, with a separate worship hall attached. Across the street, we have a thirty-room ministry building that we bought last summer. Besides the morning English service, we have Sunday school, gospel singing, and discipleship. We have challenging projects. Every month, we visit convalescent homes, and on Saturdays we go to inner-city areas where poor blacks and Mexicans live. We call this "the inner-city mission." We play with the kids, teach Bible studies, arts and crafts, and make lunch. Sometimes we go downtown to pass out religious pamphlets to pedestrians.

I'm part of the women's mission group. I take care of sick people. I've lived in Dallas for more than twenty-four years, so many people know me. If someone needs help, they tell them to call Mrs. Price. I translate for them at doctors' offices, provide transportation to the doctor, the pharmacy, the market, and so forth. I've had seven major surgeries, so I have learned a lot about the human body. I understand sick people and enjoy helping them. I think that what I'm doing is God's plan.

My life is full of miracles. The doctors said I could never have a child, and now I have a son in junior high school. He just turned fourteen. When I was pregnant with my son, I had only one ovary, I had had many miscarriages, and I was in my late thirties. My gynecologist said that my chances of getting pregnant were very small; and if I did get pregnant, I was likely to have a baby with Down's syndrome. When I thought I was pregnant, I called my doctor, but he seemed not to believe me. I waited three months and then went to see him. He was so surprised. He wrote a little article about my pregnancy in a medical journal, about the thirty-nine-year-old woman with one ovary and many prior miscarriages getting pregnant and having a baby.

When my son was two years old, he had spinal meningitis. For more than two weeks, his temperature was over 105 degrees. But he was cured, and now he is a healthy, happy boy. I know it was God's miracle.

Most of my activities are with the church. I haven't worked since my son was a year old. I've had blood transfusions many times, so I can't work full time. We're pretty well-off financially. My husband works for an oil company as an engineer; he has an important position.

There are thirteen mixed married couples like us at our church. Our pastor doesn't like the wives to come without their husbands. Mixed married couples have lots of problems, and my husband helps them out. About fifteen years ago, we had a mixed marriage church of about forty couples within the larger church. The pastor was a mixed married person himself; he wrote a master's thesis on mixed married couples. The program didn't work out very well because there were so many different levels among the people; some women were married to American soldiers, and others were married to students. They are completely different; they think and act differently, and they live different lives. We tried for about two years, but it just didn't work. Now, we try to develop programs for whoever comes to the church. Some husbands come for their wives.

I think about seventy percent of the Korean mixed married women are married to soldiers. I am heartbroken to see so many mixed marriages end up in divorce after the couple tries so hard. About eight out of ten marriages have problems and eventually break up. I would guess that more than half of the women who get divorced from their American husbands remarry Koreans. But they still aren't happy, because whenever conflicts develop, the husbands bring up the past. [Price seems to be alluding to the fact that a number of the Korean women who have married U.S. servicemen worked as entertainers on U.S. military bases in South Korea.] Mixed married couples have problems in everyday life. The first problem is cultural differences; the second is the way finances are handled; and the third is simply communication. Korean people want to increase their savings. American husbands want to go on vacations and eat out; they also like new cars. But Korean wives want to hold tightly to their money. Because of the language barrier, they can't explain their reasons to their husbands.

Another problem is the Korean emphasis on maintaining *ch'emyŏn* [face]. Koreans don't want to do something that makes them lose face in front of their friends and relatives. There are certain things you have to do, whether you want to or not, because if you don't do it, people will say something about it. For American people, if you don't feel like offering a visitor a cup of coffee, you don't have to. Korean people would do it, even if they didn't want to deep inside.

If the couple doesn't have a problem, their children do. Right now there's a couple at our church with serious problems. The mother pushes hard for the children to do well in school, but the father says, "Let them live their own lives," so the children get caught in between. Language problems between mothers and children are serious. My son speaks both Korean and English. He thinks he's a full Korean; I have to keep reminding him that half his blood is American. He hangs around with Koreans at church and with Americans at school. He's a happy little kid. I don't speak good English, so I've always spoken to him in Korean. Even if he answers me in English, I keep talking to him in Korean, and he understands. But many mothers whose English is very limited speak to their children only in broken

English. They don't teach their children Korean language and culture. The mothers and children don't understand each other. You just have to teach your children either Korean or American ways, not both. They have to know at least one culture fully. Koreans who come here only know American culture from the outside. They can't teach their children both cultures unless they know both cultures fully.

Many times, Korean wives apply different standards to their husbands and in-laws than if they had been Korean. I am not proud of myself, because at first I didn't treat my in-laws as well as I would have treated Korean in-laws. American people are human too; they want to be treated with kindness and respect. Yet they still loved me, because American people are tolerant of people from other cultures. Now I try to treat my mother-in-law just like I'd treat a Korean mother-in-law. When she had surgery, I stayed at the hospital day and night with her. Some Korean women told me I didn't have to do all that because my husband and mother-in-law are Americans. I did it because I loved my husband, and she was my husband's mother.

Soon after I came to America, I started writing to my father, and our relationship gradually improved. When I had a child of my own and became Christian, I realized how much my father had suffered because of me. I was a troublemaker, so I asked for forgiveness; and now we have a strong relationship. I brought my father over to America fourteen years ago, along with my brother, half-brother, and half-sister. They are all doing well now. My father worked here in Dallas as a janitor, and then about four years ago he moved to Los Angeles. He's eighty, but he acts sixty. He likes America and is a good Christian. He reads the Bible for two hours every morning. My mother, who divorced my father because of economic problems when I was sixteen or seventeen, and my stepmother, who doesn't get along very well with my father either, are both in Korea. I help my mother a little financially, but she pretty much takes care of herself. When my half-sister was only twelve, I brought her to live with me. Now she's graduated from college, she's married to a medical doctor, and she has a baby. I took care of my half-brother, too; he's still in school.

My older sister in Los Angeles is now my prayer goal; she's the only non-Christian in the family now. I am proud of myself because I led all of my family to Christianity except her, and someday she will be a Christian too.

No matter who you are, the most important thing is to know where you came from, who you are, and where you are going. I found the answers to these questions through Jesus Christ. I was a problem child and a troubled woman in the past; now I am a very happy person. Through Jesus, nothing is impossible.

JANUARY 1994

DREDGE KANG

Multiple–Box Person

Dredge Byung–Chu Kang was born in Korea in 1971 and grew up in the Washington, D.C. area, where his parents operated small businesses. In 1993, after attending the University of Maryland, he moved to Los Angeles, where he works for the Asian Pacific AIDS Intervention Team as the director of education and prevention services. A gold ring adorns Dredge's pierced brow, and his hair is cut close, revealing a wide forehead and clear, intelligent eyes.

Over the years, I've come to learn that my identity is fluid, and that nothing can ever truly represent who I am. But I can provide a glimmer of my essence. I've thought a great deal about what I am willing to share with others. I want to tell the truth, yet I also want to be respectful of what I perceive to be my parents' wishes. I love my family dearly, and I know they love me. I hope they try to understand my perspective as much as I try to understand theirs. I want to address stereotypes people may have of Korean Americans and of gay men, but I don't intend to be sensationalistic or to overdetermine these aspects of my self.

I am a 1.5, sometimes 1.3 or 1.9, generation Korean American. The decimal fluctuates depending on my mood. I used to feel that I missed out on growing up Korean, because my parents are Zen Buddhist-Confucian-shamanistic, and all my Korean friends had been Christian, which meant that I was out of the church loop, that I didn't take Korean classes with them, and that my family was doomed to go to hell. I realized, sometime in college, that what made me Korean wasn't church affiliation or my Konglish [Korean-English]. Koreanness is deep within me. And more than many of my Christian counterparts, I keep the traditional pagan culture alive. My mother is highly "superstitious" and believes in Chinese astrology. Although my parents didn't try to convert me to any religion, their modes of thinking are an inextricable part of me.

I've gone through a Zen phase, which seemed to please my father. But more than the practice of Zen, I think I've internalized it (isn't that the message of Zen?). And I still carry on family traditions. There's a certain night of the year—I think it's the lunar new year—when my father grinds a red stone by the light of a white candle, mixes it with water, and writes archaic Chinese characters on rice paper. One goes in the house, one in the car, and one I carry around with me always, for protection, of course. I want to learn Korean and Chinese before my father passes, so that I can carry on this family tradition.

My underwear has extra stitches in it because there's a certain day of the year when you can stitch clothing in order for it to protect you. My mother tried to stitch or get me to stitch all of my clothing, but since I am a true queen, I have so many clothes that it was impossible. So I told her we could just stitch the underwear. That way, since we wear underwear every day, we'll be protected every day. I swear by the talismans and the underwear.

I have cheated on some of the rituals. There's a night when restless ghosts, unhappy because their progeny aren't performing ancestor worship, come out, go into people's houses, and try on shoes. If a shoe fits, its owner dies. So to protect the family, you have to hide everyone's shoes in a garbage bag in the closet (that's my mother's hiding place) and place a strainer outside the door, because ghosts are supposedly inquisitive and will stop to count the holes in the strainer. If you use the new mesh strainers instead of the old-fashioned colanders with only a few holes in them, you will keep the ghosts out of your house. They will sit outside your door all night long trying to count the holes. They keep losing count, so when the sun comes up they have to disappear without having tried on any shoes. Every year, on that night, my mother calls me and asks me about the shoes. A couple of times I have lied. I have yet to experience any negative repercussions. A Korean friend of mine says it's because ghosts can't cross the ocean. But since more and more Koreans are dying in the U.S. with unfaithful children who don't feed the graves, I'll have to be more careful or buy a better strainer.

When I was about nine months old, our family emigrated from Seoul, where I was born, to the United States. We settled in an area called Kent Village in Landover, Maryland. At that time, the neighborhood was predominantly black and newly-arrived Korean, with some Southeast Asian refugees. I don't remember interacting with many white people at that time. I went to Dodge Park Elementary School's ESOL [English for Speakers of Other Languages] program. Korean was the first language I learned, although it's no longer my primary one. We lived in Kent Village till I was in the first grade; then, my parents bought a house in integrated (meaning mostly white) New Carrollton, Maryland. There, my friends were primarily Korean, Indian, and white. I got my nickname from one of the Indian kids. He was my best friend, and we shared a secret language. My code name was Driedge. We spelled it that way because we were practicing " 'i' before 'e' but not after 'c' or when sounding like 'a' as in 'neighbor' and 'weigh.'" The other kids in the neighborhood caught on quickly, and since Driedge was hard to pronounce, the "i" fell out and my name became Dredge. I've gone by many names in my life, like Mike to assimilate, and Ian (as in Echo and the Bunnymen) to be cool, but Dredge is the only name that has lasted.

My *hyŏng* [older brother] is six years older than I am and my *nuna* [older sister], seven. Of the three children, I was the one who left the ghetto early enough so as not to have an accent. My sister's accent is slightly Korean; my brother's is slightly hood.

My father told me he was a *yangban* [aristocrat] and a professor of mechanical engineering in Korea. He said he wrote a textbook that didn't sell well. My mother is from a wealthy merchant-class family. I think her father had a concubine at his country home. My mother never worked outside the house or went to school beyond middle school. When my parents immigrated to America, my father became a mechanic and my mother started working as a motel room cleaner.

My mother is a colorful person who isn't afraid to laugh. She has many stories about working as a cleaning lady. Some of these are privileged information, because they supposedly shame the family. The story I like best is the one about when she was working at Trailways bus company. I remember that her boss, who was black, would often come over to our house for dinner with his wife. When I was in college, I asked her if she remembered that, and she told me that when she started working at Trailways, she was cleaning floors, but after her boss had tasted her *kalbi* [barbecued ribs], she was washing windows.

Just as I was entering seventh grade, my parents started a sidewalk stand in the District of Columbia. They sold handbags and fake gold rings. I used to go out with them and sit at the stand all day. They have always made it clear that this is privileged information, but I am proud of our humble beginnings in America. For me, it's an indicator of our progress, not a blemish on our past.

A couple of years later, my parents bought a store in southeast [Washington] D.C., in a mostly black, lower-income neighborhood. We had a stall in a converted Safeway. It was something like a swap meet in Los Angeles, but more humble. I spent most of my weekends working and playing at the store. My cousins rented a stall next to us. First, they sold doughnuts, and later they sold shoes. After the stores opened, we never took another family vacation. I used to feel so resentful. Since my parents both worked eighty hours a week, I rarely really saw them, even if we were at the store together. I learned to be independent and became more and more distant from my parents. The culture and language gap became almost insurmountable. I no longer hold any grudges about this, because I've come to realize that my parents were doing everything they could to provide for their children.

Moving to New Carrollton allowed me to be tracked differently in school. I was eventually tracked as TAG (Talented and Gifted) and went to a prestigious magnet high school, the Eleanor Roosevelt High School Science and Technology Center. Since the "techie" portion of my high school was about twenty-five percent Asian and about seven percent Korean, I began to get more involved with other Asians. My first girlfriend, whom I dated for two years, was the first ABC [American-born Chinese] I had ever met. I hadn't thought it was possible for a Chinese person to be born here.

Right now, my mother is into hiring Vietnamese workers. Several years ago, I suggested that she hire a black woman, since most of her customers were black women. I figured they'd relate better, not have a language barrier, and feel like the business was giving something back to the community. My mother took up my suggestion. After a while, she thought it odd that the employee was offering to take out the trash quite often. Then she found out that she was taking merchandise out to her car at the same time. Next, my mother hired a black man, but he was caught later by a mall security guard who saw him stealing something from our store. My mother then hired a couple of Latinas, but she thought that they worked too slowly and didn't take enough initiative. She complained that she constantly had to tell them to do things. So she hired some older Korean women. One was older than my mother was, so she couldn't respectfully tell her to do anything. My mother said that all the others had an attitude. They felt that they were above such labor. Finally, three years ago, she hired a Vietnamese girl, who is still working for her and has become a friend of the family. My mother hired two of the girl's Vietnamese friends as well. Now, with all her stereotypes, she is happy.

After my first year of college, I came out for the first time. I was dating a coworker who was Colombian, and we came out to each other. At first, we were both bisexual. Then we came out to each other as gay and lesbian, respectively. Soon after that, I came out at the University of Maryland at College Park and started my career as an activist. Yes, I was a colored, queer, feminist, socialist, vegetarian, environmentalist, animal rights-advocating, abortion clinic-defending, meet-you-at-the-next-rally, march, protest, or whatever, button-wearing radical, militant activist.

Within a month after coming out to a straight friend with whom I often went to gay bars—it was trendy at the time for straight people to go to gay bars—I told my parents I was moving out of the house. A month later, on Christmas day, in the snow, I moved into my new apartment in Adelphi, Maryland, right across from the Jewish cemetery. I moved in with two gay men I had met the previous month, one *hapa* [Japanese for "half"] Korean, and one Spanish. We were a motley crew and did just about anything. I got heavily involved in drugs, sex, and the club underworld. I did everything I always thought I wouldn't, and I enjoyed it.

About this time, I went through my transgender phase. I really had a hard time conceptualizing gayness. I had lived all my life transmuting myself into a woman in order to have sexual fantasies. A Filipino friend of mine—Filipinos are truly fabulous drag queens—taught me everything I needed to know to be a woman. But more and more, the woman became a caricature of herself, of gender, and of me. I realized soon enough that I was not a woman but a self-loathing fag. And so, on to more drugs, sex, and fun.

Of course, I could blame everybody for all my problems: a distant father, an overbearing mother, a distant brother, a nurturing sister...and the fact that I was circumcised when I was old enough to remember it. Everything led to emasculation, and besides, I'm Asian; enough said. I took on my role as rice boy, boy toy, bottom boy, whatever. And I could have cared less what other people thought or said, because I had become tough. One thing I learned as a bottom is that it takes real butchness to be a fag.

Soon after moving to Adelphi, I moved to Greenbelt, where I started a queer people of color house. Gay, lesbian, black, Asian, white, Latino—we had it all. I lived there for two years, restructuring my life and building a home. I created a truly safe space for me and my friends, and the occasional Korean girl running away from home who threw herself at me at a gay bar, asking why all the Korean men who could dress were gay.

Eventually, the sex and drugs and clubbing pretty much stopped. The life was no longer exciting to me, and I was finding myself courting danger too often. I started volunteering at the Indochinese Community Center and the Washington Free Clinic, doing HIV test counseling. I started associating with more gay Asian men. Then I landed a job at the Korean Community Service Center of Greater Washington's Korean HIV-AIDS Awareness and Prevention Project. I started going to conferences and getting my life in order. I became a conference queen! I met gay Asian men from around the country, especially from New York, Los Angeles, and San Francisco. I had sex with a Chinese guy just because I had never had sex with an Asian before, which made me feel like I had a deficit or that I didn't respect or love myself enough to date someone who was like me. I became a theory queen —you know, post-structuralism.

During my "sticky rice" phase, I explored what it meant to be queer and Asian in contemporary America. We had terms for everyone: if you were rice (gay and Asian) and you liked white men, then you were a snow queen or a potato queen. White men who liked you were called rice queens. Every ethnicity had a term, usually related to food. The point of being sticky rice was that in a culture in which your body is devalued because it's Asian (that is, exoticized and emasculated), we had to learn to love ourselves, and that often meant fucking a brother. It was a way of empowering ourselves, of learning to make being Asian sexy. Some of my friends defined it as Asian men loving Asian men, literally. I moved away from that and conceptualized it as an attitude rather than a behavior. I'm sticky because I know what I am worth and can appreciate that, and not because I'm doing a brother. In any case, sticky rice was just another of my phases. That isn't to say that it was meaningless; I still take it very seriously. I just don't have to try at it anymore. I have internalized that message. Now I can scope out a room and notice that there are some fine-looking Asian men without being embarrassed or competing with them for the attractions of some white man that meets the GQ standards of beauty.

About this time, I came out to my mother. I had told my sister early on. Coming out to my mother was one of the most difficult moments in my life. I was shocked that she didn't know. After all, I was as queer as you could be. I never hid it.

Coming out to her, I began to cry. She told me that nothing could be that bad, unless I had a fatal disease. So I told her I was gay. She didn't cry. (I think Korean mothers cry behind their eyes.) She asked me how long I had been impotent. I tried to explain that my problem wasn't impotence, but that I wasn't attracted to women. But she assumed, because I told her I was gay, that I was impotent; that I was the woman in affairs with men; and that I would get AIDS. Our discussion wasn't very fruitful because I can't articulate in Korean and she can't articulate in English. She did, however, get across that I was rotting her soul [*sok ssŏkyŏ,* making the insides rot] and that she and Father would not be able to close their eyelids tightly when they died. In any case, she said, we were not telling Father.

The next day, Mother calls me at work and says, "I told Father." She goes on to say that impotence can be cured, and that Father was making an appointment for me with the "lower parts" doctor (that is, the urologist). They told me that they wouldn't send me to a Korean doctor, because if rumors got out, I would never be able to marry a decent Korean woman. They said they would send me to a Chinese doctor, because that's the next best thing to a Korean doctor. I was kind of surprised that she didn't put me on a regimen of ginseng and reindeer antler. In any case, I refused to go. Most of my friends who had come out to their parents were white or black. Their parents sent them all to psychotherapists, who told the parents that there was nothing wrong with their children unless their children thought there was something wrong with being gay. I was not nearly so fortunate. I think one day some of my friends and I will have to translate a PFLAG [Parents and Friends of Lesbians and Gays] brochure into Korean.

Early in 1993, I was asked to apply for a position at the Asian Pacific AIDS Intervention Team in Los Angeles. I applied and got the job, so I decided to move. In two months, I was on a plane with two suitcases full of clothes, headed for L.A. At the time, I was dating a Pilipino from L.A. whom I'd met at a conference. I didn't move specifically for him, although he was a factor. One of my rules is, I ain't movin' for no man. I'm sure I'll break that rule one day, but that'll be when I've found a husband.

In many ways, I felt as if I'd been burnt by and had burnt out Washington. I said my good-byes, the hardest one being to my best friend, with whom I'd seen heaven and hell several times. I romanticized L.A. I thought Koreatown would be paved with tacky plastic, all painted gold. There would be thousands of queer Asian men. I would meet famous people in Hollywood. I might even become Madonna's butler.

Everything about L.A. was a disappointment. I moved into a little apartment in Koreatown with a gay Puertoriqueño. I worked. I shopped at Korean businesses that charged too much for their merchandise. I looked for community. I got bored with the area and moved to Silverlake with a bisexual Korean woman. Since then, I moved in with a gay Okinawan man from Maui, and now I live with an unidentified Japanese-American *sansei* woman from Torrance.

My mother, of course, still wants me to get married and have children. She says I live in sin with women, even though I'm gay. She says my female roommates may try to come to my bed late at night to seduce me. I actually think she would prefer that. Until I remind her that I'm gay, she calls and asks if I have "the dates," meaning the years in which a Korean woman I can marry should be born.[49]

I still try to please my parents, but I also have to please myself. My father tells me that I will go to hell for having multiple piercings. It seems that I have destroyed the pressure points, unbalanced my *ki* [life force], and let all the *bok* [good fortune; happiness] flow out of me. My mother says that my bald head, multiple piercings, goatee, and expensive clothing make me look like a peasant in a potato sack . . . shaming the whole family. Not only will the Kims say bad things about me; they will say that my parents did a bad job of raising me. I, of course, will be the reason no one will want to marry into our family. While I was visiting home during the last holiday season, I conceded by growing my hair out and shaving my goatee.

Most of my life now, sad as it may seem, revolves around work. I am currently director of Education and Prevention Services at the Asian Pacific AIDS Intervention Team. I love my job. I love my agency. I love my coworkers. I just hate the hours and the stress. Most of my good friends and roommates in Los Angeles work for the same agency. This can be both a good thing and too much of a good thing. But more than anything else, working here, with friends and several new mentors, has taught me how to live a better life. Spiritually, I have learned a great deal about compassion and love.

I am now, I think, aware of all my "issues"—the baggage I carry around. Most of my friends in Los Angeles are queer and Asian. In many ways, I have made my surroundings more friendly so that I don't have to be a militant little queer anymore. That relieves a lot of stress. And I got so tired of the labels: 1.5 generation Korean American gay man. Now I prefer to refer to myself as either an MBP (multiple-box person) or a PWI (person with issues).

JANUARY 1994 AND JANUARY 1995

Causal
Connection

Doh-An Kim is the abbot of the Kwan Eum Temple in Los Angeles. He wears a gentle expression and smiles often. Born in 1937, he is imbued with a clear sense of his place in Korean history and tradition. His father and uncle founded a *sŏdang*, or a traditional learning institute that preceded the Western education system, in their native south Ch'ungch'ŏng Province; his parents met through their involvement with Ch'ŏndokyo, an indigenous Korean religion established in the late 19th century as a reaction against foreign cultural and political intrusion into Korea; and his maternal uncle died in a Taegu prison, where he was being held for participating in the national movement against Japanese occupation of Korea. His father and two older brothers were killed during the Korean War, so his family had to struggle to survive. When Kim was fifteen, he was taken to a Buddhist temple by his uncle to become a *ch'ulga-sŭng* [monk who left home].

It was no accident that I became a Buddhist monk; it was due to *inyŏn* [causal connection]. In Buddhism, we believe that life in the present world is related to the previous life and will be related to life in the afterworld.

The immediate factor related to my becoming a priest was the Korean War. Many children who were orphaned during the war didn't become monks, yet I did; this has to do with *inyŏn*. Even after I became a monk, I had many chances to return to the secular world: I attended secular universities and served in the armed forces;[50] I was a high-ranking officer in the Buddhist headquarters; I had a chance to get close to women, but I restrained myself. I never drank alcohol or smoked cigarettes. My relatives tried to persuade me to marry and return to the secular world, but somehow I resisted these pressures and remained a monk. When I used to return to our hometown for a visit, I didn't even stay one night; I just spent a few hours with my brothers and sisters and uncles, and then I left. Ever since I became a monk, I felt that my home was at the temple.

Under the Japanese colonial rule [1910-45], Korean Buddhism was forced to adopt many traditions from Japanese Buddhism. During the Meiji era [1867-1912],[51] Japanese Buddhism abolished the celibacy system, and most of the Japanese monks were married. During the Japanese occupation of Korea, Korean monks were also allowed to marry. The colonial authority appointed married monks to take charge of the major temples in Korea. In 1954, the Great Purification Campaign was initiated to restore the original characteristics of Korean Buddhism. President Syngman Rhee decreed that the legacy of Japanese Buddhism should be cleaned up in Korea. He ordered that all the temples be taken over by celibate monks. The married monks fiercely resisted the order, and there were some violent clashes between them and the celibate monks. It took several years to settle the issue by supreme court ruling, which established the legal legitimacy of celibate monks taking over the temples. My *sŏnsa sŭnim* [teacher priest], whom I followed all over the country, was in the vanguard of the purification campaign.

In 1955, we took over Pŏpju Temple in Sokri mountain from the *daechŏ sŭng* [married monks]. There were still communist guerrilla activities in the mountains.[52] Food was scarce, and life was very difficult. In 1958, I followed my *sŏnsa sŭnim* to Pongŭn Temple in Seoul, where I was able to resume my formal education. After I graduated from Tongguk University, I entered a Zen center near Seoul and started a Buddhist youth service program. Most temples are located in remote mountain areas, far from population centers.[53] Due to this tradition, even the temples located in or near cities didn't develop programs for children and youth. I wanted to urbanize some of the Buddhist practices, especially for children and youth. Through various organizations, I developed many Buddhist youth leadership programs. Later I was called to the Chokyechong administration[54] to design a registration system for temple properties in the nation. I also initiated the Buddhist literary movement, to propagate the significance of Buddhism in Korean history.

Korean Buddhist foreign missions began with the establishment of a temple in Tokyo for Koreans in 1966. The first Korean temple in the U.S. was built in Carmel, California, in 1972, and the Kwan Eum Temple in Los Angeles was established in 1974. The following year, I was sent to Los Angeles to smooth out the problems created by the Los Angeles's abbot's marriage. That's how I ended up in Los Angeles—not because I myself decided to; it just so happened, due to *inyŏn*.

When I arrived in Los Angeles, the temple was in deep trouble, paying $250 a month rent for a space on the second floor of an apartment building in Koreatown owned by the chairman of its board of trustees. The temple was bound by a ten-year lease agreement. When I took over, the rent was delinquent, so I took a job at a laundry from eight in the morning till eight in the evening and a janitorial job at night so that I could pay some of the back rent. I conducted the *pŏphoe* [Buddhist worship service] on Sundays, and the membership gradually grew until the space became too small for the services. The congregation wanted to move to a bigger location, but no one dared approach the landlord, who was also the chairman of the board. He was a powerful community leader and everyone was afraid of him. Finally, I had to confront him directly, and he said that the lease agreement was necessary to demonstrate to the Immigration and Naturalization Service that the temple was a bona fide business. He added that someone had tipped off the INS that the previous abbot, who was in this country on a visitor's visa, was working at a gas station, and he was detained by the immigration authorities as a result. I explained that the abbot had been freed from detention and the congregation needed a larger space, but this landlord wouldn't give in, so I contacted the temple members one by one and convened a membership meeting. There, I proposed that the board leadership be changed, that the temple by-laws be amended, and that the ten-year obligatory lease be dissolved. My proposal was approved by the members of the congregation. Things didn't have to end that way, but the chairman just wouldn't give in. At the general meeting, I was elected chairman of the board and abbot of the temple. We immediately started a fund-raising campaign. About twenty members of the temple made a savings pledge of $5,000 each with the Korea Exchange Bank, which on that basis loaned us $15,000. In 1976, we purchased a house in the middle of Koreatown for $25,000 and moved there.

By 1980, three more temples had been established in Southern California, and now there are fourteen temples and twenty-three places of worship. We used to hold special services, such as *t'ongil kiwŏn pŏphoe* [service for national reunification] and for Buddha's birthday. Four or five of the temples would participate together, and we would highlight Korean traditional cultural expressions, such as the Hŭngbu-Nolbu folk drama, shaman dances, and lotus paintings. We wanted to introduce and preserve Korean culture. Nowadays, these events take place separately at the different temples, although some joint services are held on Buddha's birthday, coordinated by the Association of the Korean Buddhist Temples in Southern California.

The City of Los Angeles ordered us out of our building because it was not zoned for temple activities, so we sold the building for $270,000. Then the congregation raised $100,000 more through offerings, and we bought our present building in 1986 for $800,000. The building used to be a Jewish temple, but it declined when Jewish people moved out of the area. This temple has the largest building space, 45,700 square feet, of all Korean temples in Southern California. In addition to the two main *pŏpdang* [worship halls] with three large statues of Buddha, we have a library, a gym, and a theater. We lease some spaces downstairs to merchants. In Korea, the abbot is responsible for managing the temple finances, but here the board of trustees takes charge. Resident monks receive no salaries; they rely on the temple for their daily necessities, so volunteers run errands and make meals for them during the week. They also take care of the temple, sweeping the floor and so forth.

Almost seven hundred families are registered at our temple, although only about one hundred fifty people attend the Sunday services. Some registered members come only once a year, and others rarely come. Buddhist temples never require attendance. Most of the people who do attend the services are elderly people. Middle-aged people make up only perhaps ten percent of our congregation, and young people in the Korean community generally go to Christian churches. We have adopted many worship features from Christian churches: we use an organ and sing Buddhist hymns. We pass the offering plate and deliver *sŏlpŏp* [sermons]. On Sundays, the prayer meeting begins at 9:30 A.M. and the worship service is at 11:00 A.M. Lunch fellowship is held after the service. We have about twenty children and forty high school students attending Sunday school. Our immediate priority is to reach out to younger generation Koreans. We do not have adequate English language materials for them. We need to translate the Dalma scriptures into English, but we are short of money and human resources.

We are coordinating mission strategies with other ethnic churches. I co-chair the American Buddhists' Congress with a Sri Lankan priest. There are three Tibetan Buddhist theological seminaries in America; the Chinese community in Los Angeles has a seminary for training Buddhist priests, and the strength of Vietnamese Buddhism is rapidly increasing. Last year, 13,000 believers crowded into the Buddha's birthday celebration at the Vietnamese temple in Long Beach. Thai, Tibetan, and Vietnamese Buddhists are trying to establish a seminary in Southern California to train second generation and lay leaders. Our plan is to start a multiethnic Buddhist seminary in Southern California in a few years. Only the Japanese Buddhists have not been active in the pan-ethnic Buddhist coalition, but I think they will join us soon.

Four months ago we set up a *puldang* [worship hall] in South Central Los Angeles. A black utilities employee who had been ordained as a lay leader at Hwa Om Temple in Korea donated his house. There are about 500 black Buddhists in South Central, mostly as a result of Japanese American Buddhist activities in the past.

During the riots, seventy Los Angeles Korean Buddhist families became victims. In our temple alone, sixteen families lost their livelihood, and offerings have been significantly reduced. After the riots, many of our people have been shot at their workplaces. Our temple was burglarized several times.

Sometimes, they come and ask for money; sometimes, they just come in and take things away. One of the main aims of Buddhism is to promote harmony among people. There are several black members of the kung fu training program in our gym, and three black people have joined our temple. Through these members and through the *puldang* in the South Central, we hope to promote harmony and understanding with the black community.

North Korea recently restored seventy temples; I think this shows that they are serious about preserving the Korean cultural heritage. When I visited P'yŏngyang two years ago, I saw the Yong Hwa Temple right next to the people's park near the Kaesŏnmun [Victory Gate]. There were lots of people in and around the temple, but there was no *pŏphoe* being held at the temple. I heard recently that they started holding *pŏphoe* at the temple on Sundays, and that they recently moved the Buddhist seminary from the remote countryside to P'yŏngyang. Also, the Buddhist headquarters building is being built in P'yŏngyang. All of these are positive developments for national reunification. Right now, both North and South Korea want unification, but each on their own terms: North Korea wants a unified socialist nation, and South Korea wants a unified capitalist country. As long as each side insists on unification based on their own respective ideologies, there is not much hope for real unification. They should build up common ties based on nationalist perspectives. Korean people are one people; the national division was arbitrarily imposed on them by outside forces. They should stop blaming each other and start helping each other. Buddhists like Prince Sihanouk of Cambodia, a long-time friend of Kim Il Sung, and Korean Buddhists in Japan have had a significant influence on North Korea. As a Buddhist monk, I will continue to work toward bridging the gap between North and South Korea.

In 1977, I was badly hurt in a serious traffic accident. After I had recovered, I wanted to go back to Korea, but the monks here urged me not to go, saying that we were pioneers of Korean Buddhism in the United States. They suggested that I should take a trip around the world instead. So I traveled to forty-four countries, during which time I realized both how big the United States is and how small Korea is. I decided that the United States was the place where Korean Buddhism should take root. That's when I made up my mind to stay in America.

In the United States right now, there are eighty-nine Korean Buddhist temples, serving mostly Korean immigrants. There is no way of knowing exactly how many Korean Buddhists there are. We estimate that almost half the people in Korea are Buddhists, but only about ten or fifteen percent of Koreans in the U.S. are, and most of them were already Buddhists before they immigrated. I have heard that about one-fourth of Korean Americans are non-Christians, and I think that many of these are Buddhists. We are still in the process of taking root in this country; during the past twenty years, the number of temples has increased significantly. Our membership is fairly stable; we are planning television and radio mission strategies, and we are planning to publish a Buddhist literary journal of fiction and art criticism, beginning this year.

Because we started late, we are far behind the Christian churches in terms of membership size and scope of activities, but we are gradually taking root. Our goal is to build a base for eventual movement into the American mainstream. We are making good progress; we Koreans can contribute to America by planting traditional Korean cultural elements in this soil.

JULY 1993 AND NOVEMBER 1994

EUN SIK YANG

Distorted History

Eun Sik Yang lectures at various colleges and universities and writes in both Korean and English about Korean history and politics. He says that he thinks of his life as having three parts: the first, his childhood and youth in North Korea from his birth in 1934 until 1950 when he left P'yŏngyang; the second, his young adulthood in South Korea between 1950 and 1966, when he came to the United States as a foreign student; and the third, his years in the United States between 1966 and the present. Likewise, his social concerns span the three geopolitical spheres. A solidly built and handsome man with a shock of gray hair, Yang speaks in measured tones, without gestures; his intensity is apparent only in his eyes.

Our family life became suddenly very difficult after my father died of tuberculosis. He had been a local newspaper reporter and the owner of a small socks factory in P'yŏngyang. After he died, my mother wasn't able to maintain the business, so she sold it and started a small business in the marketplace. She could barely provide for the family's livelihood or for education for me and my two younger sisters.

Until I was in the fifth grade, we had had Japanese teachers and our classes were in Japanese. After the liberation in 1945, we had Korean teachers and used Korean language in the classroom. For the next five years, we experienced sweeping changes all around us.[55]

From my early days, I tasted bitter social struggle. Since my mother's family had accepted Christianity when the American missionaries came to Korea in the 19th century, I went to church almost every Sunday.[56] When I was in middle school, our teacher asked us to come to school on Sundays.[57] I was punished for going to church first before going to school, and I protested. I was labeled a reactionary.

Many people attended churches in the north between the liberation in 1945 and the Korean War in 1950. Large meetings were held at a big central church in P'yŏngyang. I remember celebrating the release of the Christians who had been imprisoned by the Japanese for refusing to worship at the Japanese Shinto shrine. Worshipers were weeping loudly and praying, and the sermons were filled with excitement.

Christians had been imprisoned and tortured during the Japanese colonial period. People were forced to worship at the Japanese Shinto shrine. After the liberation, the Christian church was overwhelmed with the opportunity God had given the Christians. Then the socialists came with the Russian troops and started socialist programs. Everyone was wrapped in the political whirlwind. I remember it very vividly. I sided with the Christian church, since I was too young to understand everything.

After that fatal day struck us, June 25, 1950,[58] some of my classmates volunteered for the People's Army. I was only sixteen, so I was able to avoid the draft. Two or three months later, when the UN troops occupied P'yŏngyang, it was like a totally new world. Then, by autumn, we sensed the war situation reversing: the UN troops retreated, and long lines of refugees from northern areas began to enter P'yŏngyang. In December, I had to decide whether to go south or to stay with my family. I was the only son. My mother urged me to take refuge at an aunt's house across the Taedong River.[59] She heard that the river would be the defense line and that the strong U.S. and UN armies would defend the line. She thought I would be able to return home in a week or so. I went to my aunt's house. I found it empty and didn't know what to do, so I joined the long line of people walking south. There were thousands and thousands, maybe millions, of refugees. I went down to Seoul, leaving my mother and sisters behind. Of course I didn't realize the significance of what I had done. I thought we would be separated for a few days, but it actually lasted forty years.

Even though I was in the middle of a terrible refugee march, I was in a very light mood. But I soon realized that I had done an awful thing: I had left my family, and there was no way to return to them. Suddenly I was on my own, I had to make a living, not to mention getting an education and things like that.

To survive, I was willing to do almost anything. I was a helper at a *komushin* [rubber shoes] factory in Pusan. I was eventually promoted to roller man—I guess that's what you call it—I put all the material into a roller to make a very thin rubber pad from which they make the shoes. I lived at a boarding house with other factory workers. After the armistice in 1953, the factory was closed and the owners moved back to Seoul. I felt so lonely as people went back to their homes in Seoul. I went to Seoul, too, hoping to find some other way to earn money there, but I had a very hard time. Finally, I got a caretaker job at an orphanage. They didn't pay anything besides food and lodging.

One day I ran into a friend from P'yŏngyang who was already a medical student at Severance Hospital at Yonsei University. It was a shocking experience for me, since I had stopped school at the first year of high school, when I left P'yŏngyang. I tried to think of a way to start my high school education. The orphanage manager wouldn't let me go to night classes. When Sung-Ŭ Girls' High School offered me a position as a custodian, I accepted on the condition that I could go to night school. I finished high school in half a year.

Without any plan, I took the university entrance exam. I passed, but I didn't have money for tuition. The church minister donated about half the fees, so I attended Sung Sil University, but I wasn't able to pay the rest of the tuition. I had no close relatives or friends, no support system. Finally, to see if there was a God at all and to find out if he would listen to my plea, I went to a mountain every day for a hundred days to pray. If my hundred days of prayer didn't work, I was planning to take my own life.

Around this time, I met an American missionary from Philadelphia who asked me to teach him Korean. I eagerly said yes. When I told him about my wish to attend college, he offered me a scholarship in addition to my regular pay. Thus I was able to continue my education, majoring in law. I taught Korean to the missionary for about two years, and then I taught his wife for another year. Thanks to his recommendation, I was hired by Mun Hwa High School for boys in Kyŏng Ju. I had been able to practice some English with the missionary's wife, so I taught English and social studies. Three years passed, and I was not satisfied with a career as a teacher in a small country school, so I quit and went up to Seoul.

I participated in the International Youth Work Camp with fifty or sixty young people from America, Japan, Taiwan, and some Southeast Asian countries. I told two young men from America that I was interested in studying in the U.S. When they got back to the U.S., they contacted a private church women's organization called the International Christian Scholarship Foundation and helped me get a scholarship.

I arrived in California in 1966. After a year, my wife, whom I married in 1964, and my first son joined me. Because of the language, I had a difficult time at first, but I worked hard late into the night. After a year, I got a research assistantship from the Claremont Graduate School. I was a very happy man. I majored in Asian Studies. I got my master's in 1968 and my Ph.D. in 1971.

I searched for a teaching position. Unfortunately, the teaching positions created by the Vietnam War boom were closing down, and I was not able to find anything. I thought about returning to South Korea, but I had no connections whatsoever there, and my wife insisted on staying in this country. So we started a business.

My wife had been working on an assembly line, in a machine shop, as a nurse's aid—things like that. I thought of starting a publishing business, so I bought a print shop, but that was very difficult, so I closed it down after three years. Then I joined the dress contracting business that my wife was taking care of. The business prospered, so we bought a house and put two of our children into private East Coast schools.

Hoping I might get a bit of information about my family in North Korea, I wrote the North Korean ambassador to the United Nations in 1975. A reply came about a year later, saying that they had found my mother and two sisters. I was so thrilled! A photo and a handwritten letter from my mother arrived. I recognized her handwriting because she used to fill out school forms for me. I wish I could describe the moment when I opened the letter. She wrote: "They say you are alive. The moment I heard this news, my heart was beating out of control."

A letter sent by North Korean officials hinted that if I went to a neutral place like Vienna or Helsinki, I might see my mother, and all my travel costs would be reimbursed. So in 1976, I went to Vienna, supposedly to meet my mother, but she was not there. The North Koreans in Vienna assured me that my mother and sisters had survived and were all right. They said that they could arrange for me to go to P'yŏngyang to meet my mother and advised that if I went to P'yŏngyang to meet my mother, they could make all the arrangements. I asked for one day to think it over. I thought it was risky, since I had been deemed a reactionary when I was young.[60] I thought about how I had a family of my own now, a wife and three children to take care of. Then I called my wife from Vienna. She said, "This could be risky, but if you miss this opportunity, you might never see your mother again. So why don't you go ahead? It will be OK." I still appreciate that she said that.

So I went. I went from Vienna to Berlin, then to Moscow, where I stayed overnight in a hotel. When I arrived at the airport, my mother and sisters were waiting. I had not been told they would be there. I don't know whether they arranged things for dramatic effect or not. They just said, "Mr. Yang, you can wait in this waiting room while our man finds your luggage and gets the car." Then they opened a huge door. I stepped into the room and saw an official moving toward me. Then on my left I heard a woman's scream rushing toward me. An old woman was holding me so tight I could not breathe. I asked, "Who is this?" A man standing beside me said, "This is your mother."

I said, "Let me see your face, mother." But she was crying so hard that I could not recognize her. It had been twenty-seven years. When I left, my mother was about thirty-five. Now she was in her early sixties. I could not immediately tell that it was my mother. Finally, I gained control of myself and started greeting the people surrounding me, including a middle-aged woman crying beside my mother. I thanked them for making the arrangements and for the fact that my mother and sisters were living well in North Korea. Then my mother said, "Can't you remember her? This is Kyŏng-Ae." Oh my! Kyŏng-Ae! Kyŏng-Ae is my first younger sister. The other sister, Yŏng-Ae, was in the countryside; we met later. All of us spent two weeks at a guest house together. The two weeks was like a few days.

I met my sisters' husbands and their children. My brothers-in-law are working for the government, in relatively high positions. We spent day and night talking about their stories, their experiences. Again and again, they looked at the family pictures I'd brought with me. My mother had heard from the North Korean news that life in South Korea was very difficult under the capitalist system. She imagined me living under a bridge, begging for food, and then perhaps dying of hunger. "You not only survived, you finished the highest degree by yourself, and you brought such fine family pictures," she cried.

On my way back from P'yŏngyang, I was in Vienna overnight. I had some free time, so I got on a sight-seeing bus. We were taken to a large hall where wine, bread, and cheese were being served. A small band was playing music. There were about two hundred people sitting around. I was sitting near a young man from New York who said that during the 1956 Hungarian revolt, he swam across a river into Czechoslovakia and then got to New York, where he was now an engineer. He had come to Vienna to meet his parents for the first time since then. I said, "Hey, you know what kind of experience I had? It was very similar to yours." So we talked about why the world should be like this. He was about twenty-seven years old. I had waited twenty-seven years to see my mother. Then someone stood up and asked the bandmaster to play a Spanish song, and the people from Spain started dancing and singing together. I was just an outsider to this excited atmosphere. I started thinking: "These happy Europeans can visit their friends and relatives even without passports and visas. Why are Korean people so dumb? They accept restrictions imposed by politicians." It was a deeply striking experience for me.

When I got back to Los Angeles, I called a press conference. After my news was printed on an entire page, I received hundreds and hundreds of calls. One I remember at first shouting, "*Ppalgaengi* ["red one/Commie"]!" Other callers asked how could they find their families. There are millions of Korean people who are so unlucky, who die with their eyes open, because their fierce wish to see their loved ones is never fulfilled.[61] So I told them what I had done. I had to help them, because they felt the same way

I felt. Besides, I was tired of life in a small business, trying to get the children into a nice school, playing golf, going to church. I decided that helping our people with reunification of families and of the nation would be my life's pursuit.

In 1983, there had been a meeting in Beijing on Korean reunification, with six Korean American and two North Korean scholars. After that, we were invited to P'yŏngyang, where we discussed reunification with various officials. This was an occasion to meet many people, both official and unofficial. We decided that when we returned home, we would write about our experiences. In 1984, I collected the essays that were published in various newspapers and magazines and published a book called *Bundanŭl Ttwiŏ Nŏmŏ*. "Jump over the Korean division," I guess you could say in English. I think it sold over 200,000 copies. Apparently, some copies were smuggled into South Korea, too. I heard from someone that this book resulted in the new South Korean campaign "let us understand North Korea correctly."

Later, I met Im Su Kyŏng[62] in P'yŏngyang. She and Sŏ Sŭng[63] had both read the book of essays. We were happy that we made this kind of impact. South Korean people's understanding of North Korea has been so distorted. At least we initiated movement in the right direction.

I continued to be involved in these activities. I visited North Korea about twenty times between 1982 and the present. I got an audience with Kim Il Sung four times. The last time I visited North Korea was early this year, when I took my new wife to visit my mother. She was always worried about me cooking my own meals and washing my own clothes, since I lived alone for a time after my divorce. I told her that I was happily married, and that she should not worry anymore.

I thought I was at the forefront of correcting our distorted history and the division of the country, so that North and South might be brought together as one, but I was labeled as being pro-North Korea. Up until very recently, I found myself alienated from the church and from the community and harassed by U.S. authorities. Whenever I return from a visit to North Korea, I am visited by the FBI. They question me about this and that. A friend who is an editor of a Korean-language daily was told not to print my name in their newspaper. I used to be involved in a number of community organizations, such as the soccer association, the Korean Studies Association, youth organizations, and scholarship foundations. Once people from the South Korean consulate told my friends from the scholarship foundation that I should be kicked out of the board of directors. So I resigned from most of the organizations.[64]

In this and other ways, I was ostracized and prevented from getting involved with people. While making friends in North Korea, I had thought of myself as being completely shunned by the South Korean side. I was doing this work as a man of the South. But no one in South Korea can attempt such activities; because of the political freedoms American citizens enjoy, I, as a Korean American who is now a U.S. citizen, could have contact with North Koreans. But I found myself isolated in hostile surroundings. It was a sad and difficult experience. But I was doing this work out of my Christian convictions: I believed that the unification movement could enrich Korean life and strengthen the Korean state. In fact, I think that it may be the only way for Korea to survive as a small nation surrounded by hostile, larger powers. But I was cut off from expanding my work with people in the Korean American community, all because we were publicly involved in a movement for unification and tried to organize a unification association. No one offered a chance for me to write about my feelings in the community media.

At a meeting in P'yŏngyang in 1990, we decided to form an umbrella organization of North, South, and overseas Koreans in a concerted effort to achieve Korean unity. I was elected chairperson of the North American branch. The organization was called Pŏm Min Ryŏn, or Pan-Korean Alliance for National Unification. The following year, we held the annual pan-Korean conference in P'yŏngyang. The second was to be held in Seoul, but the Seoul government organization held separate conferences in Tokyo, Seoul, and P'yŏngyang. We planned to hold our meeting in Seoul again this year, but there was another misunderstanding, and an agreement was not reached in time, so separate meetings were held again. Now the validity of the umbrella organization has come into question. Since the South Korean government does not allow an organization to be formed, they regard our organization as pro-North. Now that the South Koreans are under civilian government, movement people are attempting to work with the government instead of regarding it as their enemy. Now some people are saying that our organization should be disbanded and some other more moderate organizations should be formed. There is a shift somewhat from a radical movement to a more moderate movement.

Right now, the overseas unit has regional branches in Japan, the U.S., Canada, Australia, China, Russia, and Europe. The members are writers, professors, labor leaders, religious figures. The members in North America are divided into roughly two factions: one supports North Korea, and the other contends that there should be a very close working relationship with the South Korean movement people. I'm kind of in-between. The international and domestic political situations are changing so quickly. Now the extreme left position has no grounds, or at least, they are losing ground.

The Korean division is a Korean problem, but it as also a problem of U.S. foreign policy, which has been handled traditionally by white diplomats. They did so many bad things in the name of the American national interest, and the division of Korea was one of these.

Korea has been divided for almost fifty years. America is responsible for material loss, separated families, and delay in Korean development. As a Korean American, at least I can be watchful of U.S. policy in Korea, for the benefit of both sides, Korean and American. The division created by the U.S. should be corrected, and the U.S. should make an effort to bring the two Koreas together and bring an end to the Korean disaster. We try to influence U.S. policy through letter writing, lobbying, and so forth. I am very optimistic about the prospects for the future. Understanding is expanding among Koreans. I have heard predictions of a very loose, commonwealth-type unification in the future.

Due to the changing international atmosphere, the general political mood among Koreans and Korean Americans is very different now from what it was in the past. Also, after the Kwangju incident, South Korean attitudes towards the United States and its role in Korea changed.[65] Toward the end of the 1980s, the democratic movement in South Korea changed its focus toward reunification as a focal point of Korean political problems. The mood in South Korea is reflected in the Korean-American community here.

In the early 1980s, those of us who worked actively for national unification were a very lonely voice. No one was listening. Nowadays, I am more accepted in the Korean-American community. Last year, I was invited to speak on Korean unification at a peace institute in Orange County. This year, I was interviewed by the *Korea Times*—an almost full-page interview. Over the years, we have arranged meetings of nearly 4,000 Korean Americans with their families in North Korea. These meetings between separated families means not only reunion but also exchange of information, which contributes to eventual reunification. The North Korean political system did not allow the free flow of information, but now at least they had some vital information about our side of the world—South Korea—from the relatives visiting them.

In all honesty, when you associate with North Korean people, it is not that easy to maintain your own political position. They try to buy us off through favoritism and other means. Although people may not be aware of it, we are often very critical of North Korean policies. On the other hand, there are also strong points about North Korean society. Because of anticommunist ideology and education, Korean Americans' understanding of North Korea has been very distorted. We need to come together to create an entirely new, unified Korea.

OCTOBER 1994

SUNG YONG PARK

Tasting America

Sung Yong Park operates a neighborhood market in Monterey Park.
He was born in Seoul, Korea, in December 1936 to a family of very
modest means. An avid supporter of the Republican party, his
ruddy, round face glows and his gestures become more energetic
when he talks about his participation in the Monterey Park Lions
Club and his plans to enter city politics.

In January 1951, the allied forces were retreating from Seoul, and our family took refuge in a small farmhouse in Ansan, south of Seoul.[66] One night, North Korean soldiers camped on a hill right next to the house we were staying in. They were fixing a captured dog to eat. My father helped them so that he could get a piece of meat for our family. We were starving. The North Korean soldiers were hungry, too; they were dressed in rags. The next day, U.S. jets flew over and attacked the house with machine-gun fire. The pilots apparently thought that the North Korean soldiers were hiding in the house, even though our family members were the only people there. I was with my parents, my uncle, my aunt, and a seven-year-old cousin. My father, uncle, and cousin were hit, but I was not. My cousin died on the spot, and my father died the next day. My uncle lost one of his legs. We buried my father and my cousin under the snow on a side street. My two older brothers were fighting on the battlefield, so my mother and I were left alone, and I became a semi-orphan.

Soon after that, the U.S. Army was advancing north toward the 38th parallel again. They recaptured Seoul from the Chinese and the North Koreans, and the Han River bridge was under U.S. military control. Korean civilians were restricted from crossing the bridge, but I was able to cross alone. My mother stayed behind in Ansan, her hometown, with relatives. That was in the spring of 1951, when the fighting was fierce.

One day, I was picked up by a U.S. Army truck and transported to the battle line. They were picking up able-bodied persons as laborers to carry ammunition on the front lines. These people were called *nomuja* [conscripted laborers]. I was only fifteen, but they picked me up with the others at the Map'o marketplace in Seoul. The truck stopped for a coffee break at a U.S. Army camp near the battlefront. We were not allowed to get off the truck. As I was looking around, I happened to see a former classmate. He was working as a cook's assistant. I shouted to him, and when he saw me, he told me to get off the truck right away. I said I couldn't, but he told me to jump off and that it would be OK because he was working there, so I jumped off. He took me to his quarters and told me that if I had gone with them, I probably would have been killed in battle. I stayed at the camp and became his helper in the field kitchen. That was the beginning of my long association with the U.S. military.

I moved from one military company to another as a houseboy and finally ended up in Ch'ŭnch'ŏn with the U.S. 728th Military Police battalion in 1952. I became friends with another tent boy, who was about to enter Ch'ŭnch'ŏn High School. Once, I visited his house, which was a large place with many rooms, all of which were rented out to *yanggongju* [literally, Western princesses, or Korean girls selling sex to U.S. military men]. I had been taking English lessons at a *yŏngŏ hakwŏn* [an English-language institute], and my friend's father helped me enter the Ch'ŭnch'ŏn High School. I attended school while working at the army camp.

The war ended in July 1953. In September, the 728th battalion moved to Seoul, and I went back with it. There, I transferred to Yongsan High School. The military camp was my home as well as my workplace. After three years, I entered Tongguk University, all the while continuing to work as an interpreter for the military. At the same time, I was able to get a waste disposal contract from the U.S. Eighth Army to handle the trash coming out of the Officers' Clubs. Bottles, boxes, cans, everything was money then. It was a good business; my brother returned from the army and joined me. He worked full-time, while I worked and finished college. I graduated in 1963.

I also served in the South Korean Army after I was drafted in 1958. I was assigned to the 28th division after basic training, but I was able to return to Seoul to continue with my business and my schooling. Also, I was an English-language tutor for women who had married GIs and were preparing to go to the U.S. That generated good extra income for me.

O-il-yuk [May 16, the military *coup d'etat*] was carried out by General Park Chung Hee in 1961. The new government's top priority was eradication of the nation's absolute poverty. Many people were still hungry, especially during the spring.[67] At that time, U.S. aid was the major source of revenue for the South Korean economy. Goods and money from the U.S. Army camps were also highly significant to the Korean economy then. The military government consolidated all the contracting businesses with the U.S. armed forces in Korea. There was an office in the Korean CIA to oversee this consolidation. The result was an increase in the volume of Korean goods and services to the U.S. military and an increase in foreign-exchange revenue for the Korean government. Before that, most of the supplies to the U.S. armed forces came from Japan, as did most of the U.S. aid to South Korea. The Korean War period was an important time of growth for the Japanese economy; but after *O-il-yuk*, Korea began taking over military procurement. My company, the International Electric Company, registered with the U.S. Military Goods Suppliers' Association and supplied a variety of plastic goods to the Eighth Army.

During Park's rule, two Korean Army divisions and one Marine Corps brigade were sent to Vietnam, and they stayed between 1967 and 1973. Park Chung Hee had made a deal with the U.S. government that all nonweapon supplies for the Korean troops in Vietnam would be purchased from Korea. The agreement was called the Brown Memorandum, after Brown, who was the U.S. ambassador to Korea at the time. I was on the board of the U.S. Military Goods Suppliers' Association, and my company supplied military brass, insignia fabrics, and other supplies to the Korean forces in Vietnam. It was a good time for our business.

I think that Korean participation in the Vietnam War was a landmark event in the history of Korean economic development. Hanjin, Hyundai, and Daewoo, all major corporations in Korea now, grew big during the Vietnam War era. They all benefitted from supplying goods and services to the U.S. and Korean armed forces in Vietnam. I don't think it would have been possible for the Korean economy to advance so fast during that period without the money that flowed into Korea from the war effort. About 10,000 Korean soldiers were killed or wounded in Vietnam; Korea's economy owes a great deal to these people who shed their blood there. The Seoul-Inch'ŏn and the Seoul-Pusan expressways, the first cross-country highways ever built in Korea, were built during this period. I am proud that my company made a contribution by earning hard currency for Korea during this time. By 1968, Korean exports reached the $100 million mark, and really bad poverty was eliminated from the country.

From 1945 until today, I think that the U.S. Army did a great deal to plant America in Korean soil. Americanization took place in every sector of Korean life—in politics, in economics, and in culture. Korean religion was also Americanized. Christianity became dominant; before that, Confucianism and Buddhism dominated. The Korean War was a direct outcome of Soviet expansionism during the cold war era: Stalin instigated Kim Il Sung to invade South Korea, and Truman wanted to stop Soviet expansionism on the Korean peninsula. As a result, war devastated Korea. But destruction is the mother of construction. The war became an opportunity for Korea to grow into a modern nation by providing incentives for economic development.

The military supply business was winding down by 1973, due to the termination of the Vietnam War. Many of the goods suppliers were moving to Guam; there was a huge housing boom there. Also, the U.S. bases were relocating to Guam from Vietnam, and a big typhoon destroyed most of the island's structures around that time, so there was a lot of construction money available through military and HUD housing projects. In 1974, I folded up my business in Korea and moved to Guam with my wife and two children. There, I set up the International Enterprises Construction Company and engaged in housing construction with carpenters, painters, and other workers imported from Korea.

Once you get to taste America, you are contaminated with the America disease. You want to come back to America. That's what happened to me. Ever since I visited America in 1966, I wanted to return. I had tried for a year to set up a business importing Korean lacquer and brass ware, but I was unsuccessful and ended up getting a job at a restaurant in Sausalito. At that time, my wife's application for a visa to come to the U.S. was rejected. The U.S. embassy people figured she might not return to Korea because she was pregnant. In fact, they were right; we were thinking of living in the U.S. permanently, even then.

After a couple of years in Guam, we decided to come to the mainland, and we moved to California in July 1976 when [our children] Young Han and Jung Han were in the fifth and third grade. We landed in San Francisco, and then I came down to southern California to see an acquaintance in El Monte. He suggested that I buy the Garvey Drive-in Dairy. He advised that now that I was in the United Sates, I should forget about being a *sajangnim* [company president] and start all over again with a small neighborhood market. I agreed and bought the business with $23,000 cash. Unlike other immigrants, we had the money when we came. The previous owners were a refugee couple from Hungary who had moved to this country during the Hungarian revolt of the 1950s. We opened for business on September 12, 1976. This year is the 18th year of operation. When we had our grand opening, the mayor of Monterey Park and the president of the Monterey Park Chamber of Commerce came to congratulate us, and the Monterey Park newspaper sent a photographer.

For the past eighteen years, we have opened the store at 8:00 A.M. and closed it at 9:30 P.M., seven days a week. My wife and I run the market. We really enjoy the business; every day is refreshing. I enjoy meeting people, cleaning the store, and shelving the merchandise. Our children grew up healthy and well here. Young Han went to the University of Southern California for his BA and then went on for a master's degree in urban planning at Columbia University. He married a beautiful Korean girl and lives in Portland. Jung Han went to Harvey Mudd College and is now finishing his Ph.D. in electronics engineering at the University of Michigan. I also got an MBA from the University of La Verne in 1992. These days, my wife and I play nine holes of golf twice a week before coming to the store.

Ever since we got married in 1965, my relationship with my wife has been very good. I am very satisfied with our married life, and I think that my wife feels the same way. Our *kung-hap* is very good [roughly, our personalities are well matched].

Where there's a will, there's a way. That's my life philosophy. A rolling stone gathers no moss.[68] That's another one of my mottoes. In 1979, I ventured into the real estate business. I got a general contractor's license and invested in a seventy-two-unit apartment project. Two years later, I had to file for bankruptcy because the interest rate had shot up. Fortunately, I was able to pay off the debt in three months. We bought the property in front of our market in 1982, and built a laundromat there and operated it ourselves. Then we bought the property next to my laundromat in 1985 and leased it to Weber Bread. We only own the business at our dairy, not the property, because the Jewish owner doesn't want to sell it. We're on a long-term lease.

I joined the Monterey Park Lions Club in 1982. The membership there is 90 percent white; there is one other Korean besides me, a chiropractor. There are only two blacks and two Hispanics. We meet every Tuesday. During the 1993-94 term, I was the president. Through my affiliation with the Lions, I learned teamwork, leadership skills, ways of serving the community. Also, I get to travel to other cities and states for regional and national Lions meetings.

Monterey Park and other cities will be revitalized by national business, like in Philadelphia, where the economy was deteriorating, but now the city is being revitalized. Philadelphia has a white mayor, and mainstream power is now back in that city. I think that mainstream power will reenter the inner cities and revitalize them. They call Monterey Park the new Chinatown. I don't like to call this place an ethnic town. Right now, Hispanics make up 19 percent and whites 17 percent of the residents. The rest are mostly Asians. Asians own 70 percent of the real estate here. When I moved to Monterey

Park in 1976, it was mostly white. Ultimately, it will be all mixed. Ideally, people should blend together. I think Koreans will also be dispersed all over southern California, and Koreatown will become like Little Tokyo [a commercial center].[69]

I think that federal immigration laws will change. The economy is severely impacted by the massive influx of people who have no skills and no money, especially in California. That's why Proposition 187[70] passed; it's people's reaction against AIDS, children born out of wedlock, and the breakdown of family values. People became very selfish after the equal opportunity measures of the 1960s. Women think they're the same as men, and the family is being destroyed as a result. People want to go back to [the] America [of the past]; that's why the Republican Contract With America won. People wanted a change, and there will be a change. The people's voice is powerful in this country. When the Republican party holds [presidential] power again, there will be a drastic change in immigration laws. Only those with skills and money that can help America will be allowed to immigrate.

America is my country. I consider myself an American born in Korea. As an American, I want to live in harmony with other Americans. I'm on the economic advisory council of the City of Monterey Park. I'm preparing to run for city council in two years. I have hope for America.

This country has enormous human resources and vast natural resources. The U.S. will beat Japan economically in five years. Some people say that China will catch up with the U.S., but China will never catch up, because the U.S. will not fall asleep. The U.S. will lead the world for a long time to come.

The Soviet Union fell apart because it was not able to control all its different cultural and religious groups. There are diverse ethnic, cultural, and religious groups in the United States. But here, they unite for a common cause, and they will unite to fight for freedom at any price. I oppose immigrants using their own languages here. Having a common language is our strength.

NOVEMBER 1994

KYU [MIN] LEE
Chino

Kyu Min Lee speaks English with a slight Spanish accent. He has large bright eyes and a calm, soft-spoken manner. An artist, he produces album covers, compact disc illustrations, and logos, on a freelance basis. He also writes for *Urb*, a music and culture magazine, and conducts a radio show on one of Los Angeles's largest rap music stations on Friday nights from ten to midnight. Lee was born in Seoul in 1967, lived in Bogotá, Colombia, where his father was a diplomat, and moved to Los Angeles at the age of ten with his older brother and two older sisters.

I don't think I deliberately stayed away from Koreans. From what I remember, when I came to America, it was the Spanish-speaking kids that befriended me first, when I was alone during recess. Korean people keep pretty much to themselves. I didn't see Korean kids hanging out with other races much at school. They would just kind of look at me and talk about me. They seemed to see me as an outsider because I spoke fluent Spanish, while my Korean had started to fade. I guess I wasn't really used to Koreans, either.

When I was a little kid in Colombia, there weren't many Korean people, and the ones that were there all knew each other. We'd have gatherings with other families at the Korean embassy. The kids would practice Korean and sing Korean songs. I remember being anxious to go back home so I could hang out with the neighborhood kids. At the embassy, we couldn't even run around the building too much because they would keep telling us to keep quiet. And I wasn't really into singing songs.

I never really looked forward to going to the embassy on weekends. I think it has lot to do with the way Korean people are. They compete from the time they're little kids. You could be friends with them, but they always try to be on top of you. Korean parents constantly push their kids to be the best in their class. I don't understand how Korean kids can live with that kind of pressure from their parents. In a classroom in Korea, everybody must be trying to be number one.

A lot of things about Korean culture I just could not agree with. I remember Korean kids were constantly fighting with each other over who was older. In L.A., some of the Korean kids in school and some of my older sisters' Korean friends would tell me, "You have to call me *hyŏng* [elder brother]." To me, this was silly, especially when I didn't call my own brother by such words.

I noticed that other Korean kids didn't have friends in the neighborhood; their parents were probably keeping them from having Colombian friends. My mom never told me not to hang around with Colombian kids. We would pick up sticks and run around, light fires in the park and stay out till late at night. Our parents didn't mind as long as it was the same crowd of kids. My sister is six years older than me. She started hanging around with the neighborhood teenagers, and they would have little parties. When my parents would say she couldn't go out, she'd get rebellious and sneak out the window. But Colombian kids are different from American kids. They were so innocent; to them, doing something bad would probably mean smoking a cigarette. That would be the extreme. Only one kid in the neighborhood smoked weed, and everybody knew it. They would say, "Don't talk to that guy—he's bad!" It was very safe to be a kid there. When I think about my childhood in Colombia, I think of nothing but happiness. Life was perfect for me.

In Colombia, we were made fun of just because of the way our eyes looked, but it was sort of innocent, so it never really bothered me. I remember once we came home from school and told our mom how the kids were stretching their eyes at us. She said, "When you go back to school tomorrow, squeeze your eyes together to make them round, and call them cow eyes." When we did that the next day, the kids were kind of shocked. They couldn't believe that we were making fun of them. They just kind of made fun of the way we looked, and we understood in a way, because it was probably their first time seeing an Asian person. There was no hatred behind it. At the same time, they thought all Asians knew how to do martial arts, so they were kind of scared of us. My brother was a red belt at the time. I started out with a white belt, but when it came time for the examination to yellow, I kind of chickened out. I don't know why.

We ended up in Colombia through the Korean embassy. My father was a cultural attaché in charge of establishing relations between Colombia and Korea. He also founded *t'aekwŏndo* in Colombia. He did things like teach the military police in Bogotá. They would have him come and teach big squads of people. I was always proud of that as a kid. My father became an important and respected man in Colombia. Our house was so big that it was almost a mansion. We always had a maid or two, and my father drove a BMW. Other people envied the way we lived. We got special treatment everywhere we went. People are very polite and humble to you in Colombia, especially when you are different.

When I was four or five years old, Spanish became my primary language. My sisters, my brother, and I spoke Spanish to each other. We speak English to each other now. I used to think in Korean, then in Spanish, and now I think in English. When I first came to Los Angeles, I could still speak Korean. I shouldn't have forgotten my language.

My mother brought us here to L.A. when I was ten. My father stayed in Colombia, so she had to travel back and forth. I didn't know until recently that my parents were having financial problems. My father gave up his job at the embassy because he didn't want me and my brother to have to go into the Korean military. My father reads a lot and knows history very well. He recognizes when something is wrong. He never liked war or the military, so he just didn't want us to go. But his leaving the embassy put a big financial strain on our family.

My father didn't really want to leave Colombia. I can't blame him for that. He's always been an important person there. I know how it feels when people respect you; it feels good. I wouldn't want to see him here in L.A., doing nothing. Even though the people that he taught opened up their own schools, he still has his martial arts school, and he does his journalism. But he doesn't really generate money. My mother makes money carrying things like precious stones from Colombia to Korea for people.

My mother was frustrated having us in L.A. and him in Colombia, but she recognized that he just couldn't leave all that behind. She's always been a very loyal kind of person. She practically held the whole family together. Living in L.A. was a big change from our life in Colombia. We had to do things we had never had to do before, like walk to the supermarket a mile away and then push a loaded shopping cart all the way home. We all shared one room in an apartment downstairs from our sponsor. When she saw that the money she was bringing from Colombia translated into only a few dollars, my mom got a job in a downtown sewing factory to support us. She used to leave the house at 5:30 in the morning to get to work on time. Back in Colombia, she was always at home taking care of us, and all of a sudden she had to work day and night to support us. But she made sure we were never hungry. She supplied whatever we needed or wanted. I was too young at the time to realize that life had become rough for us since moving to the United States. Because of all her efforts, she still made my childhood happy and beautiful. I never realized how sad it was for her until much later.

When we came to America, my oldest sister was seventeen, and she was left in charge of us. I can't believe that anyone expected her to take care of us. Actually, she really did good for her age. But we all gave my mom a lot of trouble at one time or another. My sister was an honor student, but she would get into arguments with my mom all the time. She moved out at seventeen and made it on her own.

Looking back, there are many mistakes I wish I hadn't made. I realize that every time I got kicked out of a school or got into trouble, it was when my mom wasn't there because she had to travel back and forth between us and our father in Colombia. It wasn't a conscious thing, but it couldn't have been coincidental either. Maybe during the times that my mom wasn't home, I didn't feel I had to come home at a certain time. I felt like I was more in charge of myself.

We lived in what is now called Koreatown. My elementary school was mostly Mexican and Korean, but somehow I ended up hanging out with the Mexican kids. In school there were big fights between the Mexican and Korean kids. I was always in the middle, translating for them because I spoke some Korean at the time. The Korean kids would get mad at me. They wondered why I was mostly hanging around with the Mexicans. I always hung out with blacks and Mexicans, so people looked at me weird. Back in those days, all the Korean kids I knew were still speaking mostly Korean to each other. Now I see Korean kids mixing in with a lot of other races.

All my friends started gang banging by the time they reached junior high school because of the neighborhood we were living in. Whatever gang was in the neighborhood, you sort of grew into it. In our neighborhood, it was the "18 St." gang. During junior high and high school, that was my company.

18 St. is probably the largest Mexican gang in the country, with maybe tens of thousands of members who don't even know each other. We had one clique in our neighborhood. I got my nickname, "Chino," which means "Chinese boy." It's funny, because "Chino" went from being an insult in Colombia to becoming my nickname, my tag, here.

At first it was all fun. We were little kids, seventh and eighth graders. We started hanging out with older gang bangers, so we were never really put into dangerous situations. That was around 1980, so the gun problem wasn't as big as today. The scariest thing that might happen would be to get jumped by a bunch of people on the street. We weren't scared of being shot; that all happened later on. Now, people just kill. They don't fight anymore; they just shoot. Crack wasn't a problem back then, but a lot of gang members are into crack now. That makes them a whole lot more violent.

A lot of gang bangers are just regular people. Not everyone joins a gang because of family problems. People are misled into thinking that every gang kid is a "troubled kid." Many times, kids join for friendships or to get girls, because when you're in a gang, you can automatically get any girl who's in the gang, since they are impressed by the fact that you are one of them. Kids join because they are just trying to fit in. They just want to run with the cool crowd. They're not good at running with the school spirit crowd, the football players and the cheerleaders; they want to run with the criminals, so that kids will be scared of them.

I went to four different high schools. I was always getting into trouble. I got kicked out of three schools. I didn't get to graduate on stage, but I made up my credits that summer and got my diploma. That was 1984. I didn't live a typical high school life, like going to homecoming, going to the prom, stuff like that.

I got kicked out of John Burroughs Junior High for stealing a bike. I don't know why I did it. It was silly, because my mom had just bought me a very nice bike. I just saw a bike without a chain on it and thought, "Hey, I'm going to take that." That was the first time I was kicked out of school.

Then I went to Bancroft Junior High. I was representing my gang. I wasn't scared to tell people that was where I was from, and I was willing to take whatever came to me for that. Even though I had no friends, I walked around saying that I was from that gang and wrote my name on the walls. It wasn't long before everybody at the new school saw me as a gangster. By the time I was in the ninth grade, everyone considered me a full-fledged gangbanger. I could go around saying I was from that gang, and my friends would back me up on it, so the whole school was scared of me. It felt good. Ninth grade was probably the best year of my school life. I kind of ruled the whole school. If I heard a kid from another gang was coming into the school, I'd go there with my friends and harass him, just to make sure that no one would threaten us. It was silly, but I thought it was cool at the time.

I was doing well in school, but in most people's eyes I was a very bad kid, always getting into trouble. My teachers knew I was good in class. My art teacher would always counsel me. He'd ask, "Are you in a gang? Do you write on the walls in your neighborhood?" I wasn't a troubled kid, so I wasn't rebellious. When someone tried to point me in the right direction, I didn't take it in a bad way. I was thankful to him for being concerned about me. He put me into the yearbook staff class, and I drew most of the yearbook illustrations. I got a standing ovation at graduation. I wore a zoot suit because I was still trying to represent my street side. It was really weird, a Korean kid wearing a zoot suit at the ninth-grade graduation and getting a standing ovation for yearbook artwork. It was like I was living two lives.

I'd hang around with my friends after school and go home whenever I felt like it. My mom was traveling back and forth from L.A. to Colombia to take care of my father. My sisters and brother knew I was hanging out with the wrong crowd, so they always got on my case, but my sisters were hanging around with the wrong crowd too, so I probably didn't listen to them because of that. The Korean Killers was the big Korean gang in the neighborhood at the time. They would always come over to the house. The gang environment was always around me, at school and at home. To me, being in a gang was not scary; it was like in Colombia, where kids in the neighborhood just got together.

My mom didn't want me to go to our area school, Los Angeles High School, which was full of gangs. She didn't know much about gangs, but my sisters told her that I ran around with a gang called 18 St. She literally picked up the telephone book and called a Korean family near the Fairfax area to ask if they would put me down as living with them. They were total strangers, but they helped out because we were Korean. I feel bad that she went that far to get me into a good school, especially since I only lasted a semester at Fairfax High. The whole gang thing erupted there because my friends were coming to visit me from other schools. Some of them were older and not even in school. They were all trespassing onto the school campus to hang out with me and a few girls from the gang. The big gang at the school, the Washington Boys, kept harassing us until we couldn't take it anymore, so one day carloads of people from our gang came in, and there was a big fight. The dean of the school tried to pin it all on me. They accused me of attracting or calling in all these people, and I got kicked out of school.

Next I went to University High School, near UCLA. That school had a lot of Mexican gangs that hated us. I was all alone there, so for a while I didn't tell anyone where I was from and just tried to do good at school. I stayed by myself at lunch and was getting good grades, until one day my friend checked into the school. He was one of those all-out crazy people. One day he got pretty badly beat up because he was going around saying what he was all about. I wasn't at school that day, but when I went back everyone was saying, "He runs with that guy," and I started getting threatened. At that time, I was already thinking, "I don't want to be involved in this." I was already in the eleventh grade, trying to think about my future. I had my mind set on going to art school and becoming an artist. So when people started threatening me, I just stopped going to school.

This time, I didn't check into another school. I started spending all my time at Fairfax, where all my friends were. I became one of those kids who hang around at school everyday without being enrolled. I feel so guilty when I think about my mom and my brother dropping me off at Uni. Thinking I was doing well, she would hug me and say, "You have a good day at school." And I would get out of the car, walk right out the backdoor of the school, and get on the bus to Fairfax.

At Fairfax, it was gang activities every day, like ditching parties. That's when someone throws a party during school hours, and you get people to ditch school for the party. I was never a drinker, even though I tried. I just turn red and throw up, so I stayed away from liquor. I tried smoking weed a lot, though. That was always around me. Luckily, I didn't get into the other things they were doing, like smoking primos, which is weed sprinkled with cocaine. They were smoking PCP. I was smart enough to stay away from that, at least. But my whole eleventh grade year was a blank.

Then my mom finally found out that I wasn't going to school. I got kicked out of University High School for truancy, and then I went to Hollywood High School. I was doing everything to avoid L.A. High School, which I knew had the most gangs. I was doing fine at Hollywood High until my gang friends started checking in, one by one. They were constantly getting kicked out of other schools, all year round. Pretty soon, we had our own little gang at school. I met a lot of new kids who were in the same gang, so we would automatically click. Eventually, we had a big fight with a gang that was already there. My art teacher even begged the principal not to kick me out of school. She thought I had potential and really wanted me to get into an art career. But I got kicked out.

By that time, I didn't want to be involved in a gang, but I was kind of trapped. When I got kicked out of Hollywood High School, I couldn't really avoid L.A. High School. At first, I tried to hang out by myself. The kids from my gang pretty much handled the school, but they weren't from my neighborhood, so they didn't really know me. Eventually, though, they heard about me somehow, so they came up and said, "Hey, man, you from 18 St.? How come you don't hang out with us?" What saved me was that there were different cliques in 18 St. I belonged to the clique called the Malditos, which is Spanish for "damned" or "evil." The Malditos was the first and highest clique in the gang. They started the gang, so all the older people were in it. L.A. High School has the Tiny Locos, which is second to my clique. Even if they were a lot bigger than me, the guys in the younger cliques respected me because I was with the older people. They couldn't really do or say anything to me. I always greeted them, but I avoided hanging around with them, and that kind of saved me at L.A. High School. I did really good in school. I went to summer school two years in a row to make up for those lost credits. I was a whole year behind, so I didn't finish until the summer after my senior year, which was really sad, because my mom called from Colombia and said she and my father were planning to come to my graduation, and I had to tell her I wasn't going to graduate on stage. That must have broke her heart.

Right out of high school, I got accepted at Otis Parsons [art school]. That made my parents very proud. My grades were so-so because I had missed so much school, but I wrote an essay about how I could do well in school if I really put my mind to it. All my friends who were in gangs knew what I was doing, and nobody really knocked me for it.

When I hear about kids saying they can't get out of a gang, I think that's really silly. Anybody can get out of a gang. You just kind of grow out of it. Once you start getting old, the younger kids can't really mess with you, and the older kids understand, because they've been through it too. If you want to get out, you just get out. You have to let go of your friends.

By 1984, the year I went to Otis Parsons, a lot of my friends were getting out of gangs and into rap music. They started break dancing and doing graffiti art. One funny thing about gangsters is that they're really into drawing. People in the gang I was in were really into writing on walls. Back then, you really had to put your name up in your neighborhood. There was some solidarity among graffiti artists—not like now, when crews are crossing out each other's names. I did a lot of graffiti. All my friends really appreciated my drawing. They usually had me draw the big things, like the block letters and old English letters. All my friends had me draw tattoos on them.

I didn't really like art school because I didn't think I was learning anything. It cost a lot of money, and my mom was breaking her back to pay for it, so I decided to quit and check into City College for a while. Then my mom wanted to open a business in L.A.

I've always had a passion for black music. Ever since junior high, I was always taping things off the radio. I saved up my lunch money for blank cassettes. I started buying records in 1979, funk and soul, and then hip hop. So when my mom asked me what I thought would be a good business, silly me, I said, "Let's open a record store." Ever since I was a little kid, she always trusted my judgment. She'd always thought I'd be a good businessman, so she decided we should go for it. So I left school and opened a hip hop music store on Slauson off Crenshaw, which is a black neighborhood. A lot of people thought I was crazy, a Korean guy opening up a store in the heart of the neighborhood. That was in 1988. Hip hop was big, but not to the point where I could sell enough records to make a good business out of it. I was breaking even, and the industry really appreciated the store. I started meeting a lot of people from record companies. It wasn't just a record store; it was a place for kids from the neighborhood to come hang out. I let them paint, and before you know it, it was like a community center. All the neighborhood kids would come hang out there and draw. That's the part I miss a lot—not selling records, but seeing these young kids get into art. The idea was good, but it was way ahead of its time. I learned that the hard way. But during the year and a half I was there, I met people in the industry, and a lot of people gave me respect for what I was doing. I got known. Everybody in L.A. who had something to do with rap music knew me from that point on.

It was easy for me to get a job at a record company after that. I started out as an intern for a company that was under Warner Brothers. After a year, I got hired as national rap music promotional director. It was all on me to promote the records that were coming out. I learned a lot about the music industry, about how corrupt it is and how the artists are exploited. I used to think that the exploitation was being exaggerated, but I got to see that the industry is really like a pimp-hooker industry. They care nothing about their artists; they only care about what they're going to sell. In fact, they don't even call what the artists turn in "music"; they call it "product."

I never got along with the guy I worked for. He was the typical industry Jewish person who was in it for the money. He cared nothing about the music. It got to the point that I couldn't stand seeing him because he was so irritating to me. I let it show that I wasn't happy there, so there was a lot of friction between us. I became friends with the artists who were on the label. They used to vent all their frustrations on me. They told me how the company was treating them. That made me hate my job even more. It came to a point where I just didn't want to do it anymore.

To me, pop music is very much on the surface; it's careful not to offend people, and it hardly ever speaks the truth—what the artist really feels. It's been through many stages; it's been cleaned up and watered down, even in terms of sound. In many cases, it's not "artists" who do pop music songs but just people with good voices that someone else fabricates into a "recording artist." I think many people who are making a lot of money aren't really artistic people. It's frustrating for real artists who are struggling and trying to make it. I've never known real art to be on top; it's always been kind of buried.

Hip hop is beyond music. It's a whole culture, a life-style. If you're really in it and understand the whole culture, you're going to be picky about what you hear. But if you're on the outside, you pretty much accept whatever comes at you. It all sounds good. To me, hip hop is not fashion; it's being yourself. Hip hop is like education; you might not have parents at home, but if you grow up in hip hop, you still know what you're supposed to do. You know right from wrong; you motivate yourself.

People who started hip hop back in the Bronx realized that killing and gangs weren't the way to survive. A whole movement started from that. It's expected that the media would attack hip hop. The good things that hip hop does aren't noticeable. Kids walking around in ghettos, or whatever you want to call them, are being touched inside. I don't think there's any negativity directly involved with hip hop. Kids don't say, "I'm going to kill somebody because I heard it in this song." Gang kids are not hip hop kids; people have to split that up. Gang kids listen to rap music, but they don't know how to analyze it. To some people, it's just music, just entertainment. It's not culture, it's not something to learn from.

I was there at the beginning, before rap music got really big, so I was able to listen to the rap records as they came out, one by one. I remember how they did them, and I've seen how commercial it's gotten. I still try to select the rap music that gives me that feel for the artist and how genuine he is. I look for a true expression rather than a formula that's being put together to make a "good song." Most of the rap music audience now is the younger kids who weren't there at the beginning of rap music, so they kind of take it for granted. They don't see it as important as it really is; to them, it's just music, it's not like a culture. To me, it's a whole culture and life-style. It's an alternative to a negative gang life, yet it's still respected and accepted in the street culture that I grew up in and was part of. Rap music gave me something to get into when I didn't want to be in gangs anymore.

It's not like I choose to be part of the street culture, but that's what I learned growing up in L.A. There was no street culture in Colombia. You either had a home or you didn't. In the United States, I found that there's a culture on the street that most people don't realize is there. They kind of brush it off as being negative or as not applying to them. When they hear about a drive-by shooting on the news, they just don't care. To them it's just a news story. They hear about gang problems and drug problems, but they think it all doesn't apply to them. But I feel that it does apply to me, because those are the people I grew up with. When I hear about the crack epidemic, I think that could have been me on crack.

My mom often regrets that she brought us all to America to all these bad things. I always try to explain to her that it wasn't really bad. If we didn't see what we saw, we would be lesser people. We are a lot more open to things. She thinks that if she'd kept us in Colombia, we would have all finished school and become doctors or whatever. I can't explain to her the benefits we got out of this, because I don't think she'd understand.

I'm happy that I've lived the way I've lived, because I can relate to many things, and most people can't. I want to be able to put out art that really reflects where I came from. I think it would be kind of shocking to the art world for a Korean artist to paint a Crip or something. I just can't wait to be able to do that. I have to learn a lot about how to exhibit art, but I think I will eventually reach my goal. Also, in the future, I'd like to teach art. Right now, I'd like to volunteer to counsel and teach art to kids in trouble. I feel fortunate that I was able to live that life and got out of it in a positive way, with big wishes and goals. Most kids who get out of the gangs are happy just to find a decent job; but my goals are greater than that. I want to leave some kind of mark, make some kind of difference before I go.

America is racist still. America pretends not to be racist, but the power structure is very white. My black friends still can't get work today, so they are selling weed to survive and pay the rent. A lot of people might say, "Oh, that's negative; don't hang around with those people." But I understand what's going on, that a black person can't get a job like I can. Anytime I want a job, I can go out and get one. The fact that I'm Korean makes people trust me. They trust Asian people when they want to employ somebody. So, seeing my friends not being able to get work hurts me a little bit. It makes me think, "How come I can get a job in this place and you can't?" I realize that Mexicans and blacks have to go through much tougher obstacles to achieve the same success Asians achieve. Since I grew up with them, I feel like those problems are affecting me in some ways.

They admire the position I'm in; they always say, "You work at a good record company. You've got your own apartment." I feel bad when they admire the things I have, because I know that I was not born with them; I achieved those things. But they can't, solely because they're black.

I never had black people treat me bad because I'm Korean. I don't think black people judge you from being Korean. They judge you on how you act, whatever you are. When I was young, I'd be the only Korean kid when I'd catch the bus to South Central and do my shopping for clothes and stuff. I'd conversate with kids on the bus and at the bus stops, and I was always accepted. I don't think my race had anything to do with it. Black people have been stereotyped so much that if you react to any of those stereotypes, it's insulting to them.

There's so much racism going on, and people don't want to see it. The media control everybody's thoughts. They make the whole society think that black people are scary. It's bad, because for a lot of people, their culture has been killed to the point that they have no motivation for anything. Not too many black people feel obligated to go to school. They feel more obligated to find a job.

Now I am concentrating on doing artwork for record companies. Since I got to meet so many people, I've had pretty steady work. But my goal now is to finish school. Finishing school and having a degree might not have anything to do with the level of success I could achieve, because you don't really need an education to move forward in the music industry, but it's a matter of self-satisfaction. Somehow I feel incomplete. This time, I'd like to go to the Art Center in Pasadena, but it's really expensive. I want to learn film. When I watch music videos, I just feel like I could make a better video. At the same time, I'd like to go to a completely different city. Here in L.A., I can't really expect nothing new. I'd like to go to art school in New York. The competition there makes people hungrier. In L.A., you can get up in the morning, get in your car, and you may not come into contact with any people. You could just see your friends and never deal with the public much.

Right now I feel guilty, since my mom did all that suffering for us to get an education. The funny thing is that none of us finished up at a big university. We all got into trouble here and there, but none of us really fell off or did really bad. Still, for some reason we never ended up finishing school. I think one of the reasons was the financial pressure. When we realized that my mom was suffering a lot to support us, it wasn't easy to just go to school and not think about it. We felt the pressure, that we needed to make money just as much as we needed to finish our education. We all became successful in a sense, not through education, but completely on our own. My brother and sisters are all paralegals now. They are all married. One sister has three children, and the other one is pregnant right now. The only problem was my brother becoming a Christian. We thought he was a fanatic, doing things for his church like passing out pamphlets. It was a problem to all of us. I think it was just a stage he went through at the beginning. Now, he seems to be a normal person. He doesn't come to the house and talk about Jesus or anything. My father used to get into deep arguments with him about how Christianity was brought upon us, and how it wasn't really a valid religion for our people.

My sisters married Koreans, and my brother's wife is Chinese. Being very Korean, my mother prefers that I marry a Korean girl, or even any Asian girl, but not a Latin girl. She thinks a Latin woman will spend up all the money and won't do anything for the home, and she worries about the divorce rate among Latin people. I've been with my girlfriend for a long time. We are just about like best friends. A lot of Mexican women feel an urge to get married and have children, but since she was born here and came from a single-parent home, she didn't feel those kinds of pressures. She wants to go to veterinary school in Texas. Realistically, I'm twenty-seven years old now; it's time for me to get married, or at least know who I'm going to marry. But it's unrealistic to think that I'll marry a Korean girl when I don't even know one.

My mom was just here in L.A. visiting from Bogotá two or three weeks ago. She said that her biggest worry is that I finish school and become financially secure. She's proud that I live on my own now, completely paying all my own bills without really having a job, but she gets nervous that work might stop coming. She wants me to finish school and get a really good art job. So she kind of left it up to me to go to whatever school I want to go to. She said she'd pay for art school. She even suggested sending me to Italy.

I'm one of those lucky people who can't complain about their parents. They have always been supportive. I think they raised us really well. If they hadn't built such a solid foundation in our minds, we would have fallen apart in the circumstances that we were living under here. We could have easily got into drugs or whatever, but we all had the common sense to know what we had to do. That's what our parents gave us.

I feel really proud to be Korean, because of my parents. There are not too many Korean people in my life besides my family. I think I got this love for Korea from my parents. They always kept Korea in our environment. Everything at home was very Korean. My mom takes me back to Korea because she wants me to spend some time with my grandmother before she dies. Going back to Korea makes me feel like I've lost a part of my life, because I can see how Korea is, and how I never got to experience that kind of life-style.

My sisters speak fluent Korean, and my brother can still speak some. I'm the one that kind of fell outside the Korean community and started hanging around with blacks and Mexicans, so my mom tries harder to teach me Korean culture.

My parents don't realize how important it is to me to learn Korean, or how hard I try to learn. They don't know that I sometimes drive around listening to the Korean radio stations and trying to remember Korean words. I try to watch Korean TV, but those shows with the young kids dancing around get too silly. Korean rap is hilarious. I'm such a critic when it comes to rap music; I'm very selective. So that Korean stuff is really funny to me. It's just their way of trying to be American, I guess.

It seems like all the Korean people that I meet through the industry, the fact that we're Korean makes us become friends automatically. That's one thing that's beautiful about Korean people. I don't know how it is in Korea, but Koreans who are away from Korea help each other a lot. There's a Korean guy in New York who's really successful. He was the marketing director for his record company, and they put him in charge of rap music. He signs the talent. Now he's starting his own record company, so he's really successful. In Dallas, there's a DJ for a famous rap group who won the annual world championship a couple of times. He happens to be half Korean and half Mexican. The whole hip-hop industry is so tight knit that we all know each other around the world, almost.

I'm not Korean American; I'm Korean. To me it's like a pride thing. It's where I was born. Already, I've forgotten most of the language; I can't speak Korean fluently, even though I can understand most of it. But I always say I'm Korean, because my parents are both Korean. I hate to hear Korean people say, "I am American."

JANUARY AND OCTOBER 1994; APRIL 1995

KATHY KIM

Starting From Zero

Kathy Kyong Sook Kim took the name "Kathy" because her home-room teacher pronounced her name so badly that it sounded like "Kong Suke." She arrived in the United States on Election Day in 1976, when she was fourteen. Her family was sponsored by her mother's younger brother, who had come as a student in the 1960s. After attending Harvard and Princeton Seminary, he became a minister, and he settled in "Illinois or Pennsylvania or somewhere" with his white American wife; but Kathy's family decided to settle in Los Angeles, where they could be close to other Korean immigrants. Poised and serene, Kathy speaks thoughtfully in a rich, melodious voice.

When my parents said they wanted to take us all to live in the United States, I was shocked. I couldn't think about coming to America when I was having such a good time in Korea. All through elementary and middle school, I was really popular and had a lot of friends. It was the best time of my life. For the first two or three years here, I was really homesick, thinking about my friends and of all the places I used to go to in Korea. We used to go to school tournaments at the Seoul sports complex, which was near where we lived. I really missed that.

I think my parents decided to come because they didn't think they could afford the expense of educating all three of us children. I guess they had talked about it for a long time before they had the courage to decide, but I didn't even know that this discussion was going on.

People told them that there weren't many Koreans where my uncle was, so we decided to settle down in Los Angeles. They did what a lot of other Korean immigrant families did: my father got a job doing janitorial work, and my mother worked as a seamstress.

In Korea, my father was the sole breadwinner. He had a small business that really didn't go too well, and my mother kept house. But here, my mother ended up making more money than my father. Once she started going to work and making money herself, she really enjoyed it. She still works as a sample maker, while my father retired a long time ago.

They talked about maybe starting a small business here, but my father was too scared. I think they prefer working for wages and having weekends. They were always home in the evening when I was growing up. We always had family meals together.

If she had been born into a different family or a different time, my mom could have been somebody like Mother Teresa. She never gets tired. I remember that she did all the cooking and cleaning, grew her own vegetables, and made all my clothes and her own clothes, too. She is really incredible; she still wakes up at five o'clock in the morning, works all day, and then comes home and cleans. Even now, she never gets tired. I tell her maybe we should trade houses for a month or so, so that she could come over to my house, work in my garden, and make my house look brand new. My father is not as strong as my mom. I think he had a lot of pain and suffering, coming down to Seoul from North Korea alone when he was only twenty or twenty-one years old during the Korean War. I remember him talking about his parents and his brothers from time to time. I even saw him crying. He told me that I remind him of a sister he loved. It was only five years ago that he was able to write a letter to North Korea. That's when he found out his parents had both died a long time ago.

Coming to Los Angeles from Seoul at fourteen was a shock for me. I started attending Bancroft Junior High School, which was mostly white, with some Latinos and black kids. My classmates looked like fully grown-up people, at least physically. I just couldn't believe how they all behaved on campus—their makeup, their clothes, their shoes. It just made me sick. When I left Korea, kids were still wearing school uniforms and short, straight haircuts. You could never put on makeup or nail polish; no one even imagined doing those things at that age. Here, the kids wanted to seem like adults by kissing, hugging, and making a lot of gestures.[71] Even the Korean kids in the eighth or ninth grade were already paired in couples. Some of them were dressing like some of the Latino kids, with heavy eyeliner and sexy clothes.

I never really wanted to belong. I didn't even try to make friends. I figured I would just study and do my thing. Nothing I saw the first couple of years made me feel good about being in the United States. I kept thinking, "I don't know why I came here; I hate L.A." I was very bitter.

Learning English was pretty tough, too. It was obvious that I had just come to this country and was learning, which was OK when I was in front of blacks or Caucasians, but I felt uncomfortable speaking English in front of the Korean kids. About half of the forty or fifty Korean students had been raised here from early childhood. The kids who had come here five or six years earlier and spoke good English really showed it off. That was the main thing that bothered me in junior high school—not being able to speak good English, and attending ESL [English as a Second Language] classes instead of regular English classes. But I did really well in math and other subjects, and I got good grades.

I didn't really talk to anyone about how I felt. My parents were busy, and so were my brothers. I took the bus every day with a couple of kids from school, but we just talked about superficial things. But I wrote a lot of letters to my friends in Korea.

After graduation, I chose not to go to the high school the kids from my junior high were going to. I wanted to start from zero, so I went to L.A. High School. I just wanted to study hard and get into a good college. At first, I didn't bother with the Korean kids; I made friends with studious and quiet Japanese and Chinese girls. It was around that time that my personality kind of came back, and I made more friends. I started getting more and more involved with a church youth group. I was elected vice president of the Korean Student Association. I was very active, staying up until two or three in the morning. After finishing my homework, I had to do stuff for the church and for the Korean Student Association. I started forgetting my friends from Korea. My letters became less frequent. Obviously they had changed too. Basically, we were growing up in two different worlds.

In my second year, I joined the volleyball team, and one of the Korean kids on the team introduced me to the Korean Youth Center (KYC) when I needed a summer job. I also got a part-time job there during the school year. The gangsters, who were my age, were on probation, so they had to do four to six hours of counseling a week; that's how they came to KYC. The way they dressed was intimidating: they had dark glasses and spiky hair. Some guys dressed like guys from Latino gangs, and some dressed like Bruce Lee, with the kung fu outfit. They would carry those *nunchakus* [sticks for fighting]. I saw them carrying guns. They were potentially scary, but as people they were very sweet guys. Some of them called me *nuna* [older sister]. We hired some of them to work with children at our summer day camp. We took the kids to Disneyland, museums, the zoo, and parks. We ran arts and crafts classes, taught history, and had Korean language classes. We worked with the youth closely, and they were very good with the kids, who just loved them and were always climbing all over them. Later I heard that they got involved in felony offenses. I remember one guy who got paralyzed in a car accident when they were going 120 miles an hour driving away from a robbery they had just committed. The driver was killed instantly. I went to the hospital to visit the guy who'd been paralyzed. Just two months before he was playing with our children. Seeing him like that really broke my heart.

I wanted to see if I could at least do something. I might not change things, but at least I could be there to provide support for a few of these guys. Jane Kim, the KYC director, really impressed me. She talked to them and visited them in jail. I wanted to be like her. I wanted to spend my life working with those gangsters. For me, the emotional aspect of doing community work is very important, more important than the professional and technical aspect. Many times, the people you are serving are victims of something. To really help them, it has to be human to human, not counselor to client.

It was KYC that shaped me and made me study sociology when I went to UC Berkeley and then come back to work in the community after I graduated in 1985. Jane asked me to apply for a job at KYC. At that time, the only staff position open was a counselor position. I thought the transition between school and work would be difficult, but I found myself really enjoying what I was doing. I created an evening adult English class, using volunteer teachers. We had seminars for Koreans trying to start small businesses. We held domestic violence workshops. It was very interesting for me because when I worked at KYC during high school, I only interacted with other youth; I never really saw the total picture, how parents go through their own transitions. I realized that in an immigrant family, everybody goes through difficult struggles. That's when I started to get to know and become determined to commit myself to work with the Korean American community.

After the initial three years of direct service, I started working for United Way in 1988. I saw how they had influence over many agencies and communities, and I thought it would be a good opportunity for me to stay involved with the Korean American community while acquiring new skills and knowledge. I started working there as the project manager for a Korean language project that was the basis for a profile study of Koreatown. I soon found out that United Way's hidden agenda was to tap Korean American financial resources. I don't think there's anything wrong with that, but my commitment was more to bringing resources from United Way to the Korean American community than vice versa. So I worked to involve Korean American community and agency leaders in the United Way system so that they could have an impact on United Way. I think the community and agency leaders were really offended by having what seemed like a giant organization come into our community to compete for the same dollars. At that time, United Way raised $85 million, while many of the community agencies had budgets of less than $20,000 or $50,000.

After a year and a half, I came back to KYC and worked in fund-raising, media relations, and volunteers' development. I was involved in a few programs, like consumer education, tobacco education, and cultural programs. I kind of managed projects. By the time I left [the Korean Youth

Center], I was actually detached from the community and the people. My interaction with the community was more like with reporters, board members, people from other organizations, and my staff. I had to package programs to attract money. The job fit me because I was not raising money for the organization; I was raising money for people in the community. It was never like begging; it was more like giving people a chance to support a good cause.

Right after the riots in 1992, I had a chance to meet the people from a group called Living Literature/Colors United. Basically, it was a group formed out of Jordan High School in Watts. They recruit high-risk youth and introduce them to different areas of theater—not only acting, dancing, and singing, but also play writing, production, lighting, sound, and music. Within a couple of years after starting the program at Jordan High, the school was free of graffiti and gang activity. That made me realize how powerful cultural programs can be, and that arts can be adapted for all kinds of issues, so that arts and social problems can really be brought together.

I went to one of their performances. It was about struggles, about gangs, about love. There were about fifty or sixty kids involved in the production. I could see right away that they didn't come from privileged families. I could also see a lot of bonding among them, a lot of love and confidence. I noticed that after each rehearsal, the kids said the Lord's Prayer in English and Spanish. A lot of the black kids had to memorize the prayer in Spanish. For me, that was going one step beyond; it was going through the hassle of learning and exposing yourself to another culture for the sake of giving the other people a feeling of pride in their culture. I had a chance to speak with some of them, and I got really motivated to somehow bridge KYC programs with theirs. It's such a different way of doing race relations work, working together as a group on a common project.

Some youth from KYC were interested in the program, but their parents were worried about them rehearsing in South Central. I told the parents that no place in the city is 100 percent safe, but that their children would be in good hands, they would be acquiring skills, and they would be breaking new ground in race relations.

Black and Latino kids are much more open about some things than the Korean kids I worked with at the Korean Youth Center. For example, I remember going to an AIDS workshop for Korean kids, and one of the birth control methods mentioned was abstinence. The director of Colors United gets condoms at Costco and hands them out to the kids. It's more realistic. You might wish it was another way, but we are human, and kids are maturing earlier. I wasn't like that, but they are, and that's the reality, so the best way is to be protected. My views on sex are more liberal than before. I think kids in Korea are too naive; they should be exposed to constructive ways of interaction between men and women as early as possible.

Four months ago, I was hired as executive director at Colors United. I spend about half my time doing grant research and proposal writing. There are four people working in the office, and we have an artistic director, a musical director, and eight or ten instructors. It's very mixed; there are African Americans, Latinos, and Anglos. At first, I was kind of scared about how I would fit into this organization as the first Asian person and as a woman. It's like a family.

It turned out that it's like a family. There are about one hundred kids involved, mostly black and Latino and a few Vietnamese kids. We are trying to expand our program to bring more Asians in. Partly because Korean people with really severe problems usually don't reach out for help, the kids I worked with at KYC didn't face the kinds of conditions kids in Colors United face. There's one Latino kid with three brothers who never get to see each other because they are all in jail at different times. When one gets out, the other two are in. We have a black kid, a very talented dancer, who just graduated from high school. When he was seven or eight years old, his father was shot to death in front of him. His mother is serving a twenty- or thirty-year jail term. He's been tossed around to different relatives, and now, after graduating from high school, he's on his own. He just got himself an apartment, and he's supporting himself. He doesn't really have any money to go to college at this point. We gave him a job at our office.

I think about the really devastating issues these kids have to face. Then I see them rehearsing or performing, their faces lit up with smiles. They are already stage professionals. For them, it's such a release to be dancing and singing their hearts out. Sometimes they do powerful, intense monologues. In the question and answer sessions after performances, they communicate so well. They're more effective than anyone else in getting support for the program. They talk about what it's done for them. It's so easy and natural to them to answer questions. Their stories are so positive and they communicate so well; they generate energy in other people. They touch hundreds of people. Those kids are really transformed by the program. In their neighborhoods, the dropout rate is like 40 percent. Their brothers and sisters are being shot and getting involved in gangs, but they have made something of their circumstances.

Most of the programs start with literature. First, they did Shakespeare. Everybody read *Romeo and Juliet* and *West Side Story* and then applied the themes to their own neighborhoods and situations. They created *Watts Side Story*, a love story between a Latino woman and a black man. The fight scenes were choreographed with karate movements and a lot of music. The kids do the reading, the research, the choreography. Last February, they took on five Hemingway books because most of them were studying Hemingway in their English classes and because there was going to be a Hemingway festival in the summer. Everybody read the stories; some people did research on his life. They took different themes from the books, the historical background, and Hemingway's biography to produce a 90-minute production called *The Life and Times of Ernest Hemingway*. Everybody contributed. Students wrote their own monologues. They combined different dance styles and jazz.

I think the best kind of interaction takes place when you are young. Los Angeles is set up structurally and geographically so that white people are here, Asian people here, Latinos here, and black people there, and people don't even feel the need to cross the boundaries to reach out. For me, it's important to accept myself and other people as individuals first, before Korean or Japanese or something else.

In some ways, I hate L.A. and what it stands for: pretension, materialism, Hollywood. I don't mean everyone who lives in L.A. is like that, but it's a kind of "dominant society" here. Cars, designer clothes—in this town, money talks. It's trendy in L.A. to act liberal and open to different races, to environmental issues, to women's issues. You have to act that way to fit in. But it's just a conversation over dinner; it's not really part of people's lives.

The Koreans in L.A. in our generation are into the life-style—the car, the perfect body, the pretty women, the nightlife. There's not much attention given to the inner spirit or to the community. What's sad is that I understand my parents' generation's need to focus on money and even be greedy to survive. But my generation is just very ignorant about what's going on in the rest of the world, in L.A., in South Central. There are people in my generation who are aware of what's going on, and they might get angry at some injustice, but they are too selfish to do anything about it.

I enjoyed being brought up in the Korean church because I liked the social networks I found there. But I've drifted away as an adult because I don't feel comfortable with what they preach in their sermons, like their concept of God as punitive. They emphasize capital expansion and conduct building fund drives. They put money into developing recreation centers that are only for their members. I don't think that they do anything that improves the conditions of people in the community.

In a sense, marrying my husband was a rebellious thing to do. He's eight years older than I am and not even established. I am not a hopeless romantic who thinks it's fine to starve with someone I love. You have to eat in order to think. But I am not materialistic, either. I wouldn't marry someone who provides material things but not emotional or intellectual things. Emotional and intellectual needs count with me. Because he freelances as a writer publishing high-quality work, sometimes we have more than we need, and sometimes we have nothing at all. He understands how I am, so he supports me by volunteering to go to parents' councils or to take our son to swimming classes.

I was attracted to his openness and respected his insights and intellect. He just can't tolerate injustice or unfairness. When he believes in a cause, he does something about it; he translates his thinking into action to get things done, and I admire that. He doesn't have the greatest personality; he can be very edgy and in your face. He can't work under anyone. I'm more accommodating. I can tolerate things and wait till the right time to deal with them.

Our child, Robin, is four. He was born with Down's syndrome. The month we found out I was pregnant, my husband did five full-page stories on Korean American disabled children. Disabled children usually go unnoticed in the Korean community because immigrants usually try to hide them from public view. While I was pregnant, I ran into a lot of Down's syndrome kids. Also, when we stopped along the ocean on our way to La Jolla once, my husband and I saw a group of Down's syndrome teenagers. I remembered all these incidents when I found out that Robin had Down's syndrome. My husband told me later that he was actually scared by them. He had some kind of premonition.

I thought it was something that could happen to other people but not to me. We heard a lot of horror stories and thought Robin wasn't going to be able to do anything, but there have been a lot of pleasant surprises. It's been really wonderful living with Robin. As we go on, we are discovering many things through him. We learn not to impose our standards on him but to accept his standards and go from there. Instead of saying, "Can Robin do this?" we wait for him to do things he's ready to do. And when he does them, we try to support him.

My parents take care of him while I'm at work, together with my oldest brother's two kids. It's strange, but after we all got married, our family got tighter. My parents have a house in Bellflower. It's only ten minutes from my house, so it's very convenient. My mom makes *kimch'i* for us, and we go there two or three times a week.

My parents-in-law live in Korea. I didn't meet them until our wedding. I think they were just thankful that their son was getting married at thirty-six, that somebody had actually said yes [to marrying him]. They didn't even mind that I wasn't Catholic.

If I had stayed in Korea, I probably would have just fit into the norm of what women are supposed to be like. If there were an organization, I would be part of it. But unless there were a strong movement that would allow me to do that, I would probably sit home very repressed. Maybe I would have gotten a teaching job or something.

Right now, I can't imagine not working. I need to have several things in my life to keep myself going: my family, my marriage, and my full-time work. I don't think that I would be completely happy being a wife and mother without doing anything outside the family. I need to have some sort of involvement in the community and in society.

JULY 1993 AND OCTOBER 1994

SEAN SUH
Dragon

Except for long strands on both sides of his handsome face, eighteen-year-old Sean Suh's hair is short. He wears his dark glasses low and tilted and has a shy smile. Over a sleeveless undershirt, he wears a baggy shirt, which he pulls open to reveal the fierce blue dragon tattoo on his back.

I got this dragon tattooed on my back because I was born in 1976, the year of the dragon. Twenty days after I was born, my dad got shot and died. Some guy pulled a shotgun on him in a bar fight. My mom didn't even tell me how he died until I was twelve years old.

I was born in Guam because my mom went there when she ran away from her first husband in Hawaii. She said he hit her and stuff like that. She went with my grandma and my half-sister, who's seven years older than me. She and my grandma opened up a nightclub in Guam, and she hired my dad to work there. He had a band, he sang, and he played all the brass instruments. That's how they met, and that's why I'm here.

My mom didn't tell me much about my dad. We don't talk that much. We just never did. When I was twelve, right after she told me how he died, we went to Korea to visit his relatives. That's where I found out that they always wanted to see me. She had been hiding me away from them. I thought I only had a sister, but I found out that I had seven uncles and so many little cousins. I found out that I was an uncle! I never knew all that. They had only seen pictures of me. They had never seen me before, but I had never even heard of them. They kept trying to touch me and buy me stuff. In Korea, I learned a lot about who I was. Up until then, I was just a kid; I didn't really care about how I happened to be here. I just worried about going out to play and stuff.

My father's relatives are really rich and have a big house. My mom says she doesn't like them because they never helped her out while we were struggling with all our money problems here in L.A. Even though she asked, they didn't give her any help. She made it on her own, by running a little hamburger shop in Venice Beach with my grandma. We came to L.A. with nothing, but she eventually bought us a house. I guess she felt she didn't do anything with her life because she married young and never finished school, so she got a realtor's license. She never made much money as a realtor. She did it for herself. She wanted to accomplish something.

I just don't see my mom as the kind of person who is close to her kids.

She's always stressing about work, having money in the bank account, making sure we're in a safe environment. She's not the kind to take her kids camping or to an amusement park. It's not because she didn't have the time. She could have taken me out places, but she didn't. I grew up with my friends; they were the ones who taught me how to live.

When we first came to L.A., we moved to Koreatown. Later, we moved to Venice Beach. Now we are in Westchester, out by LAX [Los Angeles International Airport]. When I was little, I was kicking it with Korean kids. Kids don't see color; they don't know race. They just like to play, so that's how I was. But when I got to be around eight or ten, I started seeing people's race. When we moved to Venice Beach, kids were starting to see me as different because I was Korean, and they were black and Mexican. That's when I first experienced racism, even though I still had friends. I was the only Korean kid in the junior high I went to. It was all blacks and Mexicans. Junior high was when they started dogging me, beating me up, kicking me, and calling me names because I was Korean.

I was like the skinhead in *Higher Learning,* that movie by John Singleton. He was a loser at the beginning of the picture. He wanted to get into the fraternity, and they were like, "Who are *you?*" That's how I felt. Here in L.A., there are so many different races. Everyone sticks with their own. Stuff like that could make someone commit suicide because it makes you feel so small.

When the skinhead in the movie got into a group with other skinheads, he felt like a king. My mom sent me to Bravo Medical, a magnet high school in East L.A. where all the kids were Asian. She didn't want me to just go to a regular high school. She always said that Koreans think that a high school diploma and going to a good high school are important. I was so comfortable there, because I didn't hear any racial jokes or anything like that. And it was the first time I ever knew there were all these Asian people around. White, black, Mexican, from the Middle East, I don't care. Living in L.A., I'd be more comfortable with my own people. If I was kicking it with my Korean or Filipino friends and a black guy came up to me and said, "Hey, you stupid Bruce Lee," we could all beat him up. You stay with who you're comfortable with.

I was comfortable because they were all Asian and they weren't going to call me any Asian slurs. But I wasn't accepted by them. They didn't know me; I was like the new kid in school. They used to get guys who knew everyone to pick on me to help their self-esteem at my expense. But when I got into the gang, I did it right back to them. I'm the kind of person that does back whatever someone does to me. I always want what's coming to me. If I do something wrong, I'll accept the punishment. That's where I hooked up with this one Filipino guy who was a tagger. Taggers spray-paint walls. They're not in a gang; they just color walls. Taggers aren't violent. All they care about is fame. They want other people to know who they are. That's why they write their names on the walls. I got heavily into it. We spray-painted a lot on freeways. Anyway, the tagger group partied with an Asian gang called Satanas; that means "Satan." Gangs always want to recruit people, but they don't recruit just anybody—only their friends. So I got in. The only reason I joined was because it was Asian. I don't want to join a black gang or a Mexican gang, because that's not me. Usually people are born into Mexican and black gangs in L.A. They're all around you, and you grow up together in the neighborhood. But I lived way out by LAX.

I would rather join a Korean gang because I'm Korean, but the Korean gangs all died out. In L.A., the biggest Korean gang was the Koreatown Crazies. There are a lot of Chinese and Filipino gangs. If I have to be in a gang, I would be in the biggest one, with the biggest people and the most guns. So I joined the strongest Filipino gang. It was more organized than I thought. It's the oldest one. They have old men organizing, because it's been around since the 1960s.

One of the main reasons guys get into gangs is because they get girls, like groupies. Some of the girls that are wacko get into the gangs and back it up. But the groupie ones don't fight for the gang. They have sex with the guys.

There's some good aspects to a gang that people don't really know about. A gang can teach a kid so much. If I look back now, I would still get into a gang, because when I was in junior high, I felt like an outcast. Being with my own people is where I got my self-esteem. If you don't have self-esteem, you're not going to be a well-rounded person when you're older. Before, I would never want to be away from the gang; I loved them so much. I would kill for them. I used to do a lot of stuff—burglary, mugging, carjacking, shootings.

I'm not saying that a gang is good; it's bad because you could die. Luckily, I never got shot; but God saved me many times. I can't even count how many times I got shot at. I remember one time I was sitting with my friend in the car, eating and talking at about two o'clock in the morning. This van pulled up next to us. This Chinese guy was pointing a gun at me, and then he pulled the trigger. I was sitting in the driver's seat. The window was rolled down, and the bullet hit the door, but I pretended to be dead, so he left. If he had pointed his gun down a little, the bullet would have gone right through me. I didn't even know the guy. I have to worry about all different gangs, because even if a guy doesn't know me, if I'm from a gang that he doesn't get along with, he's going to try to kill me.

A year ago, I got arrested for carrying a gun. I was going to shoot someone from another gang. When you first get in a gang, you don't really get any respect from anybody except your peers. There are these different generations, and you have friends in your same generation, but you don't have respect from anybody. The way to get respect is to put in work. You want everyone to know you, so you go out and act crazy. Respect is what everyone craves. That's why they do what they do. That's why they kill. They want people to fear them, because when you are feared, you get power, and everyone wants power.

For three or four years, my mother didn't know I was in a gang. She didn't find out until I got arrested. She didn't even know I had a tattoo. She thought I was a regular kid, because I was doing average in school, and I wasn't failing any classes. When she found out, she didn't yell or anything. She was just afraid. She didn't know how to handle me or what to do. But my *t'aekwŏndo* master talked me through it.

I started doing *t'aekwŏndo* when I was about twelve. My mom knows that I've been in trouble and that I've gotten suspended from school. I don't care if she knows. But I tried my best to hide that stuff from my martial-arts master, because he thought highly of me. He always thought I was a good kid. I didn't want to disappoint him. After he found out I got arrested, I told him everything. He started focusing on me. He's not like other adults who just tell you; he talks to you and tries to make you understand. He said that kids look at life like, "What are you going to do tomorrow?" They don't think about twenty or fifty years from now. That's why everyone drops out of school, gets pregnant, doesn't care. I was just living life day to day. He made me want to graduate from college and get a good job. He made me realize that the further I get away from the gang, the farther ahead I'm going to go in life.

He made me realize that if I stay with the gang, my life would go downhill. I'd probably only live till twenty. But if I get out, go to school, work hard for a few years, then I might live for sixty years. He said if I just have fun for the next seven years and don't go to school, the next sixty years are going to be like hell for me. If I work hard for the next five years, the next sixty will be rewarding. He made me realize that.

My master is just a regular white guy from suburbia. He's very smart and a good salesman. The words he uses, he makes people want to do what he wants. That's how he sold me on the ideas he had for me. I've never felt that way about anybody else, not even my mother. When I look back, he's going to be the first in my mind, because without him, I wouldn't exist.

To get out of a gang, you've got to grow up and learn life. Most gangsters are smart enough to be doctors, but they never get the chance to grow up because they're either dead or in jail. They don't even know the possibilities for them.

I'm trying to get out of the gang, but every time I look at this burn on my hand from getting jumped in [initiated], it reminds me that I'm always going to be in this gang because it's going to be for life, unless I get laser surgery or something. If I hadn't gotten this burn, I could get out faster. There are certain ways to get out. It takes a long time. You don't want to get jumped out. If they jump you out, they're just going to beat up on you every time they see you again, like at the store or at a party. I'm going the way where they just forget about you. I want to gradually fade out. That way, if they see me again, it will be like, "Hey, how you been doing?"

So many people want to kill me right now because I did stuff to them and they want to get back at me. I'm marked. I made a name for myself. So I can't go out much; I can't walk around by myself. I only go where I know there's no gangs. I don't go to regular parties or anything. But people trying to kill me is my least worry. I'm stressed out because I have a lot to worry about. I'm worried about finishing school. I have to do a lot of community service. I just got probation, because that was my first offense. I want to finish this crap with the community service. I also have to earn money at this hospital job I have, to help my family out. Half my paycheck goes to my family. We're really struggling right now; that's my biggest worry. After the hamburger shop did well, my mom decided to open another restaurant in downtown L.A., but that was a bad investment, and we lost everything and had to go bankrupt.

I got accepted at the university, but I got kicked out of [high] school two months ago, and now I've got to go to adult school. The school didn't want me there anymore, not because I caused trouble, but because trouble might come where I am. I was the only Asian gangster at the school. There were a couple of taggers, but no gangsters. What happened was that the Wah Ching, this Chinese gang, came to my school looking for me. I was going home in my friend's car when they cut us off and blocked us in. There were ten of them, and they hit me till I was barely conscious. I was walking in the middle of the street, and one of them hit me with his car. My friend dragged me into his car and took off.

The skinhead in *Higher Learning* blew his own brains out. I felt a lot like him, but I'm not going to go out like that. I want to finish adult school, go to community college for two or three years, and then maybe transfer to the university, if it's not too hard. All I care about is making money when I'm young, the easiest way. I want to become a Drug Enforcement Agency agent, so that I can go undercover and travel to different countries. I don't want a boring job.

When I have kids, I'm going to know exactly who they hang out with and where they are going. All the stuff that my mom messed up on. She didn't know any of my friends. She's not American; she's Korean. I'm American, and that's how it is. It was hard when I was growing up, having my mom be Korean and me being American, living in a culture that is not the same as hers. If I were living in Korea, I'd raise my kids in the Korean culture; but if I am living in America, I am going to raise them in American culture. My girlfriend right now is Filipino, but I want to marry a Korean. Korean men treat women bad; that's their culture. But I'm not Korean. I'm closer to being an American, so I wouldn't do that.

I experienced more racism from blacks and Mexicans than white people, just because they were the majority. Whatever race is in the majority, they're going to pass judgment on the minorities. Everyone is racist against each other, everyone is against everyone. Gangs are going to be around forever. Violence, prejudice, racism, it's all going to be around. You can't wipe it out of people's minds. I don't know any solutions. All I care about is my family and myself. I want to be happy. I want to be rich when I'm young, then I'll start dealing with world hunger and stuff like that. I've got to be taken care of first.

APRIL 1995

BRENDA PAIK SUNOO

Tommy's Mother

A rare third-generation Korean American, Brenda Paik Sunoo was born in 1948 in Los Angeles. She grew up near the old center of the Los Angeles Korean community. Both of her grandfathers came to Hawaii as contract laborers on the *S.S. Siberia* in 1905. Her father was born in Idria, California, the seventh of ten children in the Paik family. In 1969, before graduating from UCLA, she married "2.5-generation" Korean American Jan Sunoo. "We met because of our two *halmonis* [grandmothers] conspiring," she muses. In fact, her midwife grandmother delivered Jan's mother. Brenda and Jan lived in New York and San Francisco before returning in the late 1980s to Los Angeles, where Brenda worked for the English edition of the Los Angeles *Korea Times*. After serving as a business agent for the Teamsters Union, Jan became a mediator for the Federal Mediation and Conciliation Service. Brenda is currently senior editor for *Personnel Journal*, a national business magazine published in Costa Mesa, California.

I don't think my kids have met any other fourth-generation Korean Americans.[72] There might be Korean and Chinese, Korean and Jewish, Korean and Japanese, Korean and black, but I don't know of other full-blooded fourth generation Korean Americans. While I was working as a reporter for the *Korea Times* English edition, I started to compare myself and my kids with Korean immigrants' families. I was working with Korean American interns who were my kids' age, which meant that I was the age of their immigrant parents. That's when I started to appreciate the immigrants' sacrifices. I realized that we third-generation Korean Americans do things for our kids, but it's not a case of complete self-sacrifice. I'm more laid back, less achievement-oriented than the immigrants. It could be a class thing, or that immigrants come here with a purpose, whereas my kids and I were born here, and so I take things for granted. I didn't leave a homeland for a better world. Anyway, I started comparing and wondering if I was raising my kids right. For a while, my husband Jan and I had a sort of post-hippie mentality. We certainly didn't pressure them the way I see the immigrants' kids getting pressured these days.

Now that I'm in my late forties, looking back on what I've done, I realize that I was very idealistic in my twenties and thirties. I kind of poo-poohed the "establishment." My views had more effect on my older son, David, than on Tommy, the younger one. David was certainly imbued with our social values. He has a very strong sense of justice and pride in his heritage. He has a certain class consciousness. But I can see now that it was a little unbalanced. Sometimes I feel that certain things about David's education fell through the cracks, even though at the time we thought we were doing the right thing. When I come across all these immigrants pushing their kids to be successful, I think, "God, maybe I didn't push my kids enough. Maybe I need to have higher standards."

Both of our boys were really into art from the time they were very young. I always encouraged them by sending them to art classes and buying them materials. David likes illustration. When he looks at things and copies them, his renderings are very meticulous and beautiful. Tommy was probably following David at first, but he developed his own style, which is vibrant and imaginative, coming straight out of his own head. David wanted to be an artist after he finished high school. He was accepted at Otis College of Art and Design in L.A., but we couldn't afford it. Sometimes I feel guilty, like I should be doing more so that he can attend. Maybe an immigrant family would have found ways to make sure they sent their kids, instead of being like us. We said, "It's too expensive. I hope you understand." David worked as a waiter at a restaurant for a year and completed a computer graphics program at UC Irvine Extension. Now he says he's going to try attending community college. I'm hoping he takes to that. If he does two years there, maybe if he's still interested in art, he can go to the Art Center College of Design in Pasadena, which is very expensive. This time, if he gets in and is committed, I'll probably do a lot more to make sure he has a chance to go.

One of the reasons we couldn't afford to send David to Otis is that at the time he was graduating from high school, we moved to Orange County. That was in 1992. Tommy was just finishing junior high, so we figured if we were going to move, we had to move then, for Tommy's sake. We were concerned about all the violence in L.A. Tommy would go to a video place and someone would hold him up at knife point. Or the kids would have their things stolen or get mugged. As a parent, you get really scared. Especially after the riots, we thought things were just getting to be too much. We wanted to go where the quality of life was better. Also, we wanted to show our kids a broader world than what they were getting in L.A. Tommy and David were really into wearing the urban experience like a badge of honor. They thought it was cool. Jan and I thought it was starting to narrow their way of viewing the world.

Los Angeles was very different when I was growing up here. The elementary school I went to was largely black and Asian. There weren't many Koreans. I grew up socializing with both groups. My grandmother told me stories about the Japanese occupation of Korea, and she would get very upset when she saw me with a Japanese American boyfriend.

When you grow up with just other minorities, in a way you remain in a comfort zone. Then, when you are among whites, you do a little mental somersault. The first time I was really introduced to Caucasians was at Audubon Junior High School. I went there because our family moved to the area that is now Baldwin Hills in the Crenshaw district. All of a sudden,

I was competing with very assertive Jewish kids. I had to push myself to be assertive, but I gradually came out of my shell and became a cheerleader and a student government officer. I joined a mostly Japanese American all-girl social club called the Chanels.

There was a lot of cross-racial dating at school. I'm not saying that everyone mixed; there were the surfers here, the Asians there, and the blacks there. But it was not as polarized as today, with all this hatred. The difference was that back then we had the same socioeconomic background, we spoke the same language, we did social activities together. Sure, there was prejudice, but there was a lot more natural intermingling because we were all part of the same neighborhood. We were more homogeneous, even though there were racial differences.

Jan and I grew up in a pretty multicultural environment that included whites. It's not that Tommy and David weren't exposed to Caucasians, but they both veered toward Asian Americans, some Latinos, and some blacks. They were going to schools where English was the second language. We thought that moving would give Tommy a more competitive standard to measure up to. Tommy did well in elementary and junior high school, but he started to show that adolescent disinterest by getting a few Cs and not doing all his homework because he was distracted. We had heard that Irvine schools were excellent. Even though the students in Irvine were predominantly white, we thought it wouldn't be too much of a shock because there are also many Asian Americans, many Koreans.

The kids just hated it here at first. Tommy was at his most rebellious adolescent age. He was probably the first kid in Irvine to walk around in those super, super baggies [loose-fitting jeans]. I was astounded that he wasn't self-conscious. He didn't really give a damn; he was going to wear what he wore. He rebelled because we had yanked him away from his circle of friends. He started ditching school and running away to see his friends in L.A.

He started to change when he met other Korean kids in Irvine. Both David and Tommy had come into contact with Koreans when I sent them to Korean American summer camps—Camp Kite in San Francisco and Camp Conifer in L.A. David's two best friends now are from Camp Conifer, and when we moved to Irvine, one of Tommy's friends from Camp Conifer lived nearby. I'm proud that my children are very conscious of their Korean heritage. It's given David an anchor and a sense of his own identity, although my kids, like many teenagers, have been embarrassed by their parents. They're embarrassed by us *not* being like immigrants. Tommy's Korean American friends told him that when they call him and his dad picks up the telephone, he sounds so "white" to them because he has no accent. When we went to pick the boys up at Camp Conifer, they said, "Gosh, you two are so white!" Our kids were self-conscious that we were English-speaking, not like their friends' immigrant parents. They wanted us to stay in the back row. They tell us that their friends are always so surprised by how "Americanized" we are. I tell David's friends to call us Jan and Brenda. They always walk in, bow to us, and take off their shoes. They say, "Hello, Mrs. Sunoo." They just can't call me Brenda. I told Jan to say something because maybe they needed to hear it from the father, but Jan said, "No, I *want* them to call me Mr. Sunoo!" Therein lies the difference between a "2.5" and a "3.0"!

David has developed a very close bond with his Korean kids [as] friends. I feel very grateful to all these young Koreans who have embraced him, even though he doesn't speak Korean. They've given him a sense of his cultural background. Now he's started to criticize my Korean cooking. "How come you can't make *tchigae* [stew flavored with soy bean paste] like Mrs. Kim?" The Korean kids also introduced David and Tommy into a few Korean churches. That was good, because even though Jan and I were brought up in the Korean church, we really weren't going anymore. By the time we started thinking that church might not be such a bad thing, our kids were adamant about not going. We had given up until they met other Korean kids who were into it. I'm not worried because I don't think all of them are religious fanatics. I do see many Korean kids who go too far.

Anyway, David is pretty independent-minded. During the riots, he definitely tried to understand both sides, though he really felt bad for the merchants. He's critical of the Korean community, too. One thing he just can't accept is the whole *hyŏng* [elder brother] thing.[73] He absolutely refuses to kowtow to an older Korean just because he's older. He says a *hyŏng* [elder brother] has to earn his respect; he's not going to just give it to him because of his age. Sometimes he deliberately does things to antagonize the others, just to let them know that "Hey, I'm fourth generation; I ain't gonna kiss your butt just because you're older than I am."

David has been working all year. I'm really proud of him. He matured and learned about work ethics. Also, working at the restaurant was a major breakthrough for him because he had been somewhat self-conscious about dealing with a pretty much all-Caucasian environment.

David is twenty-one. Tommy would have been seventeen. He died last year, when he was sixteen.

At least for the year and a half we were here in Orange County before Tommy died, I feel that he did get to see another world. As much as he complained about how he hated Irvine, after he died, we were surprised by the number of friends who came by the house to express their condolences. Through his death, we actually had a glimpse of parts of his life that we would never have discovered, because teenagers are very private and possessive about their relationships. Tommy would always whisk the friends he brought home right into his room. After he died, we found out that there had been many others. They shared stories about him with us, and we found out that he was actually doing very well. One girl did a beautiful sketch of him and gave it to us as a gift.

On February 16, 1994, he was playing basketball at school when he just collapsed. The coroner believes it was cardiac arrest due to chronic asthmatic bronchitis, but Tommy never had any signs of asthma. He didn't have any genetic heart problems either. He was against drugs. I don't know; maybe it was some kind of viral condition that made his heart just shut down, like an electrical shutdown. People talk about Sudden Infant Death Syndrome, but there may be a growing number of sudden teenage deaths as well. There hasn't been much research in the area, and not many doctors specialize in teens.

It's important for parents to monitor their teenagers' health, even though the kids act as if they are indestructible. Even though it's irrational, you still feel guilty or responsible on some level, because parents are supposed to protect their kids. It's really been hard. I'm just trying to take things one day at a time. Jan and I joined Compassionate Friends, which is a national support group for parents who have lost their children. That has been very helpful, because even your friends and family can't really understand the depth of your grief unless they've gone through the same thing. I tell my friends that grief is on another level from being depressed once in a while. The grief never really goes away. You can throw yourself into your work, but you can't really escape your grief; you have to face it eventually. I'm learning day by day that you have to accept the loss. It becomes a permanent part of you.

For the first few months after Tommy died, I would not have been able to lift myself out of bed if it weren't for my job. I felt like I was pinned under a truck. The second year after Tommy died has been harder for me, in a way, because the shock cushions you the first year. You're just so depressed and exhausted, you walk around like a zombie. I'm amazed that I was able to work at a new job; probably the routine has been therapeutic for me. I put together a scrapbook of pictures and letters that people sent us. It gives a glimpse of Tommy's life. The project kept me going off and on for eight or nine months the first year after he died.

We buried his ashes only last month, on the first anniversary of his death. David felt that Tommy would not really rest in peace until his ashes were buried. Now that we have buried the ashes, I feel a certain sense of relief and peace. But I still go through moments of grief and anxiety. I'll be driving or thinking, or the wind will hit my face or I'll hear a certain song, and I just can't believe that he's dead, that he's gone.

Everything turns upside down when you lose your child. You realize that life is so fleeting, and you wonder what you have to look forward to that has any meaning. There are moments when you feel, "Well, if I die now, at least I'll be with him." You start to reevaluate and to think of things differently. You often feel very ambivalent about your own life and purpose. You do become more respectful and appreciative of life. I remember once meeting a mother who had lost her infant. She said that we have only two choices: to be or not to be, and it's true. The struggle for us is to be sure we're on the "to be" side.

The fact that he died at school has helped us heal, because the whole community came forward afterwards. The kids raised funds, and with donations from friends, relatives, and community people, we set up a Friendship Bench on the promenade of the school campus. Sketches from his sketchbooks are silk-screened onto the tile that is inlaid into the bench. Also, we set up an art scholarship in Tommy's name for an art student at his school.

Now that we are a threesome instead of a foursome, David worries about us, even though we tell him not to. He's lonely because he doesn't have Tommy, and he often goes to the graveside by himself. He sleeps in Tommy's room, and he told us not to change everything, because he wants it that way. When David drives back and forth to L.A., he listens to Tommy's music. He looks at the scrapbook now and then, too.

According to statistics, the number of broken marriages among bereaved parents is very high. When I read those statistics, I get really scared. Jan and I have been married twenty-six years. I know we're close, but we're both vulnerable, too. Jan and I are two unique individuals, and we seek solace in different ways. It's hard to have enough energy afterwards to be available to each other, and if you don't consciously work at it, your relationship will start to fray. You can't really depend on your spouse to pull you through grief. When both of you face the loss of your child, you're barely keeping yourself together. You really have to stretch to give anything to each other and to your other child. It takes a lot of energy you don't have because you're often depressed. Everyone who knows us knows that Jan and I are both very upbeat, optimistic people. We're not used to having to deal with feelings like this. It's important to know that your family and your marriage can be very fragile. That makes me more conscious that we do spend time together and that we should also give each other space. Both of us keep journals. We try not to be threatened by the fact that we grieve differently. Jan travels a lot because of his job, and it helps get his mind off of his grief. I find comfort nesting at home because Tommy was here, and I feel that his energy and spirit still reside in this house.

I'll never forget Tommy. I'll never stop loving him. I'm still his mother. The first time someone asks you how many kids you have after you've lost a child, it's like, God, what do you say? I've learned to say, "I have two children. I have one son, David, and another son, Tommy, who died last year."

Since Tommy died, I've tried to look back to see what rituals my Korean cultural heritage can offer me, but I haven't really found anything. There is a certain kind of ancestral worship, but nothing much for a child. One of the more comforting things I've come across is the Native American belief that every life is like a circle—complete, whether it's long or short. That helps me because it makes me realize that even though he lived only sixteen years, Tommy did a lot. He left a beautiful legacy of letters, journals, art, and friends. Even Jan's seventy-eight-year-old father, who's written books, been involved in Korean politics, and traveled a lot, said, "Tommy's life affected people more than anything I've done."

It's sad that in this country there isn't really a healthy attitude toward grief and death. I've become more sensitive myself; now, I have a list of not only birth dates, but also death dates, so that I can call my friends on those days because I know those days are hard for them. For grieving parents, the worst fear, besides fear of losing their other child, is that people will forget. The best thing to do for a grieving person is to ask about and remember the one who died. Just to have someone refer to Tommy is very healing to me. It validates that I was his mother.

FEBRUARY 1993 AND APRIL 1995

RICHARD CHUNG

Away From the Center

Richard Sang Hun Chung was born in Korea in 1963. He arrived in Los Angeles with his family in 1977, when he was fourteen years old. A graduate of the Art Center in Los Angeles, he is currently a designer for Ford Motor Company. Alert and focused, Chung switches effortlessly from English to Korean when he speaks.

When I was three or four years old, I could draw figures from the bottom up and could handle proportion well. Ordinarily, people draw figures from top to bottom. Also, they place the subject in a completely closed form, whereas I would draw half a ship sticking out at the corner of a piece of paper. I was expanding my imagination away from the center. I loved drawing comics and figures.

I attended the most prestigious and probably the most expensive private school in Korea. My parents wanted my brother, my sister, and me to have the best possible education. But I never liked being singled out as a "have" where there were a lot of "have nots." My parents never pushed me to be at the top of my class; they just accepted whatever I could do, which helped develop my character.

My father was one of the first to import Honda motorcycles to Korea. He was very successful at it; he was able to support the whole family, build a nice house in Samchŏngdong [an upscale residential section of Seoul], and send us all to private school. After a bigger counterpart, Samchŏnri Bicycle, got into the business, my father didn't do so well, so he tried to move into construction. We lost our house to creditors from the Honda business. I still remember them coming to our house and shouting at my parents. After that ordeal, we moved to an apartment in Hongŭndong [a working-class district in Seoul], but my parents continued to send us to the same private school.

I wasn't happy with the education system in Korea, especially the overheated competitiveness. When I was in the first year of middle school, I had to attend a *hakwŏn* [learning institute] after school every day until 10:00 P.M. Also, teachers and upperclassmen had the authority to hit students. I think it had a lot to do with the military nature of the Korean male society.

I never won any special awards at school. Students got special awards if their parents handed white envelopes of money to teachers, and my parents didn't do that. I was usually one of the top five students in my classes, but I always caused trouble, complaining about the special treatment teachers gave certain students. I knew corruption was going on. Teachers would hit me in front of the class for saying things about it.

I remember one classmate whose family was very rich. He had a private tutor and was always getting 100 percent on his papers because the teacher gave the tutor all the questions in advance. Once, I got 100 percent and he got only 85 percent on a math test, and the teacher had the whole class retake the test the following day, so that he got 100 percent. Other kids might not have noticed it, but I did. I complained to the other students that it wasn't fair and got hit when the teacher heard about it. I never saw the kids whose parents brought all the white envelopes getting hit. They would even hand out those envelopes right in front of the students. It was not a good example to set. Even today, I don't want to go back and see those teachers when I visit Korea.

Starting when I was in the first grade, my mother sent me to the YMCA on Saturdays. Every year we went to YMCA summer camp. I learned to swim at the YMCA. From elementary school all the way through high school, I was always on the swimming team. At the YMCA, I learned how to get along with other people and how to be a leader, which is usual for firstborn kids. Even when I was a little kid, I was never a follower.

When I was young, I had this image of America from the movies, so I always wanted to come here. All my uncles were already here; our family was the last to leave Korea.

We moved to Monterey Park, California. I was eager to learn English. When I went to school for the first time at a Monterey Park elementary school, I saw a Korean girl in the class. I was happy to see her and thought she would be friendly to me, so I told her my name and said I was from Korea. I asked her in Korean what was going on in class, since I couldn't understand anything, but she didn't answer. She didn't want to be singled out as another F.O.B. ["fresh off the boat"]. I was completely unaware of how Asians are treated here.

The majority of students at school were Hispanic and white. There were also many Japanese American kids. My first friends were Chinese kids who had also just immigrated and couldn't speak English either, but because we looked alike and could communicate through hand gestures, we associated with each other.

During high school, my father said that if I memorized ten English words every day during summer vacation, he would buy me a bicycle. I memorized three hundred words, and he bought me a bicycle, which helped me develop strong leg muscles.

At high school, I signed up for swimming. The coach put me on the water polo team after seeing me swim a few laps. I had never played water polo before, but he told me to just follow what the other kids were doing and I would be all right. The swimmers at the school were mostly Caucasians. There was one Chinese American on the water polo team named Jung, so I asked him to write his name in Chinese characters. He gave me a funny look and said, "I am an American." I didn't understand how he couldn't write his name in Chinese at the time, but later I understood.

The number of Korean students kept increasing, and we formed a Korean club. I was president for a few years. Most of the members had just arrived from Korea. Students who had come four or five years earlier tended to stay away from us. They knew how to speak English and didn't want to associate with us. We F.O.B.s would dress in clothes we had brought from Korea, which were a completely different style, so that we would stand out in a crowd. We weren't even aware of this. The second year, I caught up and started wearing the same type of clothes the other students wore.

High school was challenging for me because the school's academic level was high, and I still hadn't mastered English. I would try to memorize the whole text for the sections covered on the tests; otherwise, I would never know how to answer the questions. That worked pretty well, and I finished the ninth grade with a 4.0 [grade point] average.

In any society, when you don't have anything to contribute, people tend to shy away from associating with you. Because I was good at swimming and fast on the water polo team, and because I could draw all kinds of cartoon characters from American comics, the other students tried to help me, and I was able to improve my English.

I got very involved in art. The art teachers were very supportive. Most students just saw art class as a way to bump up their grades and fulfill requirements. They had neither the desire nor the talent to excel in art. But art class was my favorite. When I was a sophomore, my art teacher recommended that I take a field trip to the Art Center College of Design in Pasadena. I was especially impressed by the transportation design department display of all kinds of car designs. When I saw that, I knew that that was what I wanted to do. I made up my mind to go to the Art Center after high school.

My art teacher allowed me to draw cars instead of other assignments. She bought reading materials for me also. It was thanks to her that I chose my career. I used to go back every year to see her because of what she did for me.

I was very excited when I was accepted at the Art Center after two years at California's State University, Los Angeles. The Art Center is the most prestigious design school in the world. About half of the transportation designers in the world are graduates of the Art Center. The designers of the Mercedes Benz and the Porsche are graduates of the Art Center. I started attending in 1983. I never worked so hard in my life. Twenty-three students started with me in the transportation design department, but only twelve of us graduated.

Because American society encourages individual creativity, American designers are the best in the world. American people are encouraged to come up with creative ideas about doing and improving things. The Germans are very good at things that require precision, but they are not necessarily innovative. The Japanese tend to follow the given rules. They work well together as a group, but as individuals they aren't as creative as Americans are.

The summer of my junior year, I was able to get an internship at CALTY, a Toyota studio in Newport Beach, which was set up in the mid-1970s because Toyota realized that the best ideas came from California. They also knew that instead of producing innovative designs, Japanese designers were copying American or European ones. I worked at CALTY in the mornings and at GE Plastics in the afternoons. One of my instructors was a top designer, and he recommended me for the internship because I was at the top of my class.

When I was a junior, I was selected for one of about twelve Ford Motor Company internships for students from various schools. That was very exciting for me: Ford was one of the Big Three, and we would be in Detroit, the home of the automobile capital of the world. I worked as hard as I could; I wanted to give them a good impression of me, not only as an art student, but as a Korean as well. For the final presentation, I submitted about triple what the other students did, and I basically blew them away.

I was completing my seventh semester at the Art Center when I got a letter from the vice president of the Ford Motor Company offering me a job. I liked the vice president's ideas and philosophy, and I accepted the offer. I was the envy of my classmates and the talk of the school; Ford hadn't hired any art graduates for four or five years. They were just starting to pick up, and I was the first one to be hired. I was in the big leagues.

In 1987, I went to Dearborn, Michigan, where the Ford design center was located. I sent my first paycheck to my parents, because I was very thankful to them. My father had been a company president in Korea. He had his own car and chauffeur and many employees. He had to abandon all that to come to the U.S. and work as a chef in a hamburger shop. I really respect Dad for doing all that. My parents went through all kinds of hard work and trouble, throwing away their pride, just to support us.

I worked at the Mark 8 studio in Dearborn as one of four designers of interiors. The Mark 8 studio manager said that I had the best rating of any designer he ever rated. He liked the uniqueness of my ideas. After about three months, they transferred me to the Probe studio. The Probe studio was interesting because all the designers were minorities: besides me, there was a Chinese American, a Japanese [national], and a black. The studio manger was a Caucasian who had lost one eye. Our boss, the chief designer, was a white lady who held the highest designer position in the industry. The Probe was a joint venture with Mazda. We designed it and shipped it to Japan. We supplied the design, and they developed the engineering.

When the design was finished, the chief designer asked me if I wanted to go to Japan, so I went there for eight months in 1988. The first three months there were very hard for me because I looked Japanese but I couldn't under-stand what people were saying when they spoke to me in Japanese. Each time I tried to speak English, people would just run away. I had to do a lot of finger pointing, even to buy things.

People in Japan viewed me as an American instead of as a Korean because I came from Ford and lived among Americans. Koreans born in Japan are treated as different from Japanese. Japan is like everywhere else: "have nots" who don't have skills are ignored or mistreated. This is especially true for Koreans in Japan, although younger Japanese have less animosity toward Koreans and tend to treat them like any other foreigners.

After I returned to the U.S., I was sent to Italy for about three months. In many respects, Italy is the opposite of Japan. Whereas Japan is a very orga-nized and predictable society, Italy is very disorganized and unpredictable. It's a lot like Seoul, maybe even more chaotic. If you're moving too slowly, drivers behind you drive up onto the sidewalk and pass you. If they are in a hurry, they just ignore the red light. They are very verbal and emotional. I saw a lot of similarities between Korea and Italy. My theory is that it has a lot to do with garlic. I think food has a lot to do with personality and a people's characteristics. Japanese food isn't spicy; they don't eat garlic. Japanese people never raise their voices. On the other hand, Italians, Koreans, and Mexicans eat lots of garlic and spicy food, and they are all short-tempered.

Maybe there is some correlation. Anyway, I didn't like Italy, but I was comfortable in Japan.

When I returned from Italy, I worked very hard. After four months, the chief designer called me into her studio and told me I had been made a design manager. I thought she was joking. The youngest manager at that time was forty-one years old, and I was only twenty-six. I had only worked for the company for two and a half years. I asked her to let me think about it, because it was such a huge responsibility. A design manager is responsible for the design of a whole car, inside and out. I didn't know if I would be able to handle it. It would mean that older, more experienced designers would have to work under me. Some of them were my father's age.

I thought about it overnight, and I talked to my parents, who were delighted. I decided to take on the challenge. I told the chief designer that I would do it if she would accept the mistakes I would make in the beginning, and she agreed to that. I became the talk of the whole company. I set the record as the youngest manager in the Ford Motor Company. No one had ever been made a manger after only two and a half years. Senior designers in their forties and fifties were very disappointed; some of them got mad at me. They had been training me, and then all of a sudden I became their boss. That was very difficult for me, but I made sure that I was willing to learn and to work as a team player. I made sure that I communicated with my designers, and I didn't cross any lines. I respected their talents and distributed the work equally among the designers. Usually a manager has one project at a time, but I ended up with six vehicles. It was overwhelming. Team members were very supportive, and soon I was promoted to chief manager.

When I was sent to Japan for the second time, I went as a married man. Our two children were born in Japan. I was responsible for the design of all joint-venture vehicles with Mazda, including the Probe. It was an exciting job, since I got to look at every detail of the car. Everything you see in that car was my responsibility. There are 20,000 different parts in the car, and I had the authority to make the decisions. The model will not change until 1998; it's now one of the best-sellers among cars in its class. The Probe received the Car of the Year Award in 1992. I was very proud of that.

We returned to the U.S. in 1994, after five years in Japan. Now I am fluent in three languages: Japanese, English, and Korean. I write a monthly column in Korean for a Korean car magazine called *Car Vision*.

I've heard that I am one of the top candidates for promotion to chief designer. There are only about fifteen or sixteen chief designers at Ford working throughout the world, so I don't have my hopes up high; if it happens, it happens. I am just happy that they consider me valuable.

Japanese people are very unique; they emphasize *hwa*, which means "harmony." If you break the harmony, you break the balance of society. In America, when one has superior talent, he or she gets rewarded. That's how I got promoted. But in Japan, whoever works as part of the team will get rewarded. They'd rather make soup for ten people than a full bowl of rice for one person. They believe in group-oriented thinking. If the government tells you to save, everybody saves. They save like crazy. As a nation, Japan is rich; as individuals, they are not so affluent.

Staying in Japan helped broaden my perspectives. Japanese look at the product up close, whereas Americans look at it from afar. Because of their microspace, Japanese are forced to look at things more closely. They are also more precise. It's embedded into their national character. Throughout their history, they have enjoyed highly detailed craftsmanship. They have pride in their work and do their best, no matter how small a job they have. In Japan, even small buckwheat *soba* restaurants were passed down proudly for many generations if they made the best noodles.

But Korea has 4,000 years of history, and Koreans still are not patient. While I was in Japan, I frequently traveled to Kia Motors in Korea. I noticed that Koreans tend to have tunnel vision; they are very short-sighted. I think this is mainly due to our recent history. We were forced into many hardships and into making quick decisions, without the luxury of reflecting on our needs. That's why we are always in a hurry to take the next step, to get to the next station, to do the next task. Going from Japan to Korea is always a big contrast. Every time I go back to Korea, I look at new construction and development. There's not a single sidewalk in Seoul with smooth pavement. All the bricks are sticking out, and ladies in high heels are always falling. They could have done it better, but they were in a hurry to finish the job.

In Korea, laborers are looked down on. This is very destructive, since laborers are the main core that holds up the society. In Japan, everyone is viewed as equal. There is no kid hiding his father's education or occupation. In Korea, if they find out your father works at a construction site, they don't want to associate with you.

My wife is a born-again Christian like me. I met her in Korea. I was truly born again when I was twenty-five years old, on March 28, 1987. Before that, although I come from a third-generation Christian family, never missed a single Sunday service, and taught in Sunday school, I never really believed anything that was in the Bible. I didn't believe the story of Adam and Eve. I didn't believe anything about Noah's ark. I didn't believe that Moses parted the Red Sea. I always thought these were like fictional stories. I had lots of doubts and questions; I tried very hard to find the truth. I started to read the Bible, and I prayed with all my heart: "God, you really have to teach me about the Bible." That was about the time when I got involved in a serious traffic accident. The experience made me realize that unless I settled this issue with God, everything else was meaningless.

One year after the accident, there was a Sunday school teachers' retreat at Big Bear Mountain. We were studying the Bible, and I was reading John, chapter 15, verse 3: "You have been made clean already by the words I have given you." At that moment, something clicked in my heart—not my head, but my heart. Up until that time, I had always tried to do good deeds to make up for the sins I had committed, thinking I could purify myself by doing good. At that moment, I realized that all I had to do was believe in the words that Jesus spoke 2,000 years ago. Everything in the Bible suddenly made sense to me. That night I had a born-again experience. I received the Holy Spirit. And from that point on, I lived a different life; God became my priority.

Among churchgoers, there are those who are born-again and those who are not. They are like oil and water; they don't mix. When I went back to Detroit, I went to the Presbyterian church I used to attend the year before and told them about my experience of being born-again, but they looked at me strangely. After that, I could no longer go to that church. Instead, I found a group of born-again Christians who were meeting at another church, which I have been attending ever since. Wherever I go, whether to Japan, Korea, or Europe, I can find a church with born-again Christians, and those are the churches I attend.

Some people say that we are a cult. Even my father wants me to quit this group and return to his church. I think they say that because they have not experienced being born-again as we have.

I didn't abandon my career or anything like that, but God took over me. In serving Him, I work hard at my job. That's what's written in the Bible; I work hard to glorify God.

Faith is the solid foundation between me and my wife. Faith can supersede everything else. My wife was born and raised in Korea, so we are different in many ways; I tend to be more direct, while she's more indirect, and misunderstandings result. We argue and fight sometimes, but we always go back to our foundation. Faith covers everything. I'm very happy now, and there is no doubt in my mind that I am going to go to heaven.

JANUARY 1995

KYUNG-JA LEE

A Humble Messenger

Born in Chŏnju, Korea, in 1954, Kyung-Ja Lee was invited to the United States at seventeen by her sister, who had married an American and was living in Lewiston, Maine. She graduated from Bates College and earned a master's degree in psychology at Columbia University. While working as a psychiatric social worker in Pittsburgh, she began studying film making, and in 1985, she moved to Los Angeles to attend the American Film Institute. Her first film, *Halmani*, is the story of a young Amerasian girl's encounter with her Korean heritage as she meets her grandmother for the first time. Lee is currently working on her second film, a love story titled *Koreatown Blues*.

I had long hair, and I decided to get a haircut before making a trip to Korea. I wanted the best haircut there is, a unique, unique haircut. I got hold of this half-price coupon from a Melrose salon advertising "hair sculpting." They sculpt your hair so that you're the only one with that kind of hairdo. Mine turned out half Shogun, half punk, totally shaved in the back. It was completely new and kind of playful. I never thought it was going to offend the entire Korean nation. I didn't realize what difficulties lay ahead until I landed at Kimpo Airport and went through customs. The guys were literally scolding me for my hairdo. "*Kŭrŏn mŏri-ka ŏdi issŏ?* [What in the world kind of hair is that?]" They actually clicked their tongues. "*Sesange* [in this world]! She's going around with that kind of haircut!" They called me *mich'in nyŏn* [crazy woman].

I didn't want to make my third sister-in-law have to cook a late dinner because of my arrival, so I decided to have some *udong* [noodles] or something at this *p'ojangmach'a* [roadside snack tent]. But wouldn't you know, no one would sit next to me. They didn't want anyone to think they were with me. Not to mention that I spoke with an [American] accent. Maybe they thought I was a spy from North Korea.

My two sisters live in the U.S., but my four brothers live in Korea, so my brothers and sisters-in-law have to put up with me whenever I visit Korea. Obviously they don't want to introduce a freak to their friends. That first evening in Seoul, my sisters-in-law formed a kind of conspiracy to get rid of my hairdo and normalize me so that they wouldn't feel *chaengp'i* [embarrassment; shame]. They took me to a public bath with a beauty parlor attached to it and had me stripped and remade. My sister-in-law said she needed a little trim, and the next thing I knew, I was on the cutting board. My hair was all normalized: front and back, it was an even-looking crew-cut. But you can't really get angry at them, because it's all done in the name of love.

My mother didn't mind my "Melrose hairdo." She really gets a kick out of whatever I do. "I must have a very unusual daughter," she says. "I can't

believe that such a *t'ŭkbyŏlhan* [special] daughter came out of my belly."
I'm the last daughter, so I can get away with anything. According to Korean
tradition, the third daughter is the most pampered.

Basically, our whole family got wiped out just like most other families during the Korean War. Maybe those were actually the happiest times. If no one
had anything, you would not be discontented. When some people started to
get rich, when you could see the difference between rich and poor, that's
when unhappiness grows. It's just like when you don't have any freedom;
you just try to make the best of the circumstances. When we didn't have
anything, we actually shared with our neighbors. Now people don't share;
the custom is almost gone.

Not that sharing itself is one hundred percent pure. When Koreans fight
over who's going to pay the bill for a meal, it's very sophisticated and complicated. If you really look into it, it's extremely scientific. People secretly
remember who paid before. Everyone pretends they don't remember, but
they do. If you don't pay when it's your turn, resentment can build up.
There's an amazing continuous connection of interpersonal relationships
based upon who's paying next. I mean, no scholar can figure it out. It's not
just based on who's more successful and should pay, because pride and personalities get involved. People think, "I don't want this asshole to pay for
me." I know one guy who never paid. It gets ugly; you could become an outcast if you constantly avoid paying. People feel like killing a guy like that.
They get homicidal.

My parents grew up under the Japanese regime; they're older people, so
they have older thoughts. My father still thinks the earth is flat. He should
be in the Smithsonian. The more I think about it, it's amazing that I grew
up when I did. Between 1952 and 1960, there was the Korean industrial
revolution when Korea caught up with the West, compressing 200 years
into ten or fifteen years.[74] We grew up seeing people riding cows,[75] and then
suddenly a rocket lands on the moon. Of course, my father didn't believe
it. He said, "It's just a movie on television," and walked away. Now I'm
using a computer. It's unbelievable; we used to think chewing gum was high
tech, you know, something that you can chew for three consecutive days.
We would put it on the wall at night so that we could torture and mutilate
it some more the next day. That's how we grew up, and then suddenly it's
the 1960s and 1970s, and then my God! people have cars, and then their
wives have cars, and it's like, "What the hell's going on?"

So anyway, despite my "Melrose hairdo," I must tell you that I'm more

Korean than other Koreans my age or younger. Whenever I go to a Korean restaurant or market in L.A., they think I'm Japanese. Korean women my age act much more mature. My aura or ambience are kind of odd to them. Once I went out with these very established women in their fifties, all prominent activists in the Koreatown community and very first generation. I call people of that age *sokch'ima* [underskirt] people, meaning they are very conservative. I can wear a see-through skirt and not be bothered by it, God damn it. In a sense, I love both worlds. When these women talk seriously about how the computer age has passed them by without them even touching a keyboard, it's very poignant to me. I came from that old generation also. Fear of the unknown, the new technology. How can I hate them?

I miss the old stuff. When I grew up, I wanted the Beatles. I would try to sing along with all the Western songs. Now I go back to Korea and end up listening to the music my parents listen to, like *Sim Ch'ŏng Jŏn,* one of the most heartbreaking Korean operas.

There's the part where Sim Ch'ŏng serves her blind father a wonderful breakfast the day she's leaving to sell her body so that he can regain his sight. He says, "Why are we having such a breakfast this morning?" She breaks into tears and says, "I'm about to go; this is our last meal together." The father refuses to eat the best meal he ever had. He chokes and can't swallow. Supposedly you can only sing in that kind of opera if you cough up blood. You cry so much that you end up with a deep, choked-up voice.

I see my parents listening to this in tears after hundreds and thousands of times. My father has a little transistor radio that he probably got in the 1970s, the first transistor ever. He didn't have faith in the tiny batteries, so he got a huge battery and tied it to the tiny transistor with wires. It looks like a car battery, with greasy ooze coming out. That defeats the whole purpose, portability.

In L.A., I play *Sim Ch'ŏng Jŏn* tapes while I'm driving, and I think about my parents. It's too bad that the younger generation in Korea can't appreciate this. Right now they're into Korean rap. If it were good rap, they'd have to use "f" words, be rebellious and funky and curse everybody, but no! Korean censorship won't allow anything, so it's like, "Ah, what a beautiful morning at the window, I miss you." It's the most bizarre rap.

When we were growing up we listened to movie sound tracks, like *Sound of Music* or *Lawrence of Arabia.* I was always a film buff. When I saw *Doctor Zhivago* in Korea, I didn't sleep that night because I wanted to remember every shot from beginning to end. That was my first study of film, trying to keep the images in my head forever because I wasn't able to go back again. I got caught and almost got thrown out of school, since students were not allowed in movie theaters. We were wearing our school uniforms, which practically glowed in the dark. Even if you changed your clothes, they know you're a student by your hairdo. Your haircut was like one centimeter below your earlobe and straight. I think it all changed in the 1980s; now, kids don't have to wear school uniforms anymore or go through the unbelievable kind of suffering we went through. Even today, I sometimes wake up sweating that I didn't do the homework and am getting called on. The ultimate punishment was humiliation in front of people, being singled out. I can take anything else but that. I wonder how humiliation affects your relationships later on in life. Maybe it's why other people can have prolonged relationships and I can't.

My parents try to match me up with someone. Sometimes they call me at three o'clock in the morning and say, "We found somebody. You better come right away before anybody else snatches him. He's a lawyer with a lot of money. You've got to see this guy." Then one day, my father said very seriously, "At your age, you probably have to give up marrying a guy who never married before." But he still wants me to get married, regardless. He'd even allow his daughter to marry a divorced man. Of course my parents would like me to marry a Korean so that they can communicate with him. My mother thinks it's nice that I can visit her anytime, not having any children to go home to, but of course she cries all the way to the airport when I leave, thinking, "Oh, my poor daughter is suffering alone."

She's right. Mother's always right. I am suffering alone. I keep telling her, "Mother, it's not as sad as you think it is!" To be honest, the other day I was sitting at my window looking out at the full moon, and I thought, "What more do I need? This moment." People who have been alone so long probably get married to their solitude. It's like, this is it, this is the moment no one, no lover can replace. But at that kind of moment, you say, "It would be nice to have a man just to hold me." I haven't found a man who makes me think that I would die without him so I'd have to hang onto him for the rest of my life. I'm thinking about fate a lot.

My mother was baffled about what was wrong with her daughter, so we went to a *chŏmjaengi* [fortune-teller who divines using time and date of birth]. It was in Chŏnju, in north Chŏlla Province, where I was born. Most artists and great performers are from Chŏnju, and most fortune-tellers are also. We went early, and when we arrived at this old, dilapidated Korean traditional house, a servant is sweeping up all the dead mice from the previous night's poisoning into a mound. We had to hop over the mound at the gate. Since this fortune-teller is very famous, we had to go early in the morning to make sure that we got seen; she can't see that many people because it's draining for her. She was ninety at the time, and she goes into a trancelike state. There's no such thing as privacy. No one is safe; everyone is prey. Strangers sit around listening to her tell each other's fortunes, good or bad. It's sort of like a communal fate that's shared. It's such a wonderful thing—only Koreans do this—everyone gets in there and listens and comments. They are supportive; they hold you, they pass you a handkerchief. It works like group therapy.

I think the fortune-teller read my mother's concern that I'm still single. Anyway, she said that I was on a journey to this world from a previous world when I passed by a palace that had been burned down. I saw something, and when I picked it up and dusted off the ashes, I realized that it was the king's crown. I could have been married with children by now, but I got that crown. That means that no man can succeed with me. My expectation of men is way up there; that God damn crown has to fit. I say, "Darn, why couldn't I get an adjustable baseball cap?" What a wonderful interpretation. It's beyond artistry, you know. I am a modern woman, but I grew up under shamanism, so I totally accepted what she said.

My mother was the breadwinner in our family. She was the one who moved to Chŏnju and eventually to Seoul so that all her children could be educated in Seoul. During the Japanese occupation, she did silk trading. She had to take the train to Manchuria, but the Japanese would not allow people to carry money, so she put the gold into yŏt [sticky Korean candy made with molasses]. Then she crawled under the train to stick it on. She had such courage. Basically, she was smuggling. After the war, she had a small silk store. Her joy was putting all the silk trimmings together to make a saekdong chŏgori [Korean blouse/jacket with multicolored sleeves] for her daughters. Each streak was a different material.

My father was a good-looking guy, but he's not educated or as bright as my mother. She's the only one who can figure things out. He's much more the farmer type, simple. I appreciate that a lot more now than when I was growing up. He's good in a very visual way. His side job right now is finding tomb sites for people. In Confucianism, it's very important for your ancestors to have a good tomb site. My father can figure out where the underground water flows. My parents' tomb site has two mountains in the distance like a crow's wings spread out, and downhill it looks like a turtle sticking its neck out. It's a balance of forces, *yin* and *yang*, a perfect geological setup. They'll be buried at the neck point. You'd never see the crow's wings or the turtle's neck unless my father described them to you. He has this way of seeing things, even though he's illiterate.

My father was the stereotype of the Korean man of his time. We had a smaller house on the side of our house, and my mother came home once and saw my father's shoes outside, beside a pair of women's shoes.[76] But because he was a man, he was allowed to have a *chŏp* [concubine]. It was totally accepted. My mother said that he would not come into her quarters for months, but she would see these two pairs of shoes every time she came home from work. Two pairs of shoes. Can you imagine?

Maybe friendship kept them going for sixty years; I'm not sure. In a strange way, they miss each other when they're apart. While she was visiting here, she was genuinely worried about him, about whether he was being well taken care of. I don't think, "How stupid she is after all he did to her." But maybe there's something here I can learn from.

All my sisters live in the U.S. now, even though our parents still live in Korea. When I was young, coming to the U.S. meant being successful. It's funny: in the old days in Korea, happiness in your old age meant having all your children around you. Today, success means being busy, and the more successful your children are, the less you get to see them, because they're always so busy—right? In a strange way, what success and happiness mean gets reevaluated. If you have unsuccessful children, they hang around you. You get to have the warped joy of seeing them around.

It was great when my mother visited me in L.A. The only problem was, on the way back from the airport, my brakes went out. It was rush hour, and I was behind a bus, slowing down for a stop when, lo and behold, there was no brake. I was looking for someplace to crash into. In a sense, the L.A. riots saved us. After the riots, a lot of Koreatown mini-malls had metal fences around them. I saw a gate and smashed into it. We tipped over and landed upside down. All I remember is calling out "*ŏmŏni* [Mother]!" twice. I crawled out. I couldn't even find my shoes. Some Latino workers helped us get out. It was 103 degrees that day, the hottest day of the year, but my mother was shivering like it was winter. I learned a life lesson with this accident. My car was a cute 1976 BMW 2002, which I loved. Don't ever go for looks. Forget the outside; you have to check the brakes.

And that goes for men, too.

My mother stayed two weeks, but the first week she didn't want to go anywhere. It was sort of anticlimactic after that because nothing could match the intensity of the accident. Since then, every time I call her, she says, "Kyung-Ja, luck is with you this year." She interpreted the incident as an incredible force protecting me.

She's right; things are really going well for me. With work, it's like grabbing a star to get one company interested in your project. I've got three companies. It's unbelievable. These days, it's impossible to get an agent. I'm in the position where I can call any agency in town and they would like to sign up with me.

I walked into this agency in the heart of Beverly Hills, and got into this coffin-sized elevator made out of marble. You walk in and see the marble stairs and the artwork on the wall. I went up there and it was white, white, white. White as can be: blond hair and white people buzzing around. Then this agent in a starched white shirt finally comes and shakes my hand and takes me to his white-walled office with white blinds in the back. It was white on white. The back of the building is all white, because it's not a low-down neighborhood with graffiti or anything. He gives me a contract to sign.

Walking out of there was weird: I should have been jumping for joy because I finally arrived, but I walked out feeling like "What an asshole world this is." You have to struggle so hard to get there, and for what? The feeling was so bitter. Isn't this what I had wanted? Yet it was like being a piece of meat in the butcher shop. They're laying it out and they're weighing it.

According to the *I-Ching*[77] layout, the fish finally arrives at the ocean. It took me ten years. I've been working on *Koreatown Blues* for three years now. The film is a love story between a middle-class Korean immigrant woman and a Mexican immigrant auto mechanic in Los Angeles. It's hard to get the budget you are looking for. This is not like two people talking in an apartment; there are massive street shots and crowd scenes. My family would never comprehend the magnitude; even most Korean distributors can't comprehend it.

My goal in filmmaking is not finding some universal theme. I often see an event and think, "Oh, my God, this has got to be a movie. There's a story in there." I was working at an auto body shop and I saw the struggle of two different cultures, Korean and Mexican, and I told myself, "This has got to be a movie." That was in 1985, before the riots.

I could see both worlds. I'm fortunate that I experienced two worlds. I grew up in the Korean world; it couldn't have been more Korean, thanks to my parents. Then I had my adulthood in American life, so I flip flop back and forth. I can interpret both ways. I don't want to say my experience is better than anybody else's. I just feel fortunate that I had this dual life, and that I can understand and see the details. I'm not a historian; I have no answers. I merely share my personal experiences, observations, and thoughts.

I want to find the little nuances of life; if I can find some wisdom in these, I'd be happy. When I go back to Korea, the kinds of things I enjoy and appreciate are what Koreans call *ch'ŏn hada,* meaning low class. But that's where the most beautiful things are. A Korean dress is not beautiful when it's perfectly folded. What's beautiful is the crumpled dress worn by the woman with the baby on her back. Perhaps it's crooked and the underskirt's showing because she had to tie it hurriedly. That's spontaneous beauty.

Koreatown Blues will show what we call "immigrant culture." Like the king-size rococo bed with a silk embroidered blanket over it and the ornate teacups that you never drink from . . . the constant striving for "white world success." I document what I see and, hopefully, a certain story is going on. It's going to be a love story, with class and race differences. Can a middle-class Korean woman fall in love with a lower-class Mexican car mechanic? When it comes to love, all the rules get thrown out the window. I believe that truly.

At the same time, Korean people's fear of throwing out the rules, of cutting ties with family and community, is deeply rooted. Unlike the legendary American pioneer, we can't just pack up and say, "To hell with you; I'm starting a new life."

Where do I belong? I am really attracted to shamanism. My next project will be on the *mudang* [shaman] herself in what is neither man's world nor a god's world, but in between. The *mudang* is ostracized in Korean society, and yet God's voice speaks through her body. That fascinates me.

They say I have an American accent. That startled me because I used to think people who spoke Korean with an accent were trying to make themselves look like Americans, like showing off. How little I knew! I'm a victim of long-term American life. I couldn't help it. It seeps through you. On the other hand, strangely, I lost my Chŏlla Province dialect while I was growing up in Seoul. You used to get attacked if you had a Chŏlla accent.[78] But now I'm going back to it again. I'm happy that I may have tapped my deepest psyche after being tainted by growing up in Seoul.

I've gone through different detours in my journey to get into film-making. I always thought I would be a messenger of East and West because I understand both worlds. A humble messenger. I just hope my message will be clear and important.

OCTOBER 1994

YOUN JAE KIM

A Seeker and a Fighter

Sweet-faced and soft-spoken, Youn Jae Kim has the calm, self-possessed manner of an accomplished martial artist. Born in Seoul in 1970, Kim attended private schools and lived comfortably until his father's business suffered from government policies that protected large conglomerates at the expense of smaller concerns. The family immigrated to Los Angeles in 1988. Kim's parents operated a small Mexican restaurant in Glendale, and he entered North Torrance High School as a senior. After going on to UC Berkeley and graduating in film, he became director of an organizing project at the Korean Community Center of the East Bay (KCCEB) in Oakland.

When I first started working at the Korean Community Center almost two years ago, they told me, "There's no history of merchant organizing here; if you succeed, you will change the community. That's what I've been trying to do."

I decided I should organize first among mom-and-pop shops, because they are the most neglected, isolated, and disadvantaged of the merchants, since they are usually the most recently arrived immigrants who don't speak English well, don't understand American culture (whatever that is), and often have financial problems. They are typical of the immigrants in general because they don't have much capital, and they have to rely mainly on unlimited bodily labor, especially from family members. I knew that by working with them, we could help improve race relations in the community. But their time is limited and they generally don't know what to do. If they were organized and educated about issues, they could exert pressure on politicians to be more responsive. They could do very concrete things like take measures to prevent the escalation of racial tensions and help prevent or minimize crime in the neighborhoods, and help improve relations among communities. They could be a major voice in the Korean community, and they could change the very distorted image the mainstream society has of them: that they don't care about other people, that they just take money from the African American community, that they know nothing but work. In the end, only they have the power to change the negative images of Korean merchants.

In these times, image is very important. Even if individual Korean people are kind, especially if they are merchants, people don't believe they are sincere, because they have been overexposed to the image of Koreans as greedy and selfish. If the merchants are organized, they can change their image through substantive work, such as setting up programs for neighborhood youth, not selling tobacco or alcohol to kids, contributing to scholarships for students, and sponsoring annual picnics to show appreciation to customers. I know it would work. The merchants don't know what to do;

an organizer could help them a lot. I found that some merchants had tried various things already, and for those who had not, it was not because they were bad but because they simply had so little time, due to the nature of their businesses.

When I first started, I had no contacts, so I just started going to the two big Oakland swapmeets—the AC Indoor Mall at E. 14th Street and 26th Avenue, and the Durant Mall at E. 14th and Durant. The AC Mall has seventeen vendors; fifteen are Korean. The Durant has one hundred vendors; about forty are Koreans and the rest are African Americans, Armenians, and other Asians, like Thais and Taiwanese. I introduced myself and then visited every week. At first the merchants were very unfriendly; they thought I was a "damn radical," a member of YKU [Young Koreans United, an organization of Korean American leftists labeled by Korean community institutions as "communists"]. After four or five times, they began to give me coffee and discuss their history and problems with me. It was very difficult, because one of the swapmeet vendors also owned the property. He was suspicious that I might try to organize the vendors to demand things from him. At the same time, I was under pressure from the funding source to organize a core group. It's crazy to try to do that in eleven months. The merchants were working six days a week. On the seventh day, they would go to Sacramento or Los Angeles for merchandise. How could we ask them to attend an eight P.M. meeting? Besides, what were we able to provide for them?

The AC Mall was burglarized six times in two months. Even though they reported the break-ins to the police, they almost gave up on getting any response from them. I brought in a police technician to show them where the vulnerable points at the swapmeet were. Then I found out that the Oakland Police Department's Asian Advisory Committee on Crime had had no Korean representative for seven years. In January 1994, I joined the committee. I arranged a meeting between the merchants and the beat police. After that, they had individual contact and more frequent visits. I organized workshops featuring police technicians to help merchants with legal matters and to analyze their shops and the building so that they could figure out how to discourage burglaries. Every week, I gathered information for the merchants and made handouts for them with information not only on public safety, lease matters, and loan programs, but also on courtesy to customers: how to greet people in English, how to show respect, why they should not speak to each other in Korean in front of non-Korean-speaking customers, and so forth. Gradually, the merchants began to trust me more, and I was able to organize a core group of merchants who were willing to help lead the effort to organize other merchants.

Besides organizing a core group, the other objective of the merchant education project is to put together a resource manual in Korean. I gathered various materials and translated them into Korean. The manual contains basic information on local government resources, social services, and how to apply for U.S. citizenship; demonstrations of how to make business plans and obtain loans for small businesses; discussions of racial hate crimes, AIDS prevention, and domestic violence; and suggestions on how to relieve stress. The response was better than we expected. We had to limit the resource list to Oakland, due to lack of time, money, and manpower. But after the Korean press publicized it, we got two hundred requests in three weeks. Some people even sent postage stamps.

I've worked on several gunshot cases involving Korean merchants robbed by African Americans. One of them is a man who was robbed after he closed his hamburger shop. He handed over the money, but he got shot in the throat anyway. His daughter thinks it's because he's hot-tempered and probably glared at or said something to the robber while he was handing over the money. He may never be able to speak again. Another one is a young widow with twin three-year-old sons and a four-year-old daughter. The husband was in the back of the store when a robber came in and pointed his gun at the wife. She screamed, and when her husband came running in the robber panicked, shot him, and ran away without even getting any money. The widow didn't work at the store; she was just dropping off her husband's lunch. She has had to learn the business, and now she does it by herself. She tries to stay strong for the sake of her children, but every time she sees me, she cries. That's because I was the one who helped her right from the beginning, so I'm the one she thinks understands her most. We helped raise $6,500 in community donations for her. We also try to get shooting victims into the city's Victims' Assistance Program, which can provide $2,000 in emergency funds and help with funeral expenses and children's educational expenses.

I don't think that the merchants are greedy. Maybe they're for themselves, but they don't make the piles of money people assume they make. The people with money are fluent in English. They don't do business in low-rent areas or rely on family members. Many people in the neighborhood feel that the merchants are invading their communities and taking their money. Korean merchants are gruff in general; they aren't nice in the American way. Many first-generation *ajŏssis* [uncles] think that men should act "like men." Even if they want to be nice, they don't know how. Sometimes I get accused by my non-Korean friends when they try to read my face. They ask, "Are you mad? Do you have any problem?" When people say, "Smile," I can't. It's really tough for me to smile without a reason.

The merchants are really warm human beings struggling with real life issues. They have a lot of hopes and dreams. They never say they are living just because they don't want to die. The guy with the sweatshirt stall at the swapmeet is dreaming about selling sweatshirts in a downtown shop someday. If you get to know them, they ask you for advice about everything —family and business matters. It's a heavy responsibility for me; sometimes people ask me which summer program to send their kids to or what to do if their kids have gotten too heavily involved in some Christian church. I try to give them as much background information as possible, outlining what would be the worst and best possible outcomes, but I never advise them on what to do. I'd like them to decide.

I care about the merchants because they're an important part of the Korean community and because I want to work with people I can help empower. If I worked in an already established community, I'd be just an employee, not an owner. I feel very good about my work. The other day, after the first meeting of our newly organized entrepreneurs' council, I went out for a beer with the eight merchants, and one guy told me that his wife doesn't let him stay out late—unless it's for a KCCEB event. He said that he and his wife think it'd be great if their two kids grew up to be just like me.

I try to live my life like a seeker and to be a fighter. Living like a seeker means that I should think about things seriously and thoroughly. I should try to understand different perspectives. And I should keep looking for truth. Being a fighter means that if I see injustice, I should never step back. Instead, I should fight like a dog. If you want to win, you cannot be afraid of being hit. Now and then, I pause to ask myself which stage I am in, seeking to find out what's right and wrong, or fighting after deciding on what I think is right and figuring out the best strategies.

Non-Koreans may think that Koreans all stick together, but from my own personal experience, I know that race relations in this country are much more complicated than what you can see on the surface. I have a third-degree black belt in *t'aekwŏndo* and a first-degree black belt in *akido* (*hapkido* in Korean). When I first came to the U.S. and went into high school,

I passed the written test they made me take, so I didn't have to take ESL [English as a Second Language] classes, even though I couldn't understand a single thing anyone said. I used to study very hard in the library every day. A group of Korean students who had been in this country for about five years, but were still in the ESL classes, hated me. They made fun of me and called me names, and the boss of the group attacked me, so I beat him up in front of everyone. After that, the Korean kids at the school treated me with a lot of respect. I never had any problems with non-Korean students. Anyway, if they had tried to make fun of me, I wouldn't have understood what they were saying.

In order to survive Japanese colonization and national division, Koreans probably had to stress Korean homogeneity. But now we have to be more open. Many people ask me whether I want to go back to Korea or stay here. I think this is not the issue anymore. When I grow to be in my thirties or forties, there will be no specific boundaries and borderlines between countries. I can't be 100 percent Korean or 100 percent American. But at the same time, I can be *both* 100 percent Korean *and* 100 percent American.

SEPTEMBER 1994 AND APRIL 1995

HAN CHOL HONG
Strong Determination

Han Chol Hong [pseudonym] tells his life story as if it were a résumé. He is goal-oriented, determined, capable, methodical, and vigilant. Although he was at the top of his class, he was unable to attend a prestigious middle school because both his parents died, and he had to work from an early age. He managed to complete all his schooling by attending night school. He even finished college at Han Yang University by taking night classes while working at a construction company. Born ten years before the division of Korea, he lived through the Japanese colonization, the Second World War, the Korean conflict, and South Korea's long period of martial law. When the political upheavals after the assassination of President Park Chung Hee in 1979 and the suppression of the Kwangju citizens' uprisings in 1980 made his employment future uncertain, he immigrated to Los Angeles with his wife and three children. In Hong's view, the gamble paid off because his children's futures seem secure: one of his daughters, he says proudly, majored in medical technology and now earns twenty-nine dollars an hour as a pathologist; another daughter is enrolled in a New York medical school; and his son is a premed biology major at UC Irvine.

I was born in Hamhŭng, Hamkyŏngnam Province, in northern Korea, in 1935. Our family had an orchard; but every spring, we were short of food because the Japanese colonial authorities took away most of the produce.[79] I remember my parents keeping food and tobacco underground so that the Japanese wouldn't find it. Mother would prepare only a steamed potato for my school lunch box, and it would be spoiled by lunchtime. I was only six when she passed away.

The country was liberated when I was ten. Soviet soldiers occupied our city, and soon afterward there was a land reform program. My father was charged with dividing the land among the peasants. He had to give up his own land, and a year after the land reform, our family was ordered to leave the town. So in 1948, when I was in the fifth grade, we moved down south. We took a train to Yŏnch'ŏn in Kyŏnggi Province and hired a guide to get us across the 38th parallel. But before we could cross the Imjin River, we were caught by North Korean guards and taken back to Yŏnch'ŏn. After four days in a holding camp, we were ordered back to our hometown.[80] Instead, we hired one of the many guides who were making money helping people cross back and forth across the 38th parallel. Our guide led us to the southern portion of Imjin River, where we crossed over on foot in water that was up to our necks. Our guide led us to P'och'ŏn, Kyŏnggi Province, in South Korea. Later, we settled in Yŏngdŭngp'o, an industrial suburb of Seoul. My father passed away while I was still in primary school, so I stayed with my brother's family.

Then *yuk-i-o* [June 25, the date the Korean war began] broke out in 1950. For three months under communist rule in Seoul, we survived on pumpkin and barley soup. During the *il-sa* retreat,[81] we moved down to Taegu in North Kyŏngsang Province. We were always just one step ahead of the battle line. My brother knew someone in the military police and was finally able to get us a ride on a military truck.

We stayed in Taegu for three years, until the end of the war. I sold fruit, vegetables, and newspapers on the street during the day and attended night-school classes at Kyemun Middle School. Through high school and college, I had to work during the day, so I was only able to go to night school.[82] When we moved back to Seoul, I enrolled in Tongyang Technical High School. During the day, I worked as an errand boy at the *tong* office of Mun Rae Tong in Yŏngdŭngp'o. There were about twenty *t'ongs* in Mun Rae Tong, and I was supposed to deliver official documents to the *t'ong-jang* [chief].[83]

After I graduated, I was able to pass the civil service examination and got a position as civil engineer 4th class at Seoul City Hall. In 1963, I moved to the engineering division of the Department of Commerce and Industry as civil engineer 3rd Class. There, I supervised the construction of the Seoul-Pusan Expressway. After completing that project in 1977, I became an instructor at the Civil Service Employees Training Institute, where I stayed until 1983.

In October 1983, our family—my wife, my son and two daughters, and I moved to the United States at the invitation of my brother-in-law. The situation in Korea was not that bright at the time.[84] As soon as we arrived in Los Angeles, I enrolled at a plumbing and welding school for six months, but I was not able to get a job, partly due to problems with English. Next, my wife and I enrolled at house painting school and earned a state license, but we still had trouble getting work, so we had to do janitorial work for a while to get by.

A friend told me about a market near Western Avenue in South Central that was for sale. In April 1984, we bought the business for $90,000 with funds we brought with us and a bank loan. The price was about three times the store's monthly gross revenue, which was the going rate at the time. After operating that store for three years, we wanted to buy the building and land when the lease was about to expire, but the owner didn't want to sell, so we sold the business. Since the buyer, Mr. Yi, didn't have enough money to pay for the store, we carried the $60,000 loan for him for about four years.

After we sold the Western store, we bought another store on Manchester Avenue. It did not have a beer and wine license, but the monthly sales were good. We paid $300,000 for the store, including the inventory, the land, and the building. We borrowed $150,000 from a bank, and the rest came from our savings.

We operated that store from 8:00 A.M. to 8:00 P.M., seven days a week, three hundred sixty-five days a year. We would get up every day at 5:00

A.M., pick up the produce from the Central Wholesale Market, stop off at a wholesale general merchandise market to pick up cigarettes and sundries, and then open up the store. The only vacation we ever had was on December 28, 1988, when we sold the Western market, and March 1, 1989, when we started the Manchester store. That was the only time off we ever had, between October 1, 1984, and April 29, 1992, when *sa-i-gu* [the Los Angeles riots] disrupted everything.

After our children went to college, we hired one or two employees. Now we have one Korean and one Hispanic worker. Before that, though, we ran the store by ourselves—my wife, my children, and me. That's how we were able to minimize our expenses.

To succeed in this livelihood, I would advise newcomers to do two things: one is to minimize purchases on credit; the other is not to drive expensive cars. A lot of people got into trouble after the riots because they couldn't make the payments on their expensive cars and homes. Now their cars and houses are being repossessed. Several people I know were making house payments of $2,000 a month. Now that their monthly income is less than $2,000, they are moving into apartments. Minimizing debt is the best preparation for unforeseen events. I am successful because I have practiced this belief. We have four cars now that cost a total of less than $10,000. That's how we were able to send the kids through college.

The day the riots began, we closed an hour earlier than usual. That night, the alarm rang, but we didn't go to the store because all of the Korean radio [Radio Korea, Radio Han'guk, Korean Community Broadcasting] and television [Korean Television Enterprise and Mun Hwa Pangsong] stations were saying that it was not safe to go, and we agreed.

When we went to the store in the morning, half the stock was gone. The store had been looted during the night. We restocked the store and opened for business, but the radio and television stations kept urging us to leave, so we closed the store at noon and went home. As soon as we got in the door, the alarm company called to inform us that the store was being looted again. It was broad daylight. When we rushed back to the store, we found it in shambles. The doors and windows were broken, and everything was gone except for a few water bottles. My wife and I immediately put up a wire fence around the store and stayed right there. Mobs of people came and set fire to the store several times, but each time we put out the fire with blankets and tap water. Some of the people shouted that this was the only store left standing and should be burned down. But we stayed at the store all day and night, keeping watch. After several days, the National Guard and the police took control of the situation, and the rioters retreated. My wife kept saying that we should go home, but I said that if the store was burned down, we would lose our life base. So we risked our lives to defend the store. For a month after the riots began, we slept in the store every night to guard against arson.

The store we had sold to Mr. Yi was completely looted during the first day of the rioting. The Yis went home thinking that since there was nothing left to loot, the mobs would leave the store alone, but the next morning, they found that it had been burned to the ground.

People say that Korean stores were specifically targeted, but I don't think they were. It is true that many Korean-owned stores were burned down, but that's because many of the stores in the riot areas were owned by Koreans. Many black-owned and Mexican-owned stores were also burned. In fact, stores with "Black-Owned" signs were burned; you could still see the signs after the stores had been burnt down.

For Korean immigrants to run a store in a place like South Central is like fighting a battle. You have to have strong determination to survive. If riots happen again and the owners stay at their stores, I don't think anyone will burn them down. Rioters are also people; they won't burn down a store if they see people inside.

It took three full days to clean up our store and another two weeks to restock it. Within a week after we had restocked it, we were open for business. Altadena Milk provided us credit for dairy goods, and some other wholesalers extended credit to us for certain types of goods. The Bank of America loaned us $45,000 without interest for three years and 5 percent interest for the next three years. Friends from Korea sent us $7,500, and some friends from the church here gave us another $7,500. The Korean community relief organizations gave $3,500 to each Korean riot victim. Even though the community donations weren't enough to help restart the business, they really boosted our morale.

Before the riots, we had bought a store on Century Boulevard and leased it to an Indian merchant. It was completely burned down during the rioting, and the Indian fellow didn't want to rebuild the business, so we got an SBA [Small Business Administration] loan and rebuilt the store. We started the construction in December 1992, and reopened the store for business the following April.

Our neighborhood is changing a lot. Right now, it is about half black and half Hispanic.[85] About five years ago, it was ninety percent black. I expect the whole area to become Hispanic by the year 2000. The black people are leaving the area.

Our store is like a big refrigerator for the neighbors. Many of our neighbors do not have refrigerators at home. For me, it doesn't make much difference whether we have a beer sale permit or not. We are doing all right without it. We sell nonalcoholic beverages, foodstuffs, and various daily necessities. The neighborhood customers complain that we don't carry beer. I thought soda, bread, milk, and eggs would suffice, but many people ask for beer instead of soda. We've requested a public hearing about getting a permit to sell beer. Many neighbors have volunteered to testify in favor.

I've been in this business for nine years. During that time, I was only robbed once. I think that gunmen with concealed weapons have come to our store on many occasions, but because we took precautions, they didn't get to use their weapons. Two things are important here: one is to discourage a potential gunman from taking his gun out of his pocket; the other is to discourage gunmen from entering the store. The Western store had a little warehouse facing the main store. We stocked the warehouse with fruit and vegetables and always kept someone in front of it, facing the main store. When potential robbers come, they always circle the store and park near the front door, leaving their car with the engine running. Whenever someone like that approaches the store, we all get busy and act alert. We make it known that we are watching. Many times, they just leave, muttering "shit." I'm sure that some of them are completely innocent and have legitimate reasons for leaving their cars running, like mechanical problems with the car, but I feel that I have to take precautions. We were never robbed at the Florence store, but after we sold it to Mr. Yi, it was robbed three times at gunpoint during the first three years because he didn't take precautions.

There was no warehouse in front of the Manchester store. We were robbed once. That time, I was standing by the shelves, my daughter was at the cash register, and our employee was inside the cooler. The gunman took out his weapon, pointed it at me, and ordered me to turn around. He grabbed the money from the cash register and ran out. The whole thing took less than thirty seconds. After that, I always kept someone posted outside the door—either myself, my wife, my daughter, or an employee. After we sold that business, the new owner was robbed because he didn't post anyone at the front door. Since we reopened our current place, we have always kept someone at the main door. It doesn't have to be a paid guard. If potential robbers see someone outside the door, they get discouraged.

There are some Koreans who own twenty to thirty stores; seeing them gave me the incentive to expand. But the plan was disrupted by the riots; we have only secured two stores, and our monthly debt has increased. I'm not sure we will be able to expand more.

Doing business like this takes hard work, but I am my own boss and I own my own employment. Nobody tells me what to do. I am much better off than the people who lease a weekend space at a swap meet[86] or pay high monthly payments to a landlord. We own this business, the land, and the building. I want to continue working for as long as I can.

JULY 1993

HYUN YI KANG

No Spokesperson

Born in 1967 in the Kuro-dong factory district of Seoul, Hyun Yi
Kang imagines that if she had stayed in Korea, she would have been
working at "some multinational factory," since her parents would
not have had enough money to send her, the second girl and third
child, to college. Her family immigrated to the United States in
1976, on the day she would have begun fourth grade in Korea.
Sponsored by a maternal aunt who was married to an African
American serviceman, the family lived at first with an uncle who
was a Presbyterian minister in San Diego, moved to various housing projects in Los Angeles, and eventually settled in the nearby
suburb of Downey. Kang is completing a Ph.D in the history of
consciousness at the University of California, Santa Cruz.

I used to go with my father to translate for him at the store or bank. Once a woman asked if my father was my husband, even though I was only twelve years old. They couldn't differentiate. It was so humiliating for my father to have his daughter mistaken for his wife. What was heartless was to tell the child to translate threats and insults to their own parents, like "Tell your father that if he does that next time, I'm going to sue him," or "Why can't he speak English? This is America." I would just translate the necessary facts. It's almost like people think they have a right to be inhuman to whoever can't speak English.

My parents got into the garment contracting business in 1983, when the woman my mother was working for became pregnant and had to unload her small garment factory. My parents didn't have any money, so the woman just let them take over and pay her back later. For three or four years, my parents made more money than they had ever seen. That was when they bought a house in Walnut and I started college. But they don't know how the system works or how to take care a lot of important things. They didn't even know anything about taxes; they just thought that after paying their employees, they could keep whatever money was left. Ultimately they had to close the factory because they got into tax trouble. For the last five years, they were just working and losing money every month. I think they just stayed in there for so long because they couldn't see any other alternatives. It would have been difficult for them, with their lack of English skills and at their age, to find decent employment. So they just kept at it, thinking things would turn around, but they never ever did.

Distance has made me appreciate my parents more. After I went away to college, I started thinking about them as individuals, as people in their own right. I realized that they did the best they could, given the circumstances of their lives. Now I have a really good relationship with both of them. They weren't the best models of parenthood, but I appreciate that they never nagged or pressured me. When I told my father I wanted to go graduate school, he asked why I wasn't going to law school, but he didn't really impose anything on me.

I think my parents are very pragmatic. For example, when I started living with my partner, Paul, I think they figured it was OK as long as I was doing what I was supposed to at school and as long as Paul wasn't just a bum. My parents never pressured me to get married. In fact, for a long time my mother told me *not* to get married, not, I guess, because she was unhappy in her marriage. Other people would think it's scandalous that when Paul and I visit my parents' house, we sleep in the same room. We didn't in the beginning, but after a while we just decided that it was stupid because they knew we were living together. The next morning, no one said anything. One time they wanted to wake us up, but they couldn't come into the room. I could hear them outside telling my five-year-old nephew, "Justin, go wake up your auntie," and he was saying, "Why? I don't want to!" because he had picked up on something being weird, so I just got up and came out. Now I always try to wake up and go out first.

My parents like Paul because even though he's Korean American, he can't speak Korean. He seems like an innocent child to them. *"Aegi kat'ae* [like a baby]," they always say, *"kui yǒ wǒ [cute],"* because he speaks his bad Korean to them. They think he's harmless, *sunjin hae* [innocent, naive]. They don't sexualize him. I don't think most Korean parents would put up with it, so I'm really proud of them.

I feel some guilt about not being able to help my parents more. Ironically, I probably feel more guilty because they don't nag me or try to impose their values and desires on me. From talking to people at their church and in other places, they concluded that I would be able to make a lot of money if I graduated from Berkeley. But in today's economy, a degree from a prestigious university doesn't mean what it used to. You often need personal or family connections to get a foothold, and a lot of immigrant children don't have them, unless their parents are well off. I know many Korean Americans who move back home after graduating and end up working at the family's liquor store, factory, or restaurant. My parents try not to show it much, but I think they're really disappointed. They expected Berkeley to be a ticket to power. If I didn't have to worry about my parents, I wouldn't have minded getting just any job to support myself, because I really wanted to write full time. I was interested in studying film or creative writing, but I knew that this would not enable me to help my parents financially. I even considered law school, but I know I couldn't survive there spiritually. Going to graduate school was a compromise between what I wanted to do and financial security.

At the time I started graduate school, my parents were doing all right. They weren't making money, but at least they were able to pay their bills. Shortly after I started, they began running into financial problems. For me, just being in graduate school was hard enough, but thinking about how I couldn't do anything for my parents made me feel alone and alienated from my colleagues. I both envied and resented them for not having these kinds of worries. I've done what I could to help by giving my parents my fellowship money and taking out some student loans. It hasn't been easy, but maybe I've benefitted because I was forced to be more productive so that I could finish my degree ahead of schedule.

I've been accused by other Korean Americans of having a chip on my shoulder about class. When I was a first-year student at Berkeley, I had a Jewish boyfriend who had a Korean male friend from high school. I remember visiting his hometown and going over to his Korean friend's house. The Korean was supposed to be from a real *yangban* [aristocratic] family. His mother took the kids to piano, violin, and ballet lessons. She asked me where my parents graduated from college, and after I said that they didn't go to college, she pretended I was not occupying a physical space near her, while she lavished attention on my Jewish boyfriend.

It doesn't bother me so much that there are Koreans with more socioeconomic privileges than I have. What bothers me is that they pretend they don't have these privileges. You can't help being born into a wealthy family, but you can be conscious about how it's marked you. I have friends who bitch about not being able to go out for dinner, and in the next breath, they will be talking about renting a cabin somewhere with their family for Christmas or about how the doorman in some hotel in Europe knows their mother by her first name because she's always there. What does it mean to tell me things like that? I'm not impressed by them. It just points out how we are worlds apart. I'm the only one in my family to move away for college and then go to graduate school. I don't like that kind of ignorance about privilege.

As a kid, I always worked. From the time I was in the fifth grade until I was in the ninth grade, I worked for my uncle's wife on Saturdays. She ran a wig shop in South Central Los Angeles. She would pay me depending on the sales that day. I would wash and comb out the wigs and take care of the display case. I was supposed to sell things like fake eyelashes, costume jewelry, and beads for braids, to sweep up, and run errands for her. Another thing I was supposed to do was watch for shoplifting. I was interested in the customers, and when they would try on wigs, I would get carried away with what they were talking about when I was supposed to be watching them. Some of them looked really young to me, but when they took off their wigs, they would be balding or have white hair underneath. They would just laugh and talk, and it was much better than having to be alone with my aunt, who was constantly making snide remarks about my parents and my family. I hated that, but I didn't have any choice.

When I was older, I helped my parents at their garment factory. Most of the workers were Latinos. Working side by side, we formed a certain kind of bond, but then there's always that difference if you're the daughter of the factory owner. I felt both my privilege and a sense of shared identification. It's easy for people who aren't in the factory day to day to say that the owners are exploiting the workers. Exploitation definitely goes on, but they don't realize that the whole family is working there without getting paid, and that self-exploitation is going on. You have to finish a whole shipment, and you won't get paid until the third week, but you still have to pay your employees. My parents had to borrow money at high interest to pay the employees, but no one made sure my parents got paid. Things were further complicated by the gender dynamics between me and the Latino male workers, who were very sexual towards me. Economically, I was above them, but they were asserting their power over me by harassing me. Koreans need to declare alliance with Latinos; then they have to address the issue of exploitation and socioeconomic differences. From there maybe you can start to think about some kind of solidarity.

There are many Korean and Asian American colleagues in the academy who think of getting their Ph.D.s as part of the trajectory of their lives, whereas I have this feeling that just about everything in my life was accidental. In some ways I envy their ease, their feeling that there's no contradiction and that they're in a place where they belong. They can have an intelligent conversation with their parents in English about their projects, but every time I visit my parents, they say, "What's that program you're in at UC Santa Claus [Santa Cruz]?" There's this incredible untranslatability in my life. When I was telling my parents I was going to major in English, they said, "Why do you want to major in English? You already know how to speak English." So I told them I studied literature, and they said, "Don't do that, because you have to compete with people who speak English better than you." There's such an untraversible gulf. I really envy those people whose parents not only understand what they do, but support them aggressively. I'm hoping that the next generation will not even have to worry about these questions. I really want them to feel a certain entitlement. That's the reason I'm committed to university teaching.

I love language and literature, but coming from my background, I always have to ask myself, "What does this matter?" That's why I've chosen to do something that's really interdisciplinary. One of the commitments I've made is to write a dissertation chapter on Asian women factory workers. Next to my computer, I hung a little pencil sketch of a Korean girl factory worker, to remind myself of what I missed becoming. It's sobering and humbling; no matter what I publish, no matter what I'm able to accomplish, I live with the feeling of being powerless to help my family. Every time you think you can do something, you're reminded of where you're from.

I adjusted fairly well to immigrant life, but I was always sensitive to the feeling that we weren't wanted in the U.S. When I felt disenfranchised and out of place, I always sustained myself on the thought that after I grew up I would be going back home to Korea. When I finally went back to Korea for a visit in the summer of 1988, I had such high expectations. When I got out of Kimpo Airport and saw the freeway signs in Korean, I had an overwhelming sense that I had come home. But gradually, through interacting with Koreans there, I kept being reminded that I was not Korean. They knew I was Korean American. They said "*hyŏga torakatta* [your tongue has rolled around]," and that's why I could not speak Korean well.

I was in a two-week program at Koryŏ University, and the Korean students would make huge banners addressed to the Korean Americans reading," Go home; you're misbehaving." They would stick things on our doors that read "go back home." It was really hard. Among the few Koreans I would try to talk to and engage, the women would be rude and the men would try to hit on me. They probably thought I was loose because I was Korean American. I felt so lost and disillusioned after meeting all this rejection that I spent the rest of my stay hanging out with other *kyop'os* [Korean Americans]. They were safe. After two months, I was able to blend better. I wouldn't wear certain things. You can't wear shorts or things that show your arms. That's how they could tell right away that you're from America.

In the U.S., I had always been very self-conscious about my body and the way other people see me as strange and alien. In contrast, I just loved the anonymity, the comforting sense of invisibility I experienced in Korea.

Although I could imagine myself living in Korea in the future, I knew I didn't have a natural, stable home there either, which forced me to rethink what "home" really means to me. When I came back to the U.S., I felt committed to live here without always thinking I was going somewhere else, which was really good for me.

I've been writing my own stuff for a while now. With several other Korean Americans, I put on the 1992 Korean American arts festival, which in many ways was a response to *sa-i-gu* [April 29, the first day of the Los Angeles riots]. It was a kind of exploration of what kinds of voices were out there in the Korean American community. We did it again in 1994, when I also edited an anthology of Korean American writings called *Writing Away Here*. What's been really rewarding for me is to move beyond thinking about my own work into thinking about how I can do something to encourage other Korean Americans to write and to make films. I actually enjoy that role more; in the long run, I think it's more socially productive. Also, I can get a glimpse of the ways my own life history intersects with other Korean Americans, beyond the personal to a much more communal experience.

The good thing about cultural work is that as we produce more diverse cultural articulations, it's hard for European Americans to continue with any one unified official image of Korean Americans. It's not even ignorance, but the feeling that they don't have to know anything beyond the most superficial cultural or ethnic symbols, like food, needs to be challenged. Being a person of color in the U.S. means that you have to know how to negotiate with people—I mean mostly European Americans—who are different from you. You have to speak their language and know their history, but on the most fundamental level they don't feel that way about you. They feel like you can entertain and amuse them, but they don't have to make an effort to find out things about you. It makes me so mad that I understand the white American mind so well just by being educated in the U.S. but that I'm such a mystery, such a blank, to other people, and they don't lose any sleep over it. I want to be a thorn in the side of the way the academy enables people to ignore many things, among them Korean American history and experiences.

People who don't have any political, social, cultural sense will just believe that *All American Girl* [87] is outright representation. I'm not concerned with those people; you can't change the world. When I first saw the show, I thought we should protest it, but now I think the best revenge is to get other expressions out there to contest it. We have to maintain the critical eye, but at the same time we just have to be productive.

I'm opposed to the idea of spokespersons. I think it's ridiculous for someone with the privileges I've had in my life to speak on behalf of the Asian American women or Korean women, which I'm always asked to do. It's hard because I'm trying to negotiate questions of invisibility; but I'm also saying that I'm not the one with the answer.

Everyone has a complicated life story with many detours, twists, and turns. I'm hoping that my story resonates for other Koreans. My story probably overlaps with someone else's story, whose story overlaps with someone else's. The stories are so layered that they can't ever be separated.

NOVEMBER 1994

Y. CHANG

House of Haesun

Warm and vulnerable-looking, Y. Chang [pseudonym] has wide-set
eyes and an almost luscious smile. She wears her feelings on her
face as she speaks, almost without pausing, about her life. She has
a remarkable memory for exact dates and figures as well as for
the taste of certain foods under certain circumstances. Born in
P'yŏngyang in northern Korea in 1941, Chang has lived in Los
Angeles since 1967. Her phenomenal success in small business has
been considerably slowed by a combination of factors, including
economic recession and the 1992 riots in Los Angeles.

I never saw my mother have a happy moment with my father. I told myself that if I ever married, I would devote my life to my husband and to making the marriage happy. That's how I treated Mr. Song.[88] I lived my life for him, but he treated me as if I were nothing.

For some reason, I still keep the crystal wedding ring he gave me. But he was never sentimental about me. The day after the wedding, we sold the gold jewelry I had gotten as gifts. How could anyone sell their wedding gifts the day after the wedding? When my husband got his first paycheck, though, I remember that he bought *pulgogi* [barbecued beef] for me. My first child, Dennis, was not even a year old, and I was pregnant again. Those were happy times.

Suddenly, he announced that he was leaving for America in two days. He had taken out our *chŏnse* [rent deposit lump-sum money]. I was six and a half months pregnant, and he told me to sell our Remington typewriter at the market and abort my baby. I did as he told me to; I got $120 for the typewriter, and then I went to a clinic to abort the baby. Two days later, he left. I remember the date—it was June 9, 1966, one year and two days after our wedding. I couldn't even go to the airport because I was still weak from the abortion.

Ten months later, on March 15, 1967, I joined him with our two-year-old son. He was studying at Claremont College. I started to work the day after I arrived. In the mornings, I worked at a sewing factory in downtown Los Angeles, and in the afternoons I was a maid, cooking and cleaning the rooms at the Oriental Students' Center. I earned $100 a week from the sewing factory and $40 a week from the Students' Center, plus two meals a day. There were forty-seven students at the center. One of them became a lawyer, one runs a big assembly plant, one owns a big dry cleaning shop, and another has a sewing factory. One of them was charged with murdering his daughter-in-law.

At that time, there was only one Korean restaurant in Los Angeles, the Korea House on Jefferson Boulevard near Western. There was one grocery store, on 35th and Normandie, called Oriental Food. There were several Korean churches.

We moved to Pomona when Mr. Song's school semester was about to start. Housing in Claremont was expensive, so we rented a place for $45 a month that was in a little better shape than a garage, except that it had large rooms. That's where we stayed until Mr. Song finished his Ph.D. in 1970.

I found work as a machinist at a General Dynamics factory. At that time, the Vietnam War was escalating, and many Koreans found work as machinists near the airport. I worked there from November 1967 until 1970, when Mr. Song finished his degree. I was paid $175 a week for 60 hours of work. The pay was good, so Mr. Song didn't have to worry. He could just concentrate on his studies.

Jenny was born in January 1968 at the L.A. County General Hospital. Mr. Song was taking his final examinations. I checked myself in at around 7:00 A.M., and my daughter was born at 11:00 A.M. Suddenly, I remembered little Dennis. I had to leave him in the car in the parking lot while I went in to give birth. I didn't have the money to pay $115 a night for the hospital stay, so they said I could leave, but they were required to keep the newborn baby at least twenty-four hours. So I walked out of the hospital myself and went to the car. Dennis was drenched with sweat, as if he had just taken a shower.

When I arrived home that evening, the seven other Korean students at the Claremont Graduate School were gathered at our place to congratulate my husband about our new baby. He didn't want them to know that we couldn't afford the money for me to stay in the hospital, so he made me hide in the filthy garage until they left. It was winter, and I was shivering with cold. Finally, I fainted. I woke up in the Pomona Community Hospital with my legs all swollen. One of my friends brought me some rice straw juice. She said it was good for afterbirth fever. Miraculously, it worked; the fever went down and the swelling subsided.

As soon as I checked out of the hospital, I went back to the machine shop, intending to work, but they said they couldn't take me back because I had just had a baby. So I got a job at the Montclair Convalescent Hospital as a nurse's aide on the 11:00 P.M. until 6:30 A.M. shift. That was five days after Jenny was born.

There was only one registered nurse in that convalescent hospital, but she was the owner and was never there. On my tenth day at work, two patients barged into my office and beat me up. The next day, I was fired for not properly locking up the office. So I went back to the machine shop, where I worked for four and a half more years. I did precision drilling for part of the Apollo II project.

Altogether, before I started working steadily at the machine shop, I had had about thirty different jobs: I milked cows on a farm, packed eggs at a chicken ranch, ironed in a laundry, fed horses, sewed handbags, all sorts of things. The first year I worked, I had thirty-two different W2 forms. All the checks went directly to Mr. Song. He handled the money. He gave me an allowance for housekeeping expenses. Every morning, I made his lunch, dropped off the children at a baby-sitter's in Chino, and went to work. Then I came home and cooked dinner for the family.

In early 1968, I enrolled at Mount San Antonio Junior College. For two years, I studied business management. I would rush to school after dinner for evening classes. I was taking the children with me and leaving them in the car with milk bottles. It was difficult, but I really enjoyed school. The first semester, I didn't understand most of the lectures. I repeated the same U.S. history course three times. The second time, I understood a little. The third time, I learned a great deal.

On weekends, for a time, I used to sell goods at the Azusa drive-in swap meet. I would go there at 2:00 A.M. on Saturday and Sunday mornings in our Chevy Impala station wagon. The merchandise could be displayed from the back of the car. I usually took the children with me; they would sleep in the front part of the car. I also used to baby-sit Sunday mornings at the Claremont Presbyterian Church for $4 an hour. The people there were very nice to me. One time, I didn't know that the clocks had been set forward one hour for daylight savings time, so I got there an hour late. The children were already gone, but the church gave me $4 anyway. And I used to work for an old lady who lived alone across from our place in Pomona. She paid me $50 a month for cleaning her house and giving her a bath. When the big earthquake hit in 1971, she fell off her bed and died. I remember that after she died, eight to nine people I had never seen before suddenly appeared and took away everything. I felt very sad for her. I still keep the pearl necklace she gave me as a Christmas gift before she died. Her grandson had brought it from Japan.

When Mr. Song passed his doctoral exams, I quit the machinist job and went to downtown Los Angeles to ask a Jewish dress manufacturer if he would lend me some sewing machines and give me some homework. He agreed to pay 35 cents for every piece we completed. After four months,

I asked for a subcontract. That's how I started in the sewing business.

On March 21, 1970, I set up a sewing shop in our garage in Pomona. I named the company Hope Manufacturing. After about six months, I got up the confidence to go to the downtown Los Angeles branch of the Bank of America to ask for a loan. I told Nicole Ford, the loan officer, that I had a 1967 Chevy Impala, and she said she could lend me $500. With that money, I walked up and down the streets looking for a "for lease" sign.

The first sign I saw was on South Main Street. They were asking $450 a month for a 2,500-square-feet space. On September 21, I leased it. I had to take the Greyhound bus back and forth between Pomona and Los Angeles. It took over an hour each way. I borrowed machines and posted an ad for workers. One October day, Maria showed up with her husband, José. They were from El Salvador. We became close friends; Maria worked for me for twenty-two years, until September 23, 1992, when the shop was closed permanently. Her husband worked for us for six years, and then he got a job as a bus driver for the L.A. Transit District. He was killed in a traffic accident. I bought a burial site for him at San Gabriel Cemetery.

Anyway, after we opened the shop, I went looking for an order. I met a Jewish guy in the elevator at the manufacturers' office on 9th Street. He asked me if I could sew, and when I said I could he told me to follow him to the seventh floor. It turns out that he was a manufacturer of ladies' dresses. He said he'd pay $12 apiece when I delivered the order. He told me to take as many as I could do.

I took too many; every evening, I took work to my friends in Pomona. I couldn't finish the order within one week, and I still had to pay wages. So I went to see Nicole at the Bank of America, and she talked to the manufacturer, whose name was Sid. He told me to bring whatever had been finished, and he would pay for the finished portion. Even though he shouted a lot, Sid was a nice man.

I think I was the first Korean who started a sewing business in Los Angeles. I was stupid; I told people in Claremont what I was doing, and within three months, they all came to downtown Los Angeles to set up sewing shops like mine. I was so hurt. They became my competitors. They even took my workers. Then Reverend Noh put an ad in the church bulletin and about thirty women applied to work for me. They were all skilled seamstresses.

We sold our Chevy and wanted to buy a used station wagon. Mr. Song never wanted to ask to borrow money himself; I had to go while he waited for me in the car a block away so that no one would see him. I asked a Korean pastor to lend me $200, and his wife wanted me to sign a note promising to pay her back in three months. When she could not see me, I cried about that. I also arranged to borrow $200 from another pastor's daughter-in-law. When I arrived at their house, they were having a *kalbi* [barbecued beef ribs] party in their garden. They asked me if I wanted some. Even though I was hungry, I said no, because I felt very self-conscious. On the way out, I grabbed two pieces of discarded meat on a paper plate. Some meat was still attached to the bones. I ate it outside, crying. On our way home, Mr. Song bought two sauerkraut hot dogs. I'll never forget how delicious they were.

We were able to pay off all the debt in three months. I was very lucky; the business grew fast, and we had to move the shop to the entire sixth floor. Then the Main Street shop got too small for us, so we moved first to 9th Street. In 1972, we moved to a factory at 6th and Los Angeles Street. Our family moved first to a two-bedroom apartment and then, on Memorial Day in 1972, to a house we bought in Monterey Park. Bernard, my youngest child, was born after we moved there.

When my business got large, Sid introduced me to some other Jewish manufacturers. Sid was a nice guy, but these men were nasty. Once this guy ordered five hundred blouses; I shipped them and went to collect the check, but when I arrived at his place, it was closed. There was no forwarding address. I had more than a hundred employees, and I had to pay them on time.

I went to see Nicole, who was now at the Chemical Bank. Crying, I told her what had happened. She did a little investigating and found out that he had an account at her bank. When he showed up three weeks later, she called me, and I rushed to the bank. I shouted at him, and a crowd gathered. He was so embarrassed. He said he would pay me with a check, but Nicole made him pay in cash.

I learned a lot of hard lessons. One time I signed a contract specifying 1,200 dozen ladies' nightgowns, and I thought it was 1,200 pieces. I understood that the contract was for $15 apiece, not $15 a dozen. About three hours after I got back to my shop, the building manager told me there was a big moving truck full of boxes for me. The driver said that there were two more trucks on the way. I realized my mistake and called the manufacturer to beg for a break. He said it was my fault and made me pay the $200 shipping expenses, which was big money at that time. I cried all night, but I learned a lesson.

Sometimes I got even. There was a guy named Max who always sent fifty pieces back deliberately, to delay payment. One time I took a big order of the most expensive items at his shop. We finished all the work, but we delayed delivery as long as we could. He kept calling, since he had to ship them out to the wholesalers and department stores on time. Finally, I called him back and said, "Max, I've learned from you. I have the merchandise ready. If you bring cash or a cashier's check, covering this order and everything else you owe that's past due, you can have it. Otherwise, you can't take a single thread." Then I hung up. He arrived with a company check, but I said, "You can stop payment on this check. I want cash or a cashier's check." He cursed and bitched for two and a half hours, but he finally brought a cashier's check. I called Nicole and said that I was sending a cashier's check to her and that she should call me when it cleared. I only let Max take the merchandise after she called me. That was one time I was not cheated by a Jew.

In 1975, one of the major Korean daily newspapers started its U.S. edition. The editor urged us to buy a printing shop. He said there'd be almost guaranteed profits, since he'd have us print the newspaper regularly. So we bought a print shop in Highland. But the editor got laid off, and we had to put $200,000 a month into the print shop. Soon all the money we were earning from my sewing business was depleted because of the print shop. We were cheated and lost lots of money.

At peak times in the 1970s, my company was grossing $400,000. I didn't know much about taxes or licensing at that time. We had 120 employees, all of them Hispanic. At first, we hired some Korean workers; once, we had thirty Ewha University graduates in the shop, as well as many pastors' wives. On Fridays and Saturdays, they would call members of their church all day long, using our company phone. If I said something, they would shout, "Don't you have a mother?" I couldn't make business calls because they were tying up the telephone. It was very difficult to handle those Koreans. Sometimes they would set up their own shop and take away twenty or thirty of my workers. Or they wouldn't show up when the work was hard, just when it was easy. So I started to cut down on Korean workers. I haven't used any Korean workers since 1975. That's why I was able to last so long in business. I have contributed to a lot of Korean community causes, but I didn't employ Koreans in my shop.

Korean garment businesses were booming between 1973 and 1976. We started the Korean Garment Association because the Jewish people were selling needles, thread, and materials at too high a price, and we wanted to order them together at a wholesale price. Before the Garment Association was formed, Korean contractors didn't have much problem with the IRS or state agencies, but through the publicity and activities of the association, they discovered that the Korean contractors were making money and came after them. In the end, we trapped ourselves. We had to pay more tax and follow the labor laws, so it became much more difficult to operate.

Sewing shops really made big money in the 1970s. Contractors easily spent $10,000 to $20,000 a night at wine houses. The real peak was between 1976 and 1979. At that time, if the association decided to sponsor a community project, the members would normally contribute $5,000 to $10,000 each. For me, making $100,000 a month was easier than blowing my nose or sitting on a chair.

The main reason why the association folded is that the competition among the Korean contractors became too fierce. Everyone was dumping on price, and no one was making any profit. When I started to work on Cherokee blue jeans in 1982, we did them for $4.75 per piece; ten years later, we were making them for $3.25 per piece. During the same period, everything went up, but our profit margin went down. Koreans went to manufacturers with envelopes full of cash to buy favors. First one contractor got shaky, then another, and finally one by one, they all fell. Association board meetings became places to gather information to be used for dumping, back-stabbing, and killing each other.

What really shook up the association was when the one of the officers got the members to invest in a condominium project in Koreatown in 1982. The condos were not selling well, but he gave a rosy speech, predicting that the building's value would skyrocket when Korean athletes and tourists would crowd into Koreatown during the 1984 Olympics. Thirty-two members of the association board signed on as partners, each promising to buy a unit at $130,000 to $180,000. We would just have to make payments for one year, and then we were supposed to have the option of either buying the property or getting all the money back with interest. I thought everyone signed, but later I found out that none of the ones who gave the speeches in favor of it at the meeting signed. I ended up paying $1,820 a month for ten years, in addition to the down payment. Nobody would take the condo.

The sewing business began to decline in 1985, and it was very difficult for me to pay an extra $2,000 a month for a condo I was not using. As a result of signing onto this condo project, seven or eight members suffered foreclosure of their homes. In 1990, I was finally able to lease that condo at $850 a month to the person who owned a rice cake shop. I begged him to just take over the place; I practically gave it to him free. Later he sold it at a good price and bought a home in Hacienda Heights. It was just bad luck for me. Even now, whenever I think about how I was cheated, I get so mad I can't sleep.

After the condominium scandal, the 1.5 generation decided to take over the garment association. Now they run it, but they don't give the time and bodily energy to the association that the first generation did. They want to handle everything with money. After ten years of struggling, they realized that they could not do it alone, so now they're starting to work with the old-timers.

The new workmen's compensation law was passed in 1983. The insurance premium was $2.06 per $100 payroll. We paid $40,000 for the year. If there was no claim, 89 percent of the premium we had paid was returned to us by the insurance company. I used the $30,000 that was returned to us in November for year-end bonuses for the workers. Things went smoothly for three or four years. During that period, the premium went up to $2.75. Then, in November 1987, the amnesty law [for the undocumented immigrants] went into effect. Soon after, the workmen's compensation lawsuits began to come in. [Chang implies that she had been employing undocumented workers, who were unable to enjoy American workers' rights before the amnesty.]

Our first case was filed by a woman who said that I pressured her to do her ironing overtime. She claimed that her accumulated tension caused a miscarriage and sued for $17,000 in damages. Investigators came to our shop three times. I fought her claim; it took four years to settle the case, and in the end the insurance company paid more than $110,000. She got only $6,000. The rest went to the lawyers and investigators.

The lawsuits multiplied. By the time we closed the sewing business altogether in 1992, I had been dropped by four different insurance companies. They wanted a three hundred percent premium; we had to pay $32,900 per month for the workmen's compensation insurance. Meanwhile, we were not even making $30,000 per month. I made a mistake by not having the business incorporated when I started, so the suits were directed against me personally. It usually takes $40,000 to $50,000 to settle a lawsuit out of court. The worst time was when three law suits were filed against me in a single week. That was the year I was dropped by several different insurance companies.

In August 1992, we closed the shop for a week. After some debate, we finally decided to close the shop permanently. If I didn't work for a year, I would save $500,000 in premiums and $300,000 in deposit. If we didn't carry insurance and settled out of court for $20,000 per case, assuming that I got hit with one law suit per week, it would amount to $1 million a year. We explored all the possible options, but there was no way out. So we decided to close down permanently.

On Monday, I went to the shop and announced that we were closing permanently. I told the workers, "If you want to sue, just come to me personally. If you sue, I will have to pay $60,000, and you will only get a few thousand dollars. I'm willing to pay each of you $10,000 cash. Please help me; I'll even sell my house." I had a worker who explained to the others that I had paid his lawyers $67,000, while he got only $6,000. I cried and told them I had to close down because of the lawyers. I promised to pay that week's paycheck on Wednesday and asked them to write down their estimated work hours.

When people in town heard we were closing, they came as if to console us, but what they wanted was to get our machines free. I felt really disgusted. Not long ago a guy who owed me $60,000 suggested that I give him the machines so that he could set up a shop, with me and my new husband coming to help so that he would be able to pay his debt. I said, "I am not dead yet. Get lost in five seconds."

In good times, "gold table" was my nickname. I never refused to donate to a good cause. Koreans are always trying to take advantage of a good-hearted person like me. Once I was told that twenty-five board members of an association I belonged to had agreed to chip in $2,000 for a scholarship fund. I thought it was a good cause and sent a check in. Later I found out that no one else paid, and the money I sent was used for a golf tournament. I was so upset. When the Korean Youth Center asked for a donation, I gave $5,000. For ten years, I financed most of the Korean Studies Association operations—the seminars, the publications, the travel expenses of invited scholars, the research projects. The association folded, but that was one organization I was proud of helping. Now that I can no longer donate money, I offer my time.

When my business was booming, newspaper reporters always wanted to talk to me. Whenever there was an interview, Dr. Song would coach me for two hours the night before, because he thought he would lose face if I said one wrong word.

I cried so much because of him. He never gave me a dollar. I would not have dared to divorce him if I hadn't been on the Garment Association board. Working on the board, I discovered my ability. I realized that no one could match my ideas. At home I was nothing, but on the board, I accomplished important things and gained confidence. I realized that I could stand by myself.

He never seemed to care about me. Bernard was born in January 1973. I can never forget what happened. It was a Saturday. I was on the freeway, on my way to work, when I started going into labor. I returned home, and the labor pains got worse until the water broke. I asked a friend to take care of the children and drove myself to the hospital. Mr. Song was out of his mind because he was running for the board of directors of the Korean Association. I couldn't reach him; there were no beepers then. As soon as I got to the hospital, the baby came; the situation was dangerous. On Monday, when I was supposed to check out, Mr. Song didn't show up. He was busy dealing with the election. So I wrapped the baby in hospital clothes and took him home myself. Then I left him with my friend and went to the shop. My husband just called the hospital three times; he never bothered to show up.

In the summer of 1976, Mr. Song said that he had to go to Europe for a seminar. The following month, he called from New York to say that he had been to P'yŏngyang to see his mother and wanted me to meet him at the airport. FBI agents were questioning him. I asked him who knew about his going to P'yŏngyang. He hadn't told me about it. He said that he had told the newspaper editor who had gotten us into the printing business and that he had left him all the legal documents for the house and the print shop in case something should happen while he was gone.

At that moment, I realized that this was not the man to whom I had promised my life. That's when I started thinking about separating from him. I started putting money I saved into an account under my own name. I never felt close to him again.

After 1976, I never responded to his rages. I just ignored him. I didn't deal with him for six years. It was difficult, but I waited until Bernard started high school. Then one morning, I just disappeared. I went to see a lawyer for an annulment and had the papers mailed to him. I didn't take anything. He gave away everything that had belonged to me; I don't even have my high school diploma. He didn't even give me my own photographs.

When my business was good, Mr. Song signed off on so many charge cards. I had to pay all his bills. After our divorce, he sold our house in Monterey Park. He and the children moved first into my condo in Koreatown and later to an apartment in Beverly Hills. I paid all the rent. I supported all the tuition and living expenses for the children. When Jenny graduated from Scripps College, he would not let me attend the graduation ceremony, but he charged the dinner expenses for the guests on Jenny's card, which meant that I paid the bill.

I remarried in 1987. My new husband is also in the sewing business. He's from a Buddhist family and goes to a Buddhist temple. We worked together until our shop closed. In the future, I'd like to have a coffee shop. The workmen's compensation premium is better there, only about $2 per $100 payroll.

I didn't donate a penny for the riot victims. They dug their own grave. Koreans are killing the California economy. They don't pay insurance and they cheat on taxes. The Korean Garment Association can't touch me because I know too much. No one pays more than $250,000 a year in taxes except me. People compete until they kill each other. There used to be only a few *noraepang* [song rooms] in town, and now there are over forty. They used to charge $25 an hour, and now they charge $13. If you order *pulgogi* [barbecued beef] at a Korean restaurant, the dish is filled with water. The meat suppliers put water on the meat and freeze it so that it will weigh more.

Koreans have to earn their living honestly. They have to pay taxes and vote. Otherwise, there is no hope. These stories must be told so that people can find out how bad Koreans are. They have to know how bad they are so that they can change.

Korean businesses are corrupt. Korean media are corrupt. Korean scholars are corrupt. It doesn't matter if they are educated or not, whether they went to college or are only high school graduates. They are all the same. I am learning so much. I don't care about material possessions. The only thing I want to do is get to know some good people.

JUNE 1994

PAUL KIM

Getting Real

A twenty-year veteran of the Los Angeles Police Department, Lieutenant Paul Myung Chun Kim was born in Korea in 1950. When he was fifteen years old, after one month of high school, he moved with his family to a small town in Oklahoma, where his father, a U.S.-educated ear, nose, and throat surgeon and professor of medicine at a Korean university, had procured a hospital position. Kim does not know why his father decided to leave Korea, where he enjoyed wealth and prestige and where the demand for his surgical techniques was high. "You'd have to ask my father why we immigrated," Kim says, "I can only guess. He died in a traffic accident on a snowy day in Michigan when I was eighteen. All I know is that after he died, our lives really changed. We were rich kids in Korea, but when we came over here, it was a totally different story. That's how our immigrant life really began." After the father's death, the Kim family was splintered: one brother entered the army; one sister married; and Paul Kim entered the Marine Corps. In 1975, he joined the Los Angeles Police Department. A stylishly-dressed and handsome man, Kim speaks with a combination of ease and intensity.

207

Whatever I say, I say as an individual. I cannot represent the Los Angeles Police Department. I can't represent anybody other than myself.

What happened in Los Angeles in 1992 was different from what most people think. I know, because I've been dealing with the Korean community for a long time now. I've been in police work since 1975, and most of my time was spent around Koreatown. I was already used to the players and the issues, so what happened was not a big surprise. I wasn't the only one who felt this way; several other people were issuing strong warnings, not only to the Korean community, but also to government officials and community leaders of other ethnic backgrounds that there were problems to be taken care of. The dispute with the black community was no big secret. The city council, the county, and even the state government and the governor's office were all well aware of it. But Korean people hadn't realized the magnitude of the things they were dealing with. And they focused on being victims instead of on solving the problems. I was very disappointed that too many Koreans spent all their time trying to prove to the world that they were victims. You get promises of money, but you don't get any money that way. "Treat us, recognize us as genuine victims, victims of racism, victims of oppression, victims of whatever." That doesn't even bring positive, constructive attention to the Korean community. So what if you were a victim? Get in line; there are 10,000 victims ahead of you. That's life in the big city.

A lot of good things also came out of the riots. I was a field commander on Olympic Boulevard in Koreatown when the riot happened; I saw a lot of things firsthand. I have absolutely no doubt in my mind that Korean people are the most energetic, enthusiastic, capable people, full of passion and emotions that could be very, very positive. I am not saying this because I'm Korean; this is what I saw. Within a few days of the riot, Koreans let the word out, from mouth to mouth and through some Korean radio stations, and they began to gather at Ardmore Park for what I think they called a "peace march." They came from all over, from San Diego to Santa Barbara.

Everybody, including me, thought that they would be very hateful and resentful, and that the potential for violence would be very high. The press was openly negative about Koreans gathering in a large group. The size of the crowd grew from a few hundred to a few thousand and started over-flowing out of the park itself. I heard there were 40,000 people, but I don't think anyone has an accurate estimate. It looked like *k'ong namul* [packed together like bean sprouts, each of which has a "face"]. There were five different factions participating that day, and five different leaders. You know how Koreans always talk about how Koreans are a hopeless people who can't unite, that it's in their blood, that they always screw it up, that they don't know how to compromise or negotiate. If you have 40,000 people behind you, it could turn into a major crisis. We had information that certain gangs from other ethnic backgrounds were going to come and do a drive-by [shooting]. I had gotten all the resources that I could—police, national guard, even officers from Fort Leavenworth Federal Penitentiary, the prison guards. They were all working with me that day, but there was no way you could protect the people if something were to happen. On that day, those five groups with such different backgrounds, those five factions, were able to work together.

During that march, I saw clearly that all those negative comments about Koreans are not always true and could be overcome in five minutes. They can organize; they can be model citizens. There were Koreans with brooms and trash bags, picking up after Koreans who dropped Kleenex, Coke cans, cigarette butts, whatever. They cleaned the whole place up, including the park. Does anybody know this? I have never, never seen anybody do this kind of thing in my whole police career. And remember, buildings were still burning. During the procession, there were people from other ethnic back-grounds making a lot of comments like "Go back to Korea"—that kind of stuff. "Who do you think you are?" But the Koreans were not violent at all. They were absolutely peaceful, absolutely respectable. To me, that was very commendable. I was not the only one who was impressed. If they want to, Koreans can organize one of the largest marches within a matter of days, doing it peacefully and neatly. And yet, they lack the basic infrastructure to communicate, coordinate, and develop some kind of agenda. That's the biggest homework assignment for Koreans right now.

The reason that they haven't done it yet is that they don't think they can. They're very fatalistic. They think it's hopeless, that Koreans are hopeless dingalings who should be occupied[89] by other people. They think they should kiss up to big-power people, that that's how you get ahead. There's no agreement even about whether or not Koreans should have a common agenda. Maybe there's nothing they want in common. These things should be addressed publicly before there can be any so-called "movements." Otherwise, it's basically a shotgun approach, and the things Koreans really need and expect will not be communicated to the decision makers, who get very sporadic and superficial communication out of Koreatown now.

Many people think that all Koreans go to Harvard and get A-pluses, that all Koreans are rich. This is not so. This community has a lot of tragedies, a lot of stereotyping in reverse. We have a lot of poor and uneducated people. Their living conditions are terrible, one crowded room, everyone working two or three jobs, without life insurance, dental or medical benefits, pensions, workmen's comp[ensation]. They think that they are helping each other by just passing cash back and forth, employers not paying benefits and employees not paying taxes, but in the long run, that's very destructive. People are really living an oppressed life, mainly because they limit themselves and because no one is really giving them any emotional support or encouragement.

Take the typical Korean family. Materially, they may be well off, but in every other way, they are living in poverty. They have absolutely no life, except working. They have no family life. No recreation, no reflection on anything, no participation in the world, nothing outside of materialistic pursuit, no real sympathy for other human beings, whether Korean or not. And if they do express some courtesy or compassion, it's in terms of money. Donating money gets them off the hook.

You know how Koreans always say they are doing things for the future generation. If that's true, the best thing they could do would be to clean up the Korean image. The way we treat other people—Latinos, whites, blacks —is horrible. And we don't even see it. It's like you have a big booger on your nose, and you're the only guy who doesn't know it. We don't appreciate their culture, even though we want them to appreciate ours. We don't differentiate. To us, it's all blacks, or all Mexicans, whereas when they say that all Koreans are the same, we say, "That's not fair. I didn't come from Tongduch'ŏn;[90] I came from Seoul." Koreans don't extend the same courtesy that we expect. I used to work in a black district. My job was to crack the crack houses. We would bust in with twelve officers and arrest everyone.

Most of the time, they were black people, and sooner or later they would recognize me and we would talk. They asked, "How come when Jews used to own stores in our neighborhood, they drove their ten-year-old Toyotas and pickup trucks, wearing just sweaters and work pants, but when the Koreans took over, they park their Cadillacs in the front—not in the back, but in the front—so they can watch it? The ladies come in with big gold rings. We start to think about where the heck they made that money. And we figure they made it from us." Koreans just show it around, and people hate them. I'll be in a store in South Central L.A. talking to some store owner in Korean when somebody comes in. And they do treat him like a thief, watch him, yell at him in Korean. But these are customers! There's no recognition of their status as customers and your status as the merchant trying to sell something. It's really ass-backwards. That's why our image is so bad. Improving this image should be the number one agenda item for Koreans. If nothing else, that could be used to unite Koreans.

I'll give you another example of our image problem. Why is it that when you go to Korean bars, the guys are all drunk? Why are ninety percent of the massage parlors in Los Angeles—most of them being nothing but fronts for prostitution—owned by Koreans, with the husbands manning the front desks and wives inside? We have to admit to certain shortcomings. Otherwise, there will be no true networking and no true representation. Without networking and representation, excuse the French, but you ain't going to get shit from the system.

I've seen lots of family problems—domestic violence, substance abuse, mostly alcohol, usually by the father, but not all the time. A lot of people use dope—cocaine, marijuana. People don't realize it, but Koreans are deeply involved in the manufacturing and distribution of "ice."[91] We've seized lab equipment, cash, guns, and dope from Koreans. Many different kinds of people are involved: when you run an operation, you need different kinds of people; some of them are the gangster type, others are the chemist type. Some are for money laundering purposes, some are for the business end. Women carry the stuff. It's a combination.

You would think, with drug distribution and so many Korean massage parlors, there would be a national network of organized crime like the Mafia, but there isn't. It's very fashionable these days to talk about "gang" problems. What is called a Korean gang is really not a gang. Most of the time, it's a business group or just groups of free-spirited entrepreneurs, except that they use illegal methods. There's no indication that there's any

Korean organized crime. It's dangerous for Koreans to promote the view that there is, because the government could bring down a lot of power on the community, which would be like smashing the wall of a house to kill a fly. The people who promote the idea of Korean gangs are journalists or people who work in counseling and need to get their grant funding.

I've done probably most everything these supposed "gang" kids are doing, but when I did it, it was just what teenagers did. Most of the original Korean Killers, or the KK, are dead or in state prison. Even those kids were nice kids. They went to Berendo Junior High right here in Koreatown. At that time, the Hispanic kids wouldn't let them use the gate to leave the school grounds. They made the Korean kids climb the fence, which was degrading. So these Korean kids got together at the American Burger joint on Olympic and Vermont to figure out what to do to fight back. They were capable kids; their parents were pretty decent people. But they wanted things too fast; they got into burglarizing other Korean people's homes. Once they were making money, they started going to Las Vegas. They became really professional burglars, using younger kids. They got into dope and violence with other kids like the [Chinese] Wah Ching. Then they got into weapons. In those days and even now, the pretty Korean girls would go with the Wah Chings because they were better looking and better dressers. They treated girls better and had better cars. The Korean kids were very rough; they looked like hillbillies compared to the Wah Chings. That's how the bad feelings got started. One of the first murders between the Korean and Chinese "gangs" was the Tai Hong murder,[92] over a very pretty Korean girl who wouldn't go out with Korean boys.

You know Korean parents. As soon as the kids start dressing like "gang" or getting an earring, they think their whole world is ending and their kid is ruined. But they're not ruined. I think parents run hot and cold, in extremes. At first, they put on too much pressure, but when their kids resist and rebel and stop listening, they give up too easily. The bottom line about relationships between Korean parents and their kids is that Korean parents don't teach their kids to be independent. That's why I say they are bad parents. The number-one job of a parent is to teach their kid to be independent, to survive on their own. They give their kids money, cars, whatever it takes, but they don't give them discipline. Korean American kids lose in terms of competing on the job. They are too soft. You ask them, "You're thirty-two years old and you still live at home?" "Yeah." "How do you drive that $50,000 car?" "I don't pay anything for my housing or food, so I have money. So I get a Cadillac with a special kind of engine." The parents are too nice. They go way out of their way to do things for the kids. The kids aren't willing to struggle. They don't have the work routine ingrained in their heads. They aren't willing to put in that extra mile.

My situation was different. In Korea, I went to Kyŏnggi High School.[93] I was a good student. I was interested in my studies, especially social science, history, and mathematics.

Then, suddenly, I was in a grade school in a small town of about 1200 people in Oklahoma. I hadn't even known we were moving until the week before. The biggest industry in the town was the Indian reservation and the Indian hospital. I was supposed to be in the eleventh grade, but they put me in the third grade, and here I was sitting with these third graders and not understanding anything. I was just looking around. They put me right next to the teacher. They were trying to be nice, but I was totally humiliated and angry. People would ask me questions like, "Do they have trees in Korea?" We were the first Asians they had ever seen who were alive. They used to call me Hop Sing.[94] I didn't think it was degrading because I didn't know any better.

Even back then, I knew somehow that if I got emotional, if I just dwelled on things, nothing would change, so I just tried to be active. I tried to play football, to be a kicker. Nobody beat me up. They may have called me names, but I'd heard worse stuff from Koreans. I was resentful not so much of what they did, but because of what I couldn't do. I had been class president every year for ten years in Korea, and no one had to tell me to study. I studied on my own and liked it. Then I came here and was flunking everything. Pretty soon, the only thing I did at school was math; I just lost interest in all the other stuff.

I ended up spending my senior year in high school by myself because my family moved. They didn't want me to transfer, so they just left me there. It made me too independent in some ways. I ended up staying with a couple —the man was Irish and the lady was Polish. Now that I look back, I learned a lot of good things about this so-called American culture: how hardworking, stable, focused, and giving these people are.

After high school, I started college, but I figured I was going to get drafted; it was just a matter of time. When I went in to get my physical, the army guys looked fat and sloppy, and the air force guys looked like mailmen. But the marines had short hair, shiny shoes, pressed uniforms, and trim bodies. I always wanted things to be very professional. I wanted to do a good job at whatever it was. So I asked the guy, "What does it take to change from the army to the Marine Corps?" He said, "Are you sure you want to do that? Most marines don't come back." I said, "I think I'll come back. What's it going to take to switch?" He said, "Watch me," and then crossed out "A" and put in "MC." That was it; I was in the Marine Corps.

I think I did the right thing. It was very, very demanding, but to me it was a very beneficial experience. If I hadn't gone into the military, it would have taken me much longer to assimilate into American society and to learn about organizational life, chains of command, and so forth. I learned how to get along with people, how to survive in a large organizational setting, about leadership, about keeping your mouth shut and putting your nose to the grindstone and just getting the job done. I did pretty well in terms of physical stuff. You wear a uniform with a stiff high collar and you have a short haircut, but I enjoyed it, and I did pretty well. My company commander called me in and said they were running out of lieutenants. Too many of them were dying and not being replaced. So the Marine Corps made an exception at that time and for a few years didn't demand a bachelor's degree for officer candidates. I had just had a year and a half of college. When I was finished with my enlisted training, they said that if I scored above 500 on the GRE test and passed the physical and medical exams and the interview, I could go to officer's candidate school.

That was a very radical thing. Even I wondered how it would look to have a Korean immigrant lieutenant in the U.S. Marine Corps. You can't even picture that! It was just not acceptable; it wasn't done. It was like a female going out for NFL football. And at that time, the Vietnam War was going hot and heavy. All the instructors were Vietnam vets. I can't repeat the words they called me—every degrading thing you can ever imagine. They called me "gook" and "Mongolian fuck." They didn't want me around. They thought I didn't really care, but I did.

Lately, there was a Japanese American guy from Hawaii who accused the Marine Corps of discrimination. Based on my own experiences, I have no doubt that they probably discriminated the shit out of him, that they gave him all kinds of hard time, trying to make him quit. But the main difference between me and him, besides the fact that I was going through the marines twenty years earlier, is that he was born and raised here, whereas I had only been in this country about four years at the time I went into the marines. I didn't know I could even complain. I didn't know I deserved any better treatment. I accepted what I got and went on. All I knew was that I wasn't going to quit. I knew they couldn't kill me; all they could do was give me pain and humiliation.

I think that the drill officers thought I would quit. But toward the end, I think they were impressed. So I went to officers' candidate school. It was tough, but I knew even at that time that it was good training, that it would fertilize my soul. It was mostly physical stuff. They're not looking for any Einsteins there; they just want to know how bad you want this.

I was going to be a career marine officer. Then I heard on the radio that they were recruiting police officers, and I thought that would be a good job. It turned out that the police department really agreed with me. There was adventure and excitement, and it allowed me to do things I wouldn't have been able to do otherwise. This is a good job for someone who's interested in learning about how human beings live and don't live together. This is a laboratory in action. I could get involved in different cases of my choice, and I could see the results. The first few years, I worked in patrol and traffic. In 1979, I went to the Asian Task Force. That's when I first got exposed to the Korean community.

Right now, I'm the acting chief investigator for the internal affairs division of the Los Angeles Police Department (LAPD). I hear every complaint in the city of Los Angeles. Being a police officer in a big city like L.A. is a rough business. Last year, we had six L.A. cops shot. Danger is not a joke. You've got to do what you've got to do to take care of yourself, too. This includes hitting and shooting people. But most police officers are very dedicated. They want to serve other people; they're concerned about what's right and wrong. There are some who are bad. Police officers don't come from heaven; they come from society, so the police department has whatever sicknesses you have in the society. We have people who use dope, people who rape, steal, and extort money, people who get involved in prostitution, extortion, beatings, you name it. When you have about 10,000 employees, you're going to have a little bit of everything. Then you have people like me in internal affairs who try to help out.

Three other Koreans came to the LAPD before me. But unlike them, I knew how to speak Korean. I've been around so long, that the people I've helped think I walk on water because sometimes I make things happen that nobody else can. A police officer is sometimes in a better position than a doctor, lawyer, or judge, to actually help somebody who is desperate. Let's say somebody is trying to do you in. What good is a lawyer? What good is a judge? But then there are people who hate me. They think I ruined their lives, and I have. I put them in jail; I took their assets away—their houses and their bank accounts.

There are some Koreans who think I should help them just because they are Korean. It's very hard. I say to them, "Listen, if I use your logic, and we were in Korea, how could I arrest anybody? Everybody would be Korean." But they still say, "We're Korean. Why are you arresting a fellow Korean?" Get real. That kind of attitude doesn't work. It's difficult to be a Korean police officer in Koreatown. But there's an absolute need for it. Someone's got to do it. It's a plus and a minus, a plus because I learned a lot and had a lot of opportunities to handle different kinds of police work. Also, I was able to help people who are truly in need, helpless people, and I'm grateful for that. But on the other hand, it took a toll on my personal life. It was very, very painful, in the sense that you're being sandwiched to death. You can't make the community happy, you can't make the department happy, you can't make yourself happy all at the same time. I'm telling you, sometimes I put in seventy, eighty, ninety hours a week for forty hours' pay. Being dedicated and into public service is fine, but there's a limit to everything. I'm very grateful; I've learned a lot about the community. It's been good that I have been able to play a positive role, but there's got to be closure to everything. There's got to be some other poor Korean guy who's going to have to do this thing.

What am I going to do in the future? I'm going to hit the Lotto and buy the state of California. Actually, I'm going to try for a promotion. I am the highest ranking Asian now. I'm what they call a Lieutenant II, a senior lieutenant. This is my third attempt at the exam for captain. I think I am the first Asian to even try the captain's exam in the LAPD.

Right now I'm also a full-time doctoral student in public administration. I have a weekly radio column, and I am on the Board of Governors of the California community colleges. My kids are twenty-one, twenty, fifteen, and twelve. I don't think I am a good husband. Now that I look back, I didn't pay enough attention. At the time, I thought I was doing the best I could. Now it seems pretty obvious that there were many more things I could have done. I should have been more serious. I took life as an adventure. I didn't abuse it, but I didn't really treat it like what it is, a very delicate thing. I treated it like a Mack truck. Now I'm of the opinion that it's totally wrong to think of the husband's role as being simply to provide the material stuff for the family. They might as well go on welfare. Uncle Sam is probably the best husband you can have, if it's just a matter of providing the material stuff.

And Uncle Sam never dies.

I think America was, at one time, a rich country, and now they have the mentality of someone suffering from poverty. When you give out welfare, obviously a lot of it is being wasted; that's just human nature. But it's probably the best investment you can make. They want to save money. How much money did we spend to bail out the savings and loans? Two dollars? Let's get real. Why pick on these people on welfare? They are being picked on because they can't defend themselves.

Some Koreans think that poor people in America are lazy. Ah, lazy, my foot! If those Koreans were in the exact same situation, do you think they'd do any better? I doubt it. You go out and try to get a job right now in South Central L.A. and tell me how easy it is! If you're a forty-year-old man with a wife and two kids, and you work at MacDonald's for $4.25 an hour, would you be a proud man? You're going to end up standing on the street corner in front of a Korean-owned liquor store drinking Old English, smoking, jiving, and bullshitting. That's what I would do. I ask myself, if I was them, would I be any better? And you know what? I would be a lot worse. I would be much more violent and less patient. I would be more "give me, give me, give me." I would be pissed! If I saw all these people enjoying whatever I didn't get a chance in freezing hell to get one percent of, I might as well get violent and destroy it.

It's very irresponsible of some of those Korean people to say those guys are lazy and don't deserve anything. When they come to me and talk about how we've got to improve the situation for Korean people, I tell them, "Listen to me. How can I improve public safety just for Koreans? I can't make it safer for Koreans here and not care about the Mexicans who live next door. If you want to improve the air quality, you improve it for everyone. You can't just clean up the air that goes into Korean nostrils." That's the Korean mentality. They think if they donate money to build a police station, it should be just used by Korean people. That's why there's an image of the ugly Korean.

When are we going to get out of this "Koreatown syndrome"? Look at Motown: they don't just sell their records to black people. Look at Chinatown. You see more white people than Chinese there. Am I right? When you go to Koreatown, what do you see? Koreans. Our kids are that way. Even if they are educated here, once they reach that glass ceiling in the American company, they come back to Koreatown and become more Korean than the people born and raised in Korea! You see them in

Koreatown hostess bars, like cows coming home or something. If you ask, "Hey, you were born here, you went to Hollywood High, and you graduated from Yale Law School. What are you doing here?" they say, "I like it here. It's my cultural heritage." Give me a break!

There are lots of ways we can contribute to this society. But we're too busy fighting among ourselves to develop a cohesive group with a common agenda. Things are not getting better with the 1.5 generation because they're not admitting we have these problems; they are still in denial. The relationships between the first generation and the second or 1.5 generation are like water and oil; they don't mix. They read different books and watch different movies. I tell you, Korean immigrants spend literally millions getting churches. They buy the real estate, they pay for the building, they have lots of programs. But who's going to attend that church ten or twenty years from now? Is that a good investment? They are pouring money into something that won't be used after they get old and die off. I don't care what Korean church you mention, but do you see any young adult types there? You see little kids, adult immigrants, and senior citizens. The middle is missing. The first generation may not have the language skills or the know-now, but they have the money. The 1.5 generation isn't strong enough yet. The two have to work together whether they like it or not, but their pride and emotions get in the way. There is such a leadership gap in this community that someone has to fill it, and I would like to see it be not just a Korean leader in Koreatown but a Korean who can be a leader for whoever else is in the area, period.

JANUARY 1995

ALEXANDER HULL
Cruise Control

Tall, lean, and nattily dressed, Alexander Hull grew up in staunchly conservative Orange County. Born at St. Mary's Hospital in Seoul in 1962, Hull is a baptized Catholic and a registered Republican. In 1973, he came to Los Angeles with his family to join his father, who had immigrated a few years earlier and had set up a hamburger shop in South Central Los Angeles.

My last name is Hull. My father spells it H-o-u, but I changed the spelling because people were mispronouncing it all the time. It kept coming out "how" or "hew" or "hu." My Korean name is Hŏ Bŏm-Sŏk.

I have two brothers: Raymond is seven years younger than I am, but Paul is only one year younger. We are very competitive academically, in sports, and in our social life. If one of us achieves a certain goal, the other one feels he has to do better. I think that this makes us both reach higher levels than we would have otherwise. Paul is in Boston, finishing his Ph.D. in education at Harvard. His wife majored in education at Columbia University. I got an M.A. at Harvard myself. Paul is more academic than I am; he's the brain in the family. I take on leadership roles in a lot of things. My father always encouraged me to become a leader; ever since I was little, he always told me to think big and worldly.

We were pretty well off when I was a kid in Korea. My father worked for the U.S. Eighth Army, and my mother was a fashion designer. She was a successful businesswoman with her own shop near West Gate with twenty-five or thirty employees. Until the day we left Korea in 1973, she was making patterns.

My formal education began when I started going to a preschool run by the Catholic church. That's where the foundation of my moral character was built. I really admired the nuns; I can still remember how strict they were about moral obligations, ethics, and etiquette. I was blessed that I never got onto a bad track. I remember a story I was told about heaven and hell when I was five years old. They said, "If you do bad things, you get locked up in hell for eternity." That really set me straight; I had nightmares about hell many times. After that, I was always concerned about not doing anything bad to my parents, my elders, or in society in general.

Even up until three years ago, I considered becoming a priest. I still get very emotional whenever I enter the church; my heart starts beating fast. I consider myself very religious, which for me means being deeply devoted to Catholic teachings, doing all the right things, and following the rules of the Catholic church. Being religious means being close to God, who is some Being up there who knows and cares about you. That is what really matters. You might say that I am a typical American Catholic. I think I am pretty consistent with what the bishops dictate.

My mother has had a lot of influence on me. She always prayed for us. We were the first to open up a Korean Catholic Mass in Orange County. I set up retreat programs and camps to encourage younger kids to come to church. Now, there are three Korean congregations in Orange County, with thousands of kids attending.

I'm not as involved in the church as I used to be. I go through certain phases. Whenever I come back to the church, I get closer and more devoted to God. I was really close to God when I was a college sophomore; that was when I seriously thought about becoming a priest. Three good friends from the church are priests now. I saw so much corruption and hypocrisy in the society, and I thought going into the religious order was a good way out; but then I learned that even within the religious institution, there are also power structures that tend to corrupt people. It's the same as everywhere else. I got disenchanted and decided not to pursue the priesthood.

Celibacy was a concern for me. I tried to be celibate and concentrate on religious thoughts. I visited St. John's Vocational School, where priests are trained, and stayed with some friends who were seminarians there. Eating, sleeping, and praying with them for a couple of weeks, I learned a lot, but it was not quite the life-style I wanted for the rest of my life. I decided that there are things I could do outside the religious order that might be more effective. Still, the possibility of becoming a priest is always in the back of my mind. I'm afraid to go to Mass often, because I get too close. Sometimes I stay away intentionally. It's like running away. I don't know; someday I may just become a priest.

When my family moved to Los Angeles from Korea in 1973, I expected to see a beautiful city with nice cars and nice streets, but the area we moved into was nothing like that. My father had opened a hamburger shop at Vermont and Manchester called Tokyo Cafe. We moved to a place right behind the shop. The area was ninety-eight percent black, and gang activities were intense. It was a real culture shock for us. I had thought of America as very white and Anglo-Saxon.

I started working as soon as I got here. I was only eleven, but I was tall and could pass for fourteen or fifteen. My father was shorthanded, so I helped him after school. I took orders and washed dishes. I also went shopping with my dad at the Los Angeles central market. I learned very quickly what it is to be in the American working class.

I interacted a lot with black people, and I understood a little about race issues early on. We never had any serious confrontations with our neighbors. My father used to take his hose and clean the whole block early in the morning, and the black merchants and residents would come out, dumbfounded, wondering why this guy was doing the whole block. My father spoke pretty good English, and he could joke around with the customers. I pretty much grew up with black people, and we had pretty good relationships with them.

My father had us kids commute to Gardena, where it was ninety-five percent Japanese American. We were in America, but at school, everyone looked like me, although there were only about a dozen Korean students at the school then. I lived in a very black area and went to school in a very Japanese area. It was very funny, actually.

After about a year and a half, we moved to a mixed neighborhood in Long Beach. It was one-third Hispanic, one-third black, and one-third working-class white, and there were very few Asians. We bought a market from another Korean, and I went to Burbank Elementary School, which was pretty much a white school. I remember coming home, dropping off my books, and riding my bicycle ten blocks to my father's market, where I would fill up coolers, bust boxes, and put up stock.

I should have been in the fifth grade, but they put me back a grade because of my poor English. Within three months, I got moved up to the sixth grade because I was better in math than the other kids. People there saw us as good students. They kept putting us into a positive light like the model minority stereotype, which was good for me, because I took it as encouragement to do better.

A lot of black kids came into our market. They would shoplift little things, like candy and potato chips. Adults—even grandpas—would shoplift, too. It was a constant problem. After a while, you start perceiving everyone walking in the door, black or Hispanic, as a shoplifter. They were relying on food stamps all the time, and when they ran out of food stamps, they would shoplift. Maybe they were hungry.

One incident really changed my life. I was working at the market after school one day, and a black guy came in with a gun. My mother was sitting in the back, and my father was at the cash register. I saw bullets in the barrel. I was thirteen then, and I was really scared. I felt completely helpless. The whole thing seemed to take a very long time. My father was in charge of the whole situation; he knew exactly what to do. He said, "OK, buddy, you want money?" And then he took out all the cash and handed it over. "You want more? You want the change, too?" He wasn't scared. He stayed in control to prevent the guy from getting nervous. "You take the money. No problem," he said, and the guy took off. We had a pretty good relationship with the neighbors; he did a lot of things for them, like giving them food and letting them take merchandise on credit. But still that incident happened.

From that moment on, my view of life was very different. I was on cruise control, and after that I said, "Whoa, life could end at any time. My parents could die at any time."

We moved to Orange County, to a predominantly white neighborhood in Garden Grove, when I was in the seventh grade. I was the only Korean kid in the junior high school. One of the reasons we moved there was that my father's Korean friend decided to open a liquor store in Costa Mesa. We invested all the money we had earned for the previous four or five years into that store. My father had known this friend for twenty years; he trusted him completely and signed the contract without even reading it. It turned out that it was not a partnership; he realized that he was working under his friend, receiving a salary instead of a profit share. We decided to get out of the arrangement, but the bank had a lien on our house, and our assets were completely frozen. That was the only time that we were concerned about whether there was going to be anything on the dinner table. My mother went through a lot of hardship, because she had worked so hard up to that point, and my parents argued a lot. As the oldest kid, I tried to be strong, but it was difficult for me also. I worked at a pop and taco stand and delivered newspapers.

Then we ran into a nice Korean with the same surname as ours who had lived in Orange County for many years and owned a big nursery. He loaned us some money, and my parents opened a Korean market in Anaheim. We would drive up to Los Angeles to pick up vegetables and *kalbi* [spare ribs]. I was only fifteen, but I drove the van to Los Angeles regularly. It's very hard to circulate good merchandise. We had to throw away a lot of vegetables and meat because we didn't have enough customers. I know from experience what Korean market owners have to go through.

The issue of discrimination didn't even figure into my life until I went to high school. Except for some *sansei* [third-generation] Japanese friends I used to go surfing and swimming with, my friends there were mostly white, blue-eyed blonds. They saw me as different from the Vietnamese kids; they would say, "Oh, he's not Asian; he's Alex." But by the time I was a sophomore, things suddenly changed with a sudden and dramatic increase in the Asian population. There was a big influx of Vietnamese kids.[95] They weren't ideal students. They had been marred by the violence of war, and they were very disorganized and, in a way, angry toward the U.S. government and toward Americans. They would bring knives and machetes to school. The perception of Asian students in Garden Grove and at our high school started to change for the worse.

Nevertheless, I did my best academically and was captain of the soccer team. Then in my junior year, I ran for student body president, and the issue of race came out openly in the election debate. There were three candidates: one white female, one white male, and me. My father came to hear the debates; he was the only parent in the audience in the football stadium that day. I thought I was the most popular of the candidates. After my speech, during the question and answer session, one student stood up and said, "Alex, do you perceive any racial tension in this school?" My supervisor tried to protect me and said, "You don't have to answer that." Until that moment, I thought I was white, because my buddies were white and they treated me like I was white. I didn't think I was perceived as a minority, an Asian, or someone different from them. At that moment, it all clicked: maybe I am Asian. So I said, "I don't see a major conflict here, but I do see the differences." Something like that. The next question was even worse. It was something to the effect of, Since you are Asian, are you going to help Asians more?" They were trying to isolate me from Alex Hull, the student at Bolsa Grande High School, to Alex Hull, an Asian minority student who wanted to come into an Anglo-Saxon Protestant student body and disturb the institution. It was very dramatic for me. I walked out, very hurt and angry. But it was a good experience for me. It was an awakening. The racial issue at school got to the point where it was very explosive.

I continued on as a senior, being active in sports and serving as a member of the Western Association of Secondary Schools and Colleges accreditation committee. I was asked to write a report about the school health system. Then, in the second semester of my senior year, another incident occurred. The advanced biology teacher called out all the Asian students to go to the nurse's station to be tested for TB. I was very angry. They were isolating all the Asians. It was like holocausting. I never had a TB problem, and I was not going to go, so I walked out of the class and kicked the trash can outside the room as hard as I could. I never went to the nurse's station. The teacher was really surprised, because I wasn't usually like that at all.

We sold the Korean grocery market in Anaheim after a few years and bought a liquor store in Lakewood. Eventually, we moved down to Sunset Beach in Orange County. My parents ran the liquor store for a year and a half, and then they bought another liquor store in Sunset Beach and moved down there, to 19th Street and Pacific Coast Highway. That store was very busy. I had to work there almost every day when I was a senior in high school. Business was good. Talking about the American dream, we bought a house and had a Mercedes. But my parents were working sixteen or seventeen hours a day, every day of the week. Even our Thanksgiving dinners were brought in by neighbors. We couldn't close the store. In 1991, after having it for fifteen years, they finally sold it.

My father had bought some property during the real estate boom of the late 1980s, and when the economy shifted, he was under a lot of pressure from the payment obligations. Then one day in 1991, he came down from his office bent forward and clutching his stomach. He said, "I have stomach pains; you'd better take me to the hospital." He was taken into surgery right away for a perforated stomach. Just before they wheeled him into the operated room, he called me over, grabbed my hand very tight, and said, "Alex, you've got to stand very strong."

I did not go back to school that semester.

When I was a sophomore at UC Irvine, my mother was in a major car accident. She had a brain contusion and was hospitalized for a long time, and she had health problems for several years after that. My father could not concentrate on his business. His mind was with my mother. He needed help, so I dropped out of school to work in the store. I was nineteen at the time. This experience made me stronger and helped me understand how important it is to be financially secure; you have to have a backup plan to take care of the family when you get sick.

I was part of the family business from elementary school through college. As the eldest son in the family, my first obligation is to the family. One of the reasons I went to UC Irvine was that it was close to the business. My brother Paul also helped. He had much better grades than I did, and he could have gone to an Ivy League university, but he went to UC Irvine also. We took turns Saturday nights and Sundays. Sometimes we had to help at the store when we had term papers to write or exams to take. I wasn't able to fully concentrate on school work, but I don't regret anything, because both my brother and I were able to pursue our goals at Harvard eventually.

I think my parents accomplished their objectives in coming to the U.S. one hundred percent, because they came for our education. Our youngest brother, Ray, is thinking of switching from public administration into education also; he enjoys teaching.

During the early 1980s, there was high anti-Asian feeling because of Japanese excess exports. Customers would come in and make racial remarks, like, "You Nips, go home. You don't belong here." They were ignorant people; still, it hurt. I considered myself an American. I voted ever since I registered; I was actively involved in political parties and community affairs. I planned to do my best to improve my community and my country, which is the United States, after graduation. But hearing these comments from people who should know better—middle-class people—was mentally damaging, especially when they picked on my parents. I would just get emotionally overwhelmed.

I remember one incident when a customer walked in. We greeted him, "Good evening, sir. How are you?" but he didn't acknowledge us. He just grabbed a bag of ice cubes and proceeded to walk out the door. I said, "Excuse me, sir, you have to pay for that." "Fuck you," he said. "I'm taking this from you, you goddam Nips. You are not going to do anything about it, because you are Asians." I just exploded and argued with him until he finally threw the ice on the floor and walked out, furious.

I became aware of my Korean identity during my freshman year in college, where white students would hang around with whites, blacks with blacks, Asians with Asians. There were a lot of *yuhaksaeng* [foreign students from Korea] and recent immigrants, and they weren't the best influence for me. They just had parties and smoked cigarettes, and I didn't go to parties or smoke. I was like an oddball. I didn't belong with the white people; they were into their fraternities and they saw me as an Asian. Korean students saw me as an American. I was alone or hung around with a couple of students here and there. I was very lonely.[96]

During my senior year, in 1982 and 1983, I got involved with the Korean American Coalition[97] and started helping with voter registration in Orange County. That was the first time I became aware of many Korean community needs. As I got more involved in politics, I wanted to work in Washington, D.C., so I applied and was selected as an intern at California senator Pete

Wilson's office. Here was a little punk from Orange County who had never left California before, walking in and out of the Senate, attending subcommittee meetings, meeting all kinds of distinguished politicians, going into the White House. I would pick up the phone, request a document or some information by saying that Senator Pete Wilson wanted it right away, and the person on the other end of the line would jump, saying he'd get it there tomorrow. I was only twenty-two, and I had so much power; I felt like an invincible god.

Next I was chosen as a paid intern. I worked at the security clearing office of the State Department. We dealt with Nazi war criminals, asylum cases, defectors, Eastern European scholars, Chinese, North Koreans. I did extra work on special task forces in the evening hours. The work was interesting, but I felt I was always being watched. What was worse was that I didn't know who was watching me—the CIA, the Korean government, the Chinese, or the North Koreans. It was too intense for me to handle.

I'm a registered Republican. I have a pretty conservative perspective. I don't agree with the liberal views on Vietnam and Korea. I don't agree with the idea of pulling U.S. troops out of Korea. But in terms of domestic issues, I tend to be open-minded about the need for diversity and about the concerns of minorities, meaning not just race but also class. Many Catholics oppose abortion, contraception, gays, and so on. It has been a constant struggle for me, but through my involvement in the community, working with people of different races, I am understanding more different points of view, and I'm not as dogmatic as I once was.

Right now, I'm an entrepreneur. I work for a corporation with a retail bridal shop, a tuxedo shop, and a photo shop. My parents are involved with the bridal and tuxedo shops. I'm also involved in the Wilshire Charming School and the Excel Education Centers. In the Charming School, we train models and teach people how to dress as well as etiquette, table manners, dating manners, and so on. Our clients are professionals, students, housewives, and prospective brides. In the Excel Education Centers, we help students get into the best colleges they can. Also, I coordinate weddings, parties, fashion shows, parades, festivals, and modeling and beauty contests. I do my work right in the middle of Koreatown.

In two months, I'll be thirty-three years old. The main reason I'm still single is that I was not allowed to date when I was growing up. My mother made me focus on studying, and my father said, "Study hard now; after you've finished studying, you'll have plenty of women to choose from."

That was ingrained in our minds. We never experienced relationships with the opposite sex; we just devoted ourselves to studying, sports, and working. When I finished graduate school, I was twenty-nine; by then, most of my peers were married, and some even had kids. Like everything else, there's a certain time frame around marriage that you have to be sensitive to.

Lately, many of my friends are getting separations and divorces. They got married in their mid-twenties, had kids, and then found out it wasn't working out. In a sense, I'm glad I didn't get married early. Divorce is much more common among the 1.5 generation than it used to be. First, the ladies have become much more assertive and active in society. They are economically independent and have much more flexibility in terms of managing their time. They're not willing to take a lot of stuff from the guys. Most Korean American guys I know, except for a few, have very traditional Korean male views on marriage. This is true even among those who came here very young. They think of a wife as a second mother, and they expect their wives to take care of the cooking and cleaning. It's because of their socialization; they grew up in immigrant families and usually attended Korean churches.

In a sense, we maintain two standards. In the mainstream society, we present ourselves as liberal, open-minded males who open car doors for women and so on, but when we are within our own community, in the house, at the church, or in community meetings, our traditional male inner values come out. I think Korean American females resent that because they want to be treated as equals.

I tend to be open-minded about gender because my father is. Whenever we have a large party, he cooks. He's very sincere in helping my mother with housework. He respects women's ability to pursue their own careers. My mother was active in the 1960s as a designer; there weren't many Korean men who would have accepted that. We saw my father's example when we were growing up.

I solemnly believe in the institution of marriage. According to Catholic teachings, marriage is one of our sacraments, something that should last a lifetime. I am very cautious about who I date. There is more to it than looking at a pretty face; outer appearances last for only a certain time. I expect my future wife to be career-minded. I don't expect her to stay home, but I do expect her to be a good mother, to be there when the kids need her help. I will have to talk with her about how much she would want me to share. I am willing to share, but I don't know if it would be on an equal basis, unless she is intellectually inclined.

On the one hand, I'd like to get married soon. On the other hand, I am afraid, because for thirty-two years I have been used to this freedom. I can stay out late with my business associates because I'm single. I can spend ten or twenty hours more time working than my competitors, and I use that to my advantage while pursuing my career. In a sense, I want to be free to do as I am doing right now, but when I do a large project like an advent fashion show, I feel lonely on the way home because I don't have anyone next to me who can share the experiences I have, like, "Wasn't it great when she came out in such and such an outfit?" One of the ways I fight postmortem depression is to continue on with another project right away. I keep myself very busy and try not to think about the issue of relationships too much.

DECEMBER 1994

SERENA CHOI

Head of Household

At twenty-seven, Serena Choi [pseudonym] supports her mother and herself with her earnings as a hairstylist in downtown Los Angeles. Guarded at first, she softens as she begins to talk about her childhood. She sits with her slender shoulders thrown back when she recalls her family's struggle to make a living after arriving in Los Angeles, and there is a trace of anger in her voice. Choi was born in 1966 and came to the United States when she was eight years old.

I came here in 1975 through my first aunt, who was already here in the 1960s. My father passed away when I was almost three, and my aunt asked my mother, "Why don't you bring your kids over here? You can raise them here; it's easier, and they can learn two languages." At that time, it was hard to get a visa to come to the U.S., so we waited two years. When I turned eight, that's when we came—my mom, my brother, and me. Mom didn't have a job or anything. She never really had to work in Korea.

My father was a surgeon and a pharmacist. We had property, a house, a maid, a car. All I can remember is playing at home and enjoying life in Seoul. Then my father developed pancreas and lung cancer. I remember some moments with him, but not very many. All I knew was that he always had to smoke. When he was sick, he wouldn't let us near him. He would always say, "*Ka, ka* [go, go]." He was constantly coughing, sitting in his room. Maybe the last year of his life, he didn't really play with us.

I still have pictures of him.

When we came to L.A., we didn't know anything. Nothing! My mother did bring some money. She sold everything, and we had quite a few things. We got this room on 4th Avenue near Olympic Boulevard. It was in one of these hundred-year-old houses you can still see in L.A. It had twelve or fifteen rooms. We lived in the attic, a small little attic, sharing a bathroom with I don't know how many people. Later we moved into an apartment.

We couldn't get any help from anybody else, even though my mother's side of the family is here in California, near San Jose. My grandparents are here, too. We got here last, and it seemed like they had their own lives to live.

My mother worked at an earring factory for about three years. When I turned about thirteen or fourteen, she started cleaning apartments and buildings. During the summer, all three of us worked full time, cleaning apartments, mostly in the [San Fernando] Valley. She'd clean the kitchen, and I'd clean the bathroom. I just learned how to do it. I turned into a pro after cleaning hundreds of bathrooms.

For one year, I was cleaning apartments on weekends and during the summer. For another year, we worked at a bank every single day. It was a big bank with three floors. I cleaned the bottom level, Mom cleaned the first level, and my brother cleaned the top level. Every day after school, between 7:00 and 11:00 P.M., we would clean. We'd get home at midnight, eat a little, do our homework, and go to bed by 1:30 A.M. Then we would wake up early to go to school, come back from school, do a little homework, eat something, and then get to the bank to start cleaning.

I remember that the elevator got stuck once. The emergency alarm went off. My mother was stuck inside; I was on another floor, and my brother was on another floor. She was stuck there for about an hour, getting scared. I had to find someone to get her out. Among all those places she worked, a lot of things happened. It was very hard. Like the fumes; you don't use Ajax, you use industrial cleaners. She hurt her knees, her elbows, her fingers. They still hurt her. The skin gets really saturated all the way through, then it gets dry and splits, especially on the fingers and feet. The split skin just won't close up. It never gets smooth.

My mom is a very enthusiastic, optimistic lady. She's very strong and independent. She raised us to become human beings. I really respect her a lot. She was by herself all this time, a widow after age twenty-eight or so. My parents had just gotten married, and a few years later, he died. She just decided to live her life for us, not for herself. Being around her has made me stronger. I didn't want to live my life the wrong way; I would rather do hard work than get into something bad.

As I grow older, I want to make sure she gets all the things she never had. She says that she doesn't need anything, that she doesn't want anything, that she just wants me to be next to her, loving her; that's all she wants. But I don't think that's right. I will do whatever I can do for her, whatever she wants, whatever I can provide. It's not easy, but I just couldn't let Mom work anymore. She hasn't worked for a couple of years.

Outside work, I spend a lot of time with my mom, believe it or not, even at my age. I try to take her out as much as possible, because she's at home all the time. On weekends, once or twice a week, I take her out to dinner, to get her out of the house. I take her to places she's not familiar with—not Korean places but American ones. I like international food and restaurants, art, and things like that. I'm not really hot about Korean food and recreation.

I know I went through a lot with her. I started working at really dirty jobs when I was thirteen or fourteen years old, and I never really got to study. I wanted to study hard and go to a good college and become somebody, but I just couldn't do it.

My brother and I both graduated from high school. We worked a good solid three years with my mom. Then my brother went off to college at UCLA. He did very well; he's the studious type, very scholastic. He got a B.A. in sociology. I wanted to go to college also, but I just couldn't. After my brother graduated, he couldn't really make a lot of money, so I had to do something. I was planning to go to college and become a lawyer; that was my goal. I applied to a couple of colleges and got accepted. I just wanted to see if I could get accepted. I was pretty proud of myself. But I couldn't go because I needed to support the family. I guess the doors didn't really open up straight. Always on the left side or the right side.

About four years ago, my mom got sick and had to go to the hospital. The doctor said we had to remove her moles or she was going to end up with cancer and die. She didn't have any insurance because we couldn't afford it. For the surgery, I had to use all the cash I was saving up for school. Then my brother had a severe stomach pain, and got diagnosed at UCLA with a minor stomach ache. They said, "Drink some orange juice and we'll call you," but they never did. I was trying to take him to the USC hospital to have them check it, and his appendix burst on the way. He was dying; poison was spreading all over his body. His surgery took almost four hours, with my mother going crazy. He stayed in the hospital for three weeks. He had to skip school for a year. He couldn't walk; he always had to lie down, and for nine months, he had to change the gauze four times a day. The doctor who almost killed my brother practically got down on his knees, begging me not to sue him. I could have, but I didn't, because my brother was saved, and I figured that God had saved him, so I didn't want to ruin someone else's life. If he had killed my brother, I would probably have killed him, destroyed his career, whatever.

I went to a beauty college at night when I was in my first year of high school because I wanted to get a skill, just to get prepared for my future responsibilities. I went to night school, and then I got a license. As soon as I graduated from high school, I started working. I'm not going to say I'm the best, but I think I'm pretty good. I didn't really want to get into this field, but I did. It's been about nine years I've been doing this. It's providing me with a living, for me and my family. If I wasn't here, it would be very hard. We're still having a hard time. Whatever comes in, goes out, which makes it hard to make a living.

I don't work for the shop; I lease the space. I've worked downtown for five years and established a certain amount of clientele, and it just grew slowly from there. My customers are all professionals—lawyers, bankers, investors, high-position type people. I don't know how I ended up with those kinds of people as clients, but I did, and I feel very fortunate.

Most of my friends are married with kids. I don't really like to visit them. When I go, I take something for the kids, and something for the couple. I'm sick of doing that, but I don't like to go empty-handed. Going over there, chit-chatting about this or that, like about how I don't have a husband and am not married, I think, "Why am I here?" I stay for about an hour and then leave.

I'm going to turn twenty-seven next month. I'm going to keep working until I meet someone. I'd like to meet a Korean man who would respect my mother. That's very important to me. That's what I'm looking for. I don't care what he looks like or what he has, as long as he has that kind of mind and heart. But a Korean man would be better than an American man. It's more comfortable because we have a small family. We'll see; I don't mind being on my own. I feel OK. People who are rich have problems. They owe debts here and there, the same as me. Just because you make OK money doesn't mean that everything's OK.

When I have a little bit of time, I want to go back to school, maybe get a degree, study law if I can, or maybe psychology. I'd like to get into the psychiatric profession or into counseling or something. I realize it takes many years, but if I get situated, I would like to do that. I speak English and Korean pretty fluently. I write, read, and speak Korean. I speak English only at work, because most of my clients are Americans.

At home, I speak Korean with my mother. She still can't speak English. She understands a few words, but she can't really have a conversation. I spoke English till I got to high school. Then I picked up Korean again, and since then, I've never lost it. I would like to marry someone who can speak Korean, because I speak Korean and my mother speaks Korean. I couldn't marry someone who's not Korean because I don't want to have a mixed child. It's not being discriminative [sic] or anything like that. I want my child to look Korean.

Last year I almost got married to one man who was seven years older than me. We were formally introduced. A couple months later, he introduced me to his parents. We all sat down, traditional Korean-style, in this restaurant.

His father was on time, but his mother was thirty minutes late. She was coming from the sauna with her friend. She sat down and started counting my age with her fingers. She says, "You don't have a father?" I say, "No, ma'am, I don't have a father." She asks, "Does your family own any business?" I say, "No, ma'am , we don't own any business." "What does your mother do?" I say, "I don't let her work right now; she's kind of ill, so she stays home." "So you're the head of the household?" Her eyes just went, "You don't have a father? You grew up without a father? How were you raised?" She was trying to start an argument. The father and son interrupted her and told her to stop.

She was against me that day because I have no father, and because of my not being rich like them. I never met a woman like that before. If she'd been an American, I would have said something, but I couldn't say anything. I just shut my mouth and thought, "Let's get this thing over with. Get me out of this restaurant as soon as possible." She has everything she wants; she has three sons, and every one of them is married but him. She never attended their weddings because she didn't like the wives they chose, so she wanted her number-three son to be married the way she wanted.

Her son was like a mama's boy, as they'd call him in the American style. He wanted to follow his mother. He met my side of the family, I met his side of the family, and we were all going to meet. Of course, I had my doubts. We said our good-byes at the beginning of this year. I felt hurt that he couldn't just come out straight and say, "I want this woman to be my wife." He didn't have the courage. He even told me he couldn't do it. I just said, "OK. I have the courage to try, but you don't." So last year I thought I was going to get married, but it didn't work out. I guess it wasn't the right time and the place.

I've never been back to Korea. I sent my mother seven or eight times, and my brother went once. I would like to visit, even though I would not want to live there. This is my home; I grew up here, and I feel very comfortable here. I have my friends here, not there. I like the people in L.A.; everyone looks friendlier than in Korea. I like the work spirit and the freedom. You can speak out here. In Korea, you really can't; if you say certain things, they'll hit you.

JULY 1993

SANDY LEE

Non-Traditional and Korean

Sandy Lee was born Sandra Jane Thomsen in Oregon in 1972. She grew up in Nevada and moved to California with her mother when she was in high school so that she could establish state residency and attend the University of California. Because of California's economic problems, her mother returned to Nevada, which offered better employment opportunities. Sandy's mother came to the United States on a visitor's visa in 1971. She soon married Bruce Thomsen, a white American who had been a Peace Corps volunteer in Korea. Thomsen is not Sandy's biological father. "I pretty much figured it all out," says Sandy. "I know she was married to this man when I was, you know, conceived. But my father, who still lives in Korea, is supposedly her first love. He visited her in the U.S. once, but we have no contact with him." After a few years, Sandy's mother divorced Thomsen, then remarried and subsequently divorced a Korean man whose name Sandy has taken. When Sandy was nine years old, her mother married a man from Peru. That marriage also ended in divorce. She is currently an international marketing executive at a large Las Vegas hotel, and Sandy is a student at UCLA.

Right now there are a lot of Koreans in Las Vegas, but when I was growing up, I don't recall having a Korean classmate, or even a Chinese or Japanese classmate. All my classmates were either white or African American. So I guess I grew up always feeling different. At the same time, I felt white on the inside, pretty much the same as the white kids. Once and a while, though, I would see myself in the mirror or catch my reflection in a car window, and then immediately I would know that I was different. No one ever made me feel different. I've talked to other people about this, and they expect me to say that I was lonely and alienated, but I wasn't. I had the average childhood, except for the fact that I'm Asian.

In my sophomore year, I went to Warren High School in Downey, in southern California. Most of my friends were Asian—a couple of Koreans and Chinese and one was Japanese. They were very Christian and academically oriented. Sexuality wasn't even talked about in my circle of friends. They didn't want to talk about sex, or kissing, or anything. They talked about movies and homework.

I haven't kept these old friendships. You know how people go back to their hometown, how they meet up every Christmas break and every summer? I never really did that. I just lost contact, especially after my mother and I moved out of Downey. I don't think anyone who grew up with me in Las Vegas or Reno is ready to accept the fact I'm a lesbian. Also, since I've moved to California, I've realized how hick Nevada is. There's one friend that I would have kept, but we were just so insanely different once we reached puberty. She was very heterosexual-oriented, very promiscuous. It hurt me to see her like that, so we lost contact. If I'd stayed in Nevada, I'd be very different, consciousness-wise. And I don't think that I would have come out to myself, either.

On my first day at UCLA, at freshman orientation, I met the woman who would later be my lover for three years. We ended up living in the same dormitory during our first year, so we hung out a lot and became very good friends. We talked about certain things. She told me she'd had a relationship with a woman in high school. I had been sort of questioning my sexuality during my last year in high school. It wasn't very serious; I was just thinking that maybe I wasn't really straight, that kind of thing. When she told me about her relationship, she was concerned that I would think badly of her. She said, "I don't think I'm straight." I said, "Well, a lot of people our age don't know whether they're straight or not. I don't even know if I'm straight."

That kind of opened things up for us, in terms of communication. Once that was established, we were free to express ourselves with each other in more ways than just as friends. We broke up this past August.

Within the first year of my relationship with my girlfriend, I came out to myself as a bisexual. Then I took a course called "Introduction to Gay and Lesbian Studies." After that class, I decided to identify as lesbian. This had a lot to do with the fact that I met a lot of APIs[98] in that class. Knowing that there were other API queers out there, and that they were good people, kind of aided my identity formation. I guess I'm friends with API queers for the same reason that I had Asian friends in high school. It's just comfortable. We go see Asian films, eat Asian food, talk about certain Asian books, things like that. And whenever these things are queer, that just adds to it.

I sincerely believe that we all have heterosexual *and* homosexual tendencies, thoughts, actions, whatever. But I know I have more of a focus on women, so I decided to identify as a lesbian instead of a bisexual. When I made that decision, I was waiting for my lover to identify as lesbian also, but she didn't want to. She does now, but she didn't at that time.

After that class, at the end of my second year at UCLA, I started becoming active with the queer community on campus. I joined a student mentor group called SHOUT. We would go out to high schools and talk to classes and groups about homosexuality or about college. Then I got involved with GALA, which is the gay and lesbian organization on campus. In a lot of organizations that I've dealt with, the Asian or Pacific Islander concerns are just kind of left out. There was an established API queer group on campus called Mahu, which means "fag" in Hawaiian. It was pretty inactive. Four of us decided to restart Mahu. It turned out that there were droves of people waiting for Mahu to be rekindled. At least twenty people came every week, including six or seven women, which was really good, because most gay organizations are predominantly male. When we got together as queer APIs to revive Mahu, it was if we had ignited the political in ourselves, just by talking to each other and being together. At first, it was a social group. We'd get together for *dim sum* or go to the Hong Kong Film Festival. But eventually most of us got heavily involved in campus queer politics.

When I first came out, I used to think that I was entering into a community that would be accepting of women and ethnic groups, just because gays and lesbians were a group that was also oppressed. It was very naive of me to think that, but I did. I think that when a group that's been omitted comes to power, not only do they get included, but so does everyone else, because we know who's in the total group. When you sit at the back of the bus long enough, you know everyone who's on the bus. You know their faces, you know where they are going. But if you're always at the head of the bus, you don't know who's back there.

Now, queer APIs are starting to be included in different functions and organizations.

The relatively young Korean Americans I have met can't totally accept homosexuality, although they are tolerant of it. I haven't met a really intolerant person face to face. But recently I attended a Korean Student Association (KSA) meeting at UCLA when someone was doing a presentation about health, smoking, and safe sex, and they were just shocked when I got up and started talking about dental dams. It was a whole auditorium full of Korean Americans or Koreans between seventeen and maybe twenty-three years old, women and men. And they were totally silent. No one asked any questions about being gay, safe sex, or anything like that. Then the head of KSA got up and said, "This is not to say that KSA condones any kind of sex or smoking." This reaction was just so foreign to me. I've never gone back to KSA since.

Then there was the television show on local Korean-language television supposedly covering the topic of Korean American gays and lesbians. I agreed to be on the show because I think that as part of the community we need to speak out. We need to say yes when they ask us to come and speak about something. My mother was there with me in the studio. She didn't want to go on camera, because she said, "This isn't my thing; this is your thing." I know she hesitated because she has a lot of ties in Los Angeles. The show was in Korean, and I don't speak Korean, so it had to be translated into this little thing [transmitter] in my ear. The host was talking to me, and I had to listen to this other guy, and then speak. Afterward, they would translate it for the viewers. Something was wrong with the earpiece, so I couldn't catch most of the things he was saying. I just answered what I could understand, and then it was over. I said, "OK, thanks." Then I went out into the hallway and saw my mom attack the host verbally. She said he had insinuated that homosexuality ran in my family. She was very upset by the whole thing. I think she was concerned that people might think she's lesbian if her daughter is. I had to go her way with it.

The host was very unprepared. He didn't ask any pertinent questions or make any pertinent points. Maybe he dealt with the topic so ignorantly because he thought the entire audience was ignorant. Three or four people called in. The first caller was really nice; she said, "I don't see why we have to ask all those questions; they are just people." But a couple of the callers were really unhappy that we were on television. One guy was upset that we were calling ourselves Korean. It really caught him off guard. I know there are probably many people who'd feel upset hearing kids their sons' and daughters' ages talk about being gay. They fear it; they think it's a Western thing.

Besides me, there were three guys. I didn't really want to go on the show, but I went mostly because there wasn't any other woman on the panel. The important thing for me would have been to hear the word "lesbian" in reference to Asians and Korean women.

My mother found out I am a lesbian after I had been with my first lover for about a year. We visited her place in Studio City and were taking a bath together while my mother was at work on the swing shift. I'd beeped my mother to tell her that I was home, and then I left the phone off the hook by accident. When she came home from work, she caught us in the bath. The next day was horrible. I was saying we were like sisters and that close friends take baths together.

We lived the next year kind of in silence. I didn't talk to her. I didn't tell her what I was doing at school, in my social life, or anything. It was very different from how we used to be. At that point, I couldn't tell her what I was doing at school, because I was always doing gay stuff. I was always taking gay classes, reading gay books, going to gay clubs. I couldn't tell her these things because she was in denial about the fact that I was a lesbian.

She finally accepted it the next summer. I remember I was talking with Livia, my lover, on the telephone, and she told me that her mom asked her if she was a lesbian. I was kind of flustered. When I got off the phone I said, "Mom, Livia's mom asked her if she's a lesbian." I used it as a way to tell her I was gay. She said, "Well, is she?" I said, "Maybe. Probably." And she asked, "Are you?" I said, "Probably. Most likely." And she was like, "OK. Anything else you want to tell me?"

She holds herself responsible for a lot of what I do, and what I don't do. I think she believes that if she'd done something different, if she'd raised me differently, if she'd done one thing different somewhere along the way, I wouldn't be a lesbian.

She was not a very conventional mother. She was never in a position to tell me what life was supposed to be like, because she didn't follow any traditional pattern in her own life. That might be why she is accepting of my lesbianism. She was a single mother and a successful woman. She came here when she was twenty. She had to become Americanized, because we didn't move to Los Angeles like a lot of people from Korea do; we lived in Oregon and Nevada. She had no choice but to assimilate as best she could.

I forgot to mention that she's not full Korean; she's half Caucasian. So she really knows a lot about oppression. She knows a lot about being different and being left out. I know that when she was young, she was a child actress on live television, but I think that when she got older, she saw herself as a bit risqué for the Korean public. Like she was doing modeling and things like that, and I think she just wasn't comfortable in Korea. I don't know exactly why.

She was an only child; her parents were much older. My grandmother died in 1973, and my grandfather died two or three years later. I think she felt that once her parents died, she had nothing in Korea. The last time she visited there was in 1980. I don't think she's really nostalgic about Korea.

She's very non-traditional in her life, but she's still Korean. She dislikes everybody. She has something negative to say about every race and ethnicity, even Koreans. She still talks about wanting me to get married; she always will. She wants to have grandchildren. I told her that I could very well have children. When she asked how, I said I might have one or adopt one, but she said adoption is out of the question. She never told me that I had to get married and have kids; it was just assumed that I would, until I came out. One time I was joking about marrying this gay friend because he works for an airline and his spouse could fly free. My mom got all excited. She didn't care about him being gay, she just kept saying, "Get married! Get married! I don't care that he's gay! Come to Las Vegas and we'll have a really nice wedding." All this kind of stuff. And she still bothers me about it. I would like to take back what I said about her being accepting. I've just recently learned she's supportive and tolerant, so I'm still saying she's accepting. But she really isn't.

Still, I've become a lot closer to her than before. The one big barrier that I need to get over is being financially dependent on her. If I can do that, then I think I can really feel close to her. I still depend on her financially because I'm still in school, but at the same time, I don't feel she gives me enough money, so there's tension between us sometimes. We have this understanding that my only responsibility toward her right now is to get through school. That's the only thing I ever have to do for her my entire life: finish school. Of course this isn't true, but that's what she's making me feel right now.

My current lover is Chicana. Livia was Chinese, so I took it for granted that my lover could go with me wherever I went, but sometimes I don't feel I can invite my current lover because she might not feel comfortable if everyone else is Asian. I like getting drawn into Latino things. I think that the different groups should get together, because often we are on the same level socially.

I see the division between lesbians and gay men as more permanent in the white community than in ethnic groups, which have a lot more communication between the men and the women, probably because they are trying to establish a community within a community within a community. In my experience, there aren't enough Korean Americans for us to hang out with just Korean women.

In L.A., there's a Korean gay and lesbian group that meets monthly. It's all men. It's just amazing to be in a room with forty gay Korean men. They are the kind of people I went to Korean church with when I was a kid. There are people in the group who don't speak English. It just wipes me out completely. But every time I go, it's no fun, because there are no other women.

In general, the gay, lesbian, and bisexual community focuses on men. Women aren't as visible. Gay-bashing also focuses on gay men. I know a lot of people I could imagine doing it, just from my youth growing up in Nevada. I know a lot of people that are really racist and homophobic, and their main focus is gay men. It might be because the idea of gay men threatens their masculine idea of this culture. I know that many women are victims of hate crimes because of their sexuality. At the same time, though, I think I'm very dykey looking, and I've never experienced that kind of hate. I've never experienced racial hate overtly, either. But if I were a flaming gay man, I think I would have.

I've been thinking about how you can apply the rice queen theory to the lesbian community, and it's not quite the same.[99] It's weird when you're talking about a group of Asian cultures where both the male and the female have been emasculated or effeminized in the eyes of Western culture. As an Asian lesbian in the greater lesbian community, it might be different if I were a really feminine lesbian. I might be subject to "yellow fever"[100] or "rice-dykism." You have to be the passive partner; you have to be someone who's seen as a bottom. I have a lot of mixed feelings about rice dykes. And I'm sure there are rice dykes, but it's more subtle than just, "Come, be my slave." I think there are white women out there who are just fascinated by Asian cultures. That might be what we can translate as being a rice dyke. Fascinated by Asian women, you know. We've heard it. We've seen it. "I love rice!"

I want to be a teacher because I don't want to be a lawyer anymore. But I might just go into politics. Women's Studies classes help me theorize about things, but I'm a very elemental kind of thinker. If it makes me feel right, if it doesn't offend me personally, then I'll do it. I take everything personally too. I try to put myself into a situation and see how it works. I don't really like theory. Feminist theory had stimulated my own thoughts, but I don't know if you can say it has shaped me, because a lot of the Women's Studies readings aren't about me. They are either not about lesbians, or they're not about Asians. You can read something by a woman of color feminist theorist and really gain insight into what it's like to be a woman of color in this country, but there are things in my life that she can't write about. That's true of any woman writer. Everyone has to figure out how these theories apply to their own lives. There's been a lot written, and every woman is different. Each woman has to apply that knowledge to herself in whatever she sees as the best way. That's what feminism is about. It's meant to inspire the best in every woman. It's not to make all women strong, or all women into man-haters. It's supposed to be affirming and empowering to women.

JANUARY 1994

YOUNG SOON HAN

Second Homeland

Young Soon Han speaks thoughtfully, pausing now and then to search for exactly the right word or phrase to express her intense feelings as precisely as she can. Although she punctuates her sentences with graceful hand gestures, and the expression on her smooth face is kind and sincere, she never smiles, even during several hours of interviewing on two separate occasions at the Korean riot victims organization's temporary headquarters. Born in Taegu in 1940, she came to Los Angeles in 1970 with her husband after working in Sweden as a nurse for several years. Between the late 1960s and the mid-1970s, the U.S. Immigration and Naturalization Service technical and professional skills preferences included immigrants with medical training, such as doctors, pharmacists, and nurses. Han worked as a nurse in various Los Angeles health facilities, while her husband operated a liquor store. After her husband died of cancer, she took over the store, which was destroyed in the April 1992 Los Angeles riots.

People used to say that my husband was the kind of person who touched even a big stone before stepping on it, just to make sure it was secure. I miss my husband. With him, I had thirty-three years of happiness, counting the ten years we knew each other before we got married. Now I live in a kind of fantasy world. That's how I can survive. I am not afraid to die; in fact, I look forward to dying, because I know I will then be able to join my husband. He told me he would build a pretty house in the Garden of Eden and wait for me there.

I fell in love with him when we were teenagers. He had moved from the countryside to Taegu, where I lived, and we were neighbors. After I got a chance to go to Sweden as a registered nurse in 1964, I petitioned for him to join me. We were engaged the following year. Then we got married and moved to Los Angeles.

My husband majored in economics in college, but he wasn't able to use his skills here, so he got the liquor store not long before he died. We opened the liquor store to give jobs to our family members. By 1980, there were about fifteen of us altogether. The women could find work in sewing factories, but the men couldn't work there, so we pooled our money to start a business. My husband and I put in about fifteen years' savings. But I never worked at the store. In fact, my husband handled everything: I just gave him my paycheck from the hospital, where I was working as a nurse.

We had no idea what a liquor store was. No one drank or smoked in our family. If we had been aware that liquor was creating such a problem in South Central, definitely we wouldn't have bought a liquor store. I was asked once in an interview, "Is it true you were not aware of alcohol-related problems?" I was ashamed and shocked; for me, the liquor store was just a way to earn a living. Now I realize that there are social problems from buying alcohol.

I know that there are community complaints about the number of liquor stores in South Central. But we did not issue the liquor licenses; they were sold to us. Why did they issue so many liquor licenses in South Central?

Because there was a demand for them. One thing I am sure of, our so-called liquor stores functioned like convenience stores. Liquor sales were only thirty to thirty-five percent of the total sales; all the other items were just like in a mini-market. Many people are not aware of this fact. We also had sundries, groceries, stationery, candy, whatever is in the supermarket, just less. The liquor stores also functioned as a post office and for check cashing. The community has been suffering since we lost our stores.

The black community and the politicians claim that liquor stores create criminals. Of course I understand that we contribute some by selling alcohol. But were there no problems before Koreans came to this country? Whenever I attend public hearings, I hear people say that this problem existed for decades; how can we blame this on merchants? In the [San Fernando] Valley, there were many liquor stores owned by Koreans, but there were not the social problems. Poverty does not justify violation of other people's rights. I can understand how frustrating it is to be poor, to not have what you need in life. But hurting other people, stepping on other people's rights, destroying their livelihood, won't do anything for that poverty.

Over two hundred Korean liquor stores burned down. Few have been re-established. Are the African Americans able to start their own businesses now that the Korean businesses are gone? No. Even thirty years ago, the situation was similar; South Central has never been developed. I don't know who is to be blamed, but obviously it's not Koreans.

When my husband was diagnosed with cancer, I refused to believe he might die. I was in total denial. Maybe because I had been in nursing, I went around in a frenzy, and in the end, when he was in the hospital and tried to say something to me, I would not even let him speak about dying. Maybe he wanted to say his last words to me, but I would not let him.

I had to take over the store after my husband died. I cannot tell you how difficult it was. I had no experience with retail business at all. Finally, after about a year, I had learned how to operate the store.

On April 29, 1992, the night the store burned down, I didn't even know what was happening. I hadn't been paying much attention to the Rodney King verdict. I didn't think the issue was so serious. But some of the people from the neighborhood came into the store and said, "Mrs. Han, you'd better run now! People are coming this way, and you will get hurt." I said, "Why? I haven't done anything wrong." But they convinced me I was in danger, so I went home. That night, I kept in contact with the woman who lived in a house behind our store. She finally told me that the store had been burned down to the ground.

I didn't cry like everyone else did. I was just numb. I only cried when my sister and her husband visited L.A. and reminded me that my husband was gone and I was facing the situation all alone.

The people from the neighborhood talked to me about why the Korean stores were targeted. They said, "We don't mean you, Mrs. Han, but many Koreans treat us very rudely and look down on us. They don't treat us like human beings. They don't speak good English, and they can't communicate with us, their customers. They don't realize that the customer is king. After all, they make their money through us." The people in the neighborhood believe that Koreans learn from white people even when they were still in Korea to be racist against African Americans.

Most Korean merchants were not rude intentionally. I heard from neighbors that since their faces are expressionless, people think they are angry. Koreans are not very sociable. When I was little, I was told, "Be quiet. Obey and listen. Don't insist on putting forth your own views." Young people were told to keep quiet, especially girls. How could we learn to express our own feelings to others? There was really no communication between parents and children. Even among men, if you keep quiet, you are considered intelligent and a gentleman. Too much talking is looked down on. There is an old Korean saying that silence is gold while speech is silver. There might be some rude people, as in any community. Don't black people and Korean people fight each other within their own groups? That is not a racial problem. It's racial discrimination to say that it is. Koreans like peace. We are just not used to talking with people here. We don't know how to express our feelings. Koreans grew up in a monocultural society, without seeing blacks, whites, other kinds of people.[101] In Korea, being human means looking and acting like a Korean. Everyone else is unfamiliar and makes us uncomfortable. It's because of our nation's history—being constantly attacked by the powerful, and so many wars—that we learned not to trust other people. It's like that in Korea, but it's worse here, because you don't speak English.

Many Korean merchants have English problems. If you can talk freely to people, they will accept you. I had many good neighbors. They talked to me about their families and their lives. My main purpose as the store owner was to keep good relationships with the customers. Some of the Korean employees didn't care about the customers. They didn't speak English well, and they didn't want to learn. They would mutter that they hadn't come to

America to work in a liquor store. They felt bad.

We have to wake up and place priorities on our important issues. What is the most important, valuable? Is it money? Or something else? To me, accepting and understanding other people and other cultures is vitally important; otherwise there will be no end to fighting. We have to open our eyes wide and look at the society and at life in this country broadly. You cannot live alone. You have to have relationships with other people. There are many different cultures and ethnic groups living here. You cannot insist on your own traditions, ideas, and philosophy.

I respect African Americans, their effort in history up to now, how they fought to settle down in this country. They are a model for many minorities living in this country. There were so many great black leaders, like Martin Luther King and others. I am trying to study them. King was a role model for all of us. The leaders sacrificed themselves for equal rights and to upgrade the black community. I believe that many minority groups benefitted from black struggles, and I respect them for this.

To me, it wasn't right for the African Americans, who have accumulated their anger and resentment against white people, to take it out on the Koreans at this time. Violators will never be remembered as heroes.

Since I had had no intention of making a living through that store, I was thinking about selling it before the uprising and changing to some other kind of business, like a sandwich shop, anyway. I had paid off the bank loan for the business in 1991 by refinancing my house. Now that the business has been completely destroyed, I don't have anything, and my mortgage payment is higher than before. I have no equity in my house at all: the current house value is much lower than what I borrowed from the bank.

Those who had been in their businesses a long time probably didn't have bank loans with unpaid balances. But many victims bought their businesses just before the riots. They still have full balances at the bank to pay off. If you get an SBA [Small Business Administration] loan to start a new business, it's impossible to manage, especially now that we are in a recession; that's the first enemy we have to fight with. Among all the members of my group of Korean American victims, only three families had restarted their businesses within one year of the riots. They probably had some savings from before, plus their loans. But even they are having a hard time because of the recession. I know no liquor store owners who went back to their old places in South Central. There are many new regulations and rules all the time that make it hard to go back to South Central.

Many people in this city believe that we had lots of support from FEMA [Federal Emergency Management Agency] and the SBA and that we are all recovered. But our problems have just started now. FEMA stopped. EDD [Employment Development Department] stopped. SBA loans are not enough to relocate and restart a business. The SBA wants us to return to the old business, because it's more likely for us to be able to repay our loans. But the city is blocking us. Many victims are willing to move or convert to other businesses, but we need more money to start again. SBA loans did not include our business premium—our liquor licenses. They covered only the physical plant and inventory. It's the liquor license that is the major expense. Brokers are calling people to offer them one-fourth of what they paid for their licenses. I say, I won't sell it, I will just hang it on the wall as a memoir [memento] of the riots. If your cash is all tied up in the license, how can you relocate or start a different business?

These young people in the Korean American Interagency Council[102] have never done business, so they don't know what our needs are. How can they be in the position to negotiate for us? The most viable businesses would be the same ones they did before, because these people were not merchants in Korea and they have only this experience. Most merchants don't have the skills to get a professional job; the majority would have a hard time finding a labor job. Mostly they started working in retail stores and then started their own businesses. It's hard for them to start something else. All these Korean American social workers are trying to help business owners get into new businesses. But we cannot live on the kinds of businesses being suggested, which are not doing well lately. No one is eating fast food these days, except extremely poor people. Laundromats are only good for people who are already making their living somewhere else; laundromats are for extra money. Koreans want to work hard every day, not just do a business that you could leave alone to make money while you do nothing.

Right after the riots, we were anxious to solve the problems however we could. We wanted to grab onto something or somebody to survive. We were in shock. The main problem right now is the aftershock syndrome. When you receive a big shock, you may not feel it right away because the shock is too great. The victims are wondering day in day out, where are we going to go from here? They have a lot of problems—depression, stress, loss of memory. I know because I am a typical case right now. I cannot remember anything most of the time. It's getting worse and worse. Some people have committed suicide or died of stress. I don't see any bright future at this moment. It seems more hopeless now. I feel unworthy, desperate, miserable.

The men seem so dejected and so unhappy, sitting here in the victims' association office sighing and smoking and worrying about their families. Korean men usually support the whole family. They cannot express their depression at home, so as not to discourage the family. So they express their feelings here. We all understand each other because we are all victims. Some victims have moved to other states. I also hear that some went back to Korea. They didn't get SBA loans. They just returned to Korea, because they don't want to stay here.

Even if I could afford to live in Korea, I would have nowhere to go there. This is my country, this is my home. I feel that once you emigrate, and you are determined to live in your new country through your lifetime, you stay. We accept this as our second homeland; we can't just move away when tragedy hits. It's not like moving from one city to another within a country.

My feelings toward America have changed lately. The American spirit that I knew before I came is quite different now. I believed in freedom, justice, equal opportunity, and peace in this society, which I enjoyed for twenty years. I never complained about this country. I still like this country. There is nothing wrong with this country; the people make the trouble. To me, that's a different matter entirely.

There are shortcomings in Korean American society. There are good and bad in every group. One good part is that Koreans are hard workers and love peace. We obey the rules and generally respect the U.S. Constitution. Consequently, our hard work, such as forming Koreatowns, has contributed a great deal to American society. We are not the only ones making money by doing business. We pay high taxes as well.

After the latter part of 1970s, there was a sudden flow of new immigrants without strong leadership. There were no organizations to provide support and guidance for them. Many people say the leaders are not doing enough, that they only care about their own organizations. Who are our so-called leaders? Who picked them? The people we are told are leaders are heads of their organizations. They just declare themselves leaders. Real leaders are elected or designated and able to influence followers to go in the right direction. Leadership does not require knowledge or intellectual ability. It requires a passion to work for other people. I am not qualified for leadership. I am conservative, in the sense of being a traditional Korean woman. Men become leaders; they have the authority. They look down on and don't listen to women.

Many organizations and individuals benefitted from our tragedy. Some people became public figures after the riots. Some people got rich. It's good that someone is making money, but I wish they would return it to the community. They should give service to the community however they can, according to whatever ability they have.

JULY 1992 AND MARCH 1993

YANNY RHEE

Love Letter From a Stranger

Short, curly hair frames the serene face of fifty–five–year–old Yanny Rhee [pseudonym]. Rhee seems to relish remembering the past and thinking about the present, especially when these thoughts and memories settle on her children. Almost thirty years ago, she arrived in Los Angeles, where she married, raised her family, and has operated a restaurant since 1979. Now a widow, she occupies her spare time playing golf, visiting with relatives, and painting. Recently, her oil paintings were exhibited at the Designers Art Gallery in Glendale.

I was born in Seoul in 1939. I have three brothers, two older and one younger. Our father started and ran the only needle factory in Korea. It was in Inch'ŏn.[103] During the Japanese period, we were pretty well off. I remember living in a two-story Japanese-style house with a bath and a flush toilet.[104] My father ran the factory until the Korean War broke out in 1950, then he went down to Pusan. My older brother was in the Merchant Marine College, and the rest of the family took refuge in a farm village in South Ch'ungch'ŏng Province, where I finished elementary school. There was no electricity and no candles; I had to study by a kerosene lamp. My mother did dressmaking to support us children. After a year, we moved to Taejŏn, where our father joined us. Somehow, the Inch'ŏn factory was gone; perhaps it was demolished during the war. I was just a child at the time, so I'm not exactly sure what happened to it.

In times of crisis, a mother's head works better than a father's. It was our mother who supported the family during, and right after, the war. After we returned to Seoul in 1954, mother continued her sewing work. She made a huge quantity of men's shirts and peddled them at East Gate Market.

My second brother came to the U.S. in 1955, after graduating from high school.[105] Our parents sold one of their properties to send him. By that time, my oldest brother was pretty well established as a navigator. He helped our father start an ice plant in Inch'ŏn, making block ice and supplying them to ships. They started exporting frozen fish, too, and we were once again well off. Business went well until the 1970s, when an employee's cheating ruined it. My parents and oldest brother immigrated to the U.S. in 1973.

After studying math and physics in Kansas, my brother got a job as a computer engineer in Anaheim, [California]. He invited me to the U.S. in 1963, after I had graduated from Ewha Womans University with a home economics degree. In those days, all the girls with decent grades were majoring in either English or home economics.[106] My only goal was to become a *hyŏnmoyangch'o* [wise mother and virtuous/good wife].[107] I never even imagined a career when I applied for college; I just went along with the other girls. Now I regret majoring in home economics because I didn't learn much, and whenever something went wrong with my cooking or in other household matters, my husband used to blame me and say, "Is that all you can do as a graduate of the Ewha Womans University home economics department?"

My first year in the U.S. was very hard. I could read and write some English, but I couldn't understand what people were saying, and I could not speak. So I just smiled at people all the time. Once my brother asked me why I was always smiling at everybody. What could I do? I didn't know what they were asking me, and I couldn't say anything. Why should I get mad at them?

I met a nice white woman at a business college I attended and arranged to stay at her house for $50 a month for both room and board. Her family was very nice to me. After a year at the business college, I got a job at the company where my brother worked. At first, I was terrified of answering the telephone. People would talk so fast that I would just hand the receiver over to someone else. When I was alone in the office, I dreaded the sound of the telephone ringing. Gradually, my ears opened up and I started to understand what people were saying. I got jobs as an office worker here and there, doing mostly accounting work, until 1979, the year I started my own business.

I met my husband, David, when I was working at my first job. My cousin's husband and David's father were friends, and one day my brother asked me to go to dinner to meet David. I went, thinking he was some little boy or something, but he had already finished college and was working at an aerospace engineering company in Santa Monica. He was so shy and nervous at dinner that he couldn't eat anything; it was very funny. I wasn't thinking about marriage or anything like that. I wasn't the least bit nervous. Anyway, he called me a few days later, and we started dating. We got married in 1965 and moved into an apartment on South Ardmore. There were not many Koreans there at the time, but now that place is in the center of Koreatown.

Our daughter Susan was born in 1970, and my mother moved in with us in 1971. She took care of the baby while I went to work. Not long afterwards, my father and my older brother's family immigrated. My husband and I were having a good time: every weekend, we got together with friends to play poker or to travel to the ski resorts in Yosemite, King's Canyon, Big Bear, and Mammoth on long weekends. Our major concern was which

house we were playing poker at or where we would travel to the next weekend. Neither of us thought about saving money or anything like that; we
both had good jobs, and we spent all the money we earned enjoying life.

Suddenly, friends who had arrived in the U.S. much later than we had
begun to buy houses, while we were still living in a small Koreatown apartment. After Susan was born, our two-bedroom apartment was just too small
for us and my parents. My mother complained that she was living like a bird
in a cage. We bought a house in Glendale in 1973, and I've lived in the same
house ever since. John was born six months after we moved. Old-timers[108]
live like Americans; we don't move around so much, and we just enjoy life.
The newcomers are always buying and selling their houses, and now they're
paying the price with high mortgage payments. We don't have that problem.

I enjoyed working, but I took it pretty easy. Whenever I got tired of a job,
I'd quit and rest for a couple of months before finding another job. Once, I
was taking it easy at home for a couple of weeks when I saw an ad in the
local newspaper about a little restaurant near our house. David was visiting
Korea at the time, so I went to see the place by myself the next morning. It
looked like a good business, full of customers. When David got back from
Korea, we went to see the owner and made a $1,000 deposit. The old cou-
ple who owned the place liked us; they thought David was going to be the
cook. Several times, David told me to cancel the deal and forget about the
deposit, because he didn't think I could run the business successfully. I
thought I could handle it, and I prevailed. We bought the restaurant for a
down payment of $25,000, which we had saved up over the years.

I had no idea about American food. I didn't even know that there were so
many different kinds of bread. The previous owners trained me for two
months. I cleaned, cooked, and went to the market with them. I carried a
notebook and pencil around with me and wrote down everything they did.
After they retired, I hired a cook and worked as his cook's helper. One day,
after about six months, the cook was throwing away some bread that looked
pretty good to me, and I said something about it. He wrote a note and left
the kitchen. I thought he had gone to the rest room; but when he didn't
return, I looked at the note. It read, "I quit." I told the waitress to close the
door and asked the guests for their patience. Then I started cooking myself.
That day I had to close the shop at 9:30 A.M. Fortunately I was able to find
another cook later in the day. He worked for me for the next twelve years,
and after he retired, I found another cook who is also very good.

Trust is important, especially in the restaurant business. You have to be able to trust your employees. I have a cook, a cook's helper, a dishwasher, and two waitresses. The head waitress is my age; she started working in the restaurant when she was little, and her mother was the head waitress before her. Now, her daughter is the second waitress. Three generations of waitresses in this restaurant. I gave the keys to the waitress and cook after six months, so that they could open up in the morning. When I have to go somewhere, I leave them the bank deposit slips. When David was sick, they took care of the shop. When they can't come to work, they make arrangements for their own replacements.

The restaurant is open six days a week. The customers are mostly neighborhood residents. Many more restaurants have opened in the area lately, so there is some competition, but people like our food and our waitresses, so we are doing all right.

Susan majored in psychology at UC Berkeley and worked for a publishing company for a year, but she didn't like the job, so she quit and went up to San Francisco after she got engaged to her fiancé, Ivan, who worked there as a financial consultant. They met at Berkeley when they were freshmen. He's an immigrant from England, tall and very sharp. I like him very much; I feel comfortable with him. They come down to visit me often. Ivan used to call me Mrs. Rhee, but now he calls me ŏmma [mom].

Susan has a Korean face, but she's an American inside. It would be difficult for her to marry a man from Korea. In terms of language, culture, and values, she's more compatible with a person like Ivan than with a man born in Korea. When Ivan gave her an engagement ring, she was thrilled. She called me right away, all excited. I could sense happiness in her voice. I think they'll be a very fine couple. His parents are immigrants, humble like us.

Once Susan told me that when they go out together, people treat her as the foreigner and Ivan as the American, whereas she is the native-born American and Ivan is the immigrant with the green card. This seems to upset her a lot, but that's the kind of thing we have to go through here. Once she confided in me that she would like to have a baby who looks Korean, like her. I guess these things can't be helped.

Last Thanksgiving, Susan and Ivan came down to our family party. Our nieces and nephews are all grown up, and their language is English. One of Susan's cousins married an American [a white person], and they fit right in. Since everyone was speaking English, especially the young folks, a few English-only miguknom [American kids] blended in well. When friends of my generation get together, they speak Korean, and the English-only spouses have a hard time fitting into the group. But the younger generation English-speakers mingle very well.

My friend's son married a girl from Korea, and they have many problems. They just can't communicate with each other. He is a thirty-year-old lawyer, but he is very *sunjinhae* [innocent, pure, naive], like most of the Korean boys born here are. But people born in Korea are very tough. The two of them fight all the time, and the mother-in-law keeps saying *juketta* [I'm troubled to death]. It's the same as a Korean lady marrying a G.I. Even I have trouble communicating with people who've just arrived from Korea. I've changed a lot, too.

John is a senior at Berkeley. He's majoring in legal studies, but he doesn't want to be a lawyer; he's like me, very casual. He wants to enjoy life. He doesn't want to go on with studying for too long; he just wants to get a job after he finishes college. John has lots of friends. I think he likes Asian girls and will probably end up marrying a Korean or a Chinese.

Susan's father was a typical Korean man. He didn't help me at all with my business or my housework when he was alive. From early morning until late at night, I didn't have a moment to put my *kungdaengi* [butt] on the *ttangbadak* [floor, since people in Korea sit on the floor; here, chair]. I took the children to school, went to the shop, picked up the children, went home and made dinner, washed the dishes, bathed the children, and went to bed at midnight. That was my routine. The only time I could put my *kung-daengi* down was when I went to bed. And David would complain whenever he got back from a trip to Korea about how his friends' wives served their husbands. They would squeeze the morning juice for their husbands, help them put on their suits, neckties, and shoes, and help them take off their suits in the evening. What he didn't see was the wives in Korea sleeping during the day and having the whole day to rest. I shouted at him that I would never let him visit Korea again. Then he stopped complaining.

When David fixed or cleaned something at home, he would always shout at me that he couldn't find the tools and things like that, so I thought it was better for him not to do anything. Men are like children. When they do some kind of work in the yard, they want you to come out and watch and tell them how well they're doing. Men have inferiority complexes. If you bring in more cash than the man does, he's not happy. I guess his male ego is hurt. But if you are having trouble at your work or business, he becomes very nice. I guess that he feels he's master of the house again.

David died of lung cancer in 1989. Cigarette smoking finally got him. He was sick for about two years. He was coughing a lot, so we went in for a checkup, and eventually they discovered cancer. They operated to remove the tumor, but another tumor appeared. We went down to a well-known specialist in San Diego for treatment. During this period, I could never get enough sleep. David coughed constantly all night, and early in the morning I had to take him to San Diego. Between my sick husband, my business, and the traveling back and forth to San Diego, I couldn't find enough time to sleep, day or night. I was under physical strain, but I wasn't tired psychologically. When David got sick, all my expectations vanished. It was just unconditional giving without expecting anything in return. I had peace of mind. You are unhappy only if your expectations aren't met. When you don't have any expectations, you can't be unhappy.

Six months before David died, my cook had an operation on his leg, so I had to be at the restaurant early every morning and wasn't able to take care of David as much as I should have. By then, Susan was at Berkeley, and my mother had passed away. I know it was very difficult for David. Our [Korean] church pastor's mother-in-law learned about our hardship and volunteered to help. For three weeks before David died, she stayed with us and helped him. Then, two weeks before he died, Susan called to speak with him. I told her he couldn't answer the telephone, and the next day she was at the door with her luggage. She took a semester's leave from school and stayed by her father's bedside until he died. He was in a coma, and I was afraid to be alone with him, but Susan cleaned him up and sat beside him holding his hand and reading books the whole time. I thought it was because he was her father, but after he died, she stayed with me for six months before going back to school.

After David passed away, I started playing golf. Now I play about twice a week. My handy[109] at the Ladies Club at Wilson and Harding Golf Course is twenty-one. I also started oil painting.

One day, I got a two-page love letter from a stranger. This man had gotten my address through an art exhibition, where two of my paintings had been on display. They gave him my business address, and apparently he came by the restaurant to take a look at me, although I didn't know it. He had enclosed his photo. When I opened the letter, I couldn't help laughing. I just laughed and laughed. I'm a fifty-five-year-old widow, and a sixty-year-old man had sent me a serious love letter! He said that I would be the perfect companion for him for the rest of his life. I never met him, and I knew nothing about him. He had seen an article about me in the *Han'guk*

Ilbo [Korea Times] and had fallen in love with me. It was a story about the exhibit, with my picture. How childish he was! What would I do with a man like that?

I have my life built on relationships with the friends we had when Susan's father[110] was still alive, with my in-laws, with my brother's family, and, of course, with my two children. Last Thanksgiving, we had a family gathering at our house, and everyone had a good time. All my in-laws and their families and my own siblings' families got together. The children are all in their twenties and thirties now. We are one big happy family. These people are my world. Remarrying would change my relationships with my old friends, my in-laws, and my children. Why should I disrupt the happy little world I'm so comfortable with? Susan is engaged to be married soon, and John is a college senior. I'm happy now; I paint, I play golf, and my business is doing OK.

I would like a platonic relationship with a man, someone to talk to and walk on the beach with hand in hand. I would just like to wait for a relationship to grow. But where would I meet a man like that? They are all just interested in marriage and sex. My friends want to introduce men to me, but I just tell them I'll think about it, because if I meet with them, I know they'll be thinking about marriage, and that would be awkward.[111] If I went out with some man and suggested going down to the beach, he would say, "Oh, it's too cold down there. Why don't we go to a nice warm place?"—meaning a motel. If I were in my forties, I might do that if I really liked the man; but I am fifty-five now, and I don't have to have it. Sex is something you have to develop over time. You have to keep up with it, otherwise it becomes dormant, I guess. You only meet one or two men in your entire life that you can really fall in love with. If I ever met such a man, I'd follow what nature dictates. You can't help it. If you really fall in love with someone, what's wrong with having sex with him? It's a good thing; I think I would enjoy it.

My children are doing well, and I am healthy. I maintain close relationships with the people I used to know when David was alive. I have nothing at all to complain about.

DECEMBER 1994

JAMES RYU

Hanging Onto
My Dream

Easygoing, clean-cut James Young Bae Ryu is the publisher of
KoreAm Journal, a monthly English-language newspaper in Los
Angeles. Born in Seoul in 1961, Ryu immigrated to the United
States with his family when he was eleven years old. He lived first
in upstate New York, then in Oregon and Ohio, before moving
to California in 1981. Ryu married Tammy Chung in 1987.
They have a three-year-old son. For the first several years of their
marriage, Ryu's income was three or four times his wife's; at
twenty-seven, he was making enough to buy a house, a car, and
two other properties. Now that he has gone into newspaper
publishing, the situation is reversed. "I'm mooching off my wife,"
he jokes.

I majored in business administration in college. I never thought I'd go into publishing; I more or less stumbled into it, not because I wanted to contribute to the community but because of my interest in business. Back in 1989, I was going through a transition from my advertising and direct-mail business to the Korean business directory that my father was involved in. Once that was established, I wanted to do something different. At that time, the Los Angeles edition of the *Korea Times* was doing an English section, and they were starting a quarterly magazine in English.[112] When I saw it, I thought I'd be able to make something that second-generation Korean Americans could like. It happened that the publisher of the South Bay Korean language community newspaper was looking for someone to take over. My father wanted to try it, so he bought the paper.

Since I was helping my father out, I tried to learn all the steps needed to make a newspaper. After a couple of months, I felt I could do it in English, so in February 1990, we set the goal of producing a dummy issue of *KoreAm Journal* by the end of March. I went around asking friends and relatives to contribute ads. For the first issue, we got $2,500 worth of ads, and we thought that was big money. The dummy issue had thirty-two pages, and we printed and distributed 1,000 copies.

Everyone was telling me that it would take at least five or six years for a new newspaper to get off the ground, but I had thought I could accomplish it in a year. That was just my ego trip. A year after we started the paper, we had exhausted all our funds. We were getting three or four new subscriptions a week, and I kind of lost hope on the business side. But my friends told me they looked forward to seeing the paper every month, and people were writing to us to say that they enjoyed reading *KoreAm Journal*, so I felt some sense of responsibility to the community and some commitment to continuing the paper. I got memberships from different Korean American organizations, like the Korean American Coalition, the Korean

Youth and Community Center, and Women's Organization Reaching Koreans, and I took down lists of organizations and businesses from the Korean directory and the *Yellow Pages*. We were sending out about 1,000 copies and passing out 4,000 copies free to businesses and organizations.

Then I met Richard Choi Bertsch, who was president of the Korean American Democratic Committee. His father is German and his mother is Korean, but he speaks Korean fluently. He has several companies; his main business is in stereo equipment. He was getting involved in the community and wanted to do something the community needed. I was able to talk him into becoming a partner. He came up with most of the money we needed to continue, and he said that he could support the paper for about a year. He put a lot of money in, knowing that he was not going to get it back. He said, "Ten years from now, I want my kids to be able to read about the Korean community." For the last couple of years business in general hasn't been good, so he's had to cut back a lot; but I heard from someone else that he said he was going to contribute as long as he had a business.

Our fifth anniversary will be in April. Right now we are mailing out about 9,500 copies a month, including 4,000 to businesses. The subscriptions are growing. We decided that starting next month, there will be no more freebies. We have about 2,000 subscribers who pay $20 a year. About twenty organizations pay a $200 annual flat fee for copies of *KoreAm Journal* for all their members. These organizations use *KoreAm* for communicating with members, since each issue features organization news.

We try to come up with special topics each month. One of the first was on the gay issue. John Lee and Lucy Lim, who were writing for us at the time, deserve the credit for that issue. They came up with the names. There were four people featured altogether. Two of them didn't want their identities revealed, so we took pictures of two people facing the camera and two people in profile. Not only did readers tell us they liked the issue, but the gay issue became a topic in community discussion sessions and in other Korean media afterwards. We had calls from Radio Korea and the *Korean Central Daily News* and other newspapers wanting to know how to contact the people we interviewed. One of the people we interviewed had wanted to initiate a Korean gay and lesbian group. At that time, they only knew about eight gay or lesbian people in the whole Korean community. After they advertised their first meeting, they had about twenty-eight people. A few months ago, they told me that their group numbers about sixty now. It's good to hear.

My wife encouraged me to cover the subject. For me, it was a business decision. But afterwards, I gained a lot personally, meeting the interviewees and getting to know them. It was a learning experience for me.

When my partner was doing pretty well financially, I was thinking three or four months ahead and lining up writers. Now I am really going month to month. Our next issue will be on sexual harassment. This is a hot issue.

If you look at our 1991 issues, every month we had a section called "Race Relations." We reprinted articles from the *Los Angeles Sentinel* [an African-American community newspaper]. We wanted Korean Americans to know what was being said about us in the black media. The *Los Angeles Times* and the *Orange County Register* reprinted some of the articles written by Koreans and published in our paper. They read our paper and called us for information on the Korean American community.

The news media thrive on big events. It was good that we had an opportunity to write about the riots. People in the community wanted to write about it, and we simply provided a forum. My father and Richard both encouraged me to be as balanced as possible in my coverage. I try to be open-minded about the materials that go in. There are many articles I don't agree with, but I don't decide whether an article is acceptable or not based on my own religious or political views. In the beginning, I asked a lot of ministers to write articles. For the Christmas issue in the second year, I asked about seven ministers to write about Christmas. For six months, all I heard from my friends was, Is this a Christian paper? So I knew I had to balance things more. After we changed the format quite a lot, we have gotten letters now and then saying that the paper has become too liberal.

I am struggling. When I'm with my friends and colleagues, my pockets are empty. It's not easy to see my friends making a lot of money and paying in cash at restaurants while I have to worry about whether or not I can cover the check. My wife has to make do with a strict budget; we can't buy all the things we want. It's a tough decision to stay with this business. I can maintain my sanity and decency here, but it doesn't pay the bills.

We aren't financially solvent, but I do see gradual improvement. I'm the only full-time worker, although I do have a few volunteers. I'm not only the managing editor, but also the advertising editor. I do design, subscriptions—everything you see in the paper. I pay the bills and collect the money. I always have to keep my eyes on the overall picture. There's a lot of pressure. Every time we publish an issue, deliver it, and pay our bills, I tell my wife "I think I want to quit." The cycle is a two-week period: just before publication, I have to stay in the office six or seven days a week. I sleep only four or five hours a night. I heard that when people flirt, their brains function almost three times faster than normal. That's how it is during the three or four days before the paper is out. I'm figuring out things even while I'm sleeping.

After the publication is out, I try to relax for a day or two, thinking about how it's too much for me to handle. The next week, I start hearing people's responses. People call to say, "That was a great issue; I really liked it." I see subscriptions rolling in. Then all thoughts of quitting disappear. I am up high. For about a week or two, I feel good again. I think it's not so bad. It's sort of like women's labor in childbirth. I hear they forget all about it after delivery. That's why they keep having children, and that's why I keep on going on to the next issue. My partner and I both realize now that this is more than just a business. Our friends tell us, "Hang on to your dream."

My father told me that men tend to see the broader picture, while women are usually more detail-oriented. But I have to do both: I have to see the big picture, and I have to also look at the articles and ask why there's no title or by-line, or why something is spelled in the lower case.

My wife is a lawyer for the state. Although she makes only about half of what lawyers make in the private sector, she still makes three or four times what I make here. We share the housework. She works as much as I do, and she is not going to tolerate me watching television or reading a book while she does the housework alone. I do most of the cooking. I'm a decent cook; my wife likes my cooking. I can cook Korean and American food. I used to work at a sushi bar when I was going to college. I did a lot of chopping in my younger days. Laundry and paying the bills are my responsibilities. My wife just hands over her check to me.[113] Before, she handled the finances. When I started this business, she was always complaining that we didn't have enough money. Finally, she said she couldn't handle it any longer and told me to do it. As I was doing it, I realized what she had been going through.[114]

In my first year, I didn't make anything, period. But my wife has always been supportive. In the beginning, she was supportive because she knew I liked the business. After the second and third year, she was still supportive, even though I wasn't making any money. She likes the paper a lot. Whenever we talk about the financial stuff, she is very open-minded. She has always left the choice of whether to quit or continue to me.

At home or here at the newspaper, I just have to take care of things day by day. I stay sane by hitting golf balls during lunchtime. I would go crazy if I had to sit here eight hours straight every day; I'd worry too much. Even though I might feel depressed inside, I have to be very enthusiastic and optimistic to the writers, advertisers, and readers.

I'm pretty comfortable dealing with first-generation people. I think the younger generation needs to learn to love more and to take more responsibility. At the same time, I think the first generation needs to be more egalitarian about responsibilities. In the beginning, we got a lot of support from people in the first-generation community, even though they weren't getting any benefits in return. I am trying to change that. When I call Korean companies and banks for ads, it's like begging, and sometimes it's really frustrating. There's a limit to how much you can beg. I stay away from the word "contribution" and try to show them how they can benefit.

It's our dream that we will be able to influence people and help organize the Korean community through the *KoreAm Journal*. When Korean-language newspapers sponsor golf tournaments, parades, and other cultural events, they themselves benefit, not the community. They keep the money; I don't know what they do with it. American papers' sponsorships directly benefit nonprofit organizations. Last April, we sponsored the *KoreAm Journal* Golf Classic, and all the proceeds went to the Orange County Family Counseling Center. We need many profit-making companies doing nonprofit things.

For the past twenty years, I learned a lot about American culture; but when I think about what I do and say, I am much more Korean than I used to think. I try to take the best out of both cultures to form my own identity. After living in Oregon and Ohio, I thought I was totally Americanized. I kind of lost my ability to speak Korean, but it gradually came back after we moved to Los Angeles in 1981. Doing this newspaper business, I have to talk to a lot of Koreans, and the Korean language comes out naturally now. In order to really speak Korean, you have to think of yourself as a Korean.

JANUARY 1995

NATALY KIM

One Chapter a Day

Nataly Kim [pseudonym] was born in P'yŏngyang in northern
Korea in 1926, and immigrated to the United States at the age of
sixty. Her subdued clothing and demeanor match her quiet, deliberate way of speaking. Proper and determined, she prides herself in
being active, resourceful, and always open to learning something
new. She works as a volunteer for various Los Angeles senior
citizens' programs.

My husband returned to me after thirteen years. He had abandoned me and our three children for a younger woman. Before we married, we promised each other not to repeat what my parents and grandparents had done. I told my fiancé, I don't want anything else from you, but let us be faithful to each other. Let's end those things at our fathers' generation.

My father abandoned my mother about a year after they got married, when I was just an infant. He moved to Pusan and took in another woman. He never came back to my mother. She became a *saeng kwabu* [a living widow; a woman living as a widow even though her husband is still alive] when she was only twenty years old. My grandfather was the same; he abandoned my grandmother and moved in with another woman.

I got married in 1947, when I was twenty-two years old.[115] Before the wedding, my fiancé and I made a special trip on the train to see my father in P'yŏngyang and to deliver the *sajudanja* [traditional formal request from the groom's home to the bride's home, written in Chinese characters on rice paper]. I begged him to escort me into my wedding and to give us his blessing. During the entire wedding ceremony, I kept looking back to see if he had shown up, but he never came. I cried the whole time.

In 1973, thirteen years after my husband left me, my brother-in-law went down to Pusan and saw him lying sick and alone in his room. The younger woman had left him, taking all his retirement money and everything else. His liver and kidney were deteriorating, and he was about to die. My brother-in-law visited me in Seoul and told me about it. It was the worst time of my life. We were at the bottom of the bottom; I was struggling to support my three children. One was in middle school, another was in junior college, and the third was in the seminary. I needed a huge sum of money for tuition and fees every time a new semester began.

I was operating a one-room garment shop in a rented room in Hongjedong *taltongnae* [squatter village] near the crematory [116] where only the poorest people lived.[117] The dress shop was also my son's living quarters. I rented another room nearby for my two daughters and two girls I had hired at the shop. We didn't even have any room for my husband. We were barely surviving. Besides, I had no feelings for my husband after what he had done.

Still, I thought I should at least ask my children what they thought. My older daughter was thirteen when he left us, and she didn't want to see him again. She was very bitter. She said that if we took him back, she would leave us. Even the mention of him made her angry; she didn't talk to me for several days. Then I asked my son, who was about to be ordained as a minister. He said, "If I say no now, what would I say to God when He asks me what I did with my sick father? How could I preach if I didn't take my sick father back?" He wanted to take his father in. Finally, I asked my younger daughter, who was only three when he left and could not remember him very well. She always wanted to see her father and call him "*appa* [Daddy]."

I prayed to God about what I should do. Finally, I realized that I had to take him back. I used to pray to God to make him come back home, even if He had to punish him, and God answered my prayers. My husband was severely punished, and if I didn't take him back, I would not have anything to say to God when I went to Him later. Now I tell people not to pray to God to punish their husbands, but just to pray for them to come back without punishment. God listens to prayers, so you have to be careful what you ask.

Even though my husband had left us, I had maintained a good relationship with my in-laws, who were decent people. My brother-in-law and his wife were very supportive of us when we were struggling. My children's *komo* [aunt] was very close to my older daughter. She came and talked to her, and she finally agreed that we should take her father back; so my brother-in-law went to Pusan and brought my husband back to us.

All he had was one suitcase in his hand. He was very ill. Rent was cheap in the *p'anjach'on* [another way of saying squatter village]. We rented a room at the top of the hill for him.[118]

I had to support three households: myself and my son in the shop; my two daughters and two workers in another rented room; and my sick husband in still another rented room. It was very hard, but I took care of my husband because of my faith in God and because he was the father of my three children. I didn't do it because I had any feelings for him; it was out of my sense of duty and obligation.

Three months after my husband moved in, our son got a job as a pastor's apprentice at the Yŏnhŭi Presbyterian Church near Yonsei and Ewha universities. The church provided us with a house, and the professors and students who attended that church were very kind to us. Finally, the three parts of our family were able to live together under one roof.

My husband died a few months after we moved into the pastor's residence. The church gave him a nice funeral.[119] Later, we discovered in his diary that he had accepted Jesus Christ before he died. He regretted what he had done to me and to his children, and he prayed to God for forgiveness. My son said, "Mother, I know he is in heaven."

I attended Kidok Pyŏngwŏn [Christian Hospital] Nursing School in P'yŏngyang. I wanted to become a nurse after I saw two close friends from elementary school die, one from tuberculosis and the other from typhus. When I'd finished two of the three years, Japan surrendered and the Soviet soldiers occupied P'yŏngyang. They were stealing things and raping the women. I was supposed to graduate in February 1946, but it was not safe for me to stay there, so my grandfather came to take me to Anju, where he had arranged a teaching position for me at an elementary school. All the Japanese teachers were gone and teachers were hard to find,[120] so I became a teacher and a school nurse. That was when a friend introduced me to my husband.

My husband was from Sinŭiju. His younger brother was involved in the Sinuiju student revolt[121] and was being sought by the North Korean authorities, so we had to escape. We decided to move to the South. We risked our lives crossing the 38th parallel. After that experience, I have never been afraid of anything.

Just after my son's *tol* [first birthday], we moved to Inch'ŏn, where I started a *yangjangjŏm* [a small-scale shop where Western dresses are made and sold]. Just as business was about to pick up, the Korean War broke out. My husband and his brother escaped to Pusan right before the North Koreans occupied Inch'ŏn. For three months, the rest of the family lived under the occupation.

In September 1950, warships and air bombers were pounding Inch'ŏn in preparation for the landing of the UN troops. A church elder came by and advised us to leave town right away, because the landing was imminent; so we escaped and hid in a bean field. Shells were falling all over; I saw many people being hit by bullets, shells, and cannon bombs. People were being killed and maimed in front of my eyes. When we returned to the house, we saw the roof had been hit by a cannon bomb and the people inside were injured. We were in a basement shelter when the UN troops arrived. They shouted from outside, "Everybody come out with your hands up!" I came out first, and the others followed me. We were afraid because we did not know what was going to happen to us. After we all came out, the soldiers threw a hand grenade into the shelter and blew it up. If we had not come out, we would have been killed.

During the *il-sa* [January 4, 1951, the day the UN forces retreated from Seoul as North Korean and Chinese troops moved in] retreat, our family rented a boat with other church members and sailed to Pusan. There, I taught dressmaking while my husband worked as a customs clearing specialist for the silk export federation.

When the war ended in 1953, our financial situation got better. That's when the trouble began. My husband started to womanize. He was playing *hwat'o* [flower cards] and billiards and dancing all the time. He wouldn't go to church. Thinking back, I think I was too strict and stubborn. I was self-righteous and pushed him too hard. I thought I was always right because I believed in the Bible. I only focused on the church and the children, and I rejected everything he did that I considered improper.

People were telling me that they saw him in movie theaters and tea rooms with a younger woman, but I didn't want to believe it. I finally discovered that he had deflowered a virgin and set up a household with her. He was going back and forth between her and me. We fought every day. He wouldn't let her bear a child. I don't know why, but that's what she told me when I met her.

Finally I moved to Seoul with the children in 1960. My married life lasted thirteen years. Starting a new life in Seoul was difficult. The dressmakers in Myŏngdong[122] would not hire me because they considered my style old-fashioned, so I started to attend Narno Design School. Then there was the eruption of *sa-il-gu*,[123] and the school closed down before I could finish the course. We settled in an illegal squatter district in the outskirts of Seoul, where people are not so sensitive about style. There, we struggled for the next thirteen years. That was the most difficult period of my life. Preparing the tuition and fees for my children was the hardest part. My son comforted me by saying that it's darkest just before dawn, and God listened to my prayers. He would send me group orders for school uniforms, workers' clothing, and things like that, and I was always able to pay the children's tuition at the very last moment.

Our life changed completely after my son found work at the church in 1973. The pastor's house was nice, with many rooms and a fence around it.

I leased out the Hongjedong dress shop and helped my son with his church work. In 1974, I enrolled at a seminary, and the next year my friends at the National Medical Center asked me if I would direct the nurses' residence. My classmates from the P'yŏngyang nursing school were in charge of the nursing program there. I had that position until 1979, completing my seminary studies in the meantime. By then, my son had a church, my older daughter was a kindergarten teacher, my younger daughter was in college, and we were able to buy a modern apartment in Sinch'on.

After my older daughter married and left for the United States, I quit the medical center job and went to work for a small church in a very poor neighborhood. Since I had finished seminary school, I wanted to work full-time for the church. This church was on the second floor of a rubber plant. The congregation had over one hundred members, mostly factory workers and their families. I moved into a room attached to the church with my younger daughter. My friends said, "You're crazy. How are you going to marry your daughter off if you live in a place like that?" I told them not to worry, that God had a plan for my daughter. Then, my daughter's childhood friend started courting her. They married while we were still living at that church. Her husband has become a successful businessman, and they live in La Cañada, California, now.

I really enjoyed the work at the church. Work-related injuries were frequent among factory workers, but they couldn't afford hospital treatment. I used my connections at the medical center to get treatment for them. The doctors and nurses at the emergency room all knew me and extended treatment without charge.

Ever since 1943, when I attended the Christian Hospital Nursing School, I wanted to come to the U.S.[124] When my older daughter moved here in 1979, I really wanted to come visit. When a new seminary in Seoul offered me an administrative position, I said I'd take the job if they'd let me visit my daughter in New York every summer. They said yes, so I took the job. I was able to go to New York every year between 1981 and 1985. I got a discount on the plane fare by escorting adopted Korean children to New York.

I came here as an immigrant, permanently, in 1986. By then, my daughter was a U.S. citizen and could petition for me. My son and his family had come to Los Angeles a year earlier. He was invited by a church in which there was an internal fight. After one faction left the church, the other faction invited him, and he found himself caught in the middle of a power struggle. After seven months, he quit the job and established his own congregation. He rented out space at a Presbyterian church near Los Angeles City College owned by second-generation Japanese Americans. I was on my way to New York, so I stopped by to see how my son's church was doing. Only about thirty people were attending the Sunday services, and my daughter-in-law was working full-time as a secretary in the criminal justice building. They had three little children to take care of. That's how I ended up in Los Angeles.

Taking care of my grandchildren was very hard. They were four, six, and nine years old when I first came. I had to take my four-year-old grandson to kindergarten by bus every morning and then pick him up every afternoon. I prayed a lot, day and night, for relief from my stress. I never missed early morning prayers. The only two people who are always at the church at dawn are my son and me. For three years, I lived with my son's family in an apartment near the church. I've been cleaning the church, because I feel that it's my duty to keep God's house neat and clean. At first, my grandchildren complained a lot. "Why do you have to clean the church all the time by yourself?" Now they help with the cleaning.

In 1987, a year after moving to Los Angeles, I started teaching dressmaking at the YWCA in 1987. Also, I began doing volunteer work at the Hollywood Presbyterian Hospital and Queen of Angels Hospital. We make clothes for poor women's babies. We have a team of forty volunteers in their seventies and eighties. About twenty of us come regularly twice a month. We usually come by bus and stay from late morning to midafternoon assembling the clothing. We buy the material with proceeds from the homemade aprons we sell at the YWCA, and then make the patterns and cut the cloth at home before we come to the hospital.

Every Wednesday afternoon, about fifteen of us visit Pio Pico Library to read books to children who have to pass their time in the library after school hours because their mothers are working. Some of the children want us to read English books, and others want Korean books. We read whatever they want. The children like us. I think there should be more programs for children and senior citizens to help and enjoy each other.

I do volunteer work because I want to pay this country back for being so nice to me. I live in a senior citizens' apartment and receive a government check each month. I am very grateful for this. Also, I want to keep myself busy.

Ever since I arrived in Los Angeles, I've been taking English classes in grammar, speech, and essay writing. I made friends with a Thai student at adult school who told me I could take classes at the city college. I never knew that an old lady like me could go to college. [125]

One day, I discovered that my right hand was shaking a little, so I started writing out chapters from the Bible. Every night before going to bed, I listen to a tape of the chapter I'm going to write the next day. The next morning, I write it in English. I read one verse in Korean and then write it in English. I average one chapter a day. This way, I can understand the message much better. So far, I've finished the entire New Testament, Psalms, Proverbs, Ecclesiastes, Song of Songs, Genesis, Exodus, Leviticus, and Numbers. I will write out the entire Bible before I die. The more I write, the more I enjoy it. It's spiritually rewarding. And the shaking in my hand is completely gone.

I got my U.S. citizenship in 1991. I have been voting ever since. I became a Republican because I liked George Bush and because the Republican party is a little conservative. But in the last election, I voted against Proposition 187[126] because I know some "illegal" immigrants and the hardships they go through.

I am happy with my life in America. I feel that I have been blessed. Maybe God blessed me because I suffered so much in the past.

DECEMBER 1994

JAMES PARK
Man of the House

James Park [pseudonym] was born in Korea in 1942 and entered
the United States as a foreign student in 1969. He speaks colloquial
English fluently, and when he speaks Korean, it is sprinkled with
English words. Although he is a successful businessman and a
leader in the Los Angeles Korean immigrant community, there is
a trace of sadness in his face, and he cried when he talked about
his past.

During my early years, I was separated from my father. He worked as a clerk at the *myŏn* [rural township] office. When Korea became independent from Japan in 1945, he moved to Seoul and worked for the government property control agency. His office was in charge of transferring Japanese property ownership to Koreans after the Japanese left Korea. Whoever registered first became the new owners.

I was raised by my mother and my grandmother in a remote farm village on the western coast of southern Korea. When the communists took over Seoul during the Korean War, my father came back to take refuge in our village. He hid in the attic for the three months of communist occupation. During the *il-sa* [January 4, 1951] retreat from Seoul,[127] he fled to Pusan. There, he met a woman who was a refugee from Hamhŭng in North Korea. He took her as his concubine.

We had a very hard life. My father didn't make enough money as a government worker to support two families, so he practically abandoned us. When the South Korean government moved back to Seoul after it had been recovered from the Chinese and the North Koreans, he brought his concubine to Seoul with him. I moved to Seoul to attend middle school and I lived with my father and his concubine. I had to call her *chagŭn ŏmma* [small mom or second mom]. My mother never came to see me in Seoul because of the awkward family situation. Every summer, I went to the countryside to stay with her, and during funerals or *chesa* [memorial rites for ancestors], my father would come down to our home town alone. Everyone in town knew he had a concubine; it became an accepted fact. But accepting that fact was very difficult for my mother. She suffered a great deal. Then, when I was a junior in high school, she suddenly died. Since I was in Seoul, I never knew exactly how she died. My two younger brothers were living with her in the countryside at the time. I think she died because of my father's neglect. In remote villages, there were no doctors around. People had to travel to nearby cities to find a doctor, and transportation was very bad. She was only

275

forty-three years old when she died. I still feel terrible about it.

My mother was seventeen and my father was sixteen when they got married. My older brother was born when my father was only nineteen. When people saw them together, they would ask if the baby was his younger brother. Father was so ashamed of the fact that he had a son at such a young age that he didn't want to take my brother to the market and other places. As a result, my brother never developed much affection for our father. Also, my father's younger brother was only five years older than my older brother, and my grandmother would side with the uncle whenever they fought. When my older brother finished high school, he joined the army. The jeep he was driving went off a cliff, and he was paralyzed from the waist down. Taking care of him was a continual problem for the family, and he didn't live long.

Besides my elder brother, I have two younger brothers. From my father's concubine, I had one half-sister and four half-brothers. Two of the half-brothers drowned when a sudden heavy storm swelled a stream at the foot of the mountain where they had gone camping. Since the concubine's name could not be entered in our family registry, my half-brothers and [half] sister were registered as children of my mother.[128] After my mother's death, *jakun omma*'s name was entered into the family registry as the new legal wife of my father.

While I was staying with my father's family in Seoul, my father and step-mother would fight constantly about me. Whenever they got my report card, which was always good, my stepmother would say something and get into an argument with my father. Maybe she was jealous. Anyway, I couldn't get any money at home. Whenever I needed money, I had to go to my father's office to ask for it. I could never buy anything because my step-mother would ask where the money had come from, and they would get into a fight. It was very difficult for me to stay with them. Finally, when I entered high school, I got a job as a private tutor and moved into my student's house. My student's family was very nice to me and let me use the room all the time, so I was able to do well in high school and prepare for the college entrance examinations. Luckily, I was admitted to Seoul National University. I worked my way through college tutoring and graduated with a major in international trade.

My two younger brothers, especially the second one, are still angry at my father. On the surface, they are cordial to him, but inside, they are very resentful. They had to walk to school eight kilometers [4.96 miles] every day. They watched how our mother suffered when she was abandoned by our father. Maybe because I am the first son now, I have forgiven him.

When my mother died, my grandmother and my two younger brothers moved into my older brother's house in Seoul. The government had provided housing for him when he was paralyzed. He couldn't marry because of his physical condition, so my grandmother had to take care of him. That was a very difficult time for all of us. Maybe my outgoing personality comes from hardships I experienced at that time. I used to hang around with my friends a lot because of the problems in the family.

When I finished college, I joined the Sam Yang Company, working in the section that handled exporting sweaters. After a year and a half, I decided to go abroad to study because I wanted to escape from family problems. Also, I saw how my college *sŏnbae* [a person who precedes], who was ten years older than I was was remaining at a low rank, and I didn't want to be like him after ten years. I had ambition. Also, I wasn't a good candidate for marriage because of my family problems. I could see no future for myself in Korea.

I applied and was accepted at American Graduate School of International Management in Arizona. We called that school Thunderbird. I started the program in 1969. I had a tape recorder, a camera, and a hundred dollars in my pocket when I arrived in Los Angeles. One of my friends told me to bring a tape recorder so that I could tape the lectures and study for the tests. I borrowed money from the university to finish the program.

During two summer vacations, I went to Los Angeles to work. I stayed with a friend who was dating a Chinese-American student. She had a Hispanic roommate named Ruth. Ruth and I dated for about a year and got married in 1971.

Many people ask me why I married a non-Korean. If I had wanted to marry a Korean, they would have checked my family background, and they would have discovered that my father had a concubine, that my mother died as a result, and that I had half-siblings. I knew it would be a problem. Americans don't look at the family; they look at the person.

I found out that Ruth was more conservative than Oriental girls. I liked her way of thinking. She was from a poor family, too; like me, she had to work the whole time she was in college. Her ancestors came from Mexico generations ago and lived in Texas, where she was born and where she still has many relatives. She and her Chinese-American friend transferred to Cal State L.A., where she was a student when I met her.

Ruth never looked down on me. When I met her family, they treated me with respect. I felt comfortable with her and with her family.

At first, my father opposed my wish to marry Ruth. He wanted me to come to Korea to meet the girls he would line up for me, but I married Ruth and notified him afterwards.

After finishing the graduate program at Thunderbird, I got a job in the international banking division of the Hong Kong Bank of California. There, I saw that several customers were making a lot of money in the import-export business, and I thought to myself, "Why not me?" During my first two-week vacation, I went to Korea to meet with manufacturers. I brought back boxes of samples, quit my job at the bank, and opened up an import-export company.

I was able to start a business because Ruth had a job with the County, and we were able to live on her income.

Also, because I had married an American, I was able to apply for U.S. citizenship within three years. I became a citizen in 1976 and then petitioned for my two younger brothers to immigrate. They came in 1978. I bought a janitorial account from a friend who was leaving for another city, and I put my brothers in charge of it. Within three years, we were able to get a contract with the military. We had neither the money nor the expertise to get such a contract, but the Small Business Administration helped us.

The facilities management business has grown large; now we have contracts with the military, hospitals, and NASA all over the United States. The import-export business also grew. We pioneered the importation of Korean pears to U.S. markets. It took three years to establish the market, and then everyone jumped in. Competition became severe, and the business declined. At first, we had exclusive right to import the pears, but when other people saw us making money, they wrote letters to the Korean government asking why our company was given exclusive rights. After the government ended our exclusive right to import the pears, competitors started importing and dumping. They ruined the market. We gradually shifted to export. Now we export titanium pipes and factory equipment. Our business is pretty good.

Our philosophy is "customers first." If we're going to be late, we ship by air. We may lose money, but the next time we get a much bigger order. Sometimes we ship 100 pieces. If they say two or three pieces are missing, we don't argue. We ship the missing pieces by air. Customers are happy when they deal with us.

I always watch the cash flow and meet the payment deadlines at the bank. If I have a problem, I tell the bank in advance that the accounts receivable payment is slow. I have kept a good relationship with my bank, which is why the bank gives us a sufficient line of credit.

My business philosophy is management by delegation. One of my brothers is in charge of the import-export business, and the other is in charge of the facilities management business. My wife is the corporate secretary. I give general directions. Once I delegate responsibilities, I don't interfere with details. Korean businessmen don't know how to delegate; they want to do everything themselves because they don't trust other people. Management by delegation is the way for small businesses to grow. It gives you more time to plan the future. That's all I do—long-range planning.

When my two brothers came, my wife suggested that we give them shares so that they would take an interest in the business and work hard. I had never heard a woman say things like that. I know several friends who have problems with their siblings because they did not give shares to them. Usually their wives oppose giving anything to their siblings. They use their brothers as managers. When the brothers learn the work, they open up their own businesses and become competitors, and everyone ends up hurting each other. We gave 20 percent of the corporate shares to each of my brothers. The rest of the shares are divided between my wife and myself, at 30 percent each. We work well as partners. I am very lucky; my brothers and I are close because we suffered a lot together, and we also had good times together. When we were small, we used to fish and swim in the stream.

One thing I appreciate my wife for is that she never said no to anything I wanted to do. That's why I started the business even though I didn't have any money. I told her that since our business was doing all right, I wanted to continue with my education. She said OK, and I started the doctorate program in international business at the U.S. International University in San Diego. I took courses at their Irvine campus on weekends for two years and commuted to San Diego for one semester toward the end. I could not have made it without the help of my wife and my brothers. I finished my dissertation in 1991, when I was forty-nine years old. Since then, I have been teaching international business and import-export courses at UCLA's extension school and at a local state university. This is my fourth year of teaching, and I enjoy it very much. I incorporate my business experiences into my course material so that my students won't repeat the kinds of mistakes I made.

I spend a lot of time on social and community activities, and my wife never objects to my active involvement in the Korean community. Once, she said that while she was growing up she saw her mother stand by with a towel while her father was washing his hands. Her family is man-oriented; the women listen to the men. Whenever my wife wants to purchase something valuable, she asks my opinion. I say to her, "You don't have to ask me; go ahead and buy it if you like." But she says, "You are the man of the house, and I want to know your opinion." She puts me first and makes me feel good.

We have three daughters. When we had the first one, we said that was enough. Later, we thought we should have a son, and after seven years we had another baby, which turned out to be a girl. We said, "This is it," but four years later, we tried a third time, thinking it might be a son. But we had another daughter. My wife got her tubes tied, so we can't have any more children.

When our children go to Korea, they are regarded as Americans. When they are here, they are treated as half and half. My first daughter went to a private high school where there was only one Korean student, so she didn't have any Korean friends. But when she went to Columbia University, she met and made friends with many Korean students. Last year, we sent her to Korea for three months to study at the Yonsei University International Program. She didn't learn much Korean, but I think she enjoyed the trip. When she finished high school, she went to Spain on an exchange program and is now fluent in Spanish. Two years ago, she went to France and stayed there a year. Our second and third daughters attended public school. They have many Korean friends. There are also many Korean children at the church we go to, although it is not a Korean church.[129] I don't think our children have any problems with their identity. They know they are half Hispanic and half Korean and they fit well with both groups.

My wife and I bought an apartment in Seoul for my father and stepmother. We brothers chip in money and send a monthly allowance to them. I petitioned for all my half-siblings to immigrate to the United States. My half-sister and her husband own a liquor store and are pretty well off. One of my half-brothers has a shop at a swap meet; the other is a wage worker. I helped them buy houses, start businesses, and find jobs, and yet my father still tells me that I helped make my brothers rich but I don't help my half-brothers enough.

Some time ago, my half-brother asked me to lend him $50,000 to start a business. I asked him how much he was going to put in, and he said he didn't have anything, so I chased him away. That's not the way to start a business. I had already loaned him a good deal of money to buy a house. He has never paid any of it back, even though he bought a nice car and other things. But my father got very angry at me. Whenever my father and step-mother come from Seoul, they bring a lot of gifts for my half-brothers and half-sister, but they don't bring anything for us. They tell us not to come to the airport to meet them because they don't want us to see the packages they are bringing for my half-brothers. They are always trying to hide those things. We do everything for them, but their love goes to our half-brothers, and that creates resentment in us.

In a way, my story can be called a success story. I was born into a poor family, and I came to the United States with almost nothing. I had to borrow money to finish the graduate program, and then I paid it back and started a business from scratch. I teach at a college. I am happily married and have three children. But it is too early to really say that I am successful, because I still have an unresolved issue, which is my resentment toward my father and my stepmother. I think I forgive my father, but there is still resentment inside me.

JANUARY 1995

JAY KUN YOO
Pilgrimage

Expressive, witty, and persuasive in Korean, Jay Kun Yoo's verbal talents never found full use in America.[130] After more than two decades in the United States, he returned to Korea, where he is now a celebrated talk-show host and professor of law. "Not many people have had a life like mine," says cherub-faced Yoo. "I was born and grew up in Korea; I lived in Manchuria; I studied in the United States and became a community activist and practicing lawyer there before I returned to Korea to live and work."

282

Mother used to call me "winter vacation boy." I was conceived when my father was visiting during winter vacation and born on *ch'usŏk* [lunar harvest day], August 15, 1937. The day after their wedding, my father went to Seoul to enter Kyŏngshin Middle School. My father came home only to perform his filial duties for *chesa* [ancestor commemoration ceremonies]. I figure that my parents' total married life spanned not more than twenty days. There was no romance for my mother; her functions were to give birth to a son and take care of the household chores. The Yoo family had a big farm with many hired hands, and she was responsible for the house, the farm, and the family.

After Father graduated from Kyŏngshin High School, he went to Japan to study law. Everywhere he went, he always had a female companion, a girl-friend or a concubine; that's why he rarely came home. He even introduced five of these women to my mother, and there were many others. At the time, that kind of behavior was socially acceptable. My mother was a *de facto* widow, living with my grandparents and me.

My grandfather was also a playboy type. One day, he met a lady in a wine house and ran away with her to Pusan. Grandmother was furious. She sold the house and the rice farm and moved with me and my mother to Seoul. About nine months later, after he had spent all his money and needed the family's support, Grandfather wanted to come home, but Grandmother would not take him back.

We managed all right financially. When my father returned from Japan, he was living somewhere with another woman, but he sent money to us every month through a messenger.

From early childhood, then, I lived with my mother and grandmother, without a male adult figure in the family. When I was little, my mother often told me that since the way my father and grandfather lived their lives was not right, I should "revolutionize the family tradition." She was afraid that I might have inherited their legacy through the blood. I told her not to worry; since I had seen all the suffering that she and my grandmother had to go through, I would never live my life like my father's or grandfather's. Up until now, I have kept that promise. I believe in family; without a good family, a person cannot do anything.

Anyway, when the Korean War broke out in 1950, I was in my first year at Kyŏnggi Middle School. Father called us and told us to go to Ch'ungch'ŏng Province, saying that he would join us if Seoul were captured by North Koreans, so we took the last train leaving Seoul and made it across the Han River just before the Han River bridge was destroyed. My father stayed in Seoul with his concubine, whose mother was eighty years old. Later, we heard that the North Korean police came and took him away to North Korea. We never heard from him again.

During the war we stayed in Ch'ŏnan. I attended middle school there. My grandmother, mother and I became Christian, and the wine shop where my grandfather met his concubine became a church. I think that God wanted to take care of my mother, my grandmother, and the poor little boy He saw, so He led us to His church.

When the truce between North Korea and the UN forces was signed, we moved back to Seoul and settled in a room in a squatter area in Miari, in one of the poorest outskirts of Seoul. I remember that our room was so cold in winter that it was hard to sleep. I went back to Kyŏnggi Middle School as a ninth-grader.

As head of the household, I had to support my grandmother, my mother, and myself. From the age of fifteen, I held three jobs: every morning I got up at 4:00 A.M. to deliver newspapers before going to school; after school, I tutored middle-school pupils for money; and at night, I peddled rice cakes [ch'apssalttŏk] that mother and I made, combing through the residential areas with a wooden box on my back, shouting, "Ch'apssalttŏk!"

We joined a Methodist church in Miari. My mother went to church at dawn every day to pray. She had never gone to school, but she learned han'gŭl [Korean writing; the Korean phonetic alphabet] there. I became actively involved when I was in high school. I had won oratory contests all over the country, and I became a kind of evangelist. I was able to attract many students to the church: when we started our high school Sunday school class, there were only four students; but within a year the number grew to 150.

The pastor at the church urged me to apply for seminary school, but the school vice principal, who was a Christian himself, advised me to apply to Yonsei University's Department of International Relations instead. I was interested in politics or some type of evangelical work, and the vice principal said I could go to the seminary after graduating from the university. When I was accepted at Yonsei, I was still delivering newspapers and peddling *ch'apssalttŏk*. Most of my classmates at Kyŏnggi High School and Yonsei University never knew how my family lived. I never complained; I was always cheerful and thankful because I was a born optimist and a strong Christian.

Tosan [philosopher/sage] Ahn Chang Ho's[131] teachings deeply influenced me. I wanted to help poor kids get basic education. After the war, many children were on the streets or working full time as houseboys for American companies, shoeshine boys, newspaper delivery boys, or chewing gum and cigarette peddlers. Many of them could not afford to go to school, so I opened night classes for them. I taught *han'gŭl*, English, and mathematics. At one point, there were 160 students in the night class. Some of them were older than I was; I was only sixteen at the time. About three years ago, one of the students from my night class saw me on TV and arranged for a reunion with other students. I had taught this man how to write his name, and he is now president of a big furniture company in Seoul. It was a wonderful reunion, and we have been meeting once a month since then.

After graduating from the university, I became a Korean Air Force officer. The most prestigious job in the air force was [to be a] pilot; the next most important was ground controller, which was my job. While serving in the air force, I earned an M.A. at Yonsei University. Soon after I completed my military service, the Blue House [presidential office] was seeking high-ranking staff officers from Yonsei University, Seoul National University, and Korea (Koryŏ) University. Yonsei University recommended me, and I was hired. But on the first day of work, I was told I could not be employed there. Later, I learned that during the investigation of my background, it was revealed that a North Korean spy being interrogated by the KCIA had mentioned my father's name. I never found out what the spy said, but because of that I was classified as a security risk.

After that, I applied for a position as a journalist at the *Tong-A Ilbo*, which was the largest daily newspaper in Korea at the time. Several hundred people applied for fifteen positions. I was the only person eliminated among the 15 finalists in the final screening. I suspect that the KCIA file had something to do with it. I was deemed a security risk because of a father whose face I didn't even remember. I was heartbroken, but there was nothing I could do.

About this time, the Yonsei University president recommended me for the position of student activities coordinator at the UNESCO [United Nations Educational, Scientific and Cultural Organization] office in Seoul. UNESCO was not a Korean organization, and no one there cared about my background. I worked there for about four years. In 1966, UNESCO sent me to the U.S. for six months. Up to that time, my ambition had been to become a politician, but my trip to the United States inspired me toward community organizing. After returning to Korea, I organized the Korea UNESCO Students Association, with chapters at most of the major Korean universities. We emphasized communication and organizational skills.

In the mid-1960s, Yi Mun-Kyou, a Seoul National University graduate and progressive-minded young leader and my roommate at the Air Force Officers Candidate School in Taejŏn, organized the Haksajujŏm, a wine house gathering place for progressive-minded intellectuals in Seoul. About sixty friends chipped in to start the organization. Lee made a secret trip to North Korea to meet with North Korean leaders about national unification.[32] Most of his friends, including me, knew nothing about the trip, which was a serious violation of the South Korean security laws. When it was discovered that he had gone to North Korea, he was arrested, charged with espionage, and executed. Many of the people he knew were implicated and jailed. My name was associated with the Haksajujŏm, and I more or less had to run away to the U.S. to escape arrest. The director of the United States Information Service in Seoul helped me through his father, who was the foreign students' adviser at Brigham Young University. I got my passport and visa and left for the United States within ten days. That was in 1969.

After a year at Brigham Young, I got an M.A. in sociology. My thesis, which was on community power structures, won the award for the best thesis at the regional sociological convention. A well-known sociologist from the University of Washington in Seattle liked my paper and offered me a full scholarship in the Ph.D. program there, so I brought my family over from Korea and moved to Seattle.

I completed the course work and the qualifying examination and was teaching sociology classes and doing court interpreting when I got acquainted with a judge who encouraged me to go to law school. That was in 1971, when Korean immigration was skyrocketing. The judge said that I could always complete the sociology degree after finishing law school. I entered the University of Washington Law School summer program and finished the summer program at the top of the class of 126 students. It was unbelievable. My adviser, who was assistant dean of UC Davis Law School, asked me to come to his school.

After law school, I worked for a while for Governor Jerry Brown and State Assemblyman Art Torres, and then I was hired as a legal aid worker in Sacramento. That's when I became interested in immigration law and Chol Soo Lee's case attracted my attention.

Chol Soo Lee was charged with murdering a fellow prison inmate while he was serving a term for the famous San Francisco Chinatown killing of a Wah Ching gang leader.[133] The prison killing occurred on October 1977. If convicted of the second killing, he would be sentenced to death. I called Kyung Won [K.W.] Lee,[134] who was a reporter at the *Sacramento Union* to ask if he would be willing to work with me to bring the case to the community's attention. We went to the prison to look at Chol Soo Lee's records. He had been almost completely abandoned by the community: during the five years he had been in prison, only two people had visited him—his mother and a childhood friend.

We introduced ourselves and told him that we would like to help, but he said, "It's all over; nobody can help me now." After we had spent many hours of trying to persuade him, he broke down and wept. Up to that time, the only male figures he had ever encountered were prison guards, prosecutors, and policemen, and to him, they were all oppressors. Even his court-appointed lawyer had screwed him over.

He told us to look at his court files if we wanted to find out more about him. His court-appointed attorney refused to let us read the file, saying that all appeal avenues were closed. We persisted, and K.W. Lee cursed him to his face. Finally, he allowed us to read the file, but only in his office, so it took a month of visits several times a week to read the 2000-page file. Reading that file, it was obvious even to me, a rookie law school graduate, that the police, the prosecution, and the defense had all screwed up the case and that Chol Soo Lee's civil rights had been repeatedly violated.

K.W. Lee wrote a full two-page story about the case in the *Sacramento Union* in 1977. The full text was translated and reported in the *Han'guk Ilbo* in San Francisco, and the story was widely publicized in Korean communities all over the country. At the end of September 1977, we held the first meeting to organize a committee to help Chol Soo Lee. I went to Los Angeles, where I received enthusiastic support.

During the next six years, I made about 250 presentations to community groups all over the country. Every time I presented the case, people wanted to know if I was absolutely sure that Chol Soo Lee was innocent, if he could make it on his own should he be freed, and why I was spending all my time on this case instead of preparing for the bar examinations. I always tried to answer calmly, by presenting the facts about the trial and our reasons for being interested in the campaign.

We contacted Leonard Weinglass, who had defended Tom Hayden and Chicago Seven, telling him we had raised $30,000. He reviewed the case and said he would take it. Eleven Asian American lawyers volunteered their services free.

It was obvious that Chol Soo Lee had been politically framed. He was not a Chinatown boy. In 1973, twelve killings occurred in San Francisco's Chinatown, but no one was arrested. No one would testify at the court. At the time, the mayor was up for re-election, and he ordered the chief of police to arrest someone. Chol Soo Lee became that someone. The killing that he was accused of occurred on July 3, 1973, at the junction of Pacific and Grant streets. It was a Sunday evening, around 7:00 P.M.; the sun was still up, and there were about sixty or seventy people around. Many people at the scene witnessed the killing. Eventually, six people testified in court. Many of them said that they could not identify anyone because all Orientals look alike. The police suggested man #5, who was Chol Soo Lee. They had picked him from the California Youth Authority file, which listed about 200 supposed Asian gang members. Chol Soo Lee had been arrested for bicycle theft. One of the detectives who handled the case later testified that he had been indicted without sufficient evidence.

We organized the Chol Soo Lee Defense Committee on July 17, 1978. July 17 is Constitution Day in South Korea. On that day, we turned in *habeas corpus* to the Stockton court. *Habeas corpus* was our only avenue to reopen the five-year-old case, because the statute of limitations had all expired on higher levels of appeal. There have been more than 10,000 *habeas corpus* filed in U.S. courts, and most of these cases have been dismissed. Chol Soo Lee's was only the tenth such case that was retried. For *habeas corpus*, you have to bring evidence or witnesses that were not presented in the first trial, or else you have to bring the person who actually committed the crime. When we filed the seventy-seven-page *habeas corpus,* we listed seven grounds; the most important was that the police suggested to the witnesses that Chol Soo Lee was the culprit. Furthermore, the prosecution concealed a witness named Steven Morris, who had called the police immediately after the shooting.

Morris had described the culprit as much taller than Chol Soo Lee. The police ignored him, but we found his name on the police report. There were 760 Steven Morrises in California, and we spent $19,000 and an entire week trying to find the one who witnessed the crime. A private investigator we hired found him working as a bartender in Los Angeles. He agreed to appear in court, where he identified the policeman to whom he had reported the crime. The judge ruled that the case deserved a new trial.

When the final trial was held in San Francisco, there were fourteen lawyers sitting with Chol Soo Lee. Every day, there was a dramatic scene. A Korean Catholic priest, some Protestant ministers in clerical collars, and a Buddhist monk praying with his beads would sit in the front row, and a roomful of Koreans, many of them elders wearing *hanbok* [traditional Korean clothing] sat in the rows behind them. Each day during the two-month trial, my wife was on the telephone arranging transportation, while my mother was preparing *kimpap* [sushi rice] for over one hundred supporters. During the trial, no one tired of doing all this work. Our whole family was committed to the case for six years. The day before Labor Day, 1982, the jury's unanimous verdict was "not guilty."

We alleged self-defense in the prison killing, but it would have cost an additional $200,000 and two years to prepare for a new trial. Chol Soo Lee wanted to fight all the way, to clear his name, but we were exhausted and advised him to accept the district attorney's offer to free him without saying he was guilty or not guilty, without probation, and without compensation. Chol Soo had already spent more than ten years in prison. He finally agreed and became a free man, rescued from San Quentin's death row. It was a kind of resurrection. He is still going through hardships, having difficulty adjusting to life on the outside. We have to pray for him.

I spent six years of my life on this case because I believed he was innocent, because there had been racial discrimination in the legal proceedings, and because there had been a political frame-up involving the mayor of San Francisco. In Chol Soo, I saw another side of myself: like me, he grew up as the only child of a single mother. My father's face has no relevance to me; I don't even recall it. The only difference between us is that I was helped by God, who blessed me with a good mother and a good wife.

When I was a boy, my mother made me promise to "revolutionize the family tradition," according to which both my grandfather and my father deserted their wives for other women. My mother, my wife, and I have lived together in the same house for twenty-six years and have never even raised our voices to each other. For four years, my wife's mother also lived with us, and both mothers are like sisters. It's been a miracle; we could not be happier.[135] I believe in family, because without a good family, a person can't do anything.

For the first two years with the Chol Soo Lee Defense Committee, I was paid as a legal aid worker. For the next four years, I received the minimum wage for legal services. It was my calling; I had to finish the task to the end. My wife worked as a chemist and helped support the family. For six years, my wife and mother fully supported my work without ever once complaining. We wanted to show America and the legal system that we Korean Americans love justice and can organize ourselves to defend our rights.

I flunked the California bar examination seven times. Our whole church prayed for me each time I took the examination. When they heard that I had failed again, they could not even look at me. But I was never frustrated. I finally passed the bar on the eighth try and started practicing law in Los Angeles. I enjoyed the work, but my clients were mostly poor, and I was not doing well financially. About one-third of my clientele was non-paying. I was a church elder, and the ministers would send members of their congregation to me saying, Mr. Yoo is a nice man; he will help you. If I helped them ninety-nine times free, and then said once that I had to charge, they would hate me and think of me as a traitor. It was difficult for me to continue like this. It's a good thing to provide free services for the needy and the poor, but I had to make a living as well. That's why I returned to Korea. I thought that since I had many friends in Korea, it might be worth a try.

I worried that I might not make it in Korea, because I was just a generalist. There was nothing outstanding about me professionally. Competition was severe, and I was not used to the rules. I told my friends that I wanted to either teach in law school or become a television commentator like Walter Cronkite. In 1989, I was offered a position with MBC [Munhwa Broadcasting Company] as the host of a late-evening television discussion on current affairs. Within a couple of months, I started the job. The audience loved my voice; maybe it was from my boyhood *ch'apssalttŏk* peddling. Because of my varied educational and professional background in sociology, law, politics, and economics, I was able to lead discussions on a wide variety of topics. For the first six months, I commuted back and forth between Seoul and Los Angeles, and then I finally resettled in Seoul. After three years at MBC, I became dean of Kyŏng Wŏn Junior College and professor of law at Kyŏng Wŏn University. I enjoy this work very much.

Nonauthoritarian ways of handling interpersonal relationships, which I learned in the U.S., have been of great help in my work as a dean. I devote my energy to my work, which minimizes my longing for my children and for America.

My three children were all born in America. They are Americans. They consider themselves Americans and do not want to live in Korea. My daughters lived in Seoul for a year, but they didn't want to stay in Korea and went back to the U.S. My youngest stayed in Korea for three years and is now in college in California. My wife and I live in Korea, but we are linked to the United States: although I was required by MBC to give up my U.S. citizenship, my wife is still a U.S. citizen. She wants us to move back to the U.S. when I retire. It's been more difficult for her than for me to adjust to living in Korea; she doesn't enjoy meeting old friends because their conversations are limited to money and material possessions. Things are a little better now that she's teaching English at the police academy. Her mother and my mother, who is now eighty-four years old, still live together in California, and we still pay property taxes there.

I was able to readjust quickly to living in Seoul. In many ways, I am more Korean than many others who went to the United States to study. I went at the age of thirty-one, and my American life was always centered around Korean Americans and the Korean American community. I associated with Korean people, read Korean newspapers every day, listened to Korean radio, and watched Korean TV. In Korea, I feel appreciated; I never had this feeling of achievement or contentment in the United States. I was never able to penetrate the American mainstream. I hung onto the margins of the society, managing to survive by providing services to Korean American people.

Even so, I was surprised myself to realize how much my thought patterns had been influenced by American ways. Korea has changed a lot, but the basic relationship between men and women has not changed much. When I tell my friends that we should bring our wives when we get together, they say that is not the way things are done here. In the United States, I always went out with my wife to social gatherings, evening outings, parties, and friends' homes. Here, men often go by themselves to these gatherings. At first I felt awkward going to these evening meetings by myself. Whenever I called home to tell my wife I might be a little late, my friends called me *tchota* [fool]. My wife went to the United States when she was twenty-three. She hadn't had much experience as a married woman in Korea, and her readjustment to Korean life has been more difficult; everything seems strange and foreign to her. That's why I always try to let her know where I am and when I will be home. Nowadays, I see more and more men taking their wives to social gatherings, at last among the friends close to me. Maybe I am making an impact.

During thirty years of military rule, it became a tradition that ends, not means, are what matter. All kinds of means have been employed to get ahead in this society, to grab power and to make money, which are the only things that are respected here. Last spring, 74 percent of Ewha University students responded to a survey saying that you are a loser if you abide by the law, and 65 percent said you can only win respect by being rich.

Transportation in Seoul is terrible. It's impossible to keep an appointment on time. Being thirty minutes late is common, and sometimes you have to wait one or two hours for your appointment to show up. The air quality is homicidal: the blue skies of my youth can no longer be seen. On many occasions, I had difficulty with my voice on my television show because of the smog.

Actually, it was difficult to get used to things when we first moved back to Korea. People say I am pretty well-adjusted, but I don't feel that way; I think I am experiencing an identity crisis. Sometimes, I feel that I've been away from Korea for too long. They say that people who stay away too long become permanent vagabonds. When we are here, we long for America. When we are there, we long for Korea. But I'm a born optimist; I try to look at our situation in a positive light. The age of authoritarian rule is passing from all sectors of Korean society. I have certain strengths that I acquired in the United States, such as democratic ideals and egalitarian values, which can help me contribute to Korea. The world is changing rapidly, becoming smaller and smaller, but there aren't many people in Korea who understand America. Many Koreans who got Ph.D.s in America don't have much experience in American life; they simply spent several years in graduate school and then returned to Korea. People claim to know America, but their knowledge is very superficial. Someone once wrote two books about America after a one-week tour.

I was heartbroken when the 1992 Los Angeles riots erupted. Many of the people whose livelihoods were destroyed were my former clients. When I saw Koreatown burning on television in Seoul, I cried. I could not sleep at night. I wanted to go back to Los Angeles right away to help people, but because of my work I could not. After the riots, the Korea-U.S. Friendship Association invited several black members of the U.S. Congress to Seoul for a seminar. Koreans and blacks are not enemies; Koreans were simply caught in the crossfire of conflicts that existed for centuries between whites and blacks. I was surprised at the ignorance of the black congressmen about black-Korean relationships. Nor are there many people in Korea who can explain the nature of the Korean-black or even white-black relations. You would think that there would be many people in Korea who understand American social dynamics, but there are not that many.

In the end, it doesn't matter where you are; this world is all God's world. You just have to do the right thing and contribute your share. It doesn't matter whether you live in Korea or in the United States. Because of famine in his homeland, Jacob went to Egypt at the age of 130 to see his son. He was not timid; he spoke with pride and blessed the Egyptian king. Life is a pilgrimage, anyway; we are all wanderers, but great things are achieved by marginal people.

AUGUST 1993

YOUNG KIM

Born to Be a Soldier

Young Kim is a retired full colonel in the U.S. Army, a community activist, and a semiretired businessman. Although in his seventies, his posture is erect. He is a precise and punctual man. A second-generation Korean American, he was born in Los Angeles in January 1919, not long after his parents immigrated from Korea. Kim served in Europe with the segregated Japanese American military units during World War II and was also called to serve with the U.S. Army during the Korean War.

My father left Korea about the time Japan occupied Korea in 1910. His father had been a salt merchant in Inch'ŏn. My mother came from a farming family in Suwŏn. At that time, my parents were officially married, but they didn't live together. According to what little I heard from my father, he joined my uncle and his five or six friends when they ran away from home. They managed to get to Pusan and stowed away in a boat, but they got caught in the harbor and were sent back to Inch'ŏn. The second time, they got all the way to Yokohama, but got caught on board a ship headed for Hawaii. They made it to Hawaii the third time.

They worked, saved money, and made their way to Seattle. In those days, Seattle was the only port of entry for Asians. They got work as migrant farm workers and gradually worked their way south to Los Angeles, where the whole family worked together at a fruit stand in Alhambra, right on Fremont and Valley Boulevard. The fruit stand did very well. It was while working there with my uncle that I heard all these stories.

My mother was an educated woman. She graduated from a Methodist school in Seoul that was the forerunner of Ewha Women's University and had been a teacher in Korea. She came to America with an American missionary. Her ambition was to go to Chicago to further her education so that she could go back to Korea to teach. She told the missionary not to tell her husband that she had arrived, but the missionary said that she was a married woman and had to inform her husband. The missionary would not sponsor her to go to Chicago to study. Instead, she had to wire my father in Orange County. My father insisted that she join him immediately.

She had no alternative. Instead of going to school in Chicago, she ended up shelling walnuts in Orange County. For her, it was a terrible, terrible letdown. She cherished education and considered herself an educated woman. Before she died, she gave me her diploma from the Methodist school in Seoul. She said that it was her most precious possession.

My father was typical of many Korean immigrants I knew during that period. They fell into two categories: hardworking farmers and peasants who turned out to be better suited to America than Korea, and people with middle-class backgrounds who didn't know how to work.[136] My father belonged to the middle class category. His idea of living was sitting around drinking and talking with his friends about philosophy and politics. He participated in all the community functions. But basically, he did not know how to work. He didn't like to work.

But in other ways he was better than other people. He went to night school and learned to speak, read, and write English. He read American newspapers, two of them, every day. He knew about the American political system. That's one of the reasons I've been a lifelong Democrat. My father knew who to vote for in every election, what they stood for, and what party they belonged to, despite the fact that he wasn't eligible to vote.[137] Many of our discussions around the dinner table dealt with American politics.

But from an economic point of view, he was a dismal failure. He never succeeded at anything. He bought a pretty-good-sized grocery store from a hardworking Korean couple who couldn't speak, read, or write English. They could not communicate with customers or salespeople. Rather than losing it completely, they offered it to my father, not because he was a good worker but because he was one of the few Koreans who could speak English. They gave it to him for no money down. But my mother was the one who did all the work. My father tried, but he just did not know how to work. If it weren't for my mother, we would never have been able to keep that store.

The store made good money. It was located right on Temple and Figueroa, in Bunker Hill. We lived on top of that hill for a long time. Then we moved to a house near First and Figueroa. The Ahn Chang Ho[138] family had a big house near the corner. My father was one of the most devoted followers of Syngman Rhee.[139] Politically our two families belonged to two entirely different factions, but somehow we got along well, and the children played very well together.

In those days people didn't go to church because of religious beliefs; they went because a particular church was the one their political group went to. All the Tongjihoe[140] people went to the First Christian Church, and all the Ahn Chang Ho people went to the Methodist Church. I'm sure that the Presbyterians would be terribly upset if they knew that all the socialists and communists went to the Presbyterian Church.[141] The church you went to identified your politics.

When I was seven or eight years old in the 1920s, most Koreans lived around Figueroa and First. There were about fifteen families. The Yoon family had a dry cleaning place next to where the Los Angeles Unified School District Office is located now. The Hollywood Freeway goes over it now. Right at the corner of Grand and California streets, Danny Kim's folks had a grocery store. Up near Grand and Temple Street, I remember the Suhs' dry cleaning place. There was also a place where they made soy sauce and soybean cakes. All of them failed in business during the Depression and moved away one by one. Some moved to other parts of Greater Los Angeles, but many went back to farm work. By the time I was twelve or thirteen, there were only three or four families left.

The businesses failed not because they didn't work hard enough, but because the Korean community was not big enough. Little Tokyo and Chinatown were big enough to have their own ethnic groups to trade with, but there were not enough ethnic Koreans to keep the Korean-owned stores going. They needed to cater to non-Koreans, but in those days, Koreans would not deal with the Japanese, and the Chinese would not patronize the Korean stores. In those days, Asians were not like today; they were in isolated, hostile camps. They hardly spoke to each other. You had to depend on Caucasians, Mexicans, Jews, and other people. The overall environment almost guaranteed failure, seven times out of ten.

Our grocery store did well because we had a wonderful location and we had no competition in those early days. There was no other grocery store in any direction for four or five blocks. In the old days, what is now the court houses used to be all Victorian mansions, where rich Caucasians lived. It was the Beverly Hills of Los Angeles. Customers phoned in to order groceries. We had one of the first telephones in the area. I remember going to these beautiful mansions to deliver groceries.

As I grew older, the area became a ghetto. The big Victorian houses were divided up into apartments and boarding houses. The redneck poor whites, Jews, Mexicans, and Filipinos moved in. Chinese and Japanese also moved in. In those days, minorities were not permitted to live anywhere except in ghetto areas. Asians weren't even able to buy homes; all you could do was rent.[142] All my playmates were minorities—Japanese, Chinese, Italians and Mexicans, until the Italians found out they [themselves] were white and moved out of the ghetto as soon as they made money.

I went to Belmont High School, which was ninety percent white. Caucasians controlled all the school activities. Koreans were excluded from everything other than sports and the classroom itself. I was actually told not to participate in social activities. That's when my interaction with

Koreans increased. As a teenager, most of my social activities were confined to Koreans. By 1935, there were hundreds of Koreans in the Jefferson-Vermont area.

We had Korean teenage clubs. My sister was a leader. She and her friends organized dances, and farm boys from Fresno and Reedley would come down. They timed their delivery of fruit to markets so that they could attend the dance. My sister got some of the Chinese boys to come, too. My parents did not know about these dances. If they knew, they would not have let us go. My sister was a rebel. We told our parents we were going to have a meeting, and then we would go out and rent a ten-piece band and a big dance hall. We did that about twice a year.

When it came to socializing, each ethnic group was totally separate. My mother forbade me to play with the Japanese Americans. They were always upset when they saw me with any Japanese—Chinese maybe, but Japanese under no circumstances. We couldn't even eat Japanese food. We could not afford to eat out often, but if we did, we had to choose either Mexican, Chinese, or Italian.

We couldn't go to Caucasian restaurants because they made us feel so bad and so uncomfortable that we wouldn't go. Sometimes they would openly refuse us. If they didn't do that, they put so much salt on the food that you couldn't eat it. The fancy Italian restaurants didn't welcome us, because they wanted to get Caucasian customers, but we could go to cheap Italian restaurants. Mexicans and Chinese accepted us.

We were poor for several reasons. First, there was my father's gambling. My father went to a lot of Chinese gambling halls. He gambled for big money, and he was a lousy gambler. He was too emotional, like most Koreans. They didn't have the discipline to gamble right. One night he won $25,000. He went wild for a week and lost it all again. Then, there was his drinking. That's what he did every weekend. Twenty or thirty Koreans, mostly bachelors, would visit our grocery store on Saturdays. My mother would cook Korean food for them, and they would drink. They lived a very lonely life. The only thing they had to do was to talk about Korea and drink.

The grocery store made money, but my father always overcommitted. He kept making his pledges to support Tongjihoe. We always owed Tongjihoe money. It was really a struggle. I resented it in those days, but I can see in hindsight that trying to support the Korean independence movement was the right thing to do. My father's community activities had a strong impact on how I eventually turned out. Being politically aware, participating in community activities, going to church all day on Sundays, many of the things I do now that are important to me, I got from him.

My mother wanted me to go to college. I went to Los Angeles City College for a while. Going to school was a hardship. I had to walk from Figueroa and Temple to all the way to the campus on Vermont Avenue. I could see that other Koreans who finished college had no jobs. They had graduate degrees, but they all ended up in the fruit stands. I figured if I had to work at a fruit stand, why should I go to college?

I was born to be a soldier. I had absolutely no fear. When I eventually went to war, I was not afraid of combat, and I always knew exactly what to do. People don't realize that when I joined the army, I had an inkling already that I would be sent to a Japanese unit. When I graduated from Fort Bennington in Columbus, Georgia, they were so desperate for a new set of lieutenants that they made everyone a second lieutenant on reserve and handed everyone their orders for their next assignment. I didn't get orders. I was wondering what they would do with me after I graduated, if they wouldn't let me carry a rifle as an officer. I figured I'd end up a public relations officer or something, doing some inconsequential thing not directly related to war. Then I learned that I was going to Camp Shelby. They were holding me because the Japanese American unit was en route from Wisconsin to Mississippi. I asked for a delay and got one, so I went to Little Rock, Arkansas, and visited a concentration camp. Some of my Japanese American friends from Southern California were interned there. That was in early February 1943. I think I was the first visitor to that camp.

They kept me waiting at the gates for over an hour. They said I should go back to Little Rock, but the last bus had gone, and besides, I told them, "There weren't [any] hotel rooms." I spent eight days at that camp. I saw the way they were living. There was a family of one daughter, two sons, and a mother and father in one room a little bigger than your kitchen here. What separated them from the next family was a blanket they hung up with old-fashioned clothespins. It was really cramped, like the old army barracks— no partitions, no privacy. There was a community kitchen and a community bath. A lot of the problems with young people started because the parents had no control over their children. The children didn't depend on the parents for food. They'd form children's gangs and go to school, play, and eat among themselves. Why return to that small room—so confining!

I left the camp for Mississippi, to join the 100th Battalion. The others in the 100th were mostly from Hawaii, and they called me a *corng-kok*, a Hawaiian slang term for "mainland Japanese American". It means the sound of a coconut falling from a tree, *corng-kok!* Or when you shake it—*corng-kok, corng-kok.* They said Asian mainland heads are like that, empty.[143]

By the time I retired, I had a very high profile. I was with the 100th/442nd for two and a half years during the war. Of the line officers that led combat units or were up in the front lines like I was, and of all the line officers that went overseas with the unit, I was the lone surviving one. The life expectancy of a lieutenant in the 100th was six weeks, even including head-quarters personnel. So real life expectancy for people on the front lines could be even less—as short as four weeks. The fact that I was up there on the front lines for twenty some months meant that I led a really charmed life. Senator Inouye of Hawaii says, "You are a living legend." I appeared in all the camp papers. I had a lot of write-ups in the *Los Angeles Times*, too. So everybody, even the people who weren't in the 100th, knew me.

When I started, I was a platoon leader. Then I was executive officer of B Company. I wanted to be a company commander, but I was forced to become a battalion staff officer. I became a G2, which is an intelligence officer. After that, I became a G3, which is operations. In combat, I commanded the 100th [Battalion] in that I made the plans and issued the orders, though I didn't make any of the administrative decisions. My title was plans and operations officer for the 100th. But many people say that I was a commander.

In a battle in France, we were ready to attack a town at about eight o'clock in the evening. It was getting dark. I called Gordon Singles, our battalion commander, and gave him the details. He said, "Since you can see everything better there, and you know what you want to do, you give the orders. You direct the battle." So I did, and it was highly successful. We took the town with only two casualties, while the Germans suffered over 200 casualties. Later, I found out that the regimental commander was there when I was told to direct the battle.

Although I thought I was born to be in the army and I had all the qualities, I got out of the army because I saw no future for me there. I was a captain. I was a non-West Pointer, non-ROTC, and I wasn't Caucasian. The army was a very close-knit circle then.

About a year after I left the army, they offered me a commission. I wanted to go back, but at the time I had started a little launderette, the first one in

Los Angeles. My landlord wouldn't let me break the lease. The launderette was very successful, because hardly anyone could afford to buy a washing machine. I had twenty-five machines. The place was filled with customers, and the machines were going all the time. When the Korean War came along, the army called me again. The landlord didn't let me break the lease, but at least I could leave the business in the hands of a Japanese girl I knew. When I left for Korea, I decided I was going to stay in the army, because they offered me a commission again, and I could see the army had changed enough for me to have a real career in it.

They called me not because of my military experience but because I was Korean. They had no linguistic ability in Korean. They called up anyone with a Korean name. They sent me to the Navy Strategic Intelligence School in Washington, D.C., to study Korean. I got fairly proficient at translation. That's really where I first learned Korean grammar. There were about fifteen of us Koreans who did nothing but study Korean all day long and all night. I almost went crazy, because I couldn't master as much as they were trying to pour into me. I did not want to be a translator or interpreter; I wanted to go back to my infantry [unit]. After I'd been at the school for about three months, I made such a big fuss, they let me go.

When I got to Camp Drake in Japan, Gordon Singles, who had been my battalion commander in Europe, was the commander. He wanted me to stay in Japan. I told him I didn't want to be a translator or an interpreter, I wanted to be on the front lines, and he helped get me onto the front lines. I purposely failed the Korean language test. That's how I ended up in Korea.

When I arrived in Pusan, I first went to see President Syngman Rhee, because my mother had made me promise to when she learned I was going to Korea. I told her, "That's impossible—the country's at war, and he's the president." She said, "No, you've got to see him. Your father was a great believer who supported him, so you have to go see him." I said I'd try, and told Gordon Singles about it. When we arrived in Pusan, the provisional capital at the time, he arranged for us to get a sedan the next morning. We went to the office of the president and told his secretary that I was Kim Soon Kwon's son and wanted to see the president.

President Syngman Rhee asked me my name. He asked how was my younger sister Marion. He said, "I don't remember the names of your younger brothers, because they were too young at the time, but I do remember you. I think the last time I saw you, you were about twelve years old." Then he asked about the grocery store and about all kinds of other things.

For him to be able to know my sister's name right away and my mother's name, for him to remember my father and remember when he last saw me twenty years before was a remarkable thing, I thought. He was gracious to take time out and spend over a half-hour with us. He asked me to please stay in touch with him. I promised, but I didn't, because it was too chaotic and I was on the front lines.

After seeing President Rhee, we went to the train station. It was in late February; there was snow on the ground, and it was very cold. I saw a large crowd of Korean children swarming around the train, begging for food. They had only T-shirts on. They were trying to collect coal from the railroad track. I had never seen such a scene before. I had three days of rations with me, and I gave them all of it. Other officers in the cabin also gave theirs too. I cried a lot sitting in the train. It was my saddest day in Korea.

I was in Korea eleven months and one week: I started commanding the battalion on the first of October, 1951, and I left the first week of September in 1952. I was with the 7th Division, 31st Infantry Regiment. I was an intelligence officer and plans and operation officer before I became a battalion commander. I commanded the 1st Battalion of the 31st Infantry. My battalion was in the central area near Kŭm Hwa. At the furthest, northernmost point of penetration, we were making the last ride into North Korea. I was a major then. I think I was the first minority in the U.S. Army to command an infantry battalion in combat.

When I first arrived in the 7th Division, I was given a temporary assignment to lead a company of Korean guerrillas on a special patrol. These partisans were people from the Hŭng Nam area. They were cooperating with the American units in the north and had evacuated to the south with the Americans. They were very well-educated professionals—doctors, lawyers, school teachers, all kinds. I had great respect for them.

We went up thirty-five miles beyond the lines and stayed one night on a hilltop adjacent to a North Korean battalion. We captured some of the North Korean patrol; one of them was a Korean nurse. She was in wonderful, wonderful physical condition. When we were running, she looked at me and laughed. When I first arrived in Korea, I was thirty-two years old and not in such bad shape, but not good enough to be running like that up and down the mountains. She said, "Let me help you. Let me carry your pack. Maybe I ought to carry your gun, too." I said, "No, no. You can't carry my gun." She carried my pack. I treated her with great respect. I made sure that nobody molested her in any way.

The only time I ran into Korean civilians when I was in battle was in the mountains. When we arrived at the Hwa Ch'ŏn reservoir high in the mountains, we came upon a strange settlement. On this little plateau valley, a flat area high in the mountains, there was a very small Korean village of, I guess, a hundred Koreans. I sat there with a Korean leader who was considered the senior spokesman for the village. I offered him some C rations and K rations and things like that, and he was very pleased.

Out of curiosity I asked, "Which side are you on? Are you on the communist side, or are you on the side of democracy?" He said, "I don't know how to answer you, but let me put it this way. We are the grass, and one of you is a cow and one of you is a horse. What difference does it make which one eats us?" After a while I said, "That's a very good answer." I thanked him and went on my way. But that episode always stayed with me. I never asked another Korean peasant what side he was on.

When I came back to the States, I served on the faculty at the infantry school. From there I joined the faculty of the Commander General Staff College. After that, I went overseas and commanded an infantry battalion in Europe. They wanted proven infantry leaders to command. I was there for about eleven months.

After I retired, I became very active in the Japanese-American veterans' organization. I was the first among the veterans to demand that we support redress.[144] Japanese Americans usually try to stay away from anything controversial, but I made them take positions on important issues. Later, even the ones that were opposed to redress in the beginning became ardent supporters. I tried not to take a high profile. I would insist behind the scenes that the organization formally endorse it, formally introduce it, formally make the president endorse it.

I officially retired on disability in 1972. I was having tremendous pain stemming from battle wounds, far more pain than most people can ever imagine. When I left the army, I had eleven severed nerves and involuntary muscle spasms over much of my body. Operations were performed to alleviate my pain, but instead each operation made things more complicated and more dangerous and ended up increasing my pain. Finally, the medical doctors gave up on me. All they wanted to do was medicate me and keep me peaceful, which meant they filled me full of dope so that I wouldn't suffer so much.

By the time I came back from the service, the Korean community that I grew up in was scattered and settled all over Southern California. I found that being active in community organizations helped me to forget my pain by forcing me to concentrate on other problems.

There was a natural division between the older first and the 1.5 generation. On top of that, you've got a split between the older second generation and the young ones. The one thing that the younger ones lacked was credibility, not only in mainstream America, and with the first-generation immigrants, but also credibility with my older second-generation group. They were too idealistic. They wanted the Constitution to work like magic.

My generation has problems, too. I used to hear a lot of Koreans of my generation saying, "Why don't the Korean immigrants go home? They disgrace us. They don't know how to behave, they're obnoxious, they do terrible things, they're giving us all the terrible reputation." I used to listen to that at different kinds of gatherings of my own generation of people. They reminded me of very small-minded, parochial people who had never gotten out into the world. At one gathering, I finally got angry and said, "What's the matter with you people? Sure, you were all born, raised, and educated here. You're far more sophisticated. But the new people coming in, they're better than your parents were. What makes you so superior? Just because your parents suffered all the slings and arrows, and they were worse off than this group, and now you're in a privileged position, you don't want to give them a chance? You people are nuts. If you're going to condemn these new people this way, why don't you sit around and condemn your parents?"

Among Asians I've seen, or any group, people who try to become a part of the mainstream so much that they reject their own kind are the kind of people who have never made peace with their own identity. To me, they are bananas. They're yellow on the outside, but they think they are white. I think people who are friendly to the new generation are people who've made peace with themselves and recognize that they're not white. They are proud to be Korean, Japanese, or whatever. I find the people who are most successful in this world are people who have made that peace and understand who they are. They can see the big picture.

Sometimes Koreans of my own generation are too narrow-minded to see the big picture. We are all born egoists, whether we want to admit it or not. We tend to overvalue what we have to contribute and who we are in the world. Too many of my generation want the new Korean community to invite them, ask them for help, ask them for advice, make a big fuss over them. The new community doesn't want to do that. They don't even know that the second-generation Koreans exist in the first place. In the second place, they don't know what they have to offer.

Most people in my generation wait to be invited, often all their life, and they are never invited.

MARCH AND APRIL 1993

JANINE BISHOP

Adopted

Twenty-year-old Janine Bishop is one of the estimated 100,000 Korean children adopted into American homes since the Korean War. Many of the children came, as she did, through the Oregon-based Holt Adoption Agency, which focused at first on arranging for the adoption of the orphans and children of U.S. servicemen but eventually became the most important conduit for all kinds of Korean adoptions. Bishop was raised in Fresno, California, by a white American family. She is currently an undergraduate student at Occidental College in Los Angeles.

I was adopted when I was fourteen months old. My

parents had one biological son already who was about six or seven when they decided to adopt me. In the beginning, they tried to adopt in the U.S., through various organizations and agencies here, but they didn't have any luck because they already had a biological son. Also, my mom had been diagnosed with rheumatoid arthritis, which made it more difficult to adopt. Then one day, they saw a World Vision program on the Holt Adoption Agency on TV. That got them started looking into adoption through Holt.

It's only recently that we've talked a lot about adoption, even though they've been open about it all through my life. My mom told me about some of the obstacles they faced when they decided to adopt a child from another country. My grandmother on my mother's side was basically open, but the other family members were opposed to an interracial adoption.

My parents had decided it really didn't matter to them what child they adopted; they just wanted a daughter. They applied to Holt, but were turned down many times for financial reasons. By the time they were finally able to adopt me, my mom says, her family members' attitudes had changed: her brothers and sisters were kind of supportive. My mom once told me a funny story about how my great aunt was initially opposed to the adoption, but as soon as I arrived, she would take me around and show me off at church, acting as if the whole idea had been hers to begin with.

My mom made a point with my family that she wasn't going to tolerate any racist comments. Her attitude was that she had accepted this interracial adoption, and if anyone else wasn't going to, then she wasn't going to have anything to do with them. When I arrived—that was in 1975 or 1976—they did have a lot of problems. They went on a couple trips back East to visit some of my dad's relatives, and my mom has memories of driving through Texas and not being served because I was with them.

It's funny that people ask me, "When did you know you were adopted?" How could I not know I was adopted? I didn't look like my parents. I didn't look like my grandparents, my cousins, my aunts and uncles. I just always knew I was different. Many times I felt kind of ashamed, because no child wants to be the one who's different, the one who stands out.

I always hated introducing people to my parents, because they were going to instantly think, "Why does she look different?" Even today, when my mom and I go shopping, someone will say, "Is that an exchange student with you?" I take offense more now, because we're living in a time when people shouldn't automatically expect people to be a certain way and should accept the fact that there are interracial marriages and inter-racial adoptions.

This year, I went in to talk to a professor. He asked me my name, and when I said, "Janine Bishop," he said, "That doesn't sound like a very Asian name to me." I said, "It's not," and walked out, because he had no right to assume that it was an Asian name or not, and I didn't feel I owed him any explanations. I was probably in a bad mood that day. I ended up explaining it to him a month later.

Many times I feel kind of detached from the rest of the family, because some of my relatives are into driving the right car, knowing the right people, going to the right schools. I guess that I hated feeling that I didn't belong. It's not that they made me feel I didn't belong, but I hated to think of them ever having to explain to people, like "She's my cousin," and people would go, "Huh?" and they would have to say, "Well, she's adopted."

One of my cousins got married, and I'd see his wife's family over and over again, but they'd always ask, "Who are you?" I felt they didn't want to take the time to get to know me, even though they knew everyone else. Maybe I'm overreacting, but I just felt it was because I didn't look like them or fit in.

When I was either in junior high or high school, things started to bother me, things that happened because I looked different. People would drive by and say things like "stupid Chink" or something like that. I guess I just take it for what it is. I can't say it doesn't affect me. It would affect anybody to have people say mean things to them. It wasn't till I was in high school that I didn't want to be identified as Caucasian.

Growing up, I was surrounded by Caucasians. Most of my friends had blond hair. I felt like the guys weren't really interested in me because I was different. I was always interested in Caucasian boys, because there weren't any Asian boys in my school, anyway. Wherever I'd go with one of my best girlfriends in high school—she's blond—I'd feel like the guys would be interested only in her. I used to date the more popular guys, but I always felt it wasn't because I was attractive. I was also always afraid about the interracial thing. What would his parents think? My mom didn't wanted to scare or upset me, but she'd show that she was worried about it, because every once in a while she'd ask, "How do his parents feel that you're Korean?" I was dating this one guy, and we really liked each other, but I always felt that he was kind of ashamed of me. He'd never invite me over, and he never really wanted me to meet his parents. After we broke up and he started dating another girl, it seemed like he was always inviting her over, and that his parents knew her really well. I don't know. I guess I always felt he was kind of uneasy about me being Korean, although I never asked him about it. You don't want to be disliked by anybody, or have anybody's parents say, "You can't go out with her because..."

The older I get, the more I realize I can't avoid being Korean. Every time I look into the mirror, I am Korean. When I look at family pictures, I feel that I stand out. I guess it shouldn't bother me, but sometimes it does. Even though I may seem very American, which I am—just like anyone who immigrates can be American—I want to be distinctly Korean. I know I'm not in terms of having all the Korean traditions, but I don't want people to see me and say, "Because she grew up in a Caucasian family, and because she's very Americanized, she's white." That's not what I want anymore. When I was younger, maybe that was what I wanted, because I wanted to fit in and didn't want to be different. But the older I get, the more I don't want to be part of that ignorance that labels people and does not allow them to be who they are.

I don't know how you define who's racist and who's not. It's kind of strange that my dad has set certain limits for me. He doesn't want me to date any African American or Hispanic. In my freshman year of college, I liked an African American guy, but my dad said, "The world isn't ready for that type of interracial relationship, and I don't want you to get hurt." I guess he's right, but if you constantly live in fear, attitudes aren't going to change at all. People would say things like, "Stick to your own kind." I couldn't take the pressure. I just decided we were too different, and that I couldn't like him anymore. From then on I just dated Caucasian guys. There weren't many Asian guys at the school, but I wasn't interested in them, anyway, because I just wasn't attracted to any of them. All the men in my life have been Caucasian, so that's the kind of guy I'm most attracted to.

I've had pretty good experiences in college. My roommate loves to tell the story of when I moved to school my freshman year. She watched my parents moving me in, and my brother was putting together this big cabinet for me in the hall. She says she never realized I was different from them.

She said she just saw a family with a daughter moving in, and it never dawned on her that I was adopted. About half a year later, when we were becoming really good friends, she looked at a picture of my parents and said, "Wow! Are these your parents?" That was the first time she ever realized that I was adopted. But even today, when I hang out with a group of friends, I'll suddenly see myself as the only Asian woman in the group. They don't treat me any different, but I notice it.

I think that the move down to L.A. to Occidental College has been really good for me. When I got to college, I remember calling my mom and telling her how excited I was to meet so many Koreans. It was a chance to feel that there were other people like me around. I hadn't realized how big the Korean community in L.A. is. When I was thinking about college, I didn't want to go where I would be the only Korean. I was scared to leave California. One of my good friends from high school was showing me her dorm picture from Notre Dame. There were fifty women, all white. I started wondering how I would fit in there. Would any of the guys ask me to the dances and socials? How many Asians had they had contact with? Would they even consider dating one? I'm glad I didn't go there. I've traveled with my parents back East, and I've always felt insecure, like people are staring at me.

When I went to Korea last summer, I met thirty-four Korean adoptees from all over the United States. I was scared, but I was really excited about the prospects of being in a place where I fit in, where I didn't look different.

All the adoptees had different perspectives. Maybe it had to do with experiences, just how much exposure you had to Korean culture. My parents have tried to instill a sense of who I was, but it was kind of hard because they don't have any knowledge of Korean culture. My mom says I used to squat on the floor. But I came [to the U.S.] at such a young age that I basically lost all of my Koreanness. She tried to buy me books. She even bought me Korean Barbie doll clothes, and she'd sew pillows with the Korean flag on it. She tried, but I don't think all parents do. A lot of kids had no exposure to Korea at all. Some of them came from Midwest towns where guys didn't want to date them. They never met other Asians. Those were the ones who rejected the Korean culture that we were being exposed to. They didn't like the food and were closed-minded to a lot of things. They kept saying, "This is dirty."

I wanted to learn as much as I could. I loved having exposure to Korean culture. I had developed an idealized view of Korea, and what I found was completely different. I had expected to see people in rice fields, but Korea was very modern. Initially, I was a little turned off by people shoving and pushing, never smiling or talking. I thought people were rude. It wasn't until I had more exposure that I realized that that was just part of their culture. Maybe they don't smile at me because they are private people, not because they are unfriendly or mean. When I actually got to know some of the Korean people, I realized they were really nice, and I felt proud to be Korean. I had never felt proud to be Korean before. I realized that Korean people have a rich culture that was not something I should be ashamed of.

The trip changed my life. I want to learn the Korean language and about Korean culture, and I want to meet other Koreans. Now, when people want to know about me, I'm proud of who I am, because now I have a wonderful heritage I didn't know about before.

Holt, the agency that arranged my adoption, has a tour every year. I was lucky because the year I went, the man who established the adoption agency in Korea and who spent his whole life with Holt led our tour. He didn't just talk about the historical sites, but he could also give us insight into the adoption process, and about how Holt evolved in Korea and in the United States.

The babies' home I was from got destroyed, I guess; they put up apartment buildings where it used to be. Holt sent us to Ch'ŏngju because our home no longer existed, and they wanted us to have the experience of seeing the area. I stayed at this small babies' home in Ch'ŏngju. There was a man who was the director and three or four women who took care of the twenty children. One of the women was really interested in our lives. One little boy that she had been caring for was adopted by a woman in America, who had sent pictures back. I felt that the staff cared a lot about what happens to the babies that leave. The next morning, we all sat around a little table on the floor, eating Korean food. The women were chatting in Korean, trying to communicate with us, and I felt a real sense of belonging. It was so interesting for me to be part of that scene. It was really emotional for me, being near the city where I was abandoned and meeting women who I imagined were like the women who took care of me. For all I know, I could have walked by people in Ch'ŏngju who were related to me.

The Korean women we met at the Holt office in Seoul spoke some English and dressed in American-type clothes, but in Ch'ŏngju, the women were really Korean. To me, they were the true part of the culture that I got out of the trip.

The majority of us couldn't find any information about our backgrounds, because most of us had been abandoned. Some kids who had been in foster care were able to see their foster parents, which was really exciting for them. When I was adopted, my mom made a point of asking for every document available—like doctors' records and police records. I've looked through them. Even though she knew in her mind that there was no way for me to find my true parents, she had foresight to ask for all the paperwork ahead of time. The only reason I would want to meet my birth parents would be to find out why I was put up for adoption. And to know what they look like. As my brother gets older, I can see my parents in him.

I always wonder what my children are going to look like, and what my biological parents look like. But I don't think that finding my biological parents would fill a void in me, because I have received all the parental nurturing that I need.

I don't know how much of this is true, but my mom has always told me that the records said that I was very healthy, that they could tell I was breast-fed, that I wasn't a baby that was just about ready to die. My mom always told me that story to give me a sense that I was loved. When I was younger, I just didn't want to hear it. I thought it was corny and didn't want to think about it. But now I've reached an age when I could have a child myself, and I understand more what it means for a woman to decide to give up her child. It would be a very hard decision for me. So now, when I think about the things my mom told me about me being a healthy baby, I feel a little better about myself, that maybe I wasn't strictly unwanted and abandoned. It's something nice to keep in the back of your head.

On the way back, we got to bring four babies. That was one of the highlights of the trip. Hopefully, someday I'll be able to escort children. It would be amazing to give someone a child, to be there when a parent picked up the adopted child.

I got really interested in studying adoption in Korea, not interracial adoption, but Korean attitudes toward adopting children. From what we were told, Koreans aren't as open toward adoption as Americans, because they want their own children. We were told that adoptions are kept secret. I want to look into it, to learn more about the culture. I want to know what Korea's doing now with unwanted children.

I really want to go back to Korea. Even if I don't get a fellowship, I'm hoping to work at a home for the mentally and physically disabled as a volunteer. I want to live with a Korean family and hang out at the university with Korean people.

Last year, I took a class on emigration and immigration patterns. We had to write about our family experiences, and I didn't feel that writing about my mother's and father's relatives coming from France and England was going to be of any benefit to me. The professor said, "Well, write about your own experience." If you think about it, I'm a first-generation immigrant. So I wrote about my kind of adoption/immigration experience. At that point, before I went to Korea, I was still torn between the two cultures, feeling that I didn't fit into either one. Now, it would not even cross my mind to wonder if I should write about my relatives' immigration experiences, because that's not who I am.

Even though I feel more sure about my Korean identity, I still can't help but feel a little out of place here sometimes. And I'm always scared when I meet a guy. But now I know that I'm definitely Korean, and I would not compromise who I am for something a guy would want. If he could not accept and appreciate the Korean culture I'm trying to develop and have, then it would not work out. Before, I didn't want to be different, and it was like, "You don't have to worry about my Korean heritage or anything; it's not even an issue." Now, I feel it's so much an issue that it can't be avoided. It's going to be a subject, it's going to be something I'm interested in, and when I have children, it's something I'm going to want them to know.

I can see myself traveling to Korea quite often in the future. I can't see myself actually living there, because my family's here and I'm American, but Korea is going to be part of my life more now, and it's definitely going to be a part of my children's life, because it's important to have a sense of identity. Whether you're a minority trying to live in another place, or a woman trying to live in a male-dominated society, you have to have a sense of identity.

JANUARY 1994

KOOK KIM DEAN

Black and Korean

A tall, well–built man with a quiet manner, Kook Kim Dean chooses his words carefully when he speaks. Born in Korea in 1954 to a Korean mother and an African American father, he grew up in South Central Los Angeles. In 1982, he married a woman from Korea; they now have an eight–year–old daughter. Currently, he works for the City of Los Angeles as a mechanical engineer.

My mother has never talked about her life in Korea. She told me that my father was walking through her village and that they met that way. Neither of my parents have talked about Korea very much. One time, my brother, sister, and I offered to send my mother to Korea. We planned to pay for her airline ticket and hotel expenses, but it'd been forty years since she left, and she decided there's nothing left to recognize there, so she declined our offer. I don't think she has any relatives there. The only thing I remember is that there was mention of an orphanage in Pusan where people had known her. But so much time has passed that I don't think she has any friends in Korea now. The few friends she had at the army bases were Japanese. My father went back to Korea a few times and met some people who knew him.

When I was attending the U.S. Naval Academy, the ship I was stationed on happened to be going to Korea for a training visit, so I visited Inch'ŏn and Seoul in 1973. I tried to look up my mother's relatives, but I only had her name, and there are a lot of Kims.[145] So it was impossible to find anyone.

When I was growing up, my father always called my mother "Kinji." His family and friends also called her "Kinji." That's what I thought her name was, but later I found out that it was basically a mispronunciation of "Kyŏngja." People had trouble pronouncing her name, so she just calls herself "Kim," which is her last name and my middle name.

My mother used to prepare Korean dishes at home, but she really didn't know how to cook Korean food. What she made was based on her memory. Later on, I found out from my wife, who is Korean, that the food my mother cooked was not "genuine" Korean food. Of course, ingredients were not available.

My mother was eighteen and my father was twenty-one when they got married. I came to the United States with my parents in December 1955, when I was almost two years old. That's what I saw on an old passport. I don't have any memories of Korea. I grew up on various army bases in the

U.S. and Germany. There were very few Oriental people. The few Asian friends I remember having were Japanese. My father retired from the service in 1968, after serving twenty years.

On the army bases where I grew up, people were fairly tolerant of different people. There wasn't any overt discrimination. My father is from South Carolina. He said at the time he brought us to the U.S., we stayed at my grandparents' place when we had what were called Jim Crow laws. There were laws against marrying outside your own race. My father had married outside his race, but his wife wasn't white, so although it was a violation of the law, they let it go. My father said there were some discussions about him and my mother in the sheriff's office before they decided that it was all right.

Our family settled in Los Angeles, in the area now considered South Central or Watts, when I was fourteen years old. At that time, it was a much better place. I don't remember meeting any Koreans until I reached high school. At Locke High School in South Central, I met my first Korean. She was half Korean and half black. She had been adopted by a black family and brought to the U.S. when she was about five. We became friends. The school population was about ninety-five percent black. There were about twenty Hispanics and ten Asians out of 2,000 students.

I went to the Naval Academy for three years, starting in 1972. The Naval Academy students reflected the population in the U.S. It was about ninety percent white. There were two Asians in a class of about nine hundred people. Even though I graduated among the top five in my high school class, I was not well prepared for the Naval Academy. I struggled the whole time. I decided to quit after the third year.

Most of the time I consider myself African American. Because of the way I was raised on army bases by a Korean mother, I don't have the same speech pattern as other African Americans. This was always pointed out to me while I was in high school. African Americans pretty well accept me as one of them, even though I talk a little bit different. When I meet Koreans, I know I am not one of them, at least culturally, although I have never been treated badly by Koreans.

My mother usually prepares African American food. It's basically Southern cooking. She always spoke to me in English. She's had no chance to speak in Korean, since there were no Koreans around when I was growing up. During her first thirty years in this country, she forgot most of her Korean. Lately, she's picked up some, but when she speaks Korean, she speaks with an accent. She told me about a group of Korean women in Los

Angeles who are in the same type of situation she's in. They married African American GIs. They have meetings once a month. They go to each other's houses for fellowship. I've never met any of them, but these days, I see some Koreans coming to my parents' house on holidays. A Korean family moved into an apartment in my parents' neighborhood in Watts. Eventually, they bought the building and started a retail business in the area. They made friends with my parents, and they visit each other's homes. There are a few other Koreans living around there, but not many.

My parents have lived together for forty years. They are pretty happy together. I realize that my daddy went back to Korea for my mother when he had finished his tour of duty in Germany. To go all the way back to Korea from Germany in 1954, when there was no war going on, meant he must have loved my mother a lot. I think they've had a happy marriage. My father used to drink a lot when he was young, and they had some conflicts then, but other than that, they got along pretty well. His side of the family always respected my mother. I remember when I was growing up and my mother, my grandmother, and other members of my father's side of the family would can peaches together. It took a lot of work: you have to remove the seeds, boil the peaches, put them into glass jars, and seal the jars with wax. I remember them going out together to buy baskets of peaches. They were close with each other.

My mother and my wife basically don't talk to each other. I don't think they have much in common even though they are both Koreans. My mother came here in 1955, and my wife came here in 1982. Korea changed a lot between those two periods. My mother is pretty much integrated into Southern black culture, and my wife is quite Korean, culturally speaking.

I graduated in 1976 with a bachelor's degree in financial management from Cal State Long Beach. I found out that a degree in finance didn't pay much, so I got a degree in mechanical engineering at Cal State L.A. Now I'm an engineer working for the city sewage plant. I design pipe systems. I've always worked in the water field: for the first half of my career, I worked on the system that brings water into the city; for the second half, I've been working on the water system that leaves the city.

While I was at Cal State L.A., I encountered many more Koreans and Asians than I had before. I met my wife's cousin, Trisa, through international business club meetings. She was going to Korea, so I asked her to find me a pen pal there. She introduced my wife to me. We corresponded for two years and got married in 1982. When I went to Korea to get married, there weren't any major disagreements, even though we were culturally quite apart. My wife was twenty-five and I was twenty-eight. She was a bookkeeper at the Oriental Watch Company. She was born and grew up in a small town, although she doesn't like to talk about it. Her father was a schoolteacher.

I had a problem with my height in Korea. But because I'm six-foot-three, the chairs were too small for me and the tables were too low. My legs would not fit underneath. My head would touch the ceiling in buses, so I couldn't stand up straight. When I walked along the sidewalk, my head would hit anything that stuck out. I had to duck whenever I tried to go through doorways. Once my wife and I went to see a movie, but I couldn't sit in the chair because there wasn't enough space for my legs. I couldn't sleep at night because either my feet would hang over one end or my head would hang over the other end of the bed. I was going to stay in Korea for four weeks, but by the end of the third week, I couldn't handle it anymore and came back.

Most of my friends are black. I also have quite a few Chinese friends. We get together once in a while for birthday parties. I used to have some Korean friends; we were close when we were students, but since I am male and married and they are female, our relationships changed. I see them when they get together with my wife. My wife associates mostly with Korean friends. Since the two groups, blacks and Koreans, don't mix that much, for me it's like being split in half sometimes.

My wife cooks Korean food half the time and American food half the time. The problem is that I like my mother's cooking. That's what I'm accustomed to. My wife's cooking is different from my mother's. When I show her how I would like the food, she says that that's not really Korean cooking.

I believe that my wife is very class-conscious. She told me once that she was really upset about her mother getting into gardening, because to her the only kind of people who are into gardening are farm people, and she didn't think that was an appropriate thing for her mother to be doing.

My wife sends our daughter, Alexandra, to a Korean-language school and Korean dance classes. I wanted my Alex to be able to protect herself and control her temper, so she's also been attending martial-arts school for about nine months now. My wife wants to raise her as a Korean. She tried to select her friends for her when she was in preschool; she wanted her to play with Asian kids. There weren't any Asian kids in the neighborhood except for one Chinese boy, and Alex never got along very well with him, but my wife still wanted her to play with him. Since I'm so tall, Alex is bigger than the Hispanic kids. Kids her size are older than she is by two or three years, and the kids her age are much shorter. I know she had a bit of a problem with that, but the Hispanic kids were nicer to her than the Chinese kid. Now her friends are mostly Korean. I don't think it's working out well. About two years ago, Alex started asking me, "How come I can't play with non-Asian kids? I always fight with that Chinese boy." I told her to go ask her mother, and my wife said, "I don't want you to turn out to be a gang member." But from what I've seen, whenever she played with non-Asian kids, they always treated her nicely. They didn't beat her up or take away her toys.

About once a month, my daughter visits my parents. She plays with her cousin, who's in the same age bracket. My daughter is three-fourths Asian and one-fourth black, and my brother's daughter is three-fourths black and one-fourth Asian.

Truly, I don't think there's a real black-Korean conflict. To me, it's a fabrication of some black politicians who want to get media attention so that they can build up their own careers. Even though many Koreans do own liquor stores in poor neighborhoods, if there were no Koreans, there'd be someone else, whoever is willing to put in the money and take the risk.

I don't know Danny Bakewell,[146] but I notice that whenever he makes an appearance, he tries to emphasize conflict. That gets him the media attention he needs to advance his career. I talked with my father and some of my Korean friends about this black-Korean conflict. The two groups are equally ignorant about each other, because many Koreans form their opinions from what they see about blacks on television, and most blacks have nothing more than superficial contact with Koreans.

A lot of people emphasize the differences, but I find that there are a lot of similarities between Korean and black culture, by which I mean traditional Southern black culture. Both cultures have respect for education, for religious leaders, and for the family. There are similarities even in the way the family is modeled, with the father as head of the household and the extended family living together and supporting each other. Except for language, the two cultures are very close.

Los Angeles culture, now, is something else. When I graduated from Locke High School in South Central, at least half of the class went to college. Most of us are professionals now. Every five years, we have a class reunion, and most of my classmates are teachers, lawyers, engineers, and business people. Today, South Central is different. There used to be a black middle class, but now a lot of jobs have left the area and Hispanics have moved in. There are more Hispanics than blacks in South Central now.

Around here in the black community now, if you want to be educated, you'll be looked down on and disrespected. If you want to be religious and moral, you are not respected. In some ways I don't blame Koreans; the black culture in Los Angeles is not a healthy one. It's hard to respect a culture that de-emphasizes the value of education, religion, and the family. When Koreans see a person who doesn't respect education and morality, they don't respect that person. I think they can't understand it.

I don't think Koreans who own businesses in the black community should get out. The number of Korean businesses burned down during the riots has been emphasized, but people are overlooking the fact that many Korean businesses in South Central were not burned down. In many instances, people in the neighborhood said, "Hey, wait a minute. This guy is in our neighborhood. He respects us. We respect him. Don't burn it." Many Korean stores were protected by the neighbors. I also noticed that many stores that were not owned by Koreans were burned down. It didn't matter whether they were in a black neighborhood, in a Hispanic neighborhood, or somewhere else. I think there was too much emphasis on Koreans being targeted.

I was pretty upset when Koreatown burned. There were not many black people in Koreatown or Hollywood; most of the people were Hispanic. But to hear it from the news, the black-Korean conflict was the cause. I was wondering who was crazy. I knew it wasn't true; I saw all races on television, but the news reports emphasized that it was all blacks destroying Korean stores.

No one really wants to look at the people in the black community who emphasize education, religion, and the family. It's boring to the media to focus on some guy who works from eight to five, goes to church, and takes his family out on weekends. It's more exciting to focus on gangs, drugs, sex, and violence, which reinforces fear and stereotypes. After watching television stories about gangs and violence, my wife is really fearful.

Whenever I go to South Central, I am very comfortable. I know where I'm going. There are certain places where I don't feel safe in at night, but the same is true in El Sereno, where I used to live. There are certain Hispanic areas I would not want to go through, but there are other parts I don't have any problem with. Some of my friends from South Central didn't want to come to my El Sereno neighborhood because they thought there were gang activities there. They were afraid of drive-by shootings or that their cars would be broken into or stolen while they were visiting me. I told them that these were exactly the same kinds of comments I heard from people who didn't want to visit their neighborhood in South Central. Television creates all these bad images; a lot of opinions, true or false, are formed by the media. Politicians who want to advance their own political careers contribute to the fear and bad images by emphasizing conflict rather than similarities. We have to ask them directly, "Why would you deliberately create a situation that causes harm to so many people?"

JANUARY 1995

Year of
the Sheep

Kun Soo Kang is friendly looking and compactly built. He obviously
enjoys talking, joking, and telling stories, although he worries that
his story will not be useful because he has lived in this country for
less than one year. We meet in the offices of Korean Immigrant
Workers Advocates (KIWA), an organization comprised primarily
of young 1.5 generation Korean Americans who devote themselves
to working for immigrant labor rights and the betterment of race
relations among workers of color. In the previous month, **KIWA**
supported Kang and a group of other workers who picketed a
Koreatown restaurant that owed them two months' back wages.

I work from 6:20 A.M. to midnight every day driving a "call taxi,"[147] mostly in Koreatown. I've only been doing this for the last one and a half months, so the money isn't very good. Sometimes I make $50 all day. On good days, I make $100. The fares can range from five to fifty dollars, depending on the destination. If you work sixty hours a week, you could make $1,200 a month, or even maybe $1,500, if you get a lot of fares. I work for a company, but I drive my own car and take care of maintaining, repairing, and insuring it. I give thirty percent of whatever I get to the company. They pay for things like advertising. Sometimes they make ballpoint pens with the company's name on them. People call them for a taxi, and they refer the calls to individual drivers.

Of course, most of these Korean taxi companies aren't licensed or regulated, since they cater to Koreans. People who can't speak English can't ride in American cabs, because they can't communicate. It's hard to say how many taxis there are altogether, because the companies are all different sizes. Some of them are one-man companies, but they didn't necessarily start off that way. Maybe they started out with ten men, and each of them leaves to start his own company. There's a lot of competition. I'd say there are three hundred fifty or three hundred sixty taxi companies in downtown L.A. There's a lot of turnover. Every day, you can see seven or eight taxi company ads for new drivers in the Korean newspaper. There will come a time when they will all kill each other off. That's inevitable, because in the end, the only way you can survive is to kill someone else.

For me right now, this is not really a bad job. Many people leave their American jobs to drive a taxi. You can be on your own time a lot. After all, I can't work continuously from early in the morning until late at night. You can get started at this pretty easily. All you need is a car. I haven't even been in the U.S. for one year, and I'm doing it. But most of the drivers have been here for awhile and have had experience running a business. Usually the business failed, and the guy ended up driving a taxi because he had a car and already knew the streets in L.A. Driving a taxi is the easiest thing for him to do.

I came to the U.S. because I went bankrupt in Korea. I had a business with twenty employees. It was a beer franchise. The supply and demand just didn't match. In Korea, a small ad in the newspaper costs fifteen or sixteen million *wŏn*,[148] and you have to run these ads continuously. It was *mit ppajin toge mul pukki*, like pouring water into a bottomless jar. There wasn't enough business to match the costs. Finally, I went bankrupt. I gave up everything except my body, including my house. I had used the house as collateral to borrow money. All businesses in Korea are run that way; if you don't have cash, you use your house as collateral. I couldn't pay off my employees' wages, but no one among them cursed me, because they knew I had given up everything that I had. Besides, I had always treated them very well. From the beginning, I always paid a lot of attention to employee benefits. I gave 10,000-*wŏn* subway passes to everyone who did-n't have a car. I also bought all of them 5,000-*wŏn* telephone cards. Big companies like Hyundai often exploit their workers, but I never looked down on my employees, because I went through hard times myself. Just because I was the owner, I wasn't going to give them less and take more for myself. When I came to the U.S., all I had to my name was $3,000.

When I first got to L.A., I was hiding here and there. Then I learned that it isn't necessary to hide in the U.S. if you have gone bankrupt. In Korea, they issue a warrant for your arrest under the Fraudulent Check Regulation Law. If you get caught for something like jaywalking or smoking in a "no smoking" area, they'll run your residence card number through a computer to see if there is an arrest warrant out on you. If they catch someone, they get a reward. The guy who arrests you gets praised and is given a week's vacation. Koreans call L.A. a haven for bankrupt Koreans. So many bank-rupt people end up here.

Fortunately, my wife and I both got jobs within two weeks after we arrived in L.A. My wife got a job at Western Kaju Market, working in the section where they prepare side dishes for take-out. About five days later, I got hired in the fish section, cutting, cleaning, and selling fish. I had never done any work like that before. It was really hard work. I had to be on my feet for ten hours straight. I had to go into the freezer to take out the fish, and I had to lift heavy loads. After three days, I was ready to throw down my white apron and quit, but the other workers told me that it would take ten days for me to get used to working there, so I stuck it out, and then things did seem easier.

Even though the pay was small, we got paid on time, which was good. But employees who had worked there for three years would get the same wages as new workers—$1,200 a month, which I think is very bad. There should be a difference. Anyway, since my wife and I were both earning $1,200 a month, we were able to save some money. After a while, she heard about a waitressing job at a Koreatown restaurant, so she went there. About ten days later, we found out that the restaurant was looking for a parking attendant, so I went there too. I ended up working at another restaurant that was under the same owner.

I was never the kind of person who supported worker and student strikes in Korea. I felt that they were making things inconvenient for other citizens. I thought, "Why don't those students just study instead of protesting? Why are those workers striking? I'm sure they're getting paid enough." I figured that it wasn't my business. But now that I've been involved in picketing the restaurant for not paying the workers' wages,[149] I think there must be a reason why people demonstrated the way they did. You have to experience it for yourself to know. I put on a headband, like the demonstrators I used to see on TV in Korea.

I was an initiator, in that I was the one who insisted that we demonstrate, but I was not a leader in the picketing, in terms of figuring out strategies for people to carry out. Mostly, things were done by discussion and consensus. I didn't volunteer to be a spokesperson, but people did encourage me to speak. At first, I was embarrassed and didn't think I could do it, because there were so many people. But every day I got better at speaking, because everyday I got madder at the things that the management did.

Some of the other Korean workers didn't go out on strike with us, and neither did the Mexican workers. We got along well with the Mexicans at the workplace even though we didn't speak the same language. They don't speak English well and neither do we, so we communicate with our hands and feet. We are friendly to each other, but it is hard to get together.

Right now there are people from Indonesia, Bangladesh, and other countries working in "3-D" jobs—dirty, dangerous, and demanding jobs—in Korea. Koreans don't want to work in those kinds of jobs anymore, and there's a labor shortage. Those workers in Korea are like Koreans who come to L.A. without visas to work.

I am here on a visitor's visa, but I plan to become a U.S. citizen in the future. My father and stepmother are here. My real mother is in Korea; my mother in America is my father's second wife. They came to the U.S. together in 1987, sponsored by my father's younger sister, who I heard got to the U.S. because she was married to a black American soldier. He died before I could meet him, so I don't know much about him.

My father left my mother in the 1970s, when I was about eleven. Like all women who live by themselves in Korea, my mother had a really hard time. I stayed with my father right after they separated, but he wasn't good at raising kids because he was a man, so I went back to live with my mother after a while. It was difficult; sometimes I ate *ramen* three times a day. People say that *ramen* is more expensive than rice here, but in Korea, it's much cheaper. After eating *ramen* three times a day for a week, I could only shit water. When things started going badly at my mother's, I had to go back to live with my father.

After we kids grew up and got jobs, we started living with our mother. I had a hard time finishing school, and I had no special skills, so I did factory work. In those days, everything was manual. I lost part of my finger while I was working as a presser. In one section of the factory, they cut the sheet metal, and I was supposed to make a model from it. The press comes down as fast as you can turn the knob. If you turn the knob slowly, the imprint doesn't come out, so you have to turn it fast. I would turn the knob with one hand and put the material through with the other. One day, I was trying to impress the boss by making two models at a time, but I turned the knob too quickly and didn't have enough time to take my arm out, so my finger got stuck in the machine. Accidents like that were so numerous. That was all a long time ago. If I had to tell the story of my life, it would take all night. I suffered a lot back then, so I don't really like to think about those days.

I worked in several different factories. I also worked in stores. I worked at all kinds of odds-and-ends jobs. Even though I wasn't making much, I started saving regularly. I lived very frugally, and after ten years, I was able to buy the house I had to give up when I went bankrupt. I bought it in the spring of 1988, and I lost it last year.

I can't get a green card through my father because he isn't a U.S. citizen. After I get my citizenship, I'm going to visit Korea, but I have no plans to go back and settle down there. Maybe it's because I remember running around trying to hide after I went bankrupt there. Life is more comfortable for me here, where I can go around freely.

My kids don't want to go back to Korea either. They like it here because they only have to go to school five days a week instead of six, like in Korea. Here, there are lots of holidays and short school days. In Korea, they had to get up at dawn and come home late from school. It's much more comfortable for them here. My daughter is sixteen, and my son is fourteen.

I was born in 1955, in the year of the sheep. I met my wife on a bus while I was on leave from the army. She was a student then. I gave her my address and told her that she shouldn't think of me as someone of the opposite sex but just as a lonely soldier who wanted her to write to him. We became pen pals, and then she started visiting me. Fate is strange. After I was released from the army, we ended up working in the same building. She had a job as a dental assistant, and I was working for some relatives there. We started meeting often, but she didn't even try to introduce me to her family because she knew they would object. I wanted to marry her, but her family refused because I had nothing. I didn't even have a good job; how could they trust me with their daughter? Who would? Here in America, they let their daughters marry men who are sincere, but in Korea they have to check to see if you have a house, money, a good job, and a good education. I didn't have any of those things. But we fell in love and kept meeting. One day, I just barged into their house, carrying a bag of fruit in one hand and an envelope with some money in it in the other, hoping to meet her parents. I didn't call beforehand because I knew they'd never let me come over. In the end, I wasn't able to see them. They were very upset; how dare I just come over like that? They locked her in and wouldn't even let her come to the telephone. I told them we would not break up and that we should all meet to discuss it, but they said there was nothing to talk about.

She got out by telling them that she was just going to see me for a moment, and we eloped to Cheju Island. If I had known we were going to do that, I would have brought some more money with me. I really meant to just see her briefly, but when we met we realized that if she went back home, I would never see her again. I asked her how much money she had, and she said she had 500,000 *wŏn*, so I said, "Let's go." It was a crossroads for her: if she followed me, she would lose her parents; if she followed her parents, she would lose me. She decided to come with me. We called a travel agency, but there were no seats. They said we could just go to the airport in case someone didn't show up for the flight. It was about half an hour before the flight was supposed to take off, and at the last minute there were some empty seats, so we were able to board the plane. That was the first time I had ever been in an airplane. I came from a poor family, so I never had an opportunity to fly. I felt very dizzy.

When we got to Cheju Island, we didn't even go sight-seeing. We just went to a hotel. From Cheju, we visited Masan and Bugok. We had to borrow money after three or four days. We were gone for six nights and seven days. Everyone thought we had done everything. My wife's older sister offered to take her to a famous clinic for surgery [to restore her virginity] so that she could marry someone else. But nothing happened for six nights. If I say this in the U.S., people will think I'm old-fashioned, because people here are very liberal about sex. But even though I came from a very poor family, I am very straight. I have to admit that I tried to do it, because I am a man, but I didn't because she was afraid. Even now, I use it on her. I remind her, "What man would not take advantage of you during six nights and seven days?" In the movies sometimes, the woman sleeps in the bed and the man sleeps in the corner, but I slept on the bed and she slept in the corner. I guess she couldn't really rest because she never knew what might happen.

After that, she was totally with me. But her family would not see us, even three years after we had a baby. Maybe if her mother had been alive, things would have been easier, but her father was very strict. Korean people are like that; if it happens to other people, it's OK, but if it happens to their children, they don't like it. About other people, they will say, "Oh, well, as long as the two people love each other." But if it happens to someone in their family, they are totally against it. Of course, we're in contact with my wife's family now. I tell my children the story because it was not a crime. I took the best option available at the time; I had no choice. Who knows what would have happened to me if I had ended up with someone else? People in Korea say that a woman's fate depends on meeting the right man: if she meets the right person, she will prosper, but if she meets the wrong one, she will suffer her whole life. That's true for men as well.

JUNE 1995

YOUNG SHIN

A Higher Ground

Immigrant women's rights advocate Young Shin came to America in 1975 and settled in Los Angeles, where her brother, a certified public accountant, and his family were living. After earning an M.A. in sociology at California State University, Los Angeles, she took a job as a mental health worker in an Asian American agency in Oakland. She decided to go to law school because she wanted to acquire concrete skills to better help others, but instead of practicing law, she started working with Asian Immigrant Women Advocates, an Oakland-based organization that strives to develop leadership among low-income Asian immigrant women workers in the garment, hotel, electronics, and health services industries, so that they can protect their rights. She has been the agency's director since 1984.

I just spent a month in Korea. While I was there, some workers from Nepal staged a demonstration because they hadn't gotten paid. Apparently, they had been promised training, wages, and room and board, and then they were supposed to go back to their country. It's like the guest worker concept in the U.S. I wasn't surprised that they had been exploited and cheated, but I was surprised by the position the mainstream media in Korea took on the issue. A TV station did some investigative reporting about workers who had gotten their fingers chopped off working with the factory machinery and about workers who had gotten beaten and cursed. It was sobering to see these Nepalese workers on television, speaking the Korean phrases they had learned, such as "*Ttaeriji maseyo*" [please don't beat me]. Of course there is sexual harassment and rape of women workers. Anyway, these wrongdoings were exposed to the public. I was pleased to see that the news reporting was sympathetic to the foreign workers. In some ways Korea has changed a lot.

Here in the U.S., the history of immigrants is different. There's a lot of mistreatment of workers in the U.S., similar to what I have seen in Korea, but in the U.S. there is less guilt about exploitation. The European Americans seem to forget that they came here on the *Mayflower* and killed the Native Americans. But in Korea, people remember when Koreans were in the same situation the foreign workers are in today. I read an editorial in the *Han'guk Ilbo* [Korea Times] criticizing the mistreatment of foreign workers in Korea and recalling that it was not long ago when Korean workers were guest workers in the Middle East. And they know that some Korean emigrants are still in that situation. Just because the standard of living in Korea is higher than in the past, Koreans can't abuse foreign workers.

I went to Korea to spend time with my mom, who has liver cancer. My second brother is a psychotherapist. He and his family live with my parents in the Apkujŏngdong area.[150] My father, who's still working as a dentist, kind of helps, but we needed to hire help. We couldn't find a twenty-four-hour helper, so we had two different women. They usually came in at 10:00

in the morning and went home at 5:30. One housekeeper was living with her son and said she had to go home once a week, so, of course, we had to agree. My sister-in-law knows that she has to treat the housekeeper well, because otherwise she'll be in a bad situation. There's no such thing like in the past, when *singmo* [housemaids] were like property. We were more than willing to pay whatever the housekeeper asked. These days, housekeepers get paid $35 or $40 a day, 30,000 or 40,000 *wŏn*.

From time to time, my mom falls back on traditional ideas about maids. I had to remind her that you can't treat people like they did in the past. I told her that a housekeeper can't work around the clock; she needs a break. My mom kind of knows that things have changed, but old habits die hard.

Before, thousands of people used to be maids in Korea, and they were not treated well. But now women who do housework for wages have more economic leverage. There's more demand than supply, and they have gained respect and dignity, which I think is great. As the Korean standard of living went up, life in Korea improved for everyone, including housekeepers. It's not like in the past, with all the *kŏji* [beggars] and people working for very low wages. Now they are bringing in guest workers. Sometimes I wonder if Korea is becoming just like the U.S.

Ironically, Korean and other Asian immigrant women workers in the U.S., like garment workers, are more vulnerable, dispensable, and interchangeable than domestic workers in Korea because the industry is controlled by multinational corporations. That's why social justice work for immigrant women workers is very crucial. I work as the director of Asian Immigrant Women Advocates (AIWA).

I met my husband when I was in a training course for community organizers. Alfredo was the trainer at the Center for Third World Organizing (CTWO). We knew each other for three or four years. AIWA is a women's organization, and he used to help when we needed some muscles. Alfredo grew up in Chicago, but he lived in South Texas for a long time. His dad was from Mexico, and his mom was born here. When I first went out with him, I don't recall having any special feelings about his race. I guess because he's what you call a fair-skinned Mexican American—he could pass as Chicano, Mexican, Arab—but not as a European white. To him, being Chicano is a kind of political statement. You can't say that he has Mexican culture, although he's worked with Mexican workers. He's more attuned to what goes on here in this country, like racism. He's definitely not from mainstream white culture. His life has been with people of color. I would say he's more like mix-Mex Chicano culture. He speaks Tex-Mex Spanish. I think we got together because of our political beliefs and because we worked together in community organizing. We support each other. I can trust him and talk to him about what I do. We never compete; sometimes we argue about tactics, but many times he thinks what I do is really good. I really appreciate him for that.

I never had good luck with Korean men. I never found the right person. When some Korean men marry a Korean woman, they expect their wife to know her place; but if they married a Mexican or a white woman, they would think it's a different culture, so they would treat her better. Maybe that's what happened with Alfredo. I wasn't Mexican or Chicana, so maybe he didn't have certain cultural expectations. He might not agree with me on this. He already knew that I was active in the community; he probably married me because of that.

We both like hot and spicy foods. He loves *kimch'i*, although he lost weight when we were in Korea last time because he can't eat *miyŏk kuk* [seaweed soup]. He thinks it's boring to eat *chuk* [rice gruel] in Korea, because the Mexican kind has milk and sugar in it.

Our [identical] twins were born in 1990, when I was forty years old. Some women really want to have kids; I wasn't like that. It just happened. We were saying that if we were going to have kids, we should have at least two, so maybe it was lucky we had twins.

We were thinking of naming the girls Mira and Sora, which are Korean names, or Aisha and Maisha, which are African or Hindi names, but somehow we decided on one Korean name and one African or Hindi one. My twins want to be different from each other. Aisha calls herself Korean and Mira calls herself Chicana. Aisha loves *sun tubu* [soft tofu] and Korean dresses. Aisha thinks of herself as a girl, and Mira identifies as a boy. Maybe Aisha will be the flower girl in her stepsister's wedding, and Mira will be the ring boy.

I'm hoping to send my kids to a magnet school in Oakland, where there are kids from a lot of different racial backgrounds. Many of them are biracial, so my kids would fit right in. I really want my kids to learn about all different cultures. The common denominator in all our differences should be justice and fairness. It should not be "I'm Korean" or "you're Mexican" or Chicano. At the same time, I want them to use the strengths of both their parents' cultures. I sent them to the Korean-language school at the Oakland

Korean Community Center. We took them to Mexico several times, and they've already been to Korea more than once. At least they are attuned to different languages. Now they are enrolled at a Chinese child-care center, and they are writing Chinese characters.

I like living and working in Oakland rather than Los Angeles because I think there's more tolerance of different kinds of people here in the San Francisco Bay Area. Oakland is very multiracial, and people of different races and very different walks of life work together well here. I am energized by the immigrant community activism here.

I was out of the country when the L.A. uprisings occurred, but the situation was very disturbing to me, because it shows how the immigrant community can be squashed with all these conflicts going on in the United States. I know immigrants have to learn about and understand racial conflicts in the U.S. It's hard to take the broader view when you get squashed, and many immigrants really felt victimized. Some still have bitter feelings. People said, Why me? But the climate was boiling, and in this instance it just happened to boil over onto the Korean community.

It's a very complicated situation; that's why it's disheartening. People of all different races have anti-immigrant feelings. Blacks, Latinos, Koreans have them, and certainly the European American people have a lot. But because we are all in it together, we have to think about who really gets the most out of the poor—Latinos, Korean immigrants, people of color—fighting each other. We have to direct our anger and frustration toward the right target. Otherwise, we are going to be fighting each other, and that's not going to take anyone toward any solution.

With the racism and the growing anti-immigrant sentiments in this country, it would be very depressing to see the world only in terms of American society. I don't want my girls to have only America as their frame of reference. There are different ways of living and doing things, different kinds of politics. I always say that you have to think globally, even though you act locally. I'm not saying it's going to be easy. My daughters may not take the road that we are taking at this point, doing what people call social justice work, but I want them to understand that there is a higher ground than just knowing how to survive day to day.

Right now, AIWA is involved in a campaign to boycott garment manufacturer Jessica McClintock. We want McClintock to take leadership among the manufacturers in terms of corporate responsibility for the workers, instead of continuing to pass this responsibility on to the subcontracting sweatshop owners. We want a concrete agreement with a workers' protection clause.

Many garment worker struggles have ended in monetary compensation, but this group of garment workers wanted to go beyond that. When they saw how many supporters joined the campaign, they said, "We cannot let history repeat itself. We cannot see fellow garment workers not get compensated again. We can't have gone through a year of struggle just for money. We have to appreciate their courage. We are in for a long struggle; if we let go at this point, it will be very hard, not only for AIWA, but for other workers in the future."

Public education about immigrant workers' issues is also very important. A lot of community workers didn't like the way *Sixty Minutes* covered the McClintock boycott recently. The manufacturer was given a lot of time to talk. They cut us in an unsympathetic way. Still, having millions of viewers was important, because so often the issues we work with are invisible. How many times do people in Connecticut or the Midwest think about garment workers? Because we are immigrants and often not fluent in English, our issues are not out there.

Our workplace literacy classes are very important for building our base. Many people who come to this country, like I did a long time ago, feel a certain kind of gratitude, and don't really face up to the way they are taken advantage of. That's why education and information sharing are very important. It's very slow. Even if we win the McClintock struggle, our most important job is informing, and then educating, the immigrant women, because any agreement we reach won't be followed up on unless the immigrant women have power.

Things are getting really nasty these days. It's not necessarily because of the poor economy; the U.S. still has plenty of resources. I think it is a matter of greed. First, it was English only,[151] then it was employer sanctions, and now it's denial of education and health services to undocumented immigrants. In light of these anti-immigrant attacks, in light of global restructuring, and in light of multinational corporate exploitation, I don't think we can wait until all the immigrant women develop leadership before we start working to voice our concerns about the immediate issues affecting immigrant women workers and low-income immigrant workers.

Every society has its own shortcomings. If you think of yourself as belonging to only one society, you feel stifled. To find innovative ways to deal with challenges, you have to look at what's happening in other parts of the world. It's very important for people who want justice and fairness in any society to network and exchange information and use whatever skills they have. The bottom line is that you have to keep raising the issues of fairness and justice.

JANUARY 1995

SOOKHEE CHOE KIM

Perpetually Marginal

Sookhee Choe Kim lived in the United States for seventeen years before returning to live in Korea in 1988. In Los Angeles, she worked at a utility company for more than ten years as a revenue analyst. Her husband, who had been directing a section of a university graduate research library in Los Angeles, wanted to return to Korea when he was offered a position as a professor there. Like a number of other returnees to Korea, the Kims are separated from their U.S.-born children: their son and daughter are college students in Connecticut and New York respectively.

When I was growing up in Korea, everybody wanted

to learn from the outside. We all felt that we had to know English. Using a few English words in conversation was fashionable among educated people. Coming back to Korea after twenty years, I see that it has changed completely.

We moved back to Seoul from Los Angeles in early 1988. At that time, Seoul was getting ready for the 1988 Olympics. The slogan posted everywhere was, "The world to Seoul and Seoul to the world." I didn't take much notice of it, but later, when I heard people saying, "What is truly Korean is truly global/cosmopolitan," somehow, it didn't sound right to me. It's fine to have some pride, but it's too much to equate Korea with the whole world. This kind of thinking is still being promoted by the mass media in Korea.

There is a positive aspect to it all, though. In the past, Koreans didn't pay much attention to their own treasures, like *p'ansori* [Korean vocal music narratives]. Now, they are taking pride in their roots and cultural heritage. This is a good thing. But the reaction has been excessive. Somehow, it has generated a hostile attitude toward America. These days, I encounter people who say privately that Russia is closer geographically and maybe even culturally to Korea than the U.S., and that Korea should develop closer ties with Russia than with the United States. I don't like to hear comments like that.

Many government officials and scholars who go abroad seem to look only for bad things, like dirty streets in New York City and beggars in Los Angeles's skid row. They return and say that the downfall of the U.S. is imminent. People in Korea live and eat well now, so they seem to think there's nothing they can learn from the U.S. They form their opinions from relatively short, superficial visits to America. They hear things from uninformed interpreters or people in [L.A's] Koreatown, and they come back to Korea with all kinds of twisted opinions. People who don't really have firsthand experience claim to know everything about America. It's disappointing to hear these kinds of remarks all the time.

Somehow, it feels like a personal attack on me. Sometimes I feel like fighting back. Maybe I have become too cosmopolitan myself. When I was living in America, I would get angry if someone said bad things about Korea. Now that I've returned to Korea to live, it really hurts me when someone says bad things about America. But I can't openly express that in Seoul. When we get together with people of similar backgrounds, like other expatriates from America, we can talk about these things.

I remember attending a lecture by a man who spoke English well and had lots of contacts with people from other countries, including Americans He had worked in several first-class hotels in Seoul for many years. He had just returned from a two-week tour of America and was talking about a nursery being attached to a high school in Orange County. He said that the nursery was for the babies of unwed pupils at the high school. I had never heard of such a thing before, so I asked him if he himself had seen it. He said he heard about it from a Korean minister at a Los Angeles church. I said that there are children born to unwed teenagers in the U.S., but I didn't think things were so bad that they were building nurseries for high school students. He got very agitated and asked me why I got so upset at him mentioning something bad about America. There are so many people like him in Korea.

Both of our children were born in Los Angeles. Our son, who is twenty, is at Wesleyan College in Connecticut, and our eighteen-year-old daughter is starting her freshman year at Columbia. When we came back to Seoul, we sent our son to Phillips Academy and brought our daughter back with us. She attended the Seoul Foreign School, but she didn't like the school and had a hard time making the transition and wanted to go back to the States; so after a year, we sent her to boarding school at the Phillips Academy.

I've been teaching English at a junior college here. When I was in the United States, I did not particularly enjoy working. There was always a lot of stress at work. Here, I realize how convenient it is to use one's own native language. In America, I always was self-conscious about my accent, about writing reports, about my clothes, about what kind of food I should eat that didn't smell. There was constant pressure. Here, I don't have to worry about those things.

But there are different kinds of pressure here in Korea. You have to conform to the expectations of others in terms of dress, mannerisms, and ways of interacting. Sometimes, I'd like to ask my students about my teaching, but I can't, because professors don't ask students questions like that. If I did, I'd be ostracized by my colleagues. They don't like you being different.

I didn't realize this when I first got back to Korea. No one said anything to me then, but now they keep telling me that I've changed a lot since I first got here, which means they didn't like the way I behaved at first. The fact that I have to be conscious about these things all the time really bothers me.

People who live in America are usually frank and straightforward. In Korea, people don't say what they think right away. There's always something they're holding back when they speak. You have to try to figure out what that is. They don't listen to you straightforwardly, either. Everyone is paying attention to what other people might think of what they are saying. In meetings, people don't say what's on their minds; they go home and do their real talking on the telephone with a few people later.

When I first returned to Korea, people took my words in a thousand different ways. When I said something about America, they thought I was bragging about it. They always wanted to know whether I came back because I didn't like America. What they wanted was for me to give up my American identity and become totally Korean. They want to force a choice on you—either America or Korea. They cannot tolerate someone being both Korean *and* American. They hate the binational or cross-national outlook. They fear that a dual perspective might be superior to their monolithic outlook, and they can't tolerate that. Either you have to come back and live like them, whether you like it or not, or you have to go back to America.

This does not mean that they love Korea any more than I do. It just means that they can't tolerate the fact that I am a little different from them and have a few more choices than they do.

Now I'm very careful when I talk to people. I try to avoid mentioning anything about America.

Women enjoy a certain degree of power here. They're in charge of the household budget and the children's education. Most men hand their paychecks over to their wives. Men here get lots of extra income by doing things like giving lectures at seminars or writing articles for magazines. Company men get travel allowances. They use their extra income for evening outings to drinking places, but they deliver their paychecks to their wives, who control the money in the household. Korean women in the U.S. have to work outside the home and also do the household work. They have a much more difficult life than women here do.

That does not mean that women here are happier. Physically, they are more comfortable. They don't have to work. They can use the money their husbands bring them. They have plenty of time to meet with friends to chat. In the States, I never got to meet a personal friend for lunch. Not even once. On Sundays, we went to church and ate with the people there. It was a family gathering. Here, women go out at 9:30 A.M. When I first got back, I didn't know where they were going. When I would call my friends in the morning, they were already gone. Later, I found out they were out meeting friends. There are things happening every day. If you go to upscale restaurants in Seoul during lunch hours, eighty percent of the clients will be women in nice dresses. They go out every day.

Some women do volunteer work, but they are a very small minority. Most of the women in their 40s and 50s go out with their friends for a good time. I think they go out every day because they feel empty inside. If they felt full inside, they'd look for more meaningful things to do. They always have to talk about which places they went to yesterday, what they bought, what's going on in real estate and at the stock market, things like that.

During the first year, I met with my old friends often, but now I don't meet them anymore. The conversation is always the same. They just talk about their own stories. Everyone is talking, and no one is listening. They are just relieving their stress. There is never any point. They talk about money, how to make more money, the prices of apartments. That's all they talk about. The amounts they talk about is in the billions. I get dizzy listening. They say that everyone in their 40s and 50s should have at least two billion *wŏn*. They complain about the president forcing government officials to make their private assets public. They say that since everyone has at least two billion *wŏn*, why bother? In the U.S., it's rare for anyone to have $100,000 cash. Here, it's no big deal. I feel so poor among them, so I don't go out with them any more.

Recently, I quit teaching because the school was too far away from home and commuting was exhausting. Now I'm taking it easy at home, reading books, watching television dramas, and writing. I belong to a group of essay writers. Writing essays helps me sort out my thoughts. I write about my youth and about my life in the U.S. It's different from writing a novel. Some of my writings have appeared in an anthology published by the club.

I didn't even try to get into a Korean social circle. The only social life I have is with the people who belong to the essay writing club. Am I lonely here? In America, we were accustomed to our marginal status and learned how to cope with it. I am OK by myself; I can have peace of mind, even if I'm not accepted. So I don't feel lonely. Anyway, it's not so much that they don't accept us as that we don't want to establish a full partnership with them. I can't pretend to enjoy their life-style.

I don't belong to either Korea or America. When I was in the U.S., I didn't feel that I really belonged there. Here, I don't feel that I belong either. I'm perpetually marginal. But if you look at it from the positive side, you belong to both. Right now, Korea is my home, but my future home is where my children will be, which is the U.S.[152]

SEPTEMBER 1993

BONG HWAN KIM

As American
as Possible

Bong Hwan Kim, director of the Korean Youth and Community
Center in Los Angeles, was born in Korea in 1958 and grew
up in New Jersey. In 1982, Kim moved to Oakland, California,
where he began working in the Korean American community before
settling in Los Angeles in 1988. He has won numerous awards from
such organizations as the NAACP and the Pacific Center for
Violence Prevention for his community service and advocacy work.
Kim attributes his interest in social justice in part to his parents'
activism. His father, a chemist, and his mother, the proprietor of a
frame shop, participated actively in the overseas Korean movement
to protest the excesses of the South Korean military dictatorship of
the 1970s, and Kim recalls hearing many family discussions of
human rights issues when he was young.

342

I am always amazed at how pervasive the stereotype of Asian Americans as a model minority is. When European Americans start up conversations with me at airports, they invariably assume that I am an engineer or have something to do with computers. When I tell them I work with Korean American gangsters in Los Angeles, they get this blank look of total bewilderment on their faces. It's so far from their expectation of what I am supposed to be. I am very conscious of the way people perceive me just based on what I look like.

For the past thirteen years, I have been working for Korean American organizations in California, first for the Korean Community Center of the East Bay in Oakland, and now at the Korean Youth and Community Center (KYCC) in Los Angeles. When I was growing up in New Jersey, I never imagined that this kind of work would be possible. And I didn't dream that I could feel so at home with being a person of color in America. Throughout my childhood, I associated mostly with whites, but all through my adult working life, I've associated mostly with people of color, both professionally and personally. My current work on behalf of poor and immigrant communities often pits me against homeowners' associations, which are predominantly white, and white business leaders, who have the most access to political power and economic resources.

At this moment, it's hard for me to imagine having to live and work exclusively among people who thought the way people thought when I was back in New Jersey. To tell the truth, now that I know how much better I feel working in racially diverse groups, I am uncomfortable in a group of all white folks. Having grown up with white folks, I think I got to know "white culture" pretty well. I have to admit that I have a stereotype in my mind of white folks who have little contact with people of color still believing they're superior. I feel a strong kinship with other people of color because of the experiences I have had growing up as a Korean American in this society.

The Bergenfield, New Jersey, community where I was raised was a blue collar town of about 40,000 people, mostly Irish and Italian Americans. I lived a schizophrenic existence. I had one life in the family, where I felt warmth, closeness, love, and protection, and another life outside—school, friends, television, the feeling that you were on your own. I accepted that my parents would not be able to help me much.

I can remember clearly my first childhood memory about difference. I had been in the U.S. for maybe a year. It was the first day of kindergarten, and I was very excited about being able to have lunch at school. All morning, I could think only of the lunch that was waiting for me in my desk. My mother had made *kimpap* [rice balls rolled up in dried seaweed] and wrapped it all up in aluminum foil. I was eagerly looking forward to having that special treat. I could hardly wait for lunch time. When the lunch bell rang, I happily took out my foil-wrapped *kimpap*. But all the other kids pointed and gawked. "What is *that*? How could you eat *that*?" they shrieked. I don't remember whether I ate my lunch or not, but I told my mother I would only bring tuna or peanut butter sandwiches for lunch after that.

As a child you are sensitive; you don't want to be different. You want to be like the other kids. I was made to understand that I was different, and that the difference was negative. They made fun of my face. They called me "flat face." When I got older, they called me "chink" or "jap" or said "remember Pearl Harbor." In all cases, it made me feel terrible. I would get angry and get into fights. In high school, even the guys I hung around with on a regular basis, would say, "You're just a chink" when they got angry. Later, they would say they didn't mean it, but that was not much consolation. When you are angry, your true perceptions and emotions come out. The rest is a façade.

They used to say, "We consider you to be just like us. You don't *seem* Korean." That would give rise to such mixed feelings in me. I wanted to believe that I was no different from my white classmates. It was painful to be reminded that I was different, which people did when they wanted to put me in my place, as if I should be grateful to them for allowing me to be their friend.

Part of growing up in America meant denying your cultural and ethnic identity, and part of that meant negating your parents. I still loved them, but I knew they were not going to be able to help me outside the home. Once when I was small and had fought with a kid who called me a "chink," I ran to my mother. She would say, "Just tell them to *shut up*." Or my parents would say that the people who did things like that were just "uneducated." "You have to study hard to become an educated person so that you will rise above all that," they would advise. I didn't really study hard. Maybe I knew somehow that studying hard alone does not take anyone "above all that."

I was a kind of natural athlete, and I enjoyed every kind of sport. My parents encouraged my interest in sports, indulging and nurturing all my boyish enthusiasms by sparing no expense whenever I needed equipment. Probably sports saved me from complete lack of self-esteem as an Asian growing up in New Jersey in the early and mid-1960s. Through sports, I got lots of positive feedback and was able to make friends with white boys, who respected my athletic abilities even though I was Asian. In high school, I was elected captain of the football team, and my girlfriend was captain of the cheerleaders. I was not particularly good in school. My parents were upset, but I didn't pay much attention to them.

I grew up thinking that "American" meant "white," and whatever was not American and not white was not good. I wanted to be as American as possible. I drank a lot and tried to be cool. I convinced myself that I *was* "American," whatever that meant, even though I wasn't white. But I was always hounded by a nagging sense of inadequacy, by the sense that I was less than a man, which I kept trying to compensate for by pursuing sports.

I tried to avoid the few other Asians at school. The guys were pretty much nerds, the studious type—Chinese Americans who played tennis. One of them played golf, but they weren't into the macho sports that get you accepted. When I met another Korean guy in college who was athletic, I was guarded and rejecting. It's strange: if I had met him at the Korean church, I probably would have befriended him, because the church was a familiar environment that felt like an extension of my family, so there wasn't that strong backdrop of white male standards to measure people against.

Back then, I thought of white women as the epitome of womanhood. But at the same time that I viewed white women as ideal, I knew that they viewed Asian men as less than ideal. I clearly remember wanting to avoid Korean and Asian women. I had the feeling that I was superior to them. I know now that I avoided them because they reminded me of my own inadequacy as an Asian male. At the same time, the Asian woman was probably trying to avoid me, because I reminded her of her inadequacies vis-à-vis white people.

Thinking back to how pervasive that feeling of wanting to belong to whatever was popular or cool at the time, I realize that I should have been with other people who were on the fringes, like the artist types, who rejected social conventions and didn't care what was popular or cool. If I had gotten

345

to know them, I probably would have had a much more meaningful experience then and much better memories now. But you have to be confident to enjoy being on the fringes.

When I got to college, sports failed to be a way of leveraging acceptance into circles I would not otherwise be allowed in because of my race. I was thrown into a kind of identity crisis. I tried to imagine what I might be doing in ten years, to think about the kind of life I would be living in this society, but I just drew a blank. Now I realize that I was facing the knowledge that you can't really participate in society if your humanity and your sexual identity are always in question. You are just too distracted to find a goal, much less focus on it. I became very depressed. I hated even getting up in the mornings. Finally, I dropped out of school. All the while, I knew underneath that I'd have to reconcile myself someday, to try to figure out where I could fit in a culture that never sanctioned my identity as a public possibility. What helped me get out of my depression was going to Korea. I went there hoping to find something to make me feel more whole. Being in Korea somehow gave me a sense of freedom I had never really felt in America. It was a physical space in this world where I would not be rejected simply because of what I looked like, where I did not have to always look over my shoulder, wondering if someone was out to get me for being different. Being in Korea also made me love my parents even more. I could imagine where they came from and what they experienced. I began to understand and appreciate their sacrifice and love and what parental support means. Visiting Korea didn't provide answers about the meaning of life, but it gave me a sense of comfort and belonging, the feeling that there was somewhere in this world that validated that part of me that I knew was real but that few others outside my immediate family ever recognized.

After spending a year in Korea, I returned to finish college, and then I packed up and just headed for California. I had always wanted to go to the West Coast, not only because of the mystique of California "freedom" but also because I heard that Asian Americans had a stronger presence there. I wasn't much into career planning; I still have trouble planning my life over five-year time spans. I wasn't looking forward to getting a job in the mainstream labor market, but I was anxious to find out what the "real world" was like. In California, I had the opportunity to work in the Korean American community and be accepted for what I was. I met Asian Americans of all kinds, and I learned to appreciate Korean American women.

When I was young, the places where I could be a full human being were at home with my family, at the Korean church, and in Korea. It makes sense that I work in the Korean American community now. But I don't think that self-ghettoization is a good thing. In Los Angeles, I run into many Koreans my age who deliberately segregate themselves from non-Koreans. America should not be a society where people don't want to associate with each other. My optimistic side says that this is a transition period in which we are moving away from old paradigms in favor of creating something new, although I have no concrete reasons to be optimistic, what with the current immigrant bashing and backlash against people of color.

Three years ago, I would not have guessed that anti-immigrant sentiment would be this strong. Opportunistic politicians are appealing to majority white voters by simplistically pinning the blame for the nation's social and economic problems on immigrants, most of whom are Asian and Latino. That way, they can also maintain their traditional constituencies. If the current House and Senate version of the welfare reform bill goes through, legal immigrants would be cut off from most government services. Most recently, a government-sanctioned private commission on immigration reform headed by ex-Congressperson Barbara Jordan has been calling for a major overhaul of immigration policy to cut back the number of immigrants allowed into the country by one-third and to eliminate the fifth preference, which gives priority to family members.

At the same time, social services for the poor are being cut back. We are going to be forced to rethink traditional approaches to community development, unless a major tax reform is approved by voters, which is highly unlikely in the current climate. In some respects, Korean and other Asian American communities are relatively better off than other communities of color, given Asians' strong belief in self-help and relatively lesser reliance on agency services. But being relatively better off in a world where most people around you are continuing to sink into poverty will eventually wear you out also.

Asian Americans are juxtaposed between white "haves" and black and brown "have-nots," and we are classified as model minorities in that context to justify the unequal distribution of wealth and power. Asian American successes in education have been used as a rationale to do away with affirmative action programs for African Americans and Latinos. Instead of allowing ourselves to be used as a rationale for dismantling these programs, we need to assert our own opinions and positions in the public policy arena, not only for the benefit of African Americans and Latinos but also for the Asian Pacific American poor, who are being swept into conceptual invisibility by the pervasive stereotypes of Asian American "success." It doesn't benefit us for whites to believe we are smart or "better" than other people of color. Instead of mutely accepting a designated place in the social hierarchy, we must work toward a completely different social structure based not on hierarchy but on social justice and equality, as espoused in the U.S. Constitution.

The stereotype of Asians as goody-goody conformists is so pervasive. Immigrant Korean parents often view themselves as sacrificial lambs, believing that even though they'll go to their graves as deaf, dumb, and blind, they are doing it so that their children can achieve the so-called American dream. Their kids work incredibly hard, knowing that only they can vindicate their parents for their sacrifice. In the end, they may think that as Korean Americans with college degrees they are fulfilling their parents' expectations according to the myth of the American dream. But instead, they become the target of resentment from all sides: white resentment and fear of Asian yellow peril takeover and black and brown resentment because of the perception that Asian Americans are honorary white people unconcerned about social justice issues.

People don't realize that a large percentage of Asian immigrants are from the middle classes of their homelands. When they come to the U.S., they suffer socioeconomic decline but, ironically, this decline is perceived as achievement. The Southeast Asian refugees who didn't come from the middle class share a lot in common with Spanish-speaking working-class immigrants. Those Asians who don't conform to the model minority stereotype are invisible in the mainstream society. There are going to be more and more Korean American high school dropouts and juvenile delinquents succumbing to urban deterioration. There's only so much that the much-touted "family values" can do to defend against these pressures. The family unit can't operate all alone, in a vacuum, indefinitely.

We can't dismiss what happened to Korean Americans during the 1992 Los Angeles riots as a fluke or an aberration in a social system that is otherwise basically working fine. Institutional neglect of urban poverty and lack of effective political leadership allowed the social environment to degenerate to the point where Korean Americans could be scapegoated for conditions that we neither created nor had any control over. I continue to remind Korean Americans that unless those conditions are changed, such a thing could recur.

348

At the time of the riots, African American communities were politically strong but economically frustrated, Asian American communities were economically stronger and politically invisible, and Latino communities were both politically and economically disenfranchised. Ultimately, we need a multiracial coalition that supports true equality and enfranchisement. The toughest part will be convincing those with the most that even if a redistribution of power means no gains for them in the short term, the society as a whole will be better for everyone in the long term.

Every issue comes down to a convoluted configuration of class and race. I can see myself taking the Central American side in the future on affordable housing, playgrounds, social services as opposed to high-rise office buildings proposed by Korean developers.

It's hard to imagine what happened in April 1992 as a Latino-Korean conflict. Many Korean merchants feel lingering resentment at the role Central Americans played as looters. The traditional Korean love-hate relationship with the poor spills over into attitudes toward Latinos. Like many Latinos, Koreans are immigrants from a homeland decimated by colonial subjugation and U.S. cultural imperialism. As struggling immigrants, they have much to share: I often see working-class Koreans working side by side with Latino laborers, speaking a combination of Korean and Spanish, eating spicy foods together. But the majority of Korean immigrants want desperately to regard themselves as belonging to the middle class, as better than Latinos, whom they believe they have to exploit in a capitalist society.

After the riots, KYCC worked to organize neighborhood based focus groups between Central Americans and Korean Americans, with the goal of putting together a multiracial planning council in Koreatown. We hired a community organizer who was active in the movement against the military dictatorship in El Salvador to conduct block-by-block canvassing in the neighborhoods. This project required a delicate balancing of Central American street vendors who might be exiled fighters against fascism in their homelands with Koreatown's richest and most capitalistic developers. It failed because KYCC lacked an infrastructure within the Central American community. We have begun to address ways to build coalitions by revising our organization mission statement to incorporate *all* Koreatown residents—many of whom are Latinos—as our constituency.

We also worked to ensure fairness to both Korean and African American communities by responding to the African American community's call to reduce the number of liquor stores while at the same time being mindful that the ruined Korean merchants need to regain a means of livelihood. We set up a liquor store conversion project to help burnt-out Korean and African American liquor merchants establish other businesses that would serve community needs. We were able to get the city council to waive costly sewage hookup fees for conversion of liquor stores to laundromats and other businesses. Another avenue we have been pursuing is technical assistance to help liquor store owners improve their sales of nonliquor items, thereby reducing their dependence on liquor sales. If you compare a Korean immigrant-owned store to, say, a 7-Eleven Store, you see how poorly managed the Korean store is. In the 7-Eleven, each item is located in exactly the same place, so that the delivery man knows exactly where to go. Most immigrant merchants don't keep inventory, so when a shelf space gets emptied, they just put anything in there. We're working with the Korean American Grocers Association to help them provide better technical assistance to their members. Many merchants know that dependence on liquor sales is unhealthy for the community and for them. Poor people who don't have cars rely on the local convenience store for things like produce and dairy products. And liquor sales are a magnet for crime, for residents and merchants alike.

I think that all our strategies have to have a fundamental economic base. People in South Central don't want to talk about improving race relations between African Americans and Asian immigrants unless you're talking about jobs. That redefines how we should approach improving relationships. There are people who still focus on trying to get people to know each other better, which is OK if you are dealing with mostly middle class people in various organizations and institutions. But if you really want to get to the root of a problem, you have to talk about economic development. You have to address the deep, institutional inequities that give rise to violence among people.

I hope that the riots had a profound impact on Korean American community perceptions of our own needs. There had not been a collective longing for leadership before. People were fighting over credit and titles. It was bad, but the community was doing all right economically, and that's all that seemed to matter. The American dream of Korean immigrants was based on economic rather than political wants. That's the desire that capitalism engenders, both in Korea and in the U.S. Korean Americans played by the rules of the game that were already set up. The rhetoric in the U.S. is about inclusiveness, about everyone, no matter what color, being rewarded for working hard and minding his or her own business. The ideals are great, but the reality is about political powerlessness for people of color in a hostile and racist environment.

What stands between Korean Americans and the promise of the American dream is racism. For immigrants of color, the prerequisite for becoming American has been leaving your culture by the door. But you can give up your culture and still not be accepted. You'll be hated instead, in a society that blames you whether you "succeed" or "fail" in your efforts to attain the American dream. I think it's a trap. We have to ask ourselves, What do we have to give up? What if there's no "there" to enter into after you have given everything up?

It's crucial for Korean Americans to participate in the decisions that affect our lives. That's why we have programs to help Korean immigrants become U.S. citizens and campaigns to get people registered to vote. We also have leadership development internship programs for Korean American youth, because they can serve as bridges between the immigrant families and the society at large, and because they could become key agents of change in our community in the future.

I can't understand why so many young Korean Americans have conservative values, why they give themselves up to the status quo. It's disheartening that so many of them want to go into the legal profession, which in my view is the upholder *par excellence* of the status quo. It's all about manipulating the rules of the game, which implies accepting the rules of the game and becoming part of a network of colleagues whose power and privileges are dependent on locking lay people out of even knowing the code words or the logic that lawyers monopolize.

To many Koreans and Korean Americans, leadership is equated with social status, professional qualifications, and advanced degrees. That's why attorneys and academics with no record of involvement in the community can be so quickly accepted as spokespeople. Many Korean immigrants are only interested in the person's credentials, not in her or his track record. Perhaps it's a holdover from Korean Confucianism, which places so much emphasis on social status.

The people that I admire the most are those who are committed to social equality and justice and have attained a position of influence to make a difference both within their own community as well as the public dialogue, but, most importantly, go about their work in a humble fashion. This is not to say that I measure up to those standards. But those are the standards I aspire to and by which I assess the effectiveness of others as well.

The powerful have to be held accountable. I distrust power, no matter what color or how well-intentioned. I don't buy this American individualism stuff. Individual success stories don't translate into well being for the Korean community as a whole. If we accept the rules of the game as they are, we are doomed. The game should be about creating a humane and just society, where people can provide their unique perspectives and do their part to build a better world. Korean Americans could be an enrichment instead of a "problem" that needs solving. I want to believe that those who have been on the outside can bring that outsider perspective in and transform America.

DECEMBER 1992, MARCH 1993, AND JUNE, 1995

APPENDIX A
Elaine H. Kim

Koreans often tell me that I don't "look" Korean. My spoken Korean is clumsy and comical. And my personal history doesn't resemble that of many other Korean Americans. Born in New York and raised in Maryland at a time when Asians on the East Coast were relatively few and U.S.-born Korean Americans were all but invisible outside Hawaii, I belong to the "lost generation," the descendants of early Korean immigrants who, K.W. Lee says, are "gone with the wind." My family consisted of my father, my mother, and my brother; none of my other relatives came to live in this country. The Koreans I encountered were mostly some aging bachelors who died alone far from home and a few foreign students studying engineering and planning to return to Korea after completing their studies. There was no regular Korean church nearby, and even if there had been one, we may not have attended much: Because of my father's low opinion of Koreans who got their U.S. degrees by studying theology with the help of American missionaries, our family was militantly non-Christian, which in the 1990s, when the vast majority of Koreans in this country devotedly attend Christian churches, would make us considered by many to be not Korean American at all.

When my parents died in Oakland in 1989, they were both almost ninety years old. They had not only experienced America through the Roaring Twenties, the Great Depression, and the Second World War, at a time when there were few cars, no televisions, and no chance of justice for Asians in the United States; they also knew a Korea that has long since vanished. Their American experiences directly contradicted the American Dream, according to which the immigrant steps onto an escalator that moves her from East to West, from primitive, uncivilized native to successful U.S. citizen, closing the door on her past forever and leaving her legacies and memories behind. In the end, neither my parents' stories nor their bodies found a home here. My father never became a U.S. citizen, even after living sixty-three years in this country, at first because he was not allowed to, and later because he chose not to. My mother, who we believe was born in Hawaii or at least arrived there when she was an infant around 1903, was prevented by law from voting or exercising other rights of a U.S. citizen until she was almost fifty years old, when the McCarran-Walter Act[153] was passed. By that time, she was not interested in being "American." Even though her best language was English and she only visited Korea for the first time when she was sixty years old, she thought of herself as Korean, as other Americans frequently reminded her she was. Both my parents were buried in Korea, in accordance with my father's wishes. I had the heartbreaking task of sorting through their worldly goods. Their nine decades of life in America amounted to a small pile of harassing letters from the Immigration and Naturalization Service, some receipts crumbling with age, and a little stack of faded photographs and yellowing sheets of personal correspondence, all tantalizingly unrevealing about who they had been. I did not know who the faces in the photographs belonged to, and I could not read the letters.

I struggle for whatever I can learn about the past. Korean Americans of my generation had so little to call our own in America. We might stare into the faces of unknown people in our family albums or interrogate our parents, who connect us to a past we have no other way of knowing. Korea was always a topic at home, but it did not seem to exist anywhere else. When I was growing up in Maryland in the 1950s, most people I met asked me "what I was" and didn't know that Korea was not a province or state in China. Our American "world" history classes began with Greece and Rome and ended in the U.S. I recall those rare occasions when teachers mentioned China in the classroom because they always looked at me, as if I knew more about China than anyone else did. It didn't matter that I wasn't Chinese, or that I had learned just as little about China as my classmates, since I had never lived or gone to school anywhere but in the U.S. Meanwhile, when I complained to my father about being called "chink" by my classmates or about their parents, who would not let their children play with me, he would say, "Just tell them that you're Korean." That, he thought, would take care of everything.

The immigration of most Korean Americans today was made desirable by shifts in global geopolitics and possible by changes in U.S. immigration quotas after 1965. This Korean American experience emerges from so-called post-colonial, divided, industrialized, and Christianized South Korea and from post–civil rights U.S. American culture. When contemporary Korean Americans learn about my background, they think I am the quintessential "sister outsider," the sister from another planet, a person fallen out of time. But as visual artist Yong Soon Min has said, "The more a thing is torn, the more places it can connect."[154] On a deeper level, perhaps there are lines of affinity between my background and that of other diasporic Koreans, whose twentieth-century life circumstances, including their migration to the U.S., are rooted in colonization and war, both hot and cold. And perhaps we are linked in some way by the outlaw identities that we sometimes try hard to conceal, especially from each other.

My father's family was scattered across the world by the impact of Japan's annexation of Korea in 1909. Both he and my half-sister were jailed by the Japanese police for anti-Japanese activities and anti-Japanese thoughts. His older brother fled to China, where he fought in the resistance movement against Japan until his death. My aunt became a communist and, after the Allied defeat of Japan, moved to P'yŏngyang, where my cousin says she was killed when the U.S. used bacteriological warfare on North Korea during the Korean conflict.[155] My father's hometown in Kangwŏn Province was cut in two when Korea was divided by the world's superpowers after World War II. He was the one who came "West," first to Japan around 1917, and then to the U.S. as a foreign student in 1926. Since persons born in Asia were prevented by law from immigration and naturalization, he remained in this country throughout the Japanese colonial period in Korea by staying enrolled at Columbia University until he was almost forty years old. Finally, he and other Koreans literate in Japanese were granted permanent resident status by special congressional bill when they were hired as translators during World War II. Like so many other Korean sojourners of his time, my father struggled all his life with underemployment, waiting on tables in Chinese restaurants, peddling Japanese novelties, working for the South Korean embassy, and finally starting his own small business.

At the end of the Yi dynasty, many Korean families were scattered, like my father's family, and many family members found themselves ascribing to opposing political ideologies, like my father's brothers and sisters. When I was growing up, I heard a lot about my father's history, but no one said much about my mother's background. I figure that my maternal grandmother, a country woman, fled Korea to Hawaii, pregnant and alone around 1903. My mother looked like a person of mixed racial heritage. Could the father she never knew be one of the Russian soldiers who was sent to the Korean peninsula around the time of the Russo-Japanese War? Was my grandmother seduced? Was she raped? Perhaps she considered jumping into a well, like No Name Woman in *The Woman Warrior*,[156] but was saved by the tiny window of opportunity opened when the Hawaii Sugar Planters Association recruited briefly in Korea to counter the efforts of Japanese sugar workers in Hawaii to organize for equal wages. I can only imagine the background story, since my grandmother returned to Korea, where she died before I could ever meet her.

My migrant farm worker mother ran away from the abusive older husband she had been matched with at seventeen, leaving her son behind and moving from California to Chicago, where she worked in a five-and-ten-cents store. She married my father and gave birth to two children when she was around forty years old. My father always emphasized her educational accomplishments: After meeting him, the story goes, she enrolled in the ninth grade; within three years, she had won a full scholarship to Mount Holyoke College, from which she graduated in 1938. But hers was no "model minority" success story; like other Asians in the U.S. at the time, she was never able to obtain employment commensurate to her education. She sold Avon cosmetics and the *World Book Encyclopedia* door-to-door and earned money on the side researching and writing ghost master's theses for Chinese foreign students.

A few years ago, a Korean immigrant acquaintance informed me that people were saying bad things about me. I learned that they were talking about my being descended from sugar plantation workers and migrant vegetable pickers. Strangely for them, perhaps, I am very proud of this ancestry, and I am proud that I may be descended from a long line of "bad women."

In a larger sense, even this gendered and impossibly marginal heritage may be more "mainstream" than it as first seems. Every Korean American family I know has a huge cache of skeletons in its closet. Isn't it likely that most immigrants to a new land do? Many early Japanese and Korean picture brides, for example, left their homelands behind to marry men they had never met and to live in a foreign country where they could not even speak the language. At least some of these women must have been escaping something; some of them must have been women with a "past"—a failed love affair, perhaps, or a child born out of wedlock.

Eight years ago, when I was conducting interviews in Seoul, whenever I was told about a scandal and asked what happened to the parties involved, the answer was invariably, "She moved to Los Angeles," or "She's living in New York." Korean Americans are people with a "past," or at least sons and daughters of people with a "past"—women and men escaping from their pasts.

Many Korean Americans look down on Korean women who marry U.S. servicemen, sneeringly referring to them as *yangsaekssi*. [Western "girlies"], *yangkongju* [Western princesses], or *yangkalbo* [whores of the West], which implies the epitome of female "badness"—both betrayal of nation and prostitution. But they are overlooking the people who made their American lives possible, for although few will openly admit it except when asked, it is likely that the immigration of the majority of Koreans in the U.S. today can be traced to a near or distant female relative who married a black or white American military man. It turns out that most of us are probably descended from a long line of "bad women." Perhaps we need to reexamine our notions of "bad women," so that we can find out just how we are connected.

Because I spent my early years living as something of a freak within mainstream American society, which decreed that there was no way to be "Asian" and "American" at the same time, I often longed to be held securely within the folds of a community of "my people." Like many other U.S.-born Korean Americans, I was changed forever when I visited Korea at the age of twenty and saw my relatives for the first time. Finding myself among so many people similar to me in shape and color made me feel as though I came from *somewhere* and that I was connected in a normal way to other people instead of being taken as an aberration, a sidekick, or a mascot whose presence was tolerated when everyone was in a good mood. But like other U.S.-born Korean Americans, I came to understand that there is no ready-made community, no unquestioned belonging, even in Korea, for as soon as people heard me speak or saw me grin like a fool for no reason, as soon as they saw me lurch down the street swinging my arms, as soon as they noticed me looking brazenly into people's eyes when they talked, they let me know that I could not possibly be "Korean."

The African American-led civil rights movement of the 1960s made it possible to imagine that a person like me could be an American, and I have been committed to equality and the creation of self-determined identities and futures for Americans of color ever since. Attempting to uncover buried knowledges and viewpoints reveals our connectedness as well as our heterogeneity. It is at times a labor of sorrow, because it continually brings us face to face with experiences of dislocation and damage that brush History against the grain. At the same time, it is also a labor of joy, because it brings into view the natural grandeur of people's struggles for dignity in the most challenging circumstances, and because it inspires us to grapple with the question of why stories of such struggles are so often missing from the dominant discourse to begin with. For me, learning about other Korean Americans' viewpoints and experiences is especially exhilarating, because they demonstrate so clearly that there has never been just one way to be Korean, American, or Korean American.

APPENDIX B
Eui-Young Yu

The other day my uncle took me to a remote mountain in Kyŏngsang Province where my sixth-generation grandfather is buried. Though I live in Los Angeles, I was in Seoul writing the seventy-year history of the church that I grew up with, and my father pastored for a good deal of his life. My uncle thought I should learn more about our ancestral roots since I am writing a memoir about my father, who passed away in 1988. Thirteen generations ago, my ancestors moved to the southern province from Seoul when the Manchus captured it in 1636.[157] They became farmers and gradually moved up north over the generations.

It was in my father's generation that the Yu clan finally made it back to Seoul. It was a good feeling that I finally encountered the grandfather six generations before me, although he had been dead for more than 100 years. The grave site was near the top of the steep mountain, and it took us a while to hike up there. It was beautiful. You could see chains of mountains stretching far to the south. Believing that a good grave site on a high mountain would bring blessings to his descendants, he wanted to be buried there.

I was born and grew up as a preacher's kid. My father became a Christian when he was twenty. My grandmother was struck with diphtheria. No one in the village would come near her house except a Christian lady in the neighborhood who cared for my grandmother day and night. Finally, grandmother recovered. My father was so impressed by the neighbor's love and care that he went to her church and received Christianity. He worked his way through a seminary school and became a Presbyterian minister. My father wanted me, his eldest son, to become a minister, but by the time I reached college, I realized that it was not for me. Never as faithful as my father wanted me to be, I have also never strayed far from the Christian faith. I find peace and comfort in it. My Christian upbringing forms the foundation of my values.

What were my first encounters with Americans? I was a second-grader when American soldiers rode in on a big military truck near my village outside of Seoul. It was in September 1945, immediately after the Allied defeat of Japan. They threw candy and gum to us. Sometimes they would throw down their ration boxes. At times, they gave us a ride on a jeep. I was very impressed. But once, when I was a third- or fourth-grader, I was almost hit by a rock thrown by some U.S. soldiers on a military supply train. They were throwing rocks at the children and laughing. Another time, my father was walking home from the evening church service when the driver of a U.S. military truck stopped his vehicle, got out, and beat him for no reason. My father spoke some English and tried to say something, but it didn't do any good. I just couldn't understand why someone would just attack him like that.

I barely escaped death several times from U.S. bombings during the Korean War. I was in the seventh grade when the war broke out. During the three months that Seoul was under North Korean control, our family was hiding in a farm village away from Seoul fearing that the communists might harm my father. I would see many decaying corpses by the side of the road while I was walking to the market to barter my mother's clothing for food and grain. That's how we survived during three months of hiding under the communist occupation.

Once, my father and I were in a farm field when squadrons of attack planes started hovering overhead. I was absolutely terrified; I could even see the faces of the pilots. I was carrying a big bag of grain, and my father told me to stand still in the middle of the rice paddy. We thought that if we started running, they might shoot. They circled five times and then left. Later, we heard bombs exploding and saw people carrying wounded bodies on handcarts down the mountain road.

Toward the end of the three months of communist occupation, we were famished. My five-year-old brother tried to eat some raw wheat. It troubled his stomach. He was sick all night and by the next morning he became unconscious. My father ran to all the nearby villages to look for a doctor, to no avail. That evening, my brother stopped breathing. The next morning, U.S. tanks and trucks rolled into the village. They came one day too late.

When we returned home to Seoul, we learned that my uncle (my mother's brother) had been killed by the communists. He was considered an enemy of the people because he owned a hardware store and was rich by their standards. We also saw half of our house destroyed by an American bomb. The house was bombed during a battle between UN and North

Korean forces. Half of our church was also destroyed.

I came to the U.S. on the *S.S. Sultan*. When I arrived in Honolulu in June 1963, I cried because it was so different from Korea, so beautiful and afflu-ent. I was overwhelmed by the difference.

After disembarking at the Oakland Naval Station, California, I boarded a Greyhound bus to Tennessee with Billy Joe King, an American soldier I had befriended when he was in Korea. Many years later, I remembered how Billy Joe led me to the back of the bus, where all the blacks were sitting, and I thought about what it meant. Billy Joe had been stationed with a mili-tary police unit in front of our village in Yŏngdŭngp'o, Torimdong, and my brother invited him to our house after he visited our church. We treated him like a brother. Billy Joe and I had the same birthdate: October 29, 1937. He was a true Southern gentleman and a good Christian; we are still good friends to this day, even though we live on opposite coasts.

I had graduated in sociology from Seoul National University and was making plans to study abroad. When it was time for me to come to the U.S., Billy Joe suggested that I live for a while at his family's house in Denmark, Tennessee, fifty miles from Memphis, for a year, taking classes at the local college and polishing up my conversational English. Billy Joe's family treated me like their own son. I was pretty good in English from middle school onwards. In fact, English was my favorite subject. When I was in the tenth grade, I had memorized the Gettysburg Address.

Still, I have had complicated feelings about the U.S. all along. When I was in college, I studied about how the U.S. and other world powers divided up our country, and I wondered how American people would feel if Korea cut their country in half.

After staying with Billy Joe's family for a year, I went to graduate school at the University of Pennsylvania on a full scholarship. I met my wife, Julie, in 1965. She was studying math at Temple University. She's now a high school math teacher. I finished my Ph.D. in demography in 1969. I planned to go back to Korea after a couple of years, but I took a job teaching at Cal State Los Angeles. When I was offered a position at Seoul National University in 1971, I turned it down. We'd bought a home in Monterey Park and had a new baby, and Julie had a job as a computer programmer at Xerox. She really didn't want to go back to Korea. Also, I had six younger siblings, four of them still in school, and I knew if I went back I'd be responsible for all of them on a teacher's salary. Eventually, I brought my family members to the U.S. I have never regretted not going back to Korea, because I have been able to be more productive here.

It took five or six years for us to feel at home in Los Angeles. There were a few thousand Korean Americans then, and Koreatown extended between Vermont and Western on Jefferson, in an area that is now referred to as South Central. People in the Korean community were very supportive of me; I was placed in positions of responsibility right away. I was both a scholar and a community worker all along. The growth of the Korean community in Los Angeles was fascinating, a new urban ethnic community unfolding in front of my eyes. I wrote articles and focused my teaching on it. At first, my research concerned urbanization and migration in Korea. Toward the end of the 1970's, I shifted to Korean American issues and race relations. It is disheartening to see starkly contrasting worlds coexist in American cities, compartmentalized clearly by race and class, without much human interaction.

Whenever I see the videotape of the Rodney King beating, I feel strongly that a great injustice was done. I fully understood the anger coming from the black community. After many years of legal and social segregation and oppression, they experienced only small gains after the civil rights movement of the 1960s. At the same time, I was afraid for the Korean merchants in South Central because of the mutual ignorance and lack of understanding between African Americans and Koreans. The first steps toward building a bridge are open expression and communication. I am happy to be part of a project that contributes to this cause.

I realize that I don't have many years of research life left. My goal is to serve the community and humanity, to promote human welfare and well-being. I cannot stand by while someone is being mistreated.

Brief Overview of Korean and Korean American History

5000–900 B.C.
Prehistoric period.
Neolithic people first appear on the peninsula that is now Korea.

900–60 B.C.
Walled-town states and confederated kingdoms period.
Walled-town states, such as Puyŏ, Old Chosŏn, and Chin, emerge. Old Chosŏn combines with other walled-town states to form a single confederation, which becomes a formidable independent power in northeast Asia. Samhan states emerge in the southern part of the peninsula. Han China takes control of the area north of the Han River in 108 B.C.

Rice is cultivated. Bronze culture merges with iron culture.

60 B.C.–668
Three kingdoms period.
Koguryŏ, having ousted a large Chinese colony called Nangnang, occupies the region centered around the middle Yalu River and the Tung-chia River basin; Paekche emerges in the southwestern part of the peninsula; and Silla appears in the southeast. The three kingdoms evolve into aristocratic societies under monarchic rulers. The allied forces of Koguryŏ and Silla repel a Japanese invasion in 400. In the mid-seventh century, Koguryŏ engages in long, bloody wars with Sui and T'ang of China. Internecine wars erupt among the three kingdoms, and Silla allies with T'ang to annex Koguryŏ and Paekche by 668.

Buddhism becomes the state religion, first in Koguryŏ and Paekche and finally, after much struggle, in Silla.

668–918
Period of unified Silla.
Unified Silla enjoys a long period of political stability. Buddhist culture flourishes. *Hyangga* poets express the people's religious feelings in lyrical poetry. Silla aesthetics are based on idealized harmony with nature. Maritime activity flourishes. A large Silla community settles on the Chinese Liaotung peninsula.

918–1392
Koryŏ period.
Wang Kŏn, a regional warlord in the Kaesŏng area, establishes the Koryŏ dynasty with its capital in Kaesŏng (north of what is today *p'anmunjŏm*, near the 38th parallel) and consolidates the three warring nations. Koryŏ emerges and continues its hereditary aristocratic rule until 1392.

The civil service examination system is imported from China, and a new type of class society emerges. Several notable slave uprisings attest to the oppressiveness of the class system. Buddhism is integral to people's everyday lives and is the major creative force shaping Koryŏ's cultural achievements. Artisans produce delicately colored, highly refined celadon pottery. Koryŏ University is established in 992. Literature written in Chinese flourishes. Publication of Buddhist scripts with wooden blocks begins. Women enjoy great freedoms and inheritance rights equal to men's. As in the Silla period, uxorilocal marriages are common. The literature of the period contains expressions of love and sexuality, thus reflecting the liberal ethos of the society. Because of trade with the Saracens, Koryŏ is introduced to the Western world, whence the English word "Korea" originates ("Corée" in French and "Corea" in Spanish).

Invasions of Koryŏ. Khitan (a tribal state in northeast China) mounts three invasions of Koryŏ between 993 and 1018. Khitan forces are crushed. Large-scale peasant and slave uprisings against government officials' oppression break out between 1181 and 1198. The military takes power in 1170 and rules the country for a century. Japanese *waegu* [armed bandits or pirates] raid the Koryŏ coast frequently between 1213 and 1259, devastating farm villages. After 1350, the coasts are all but deserted. The Mongols begin a series of invasions between 1231 and 1235, taking over Koryŏ's northeastern territory and seizing 200,000 captives, including many women. The Mongols conquer Koryŏ in 1259. A large number of women and girls are sent to the Mongol court, which demands them as tribute. The Mongols

establish the Yüan Dynasty in 1271. The last Koryŏ resistance to the Mongols takes place on Cheju Island, off the southern coast of the peninsula, and is subjugated in 1273. A succession of Koryŏ kings is required to take Yüan princesses as primary consorts, and sons born to these queens succeed to the Koryŏ throne.

1392–1910

Chosŏn (Yi) Dynasty period. Koryŏ general Yi Sŏng-gye succeeds in a *coup d'etat* against the Koryŏ king in 1392 and establishes a *yangban* [*literati* ruling class] bureaucratic state. The capital is moved to Hanyang (today's Seoul).

Class society. Neo-Confucianism, which is based on strict hierarchical order among social classes, between the genders, and according to age, is imposed as the state ideology. However, the Confucianization process takes about 250 years to take root. By the mid-seventeenth century, women are divested of the right to inherit property; segregation of the sexes and rigid gender hierarchies are firmly in place. *Han'gŭl*, the Korean writing system, is promulgated in the fifteenth century. *Han'gŭl* is used by a very small number of commoners and by women of some social standing, while the Chinese classical writing system is reserved for men of the *yangban* class.

Invasions of Chosŏn. Japanese warlord Toyotomi Hideyoshi invades Chosŏn between 1592 and 1598, during which the countryside is devastated by pillage and slaughter. The invasions are finally halted by combined Sino-Korean resistance. The Manchus invade Chosŏn in 1627 and 1636, ravaging the northern part of the peninsula. Large numbers of women are sent to Manchuria as tribute. Many of them are returned, precipitating a social crisis because they are considered *hwanhyang nyŏ* [promiscuous women] not fit as wives, even though their "condition" does not result from their own actions.

Social criticism. Contact with foreign societies results in the importation of new farming technologies. Number of landholding farmers increase. Cottage industry grows as a result of tax reforms. As a market economy culture begins to evolve around market towns, critical social views develop, including new religions that promise social transformation. Sirhak [practical learning], which emphasizes agrarian-based social transformation and land reform emerges. In the late eighteenth century, Catholicism, which is named Sŏhak [Western learning], is embraced by marginalized *yangban* and, later, by large numbers of women. In the latter nineteenth century, Tonghak [Eastern Learning] proliferates, advocating equality for all human beings, regardless of gender, class, or age. Movements for social reform lead to peasant uprisings.

Contact with the West. In the seventeenth century, Crown Prince Sohyŏn becomes acquainted with a Jesuit missionary while being held hostage by the Manchus. He brings a number of works on Western science to Chosŏn. In the late eighteenth century, Catholicism is gradually introduced by Chosŏn scholars acquainted with Jesuit missionaries residing in China. Catholicism is outlawed in 1785, and Chosŏn Catholics go underground. English merchant ships begin appearing off the western coast in 1832. French warships and Russian armed vessels appear off the coast in 1846 and 1854, respectively. For the next two decades, Western nations repeatedly attempt to establish commercial and diplomatic relations with Chosŏn, but all overtures are rejected. In 1866, the Chosŏn monarch launches a full-scale campaign against the Catholics; nine French missionaries and about eight thousand Chosŏn converts are killed. Chosŏn attacks a fleet of French warships that enter its waters to inquire after the fate of the missionaries. In the same year, a U.S. trading ship called the *General Sherman* sails up the Taedong River to P'yŏngyang and is set afire by a mob of local residents and soldiers. All on board are killed. In 1871, a detachment of the U.S. Asiatic Squadrons dispatched by the U.S. Navy is met with fierce resistance. Taewŏn'gun, the staunchly isolationist de facto regent, relinquishes his decade-long hold on power in 1873. Nine years later, the Corean-American ("Corea" was changed to "Korea" by Japan, because "J" comes before "K" in the Western alphabets) Treaty of Amity and Commerce is signed in Inch'on, and the first U.S. minister arrives in Seoul in 1883. In the same year, Great Britain, France, Italy, and Russia establish permanent legations in Seoul. An eight-person Chosŏn diplomatic mission is sent to the U.S. One member, Yu Kil-chun, stays on as a student at the Governor Dummer Academy in Massachusetts, becoming the first Korean to study in the U.S. Yu later returns to Korea, where he helps launch dramatic reforms. The first Protestant missionaries arrive in 1884-85. They establish modern educational institutions, such as Ewha Haktang, Paejae Haktang, and Chosŏn Christian College, which later evolve into Ewha and Yonsei Universities.

1876–1910

Japanese encroachment and the end of the Yi Dynasty.

Japan sends three warships with eight hundred soldiers to Kanghwa Island in 1876, demanding that Chosŏn enter into treaty negotiations. The Treaty of Kangwha, which permits Japan to survey Chosŏn's coastal waters at will and authorizes establishment of Japanese settlements in three open ports, Pusan, Inch'ŏn, and Wŏnsan, is concluded. Informal Japanese domination begins. As the Japanese presence increases, rural Chosŏn sinks into misery, and popular uprisings break out in many areas in the 1890s. The 1894 Tonghak uprisings against increasing foreign encroachment as well as government corruption constitute the largest-scale peasant insurrection in Korean history. The Chosŏn government appeals to China for help against the Tonghak rebels, but when Chinese troops land on the peninsula, Japan also sends its army, leading to the Sino-Japanese War in 1884. Victorious in 1895, Japan takes virtual control of all internal security matters in Korea.

In response to Russia's increasing presence in Manchuria and Korea, Japan attacks the Russian installations at Port Arthur in 1904. In the secret Taft-Katsura Agreement of 1905, U.S. President Theodore Roosevelt recognizes Japanese domination of Korea as *quid pro quo* for Japan's recognition of U.S. hegemony in the Philippines. Japan imposes the Protectorate Treaty on Korea in 1905, taking full authority over all aspects of Korea's foreign relations, foreign trade, and defense matters. The Korean army is dissolved in 1907. In 1910, Japan formally annexes Korea, commencing three and a half decades of brutal colonial rule.

Korean Migrations. Koreans begin to migrate to northern China and into the maritime provinces of Russia after the end of the Sino-Japanese War in 1884. The numbers increase to tens of thousands when Korea is annexed in 1910.

Mass migrations are again triggered in the 1930s, when colonial land policies in Korea uproot millions of farmers. During this period, hundreds of thousands of Koreans migrate to northern China, where two million Korean Chinese descendants of these emigrants still reside. In 1937, two hundred thousand Koreans who had moved to the Russian maritime provinces are relocated by the Soviet government to Kazakstan and Uzbekistan for security reasons. Currently, about half a million Korean Russians live in the former U.S.S.R. During World War II, Japan forcibly conscripts Korean men and women to Japan and various Japanese military outposts in Asia as laborers, soldiers, and "comfort women," or sex slaves for Japanese military men. By the end of the war, there are more than two million Koreans living and working in Japan. By 1945, approximately one-fourth of the Korean population is living outside

Korea. Many return to Korea after the liberation, but about 700,000 Korean nationals still reside in Japan.

Koreans in America. Due to U.S. immigration restrictions, the Korean population in America has been, until quite recently, very small compared with overseas communities in China, Russia, and Japan. Although several dozen students and ginseng merchants have already gone to the U.S. by way of China after 1884, the first significant group of Koreans to migrate are recruited as laborers by sugar plantation owners in Hawaii, who wish to break up Japanese immigrant workers' organizing efforts there. Between 1902 and 1905, about seven thousand Koreans, the majority of them men, sign up to work on sugar plantations in Hawaii. In 1905, about one thousand Korean laborers arrive on the Yucatan Peninsula in Mexico to work on henequen plantations. Emigration to the West is terminated after the Protectorate Treaty with Japan is enacted, but between 1905 and 1924, about five hundred Korean students and political exiles arrive in the U.S. by way of China and Europe. During the same period, about eight hundred picture brides land in Hawaii and another two hundred arrive on the U.S. mainland. Since U.S. immigration officials consider Koreans Japanese nationals after the annexation, Korean picture brides are allowed into the country during the period when picture brides are arriving from Japan as a result of the Gentlemen's Agreement between the U.S. and Japan. Between 1908 and 1920, the Gentlemen's Agreement permitted the entry into the U.S. of immigrants who are not

specifically laborers. Presumably, Japanese officials allow them to emigrate because they hope that the presence of women will calm the political passions of the exiles in America, who are vociferously protesting the annexation of Korea.

Because they begin immigrating later and are stopped from coming to the U.S. earlier, the number of Koreans in the U.S. remains much smaller than the Chinese and Japanese. In the 1930s, approximately 650 Koreans in Los Angeles County form a community in the area between Adams and Slausen Boulevards and between Western and Vermont Avenues, now called South Central Los Angeles. Despite their small numbers, Koreans are targets of anti-Asian violence as well as anti-Asian legislation. Korean farm workers are attacked in Hemet Valley, California, in 1913 by an angry crowd of white workers who mistake them for Japanese. The same year, California passes the Alien Land Act, which prohibits immigrants ineligible for citizenship—that is, Asians—from buying property. Koreans, like other people of color, are subject to both employment restrictions and housing segregation. Thus, many Korean Americans engage in tenant farming and in small businesses, such as barbershops and rooming houses, that cater to people not permitted to use facilities reserved for white people. In 1924, the U.S. Congress designates Asia as a "barred zone" from which immigration is totally prohibited. About three hundred Korean students are admitted with Japanese-issued passports between 1925 and 1940. They are allowed to remain in this country as long as they continue to register for school. No Korean-born person can become a naturalized U.S. citizen. No Korean immigrants are admitted into the country until 1952, when the McCarran-Walter Act is passed. This law reformulates the 1924 barred zones and national origins restrictions allowing, among other things, East Asians to apply for U.S. citizenship.

The fact that they are never able to become Americans may serve to encourage Korean American participation in the movement for Korean independence from Japan. Koreans in Hawaii and on the mainland U.S. establish churches and organizations, such as Taehanin Kungminhoe [Korean National Association] which becomes the "official agent" of Koreans in the U.S. until the end of World War II and which provides financial support for the Korean provisional government in Shanghai between 1919 and the 1940s.

1907–1945

Resistance to Japanese colonization.

Resistance to Japanese colonization is a Korean preoccupation during most of the first half of the twentieth century. After Japan disbands the Korean army in 1907, Koreans organize ŭi-pyŏng [righteous army/people's volunteer army]. By 1910, almost three thousand clashes occur between the Korean guerrillas and the Japanese Army, and more than 17,600 Korean fighters are killed in battle. Patriot An Chung-gŭn assassinates Ito Hirobumi, a Japanese statesman responsible for forcing Korea to accept the Protectorate Treaty, in Manchuria. On March 1, 1919, the Declaration of Independence, signed by thirty-three

national representatives, is read at Pagoda Park in downtown Seoul. The movement for independence is called *sam-il undong* [March 1 movement]. Demonstrations and rallies are held all over the country for months, with over one million Korean people participating, including many young people and women, as can be seen in photographs of the period. Thousands of Koreans are killed, injured, and imprisoned by Japanese police. In 1929, another large-scale uprising is ignited among students in Kwangju and spreads across the country. Throughout the colonial period, Koreans — including many women — participate in armed resistance efforts in Manchuria, China, and Siberia. Especially during the 1930s, anti-colonial socialist movement activities proliferate in both Japan and Korea, where there are numerous tenant farmer disputes with Korean and Japanese landowners and factory worker strikes against mostly Japanese factory owners.

Korean American independence movement activities.
Inspired by U.S. President Woodrow Wilson's Fourteen Points Declaration, which includes respect for the self-determination of peoples, Koreans in the U.S. participate actively in efforts to draw world attention to the Korean people's desire for national independence and their opposition to colonization of Korea by Japan. On the eve of annexation, thousands of Korean laborers in Hawaii sign a petition to U.S. President Theodore Roosevelt advocating independence for Korea. Two Korean expatriates in San Francisco assassinate a pro-Japanese American advisor to the U.S. foreign office in Seoul. During the

Japanese occupation period, Korean American laborers donate significant portions of their wages to support the Korean provisional government, which has been established in Shanghai. Korean political leaders subscribing to different paths toward Korean independence move between the U.S. and China in their struggles against Japanese colonization. Ahn Chang Ho (An Ch'ang-ho) travels between the U.S. and Korea between 1899 and 1913, when he establishes Hŭngsadan, an organization that advocates the regeneration of the Korean national character. In 1919, Ahn joins the provisional government in Shanghai. He is arrested by the Japanese police in 1935 and reportedly dies in a Japanese prison three years later. Another independence movement leader, Pak Yong-man, arrives in the U.S. as a student in 1904. An advocate of military resistance against Japan, he establishes Korean military training centers in Nebraska, California, Kansas, and Wyoming. In 1914, the total number of Korean cadets reaches 311. After 1919, Pak moves his base to northern China, where he is assassinated in 1928. Syngman Rhee arrives in the U.S. in 1905, studies at Harvard and Princeton, and becomes an advocate of international diplomacy as a path to national liberation. Rhee's followers establish Tongjihoe [Comrades' Society] in 1921. Rhee sets up and pastors the Hanin Tongnip Kyohoe [Korean Independence Church] in Hawaii in the 1920s as a base for his political activities.

1945–1953
Liberation, division, and war in Korea.

Near the end of World War II, the U.S. State-War-Navy Coordinating Committee decides to divide the Korean peninsula into two occupation zones, with the north under Soviet control and the south under U.S. control. Meanwhile, the Koreans establish the Committee for the Preparation of Korean Independence (CPKI), which quickly develops as a new national government. People's committees of the CPKI assume control of the local administrative operations in all parts of Korea. Delegates convene a meeting and announce the formation of the Korean People's Republic (Chosŏn Inmin Kŏnghwaguk). Soviet troops have already mobilized at the northern border, and U.S. troops land in southern Korea. The U.S., suspecting its leftist tint, refuses to recognize the Korean People's Republic, outlawing it instead and setting up the United States Army Military Government in Korea (USAMGIK). By the end of 1946, most of the people's committees in the south are gone. Syngman Rhee returns to Korea from the U.S. and is placed as top political adviser to U.S. Lieutenant General John R. Hodge, who has been placed in command in Korea. Meanwhile, Kim Il Sung, a guerrilla fighter in Manchuria in the 1930s, takes control of northern politics and implements socialist reforms through the channels of the people's committees in the north.

Separate elections. For all practical purposes, Korea is divided into two halves at the 38th parallel. Massive migration of Koreans from the north to the south begins. A U.S.-backed campaign to repress the left begins in the south. Although Southern nationalists fear that separate elections will lead to permanent division of the country, U.N.-supervised elections are held in the south in 1948. The U.S. backs Syngman Rhee as a staunchly anticommunist conservative. The Republic of Korea (ROK) is established in the south, with Syngman Rhee as its first president. Ten days later, elections are held in the north, and the Democratic People's Republic of Korea (DPRK) is proclaimed, with Kim Il Sung as premier. The U.S. has no official diplomatic relations with North Korea, and Koreans who come to the U.S. after the national division are all from South Korea, including refugees to South Korea from North Korea's authoritarian rule. Thus, Korean American immigration after the national division is strongly linked to economic, political, and social conditions and events in South Korea.

Civilian uprisings. The implementation of separate elections triggers a massive uprising on Cheju Island. The uprising is brutally suppressed: The last people's committee is destroyed only after a sustained South Korean government assault. Fighting devastates three-fourths of the island's villages and leaves tens of thousands of people dead. Many Cheju Island people take refuge in Japan. Thousands die during the Yŏsu- Sunch'ŏn rebellion in South Chŏlla Province, which begins when the Korean military revolts against deployment to Cheju Island. Atrocities are committed in the name of both the right and the left. The military rebels are joined by hitherto underground leftists, and the rebellion leads to several years of guerrilla warfare in the Chiri Mountain area.

Civil war in Korea. The Korean War erupts in 1950. The U.S. enters the war on the side of South Korea, and China enters in alliance with North Korea. Three years of fighting bring ruin to both halves of the country. Cities and towns are reduced to ashes, and millions are rendered homeless. Approximately three million Koreans and almost a million Chinese are killed, wounded, or missing; about 34,000 Americans lose their lives, as well as 1,300 British and 1,900 other U.N. participants. Hundreds of thousands of refugees from North Korea flee south. Many believe they are separated from their homes or family members only temporarily, only to find themselves prevented for decades by the permanent partitioning of the country from returning home or being reunited with their families in the North. Feeling cut off from their families and their places of origin, many northerners emigrate later to other countries, including the U.S., as opportunities arise. A truce is signed in 1953, but U.S. troops remain on the peninsula up until today. Immigration of thousands of Korean wives of U.S. servicemen begins. The U.S. Congress passes a law allowing intercountry adoption of Korean children by American families. Currently, an estimated 100,000 Korean wives of U.S. servicemen and 100,000 Korean children adopted into American families live in the U.S.

1961–1987

The military dictatorship period. After seven years, the Syngman Rhee regime is toppled by massive citizen protest against injustices and government corruption. *Sa-il-gu* [April 19], meaning the movement that begins on April 19, 1960, erupts when tens of thousands of college and high school students march toward the South Korean presidential mansion to protest rigged elections. Demonstrations spread across the country when police fire upon and kill 130 students. Within one week, Syngman Rhee is deposed. In 1961, the *o-il-yuk* [May 16] *coup d'etat* takes place when Major General Park Chung Hee seizes power and places the South Korean military at the helm of the country's politics for the next three decades. The military government launches a series of export-oriented development plans that propel the country into rapid modernization and economic growth. These plans require "austerity," meaning hard work and deferment of gratification as well as indefinite suspension of many democratic rights. Millions of rural people, many of them women, are drawn into labor-intensive urban factories, where they face intense labor exploitation. Female textile workers organize a number of spectacular strikes in the late 1970s to protest low wages and poor working conditions, but these are brutally suppressed. Park spearheads normalization of diplomatic relations between South Korea and Japan, thus opening the era of multinational industrialization. The acceptance of Japanese capital and investment after 1965, along with U.S. investment and South Korean profits from the Vietnam War, lays the groundwork for the contemporary South Korean economy.

Emigration during the military dictatorship period. In 1962, the Korean government passes the Overseas Emigration Law, which encourages emigration as a means of controlling population, alleviating unemployment, earning foreign exchange, and acquiring knowledge of advanced technology. Among those prohibited from emigration are draft resisters, political dissidents, high government and military officials, and people with assets over $100,000. Also, the Korean government arranges labor contracts with various countries, including West Germany, Thailand, Uganda, and Malaysia. Korean nurses and miners go to West Germany on a guest-worker program between 1962 and 1970. In 1963, Koreans begin migrating to Brazil as agricultural workers. By the 1970s, Korean immigration to South America has spread to Uruguay and Paraguay. Koreans are also trying to settle in Argentina. Due to a shortage of medical manpower in the U.S., Korean nurses and doctors begin to move to the U.S. with work permits. In 1965, the U.S. Congress passes an Immigration Act that abolishes the national origin quota system and adopts a new immigration structure based on family ties and employment skills. As a result, immigration from Korea rapidly increases. The U.S. Census counts almost nine thousand Koreans in Los Angeles County and 70,000 in the U.S. in 1970. By 1990, the official count is about 145,500 and almost 800,000, respectively.

Martial law in South Korea. In response to growing dissidence in South Korea, Park Chung Hee imposes constitutional revisions, euphemistically called Yusin Hŏnbŏp [Revitalization Constitution], in 1972. These revisions allow unprecedented executive powers, allowing Park to rule by decree and expanding his power to disband the National Assembly. One of the executive decrees promulgated during the Yusin era makes it a crime to criticize the government, punishable by seven years to life in prison. During the 1970s, many Koreans leave the country because of economic difficulties stemming from the export-oriented economic policies that favor *chaebol,* or business conglomerates, as opposed to labor or smaller enterprises. Others migrate to escape from the kinds of constitutionally-warranted terror brought forth by the Yusin Hŏnbŏp. Meanwhile, fearing the possible loss of U.S. government and military support, the South Korean government steps up Korean CIA terrorism and surveillance activities designed to suppress criticism of its policies among Koreans in the U.S. At the same time, the South Korean government offers funds to U.S. universities, newspapers and news magazines, and television stations. In 1976-1977, several U.S. legislators are implicated in a South Korean influence-buying scandal involving lobbyist Pak Tong-sŏn.

Denouncement of military rule. Park Chung Hee is assassinated in 1979, and power is seized by several South Korean Army generals. In 1980, the Kwangju Uprising begins as a peaceful demonstration calling for an end to military rule. The demonstrations spread and are violently suppressed by the military. An estimated 2,000 civilians are killed. Since a U.S. general is in ultimate control of the Korean Armed Forces,

many Koreans believe that the U.S. is partly responsible for the tragedy. Anti-U.S. sentiments begin to spread in South Korea, and demonstrations against U.S. Information Services offices continue for many years. A sweeping national culture movement develops to challenge dominant U.S. consumer culture. Meanwhile, citizens continue to demand democratic elections.

Popular demands for democratization. As opposition to continuing military rule intensifies, nationwide protests are sparked in 1987, after a dissident college student dies while being tortured by police. The protests culminate in the June, 1987 uprising, in which students, workers, and ordinary citizens join forces to demand democratic elections and civilian rule. Tired of years of austerity and privation, during which they bore the burden of South Korea's rapid economic development, workers for Hyundai and other major manufacturers strike all year for better wages, better working conditions, and the right to organize. General Roh Tae Woo, hand-picked successor of General Chun Doo Hwan, is elected president. Four years later, Kim Young Sam wins the presidential election in South Korea, bringing civilian government to the country for the first time since 1961. The new government exposes the corruption that characterized the previous decades' military regimes. Although many of the economic and foreign policy positions remain the same under the new government, Korean society becomes more open as the power of the military declines. Labor movement demands result in increased rights for workers. Citizens are permitted to travel abroad more freely in the 1990s, with increased contact perhaps resulting in more tolerant attitudes toward peoples of other cultures. The women's movement continues to score major victories in the arena of social policy, such as equal inheritance rights and an end to forced resignation from work upon marriage. Election results in 1995 support autonomous regional governance for the first time in fifty years. Decentralization presents the possibility of an end to decades of massive exodus from the countryside and from other cities and towns into Seoul, where more than one-fourth of the population of the country lives and where traffic congestion, air pollution, and other urban problems are making life there increasingly difficult.

North and South Korea. Both South and North Korea are admitted to the United Nations as member nations in 1991. In a conflict between the International Atomic Energy Agency and North Korea, the U.S. intervenes and negotiates a settlement with North Korea to improve relations in exchange for North Korea's promise to utilize nuclear power for peaceful purposes only. In the midst of the negotiations, Kim Il Sung dies. The possibility of a summit meeting between his son, Kim Jong Il, and South Korean president Kim Young Sam is discussed.

Koreans in the U.S. today. The liberalization policies of the new civilian government, together with the movement away from centralized government, may ultimately lead to decreased Korean immigration to the U.S. At the same time, anti-immigration sentiments in the U.S. might result in immigration reforms that would cut Korean immigration substantially by eliminating certain family preference categories. Moreover, reports reaching South Korea about race discrimination and racial tensions, economic difficulties, and social alienation, especially after the 1992 Los Angeles riots, may seem to be discouraging continued immigration to the U.S.

A significant proportion of those with professional and technical backgrounds who arrive in the 1970s and 1980s are unable to find employment in the U.S. commensurate with their education, skill level, and work experience. Many become self-employed small business owners, often in poor and minority communities, where start-up costs are comparatively low, and where established mainstream businesses and large corporations are reluctant to invest. Between 1981 and the present, disputes between Korean merchants and African American customers develop into boycotts of Korean stores in New York, Chicago, and Los Angeles. Korean shopkeeper Soon Ja Du kills an unarmed African American teen-aged girl in her South Central Los Angeles store in 1991. Tensions between Los Angeles Korean and African American communities intensify, exploding when Du is released on probation by a white judge. Political protests against the verdict in the case of the white police who beat African American motorist Rodney King escalate into riots in Los Angeles on April 29, 1992. Three days of rioting result in fifty-eight deaths and nearly $1 billion in property damage. Around 2,300 Korean businesses are damaged or destroyed. The Los Angeles riots constitute a turning point in the identity formation of many Korean Americans, especially young Korean Americans for whom America is the home of the heart. After the riots, small but concerted efforts continue in Korean American communities around the country to improve relations between Korean immigrants and people in African American, Chicano, and Latino communities. Korean Americans work increasingly in coalition with other groups against race discrimination and hate violence. Participation increases in local, state, and national political campaigns and programs. In the 1990s, a number of young Korean American film makers, playwrights, novelists, poets, and visual artists burst onto the American cultural scene, expressing new sensibilities and aesthetics. Korean American women form organizations to ensure equal participation for women in Korean American community politics and to work in coalition with other women's groups and groups from other communities on various social and political issues. Some young Korean Americans turn their attention to transnational labor issues, protesting layoffs of mostly Latino workers in Los Angeles by the new South Korean owners of a large Los Angeles hotel in 1993 and launching protests against South Korean factory owners in Guatemala for their brutal attempts to prevent worker organizing there in 1995. Korean American participation in these

issues gesture away from traditional Korean nationalism and toward transnational alliances rooted in broad-based social justice concerns.

Notes

[1] By "1.5 generation," Korean Americans usually mean those who were born in Korea but who were educated mostly in the U.S. Most Korean Americans in the 1.5 generation speak both Korean and English, with varying degrees of fluency. A second-generation Korean American, of course, is the U.S.-born child of immigrants.

[2] See Appendixes A and B for Kim's and Yu's stories.

[3] See Appendix C for "Brief Overview of Korean and Korean American History."

[4] An important nationalist leader in the Korean American community at the turn of the century who advocated individual self-improvement and education as a means to restore Korean national autonomy. Please see "Brief..." for more details.

[5] March 1, 1919, movement for Korean independence from Japanese colonial rule.

[6] Literally, letter hall; a traditional private school for learning Chinese ideograms and other subjects.

[7] The first modern high school in Korea, established in Seoul by American missionaries.

[8] *Chigyekkun*, or men who hired themselves as porters; they carried loads on wooden A-frames on their backs.

[9] To be relegated to the Chŏlla provinces, where Kwangju is located, was thought of as being sent to the hinterlands in exile because of social neglect and poverty there. Discrimination against Chŏlla province people is centuries old. After the three kingdoms, Paekche, Kogŭryŏ, and Silla were unified under Silla with the help of the Chinese T'ang dynasty, Silla rulers' resentment and distrust continued against Paekche (later, the Chŏlla provinces) and Kogŭryŏ (later, northern Korea). Chŏlla Province people were officially discriminated against in all sectors of Korean society since the beginning of the Koryŏ dynasty, when the dynasty's founder, Wang Kŏn, decreed that no Chŏlla people could be hired in the government. Discrimination intensified in modern times after the 1961 South Korean military coup d'état, which heralded more than four decades of rule by Kyŏngsang provinces men.

[10] Native Japanese descended from a social caste relegated to unclean but necessary work, such as handling the dead and butchering meat, and prevented from marrying or living outside the group.

[11] Beginning in the late 1930s, Koreans were pressured to adopt Japanese names, in keeping with the Japan-Korea oneness policy of one-way assimilation.

[12] The Chinese character for *gold* is also the character for *Kim*, the most common Korean name.

[13] Women, mostly Korean but also from other Asian countries, who were forced into sexual slavery for the Japanese

military during World War II.

14 During the war, hundreds of thousands of Koreans went or were taken to Japan as forced labor to work in Japanese mines and munitions factories.

15 One of Korea's best known poets, Kim Sowŏl (1902-34) wrote *Yŏngbyŏn-ŭi Jindalrae*, or *Azalea of Youngbyun*. Buddhist thinker, independence fighter, poet, and author Han Yong-un (1879-1944) wrote *Nim-ŭi Chim-muk*, or *Silence of the Lover*.

16 The three other highly respected universities were either established by Western missionaries, as in the case of Yonsei and Ewha Womans universities, or run by the government, as in the case of Seoul National University. Korea University was considered independent. Lee calls it "a bastion of cultural nationalists."

17 One of the largest leftist military rebellions occurred in Sunch'ŏn, a southwestern coastal city in South Korea.

18 A South Korean Army general who masterminded the *o-il-yuk* (May 16, 1961 military coup d'etat,) and ruled the country until 1979.

19 Kyŏnggi middle and high schools were considered by many to be the most reputable and difficult to enter public schools in South Korea through the mid-1970s.

20 To encourage the spread of Christian religion among Koreans, U.S. missionaries offered scholarships to those who would study Christian theology at U.S. colleges and universities. Many Korean Americans who came to the U.S. between 1924 and 1952, when general immigration from barred zones such as Korea was prohibited, came as students, with the help of American missionaries.

21 Literally, comrade society, the name for the overseas group that supported Syngman Rhee.

22 Chol Soo Lee was on San Quentin's death row, accused of a Chinatown murder, when K.W. Lee ran an investigative series on the case for the *Sacramento Union*. Poor, uneducated, and without social networks, the young prisoner seemed utterly powerless even within what Lee saw as a voiceless and invisible Korean immigrant community. K.W. Lee wanted to continue to write about the case in *Koreatown*, not only to gain support for the movement to have the case reopened, but also to help educate people in the Korean American community about social justice. Lee's news stories and, later, his involvement in the community-based effort to have the case reopened were critical to Chol Soo Lee's eventual release from prison. See Jay Kun Yoo's story in this volume.

23 The reported crime rate in Koreatown, which is part of the high-crime Rampart/Wilshire police precinct, is one of the highest among Los Angeles neighborhoods.

24 Danny Bakewell, a leader in the Los Angeles-based Brotherhood Crusade, organized a series of demonstrations and protests against Korean stores in South Central Los Angeles demanding, among other things, that every Korean store hire at least one black employee. Bakewell has posited himself in various media interviews as a spokesperson for black community interests. In the minds of many Korean community leaders, Bakewell's role in South Central Los Angeles is comparable to that of Reverend Al Sharpton in New York.

25 Lee is using the term *mandarin*, which signifies prerevolution China's high

government officials, who had to pass examinations on the Confucian classics, to refer to Korean immigrants who came to the U.S. as foreign students and stayed on to become physicians, professors, and so forth.

26 Lee is referring to the last of the three Korean dynasties, which spanned the period between 1392 and the early years of this century, when Korea was colonized by Japan. He is also invoking the Korean neo-Confucian mores and values that dominated the period.

27 Neo-Confucian elitism in Yi Dynasty; *yangban* belonged to the aristocratic class.

28 Established in 1905, the San Francisco Korean Methodist Church is the oldest Korean church in the continental United States. Lee is referring to the sale of the church building by its contemporary congregation, which wanted a larger site. In 1994, a number of Korean American organizations and individuals have attempted to have the old building designated as an historical landmark.

29 The first wave refers to those 7,000 Korean laborers who came to Hawaii between 1903 and 1905 and 1,100 picture brides who came between 1910 and 1924. The second wave refers to 6,500 Korean wives of U.S. servicemen, 6,300 Korean orphans adopted into American homes, and 6,000 Korean students who came between 1950 and 1965. The third wave refers to Korean immigrants who came after 1965, when the U.S. immigration quotas were altered.

30 One reason for the preponderance of Korean clergy is that U.S. colleges offered full scholarships to Koreans who would study Christian theology. For the most part, expensive foreign

schooling was otherwise almost unattainable for even upper-class Koreans before the 1950s. In the minds of many older Korean people, Western Christianity is almost synonymous with educational opportunity. Christian missionaries established schools and colleges in Korea; among these are two of the largest and best-known universities in the country, Ewha Womans University and Yonsei University. In particular, many Koreans credit American missionaries for opening the door to education for women. Until recently, many Koreans viewed the Christian clergyman as the epitome of Western modernity and education.

31 Until recent decades, it was common for well-to-do men in Korea to have more than one wife. Usually, his first marriage had been arranged by his parents when he was young, and his second marriage was to a woman of his own choice.

32 The area directly above where the briquette is inserted.

33 We are not able to verify such a policy.

34 Lieutenant General John R. Hodges was commander of U.S. occupation forces in Korea between 1945 and 1948. He was in charge of the U.S. military government, which facilitated the installation of Syngman Rhee as the President of South Korea. The election of a separate President in the South helped pave the way for the long-term division of Korea, which had been determined by the U.S. and the U.S.S.R., into separate states. See "Brief Overview of Korean and Korean American History" in Appendix C.

35 Since Korean immigration occurred mostly after 1965, U.S.-born Koreans Stella Koh's age are rare.

36 The 1992 Los Angeles riots.

37 Korean grocer Soon Ja Du whom Koh calls "Du Soon Ja" because Koreans say the family name (Du) first, received a suspended sentence from white judge Joyce Karlin for shooting African American teenager Latasha Harlins in the back in 1991 after an altercation over a bottle of orange juice in Du's store in South Central Los Angeles. The incident and the sentencing contributed to further deterioration of African American-Korean relations and the targeting of Korean stores during the Los Angeles riots.

38 A military coup d'etat in South Korea in 1961 established what was to become three decades of martial law. Curfews and daily drills were imposed, and neighborhoods were organized into defense units. During Ku's childhood and youth, there were innumerable civilian protests against martial law and for free elections; these were brutally suppressed, and tear gas was routinely used to disperse demonstrators.

39 Since 1992, approximately one southern California Korean merchant has been killed every month during a robbery attempt.

40 Eui-Young Yu estimates the number to be three thousand.

41 Between 1945 and 1947, travel between southern and northern Korea was not completely restricted.

42 A well-known independence movement guerrilla hero who later became principal of the P'yŏngyang Political Military Academy, Kim Chaek (1903-51) was born in northern Korea and moved with his family to Manchuria. He joined the Chinese Communist Party in 1927, engaged in anti-Japanese guerrilla activities in the 1930s, became an officer in the Soviet Army, and returned to

Korea after Japan's surrender in 1945. He was killed in action during the Korean War.

43 Kim Ku was a nationalist leader in the Korean provisional government in Shanghai; staunchly anticommunist, Syngman Rhee was the U.S.-endorsed president of the first South Korean republic after the national division.

44 Nationalist leader who opposed the division.

45 People's Committees [inminuiwŏnhoe] functioned as local party organizational units in both northern and southern Korea during this period.

46 The Holiness Church is the third largest Protestant denomination in South Korea, after Presbyterian and Methodist. Unlike the other two denominations, the Holiness Church evolved in Korea. In 1907, two Korean graduates of the Oriental Missionary Society Bible School in Tokyo started an evangelical mission in Seoul.

47 It has been estimated that virtually every Korean in the United States donated the equivalent of one month's wages each year between 1919 and 1945 to the Korean independence movement. Their donations supported the Korean provisional government in Shanghai. This is particularly impressive in light of the fact that most Koreans in the U.S. at that time were menial laborers earning meager wages.

48 According to Korean history books, women carrying rocks in their aprons at Haengju on the north bank of Han River fought Japanese invaders and helped win triumphs during the Toyotomi Hideyoshi Invasions (Imjin Waeran) in the sixteenth century. Actually, however, this story was probably created to inspire Korean nationalist sentiments. The Chinese

characters for the 16th century province name Hangju, do not mean *haengju* (apron).

49 According to Chinese and Korean astrology, Dredge was born in the year of the pig and should marry someone born in the year of the rabbit, sheep, or tiger.

50 At the time, Buddhist monks were not exempted from military service in South Korea.

51 The reign of Japan's Emperor Jutsuhito, 1852-1912, is traditionally regarded as the historical era during which Japan transformed itself from a feudal state into a modern industrial nation.

52 When the U.S. forces landed in Inch'ŏn, many North Korean soliders and South Korean leftist guerillas fled to the T'aebaek mountain chain. They continued to engage in guerilla activities in the southern part of South Korea many years after the truce was signed in 1953. One of the bigger mountains in the chain is Sokri mountain.

53 This was due to the exclusionary policy of the Yi dynasty toward Buddhism, which was viewed by the ruling group as threatening to Confucianism.

54 The main Buddhist denominational body in Korea.

55 For background information about the Japanese occupation of Korea and the period following liberation from Japanese rule, see "Brief..."

56 Christian doctrines of equality before God were often appealing to people living in the northern provinces of Korea because historically they had been excluded from central government favors.

57 The communists in North Korea generally looked askance on Christians

and Christianity, which were often viewed as tied to Western imperialism.

58 The first day of the Korean War.

59 The Taedong River is in North Korea; it runs through P'yŏngyang.

60 Going to North Korea in the mid-1970s was also risky because even Korean Americans with U.S. citizenship were not exempt from the reach of the South Korean Central Intelligence Agency. Up until the assassination of President Park Chung Hee in late 1979, the South Korean government used various intimidation tactics to prevent Korean Americans from even having neutral opinions about North Korea as well as bribes to foster favorable attitudes toward South Korea. Also, hostility between the U.S and North Korea meant the absence of diplomatic relations and protection for U.S. citizens visiting there.

61 An estimated ten million Korean families were separated by the partition of Korea.

62 Im Su Kyŏng, a South Korean college student, went on an unauthorized visit to North Korea in 1989 as a representative of the [South] Korean College Student Association. She received a hero's welcome in North Korea, but she was jailed in South Korea after her return to Seoul. Released in 1993, she now attends graduate school.

63 Sŏ Sŭng, a Korean Japanese university student, served 19 years in a South Korean prison for alleged leftist activities.

64 Starting with President Syngman Rhee in the late 1940s and continuing into the late 1980s, anticommunism and fear and hatred of North Korea was promulgated by every South Korean government through legal, educational,

political, and cultural institutions. South Korean government policies branched into Korean-American life through Korean CIA activities abroad. South Korean consulates advised members of the overseas community not to associate with people suspected of procommunist leanings.

65 Massive civilian demonstrations protesting martial law and demanding democratization were violently suppressed by the South Korean military, resulting in hundreds of deaths and injuries in Kwangju in 1980. Because the South Korean military had always been under U.S. armed forces command, many Koreans and Korean Americans believe that the U.S. supported the massacre. This belief was strengthened when newly elected President Reagan chose to extend his first state invitation to Chon Doo Hwan, the military officer who proclaimed himself president of South Korea in 1981 and whom many held responsible for the Kwangju tragedy.

66 For background information on the events Park describes, see "Brief..."

67 The months of March and April, just before the spring barley harvest season, were a period called *pori kogae*, during which many people struggled to survive without enough food.

68 Mr. Park says these adages in English.

69 Los Angeles Little Tokyo features restaurants, hotels, and shops rather than housing and residential neighborhoods. As such, it is less a community than a commercial center for tourism.

70 A California state initiative to limit entitlements for people believed to be undocumented immigrants.

71 At the time of her immigration, most middle and high schools in South

Korea were sex-segregated, and men and women rarely touched each other in public.

72 Sunoo's sons are fourth-generation Korean Americans because they are the great-grandchildren of immigrants. First generation means immigrant; second generation means U.S.-born offspring of immigrants. Since Jan's father was an immigrant and his mother is U.S.-born, Brenda calls him "2.5."

73 South Koreans generally discriminate among themselves according to age (among other things); thus, male students and youth are supposed to call upperclassmen and elders—even if the age difference is fairly negligible—*hyŏng*. The elder calls the younger by his given name. According to this system, equality between individuals is based on sameness. Two sophomores or two seniors can call one another by name, but a sophomore cannot call a senior by name. Traditionally, the *hubae*, or successor, is supposed to treat the *sŏnbae*, or predecessor, with respect and deference, while the *sŏnbae* treats the *hubae* with paternal affection. The stronger are encouraged to protect the weaker, who are supposed to be loyal. This system operates to a lesser extent among female students and young women; in this case, the elder is called *ŏnni* [elder sister of a female]. It also functions across genders: younger males call older females *nuna* [elder sister of a male], and younger females call older males *oppa* [elder brother of a female]. These practices are supposed to encourage familial affection and closeness.

74 Actually, industrialization took place during the 1970s and 1980s, rather than the 1950s and 1960s.

75 Lee refers to the oxen used to plow rice

fields. Until the 1970s, farmers occasionally brought goods into the cities on oxen as well.

76 Korean people leave their shoes outside when entering a house.

77 An ancient Chinese book of divination.

78 As mentioned in note 9, people from the Chŏlla provinces have faced official and unofficial discrimination, especially from the central government for centuries. In contemporary times, presidents from Kyŏngsang Province have prevented people from the Chŏlla provinces from obtaining high office, which helps explain the massive support in the Chŏlla provinces for native son Kim Dae Jung, the opposition leader who made several unsuccessful bids for the presidency. In popular television dramas until only recently, most powerful people spoke with Kyŏngsang Province accents, while criminals, uneducated people, laborers, and servants were often characterized as having Chŏlla Province accents.

79 During the Japanese colonial occupation (1910-45), Korean agriculture was converted from subsistence farming to one-crop rice production for export to Japan. Particularly during World War II, almost all Korean crops were confiscated and taken to Japan.

80 During those chaotic times, families were often ordered out of their hometowns; at the same time, they were not permitted to leave North Korea.

81 The *il-sa* retreat refers to the January 4, 1951, Chinese recapture of Seoul. For more information, see "Brief...."

82 Poor and working-class children often attended night schools because they had to work during the day. Night schools were usually held from 6:00 to 10:00 P.M.

83 Korean cities are divided into administrative units called *ku, tong,* and *t'ong.* There were eight *ku* and hundreds of *tong* at the time Mr. Han was working in the *tong* office. A *t'ong* is the smallest administrative unit. Each *ku* has a head, or *kuch'ongjang,* appointed by the city mayor, who is in turn appointed by the president. Each *tong* and *t'ong* has a chief.

84 As a civil engineer 3rd class in the Department of Commerce and Industry, Mr. Han's level of employment was high at the time. Chon Doo Hwan, who had seized power and become president of Korea, reshuffled the government bureaucracy, and placed his military allies in key positions.

85 Most of the Korean immigrants we interviewed used the term Hispanic, not Latino, which leads us to conjecture that they rely on Korean language newspapers for their knowledge of this community.

86 Swap meets began as flea markets— weekend outdoor operations in which spaces were rented to individual merchants selling T-shirts, sunglasses, athletic shoes, and other such goods, many of them South Korean-made. Currently, swapmeets are open all week in buildings with stalls rented out to individual operators.

87 A weekly half-hour situation comedy on commercial television aired between 1994 and 1995, featuring the Korean American comedienne Margaret Cho as the central character.

88 Korean women often refer to their husbands as "Mr. Such-and-such."

89 Kim is referring to the 1910-45 Japanese occupation of Korea. For more information, see Appendix C

for "Brief ..."

90 The slum area around a U.S. army base north of Seoul, where prostitutes traditionally plied their trade.

91 According to Paul Kim, Koreans have been doing business with Japan since the last part of World War II, manufacturing *hiroppon*, an amphetamine used in Japan and Korea. The drug is usually in powder form that can be turned into liquid. Manufactured on small islands off the southern coast of Korea, it is smuggled into Japan on speedboats. Kim contends that the *yakuza*, or the people involved in organized crime in Japan, are involved in both manufacturing and distribution of the drug. He says that Koreans have set up laboratories in the Philippines, South America, and the U.S., where motorcycle gangs such as the Hell's Angels traditionally made the drug in bathtubs. "Their methods are crude, so the purity level is low," Kim says, "whereas the Koreans approach it almost like chemists, so there's more demand for Korean-made 'ice.' Koreans are probably the best chemists in the world in terms of making 'ice,' or crystal menthathethanimin, because they've been making it the longest."

92 A 1979 incident in Los Angeles Chinatown.

93 South Korea's best-known high school, known for its difficult entrance requirements at the time.

94 A grotesquely cowardly and comical pigtailed Chinese servant on the television show *Bonanza*.

95 Orange County was the main receiving station for Vietnamese refugees in the continental United States after the Vietnam War.

96 Despite the vivid presence of people of various races, many Koreans in Los Angeles continue to think that American means white. African Americans, Latinos, and Chicanos don't automatically come to mind in discussions of this sort.

97 A Los Angeles-based political advocacy organization founded by 1.5 and second-generation Korean Americans in early 1983.

98 API stands for Asian/Pacific Islander.

99 "Rice queens" refers to non-Asian gay men who want Asian men; "rice dykes" are non-Asian lesbians who prefer Asian women.

100 "Yellow fever" usually refers to white men's desire for Asian women or men. Although the term emerged to describe relations among heterosexuals, it also exists in the gay community. According to Sandy, the issue is one of power and control. Asian men are feminized whether they are gay or straight.

101 Government-imposed travel restrictions designed to prevent the outflow of capital, together with the insufficiency of personal funds, prevented most South Koreans from traveling until the late 1980s, resulting in lack of exposure to many of the world's cultures. At the same time, Japanese and U.S. economic and political involvement in South Korea meant that South Korean society was disproportionately influenced by Japanese and U.S. cultural attitudes and practices. Finally, one of the outcomes of decades of anticommunist social policy in South Korea was the national security laws, according to which aiding the "enemy" (communism and North Korea) has been harshly punished. Until the mid-1980s, one sure way of aiding the "enemy" was to

criticize the U.S., which was deemed the "friend," and information about U.S. racism—as well as about African Americans, which often implied criticism of the U.S.—was not readily available to most South Koreans, who learned instead about American principles of democracy and equality and about the greatness of Abraham Lincoln.

102 A consortium of Korean American social service agency representatives, established to cooperatively address postriots problems in the Korean American community. Han is referring to the consortium's attempts to help burnt-out liquor store owners become engaged in different kinds of enterprise, such as laundromats and fast food franchises.

103 The port city of Inch'ŏn was one of the major industrial centers in Korea under Japanese rule.

104 During the Japanese colonial period, many Japanese settled in urban areas in Korea, living separately in residential sections built especially for them. Usually homes were graded according to the rank and wealth of the residents. Some well-to-do Koreans lived in Japanese neighborhoods.

105 At that time, immigration sponsorship requirements were not strict for foreign students. But since most Korean people were very poor, only a few could dream of studying in America.

106 An English or French major was considered appropriate for young women who hoped to marry upper middle class or upper class men who might be diplomats or businessmen for whom English- and French-speaking wives might be at least suitable adornments, if not professionally

useful.

107 Korean translation of a phrase used to designate the role of women in modern Japanese nationalism. While the Korean version of the phrase places the "wise mother" first to fit better the Korean way of thinking about women's roles, in Japanese the "good wife" comes first.

108 Rhee seems to be referring to Koreans who immigrated earlier, perhaps before the late 1970s.

109 Some Korean people say "handy" for handicap.

110 Korean people often refer to each other as the father or mother of a first-born child. Sometimes women refer to their husbands as "baby's Daddy".

111 Traditionally, Korean men are quite dependent on women to take care of household matters, and when left alone become almost completely helpless.

112 Shortly afterward, the English-language magazine publication was halted, and after the Los Angeles riots reduced Korean small business advertising in the paper as a whole, the English section of the Korean newspaper has been operating with a one-person staff.

113 Traditionally, wage-earning husbands in Korea hand their paychecks over to their wives, who pass back a sundries allowance to them and use the rest to operate the household, make investments, take care of the children's education expenses, and so forth.

114 It is commonly argued that the fact that women are given the responsibility of handling household finances is a sign of female social power in South Korea. Others argue that trying to reconcile expenses with income is an irksome task that husbands prefer not to handle, particularly in light of traditional

Confucian gender roles, according to which women handle mundane survival issues so that men can be free to think and philosophize.

[115] Mrs. Kim said she was twenty-two in 1947, even though she was born in 1926, because in Korea, a person is one year old at birth. After that, s/he gains a year every new year. Thus, a person born on the last day of the year becomes two years old on New Year's Day, but a person born on the first day of the year has to wait until the next new year to become two years old. Currently, when people are asked their age, they often give two ages, a counting age and a full age, or a Korean age and an American age.

[116] There was only one crematory in Seoul at the time.

[117] Traditionally, only the outcast class engaged in grave-digging or crematory work.

[118] The higher up the housing, the cheaper the rent in Korean cities. The most desirable residential areas were closer to the center of the city. In the days when people had to fetch water from a well below, living on top of a hill was inconvenient. Also, transporting anything along narrow, steep, and winding roads in hilly areas made them less accessible.

[119] A "nice funeral" means that there were many mourners, who were mostly church members and friends of the children.

[120] During the colonial period, Japanese took up most of the middle to high-level posts in government and education in Korea. See "Brief..." for more information about the Japanese occupation of Korea.

[121] In November 1945, an anti-Soviet,

anticommunist student revolt took place in Sinŭiju, a town on the North Korea-China border. Soon afterwards the Russians came into North Korea.

[122] The central commercial and business district of Seoul at the time.

[123] Sa-il-gu denotes the April 19, 1960 student protests against widespread corruption in the Syngman Rhee government in the previous month's general elections; the uprising resulted in the Rhee regime being toppled after thirteen years of authoritarian rule.

[124] Although most American missionary doctors and nurses were evacuated from Korea in 1943—during World War II—their influence was still strongly felt.

[125] Older people don't attend college in Korea, where people are generally expected to be engaged in age-appropriate activities. This explains why it is difficult for women and men to marry after they pass a certain age, and why blue jeans are frowned on when worn by middle-aged people. Because proper sequence and hierarchy are important, it is considered awkward and undesirable for older company workers on the same employment track to be supervised by younger workers.

[126] The California state initiative to limit entitlements to people assumed to be undocumented immigrants.

[127] For more information, see "Brief..."

[128] Although polygamy was socially sanctioned, it was legally prohibited. Thus, children born to concubines or other women were registered as children of the first wife, who was the legal wife.

[129] Some parents send their children to English-language non-Korean churches

while they attend Korean churches. Most Korean churches conduct their services and activities in Korean, and English-speaking Korean children have no place in them.

130 In Korea, he is known as Yu Chae-kŏn.

131 Nationalist leader Ahn Chang Ho (An Ch'ang-ho) advocated Korean self-development in preparation for eventual independence from Japanese colonial rule. Ahn was active among overseas Koreans; he founded the Hŭngsadan, a political organization in which many early Korean Americans actively participated. He died in a Japanese prison in 1938.

132 In stridently anticommunist South Korea, all contact with North Korea or North Koreans was strictly forbidden for decades, especially after the declaration of martial law in 1972, when speech, writing, and actions interpreted as aiding the enemy were punishable by death. South Korean law prohibited its citizens from even reading or speaking anything but unfavorably about North Korea. In the 1960s, when Yi Mun-Kyo traveled to North Korea, the flames of anticommunism were vigorously fanned by the South Korean government: even the Far Eastern editions of *Time* and *Newsweek* that featured the 50th anniversary of the Bolshevik Revolution were censored, and South Koreans were prevented from listening to music composed in Russia after 1917 because it was "communist music."

133 The Wah Ching, which means Chinese Youth, began forming in San Francisco in the early 1960s. Members were Hong Kong-born youth, many of whom had dropped out of school. By 1967-68, the Wah Ching were well-organized and somewhat politicized. Members became involved in petty crime in the early 1970s, and by the mid-1970s a number of killings took place between the Wah Ching and rival groups. These activities threatened the Chinatown tourism industry, which was important to San Francisco's economy, and police were under a great deal of pressure to make arrests. For a discussion of the Wah Ching, see Stanford M. Lyman, *Chinese Americans*, New York: Random House, 1974.

134 See K.W. Lee's story in this volume.

135 Yoo considers his family situation a miracle because among Korean daughters-in-law, there are many complaints about the difficulties and frustrations of *sijipsari*, living with parents-in-law, especially mothers-in-law. Moreover, many Korean women are reluctant to marry widows' sons; they fear that widows will become meddling, domineering mothers-in-law because they pin all their hopes on their sons. Also, the husband's mother and the wife's mother do not generally have a sisterly relationship, since mothers are likely to be sympathetic to their daughters' complaints about their mothers-in-law.

136 Members of the *yangban*, or aristocratic classes in Korea, disdained manual labor, and mercantile activities were traditionally looked down upon in Korean society.

137 Foreign-born Koreans were not eligible for American citizenship until 1952, and, therefore, they could not vote.

138 See note 131.

139 Syngman Rhee was a rival of Ahn Chang Ho. Supported by the United States, he became the first president of the Republic of Korea in 1948, after the

national partition. Rhee was deposed in the wake of massive student-led political protests in 1960.

140 Tongjihoe was the political group founded by Syngman Rhee when he was living as a political exile in the United States.

141 Many early Korean nationalist leaders, inspired by the Bolshevik Revolution and by Karl Marx's writings, were sympathetic with socialism and communism.

142 Alien Land Acts passed in 1913 and 1920 prevented all aliens not eligible for citizenship, including Japanese and Koreans, from owning land in California. Similar laws were passed in a number of other states.

143 Another pronunciation and spelling of this word is *kotonk*.

144 Kim is referring to the Japanese-American movement to demand an official apology from the U.S. government for violating Japanese-Americans' constitutional rights during World War II.

145 Approximately one-fifth of Koreans have the surname Kim.

146 A black entrepreneur and self-appointed community leader who spearheaded efforts to boycott Korean-owned businesses in the black community. See footnote 22 in K.W. Lee's narrative.

147 "Call taxis" in Los Angeles and New York are operated by Korean-speaking drivers and dispatchers. Customers call to arrange to be picked up and taken to their destinations. Unmarked and meterless "call taxis" are operated by individuals at negotiated rates.

148 There are about 760 *wŏn* in a U.S. dollar.

149 In early May 1995, some of the workers, who had been laid off when the restaurant's ownership changed hands, picketed the restaurant after their attempts to procure two months' back wages were unsuccessful. Wages were about $600 a month for twelve hours of work per day, six days a week, and a total of $8,000 was allegedly owed. Although some diners did cross the picket lines, many did not, because many customers were regulars who recognized and wished to support the workers. After only five days, the back wages were paid in full.

150 An affluent district considered the Beverly Hills of Seoul.

151 Shin is referring to a 1986 state proposition, the initiative to instate English as the official language of California, which many believe was an expression of resentment against the many Asian and Latino immigrants who came into the state after 1970.

152 Sections of this story appear in *The State of Asian America*, ed. Karin Aguilar-San Juan, Boston: South End Press, 1993.

153 Passed in 1952, the Immigration and Nationality Act (the McCarran-Walter Act) established tiny national origins quota for Japanese and Koreans and enabled Koreans to become naturalized U.S. citizens.

154 Min quotes from a Meredith Stricker poem in her interview in Valerie Soe's film, *Art to Art*, Asian Women United of California, 1993.

155 North Koreans allege that the U.S. use the germ warfare during the war.

156 A 1976 novel by Maxine Hong Kingston.

157 *pyŏngja horan*; please see "Brief..."